THE DANCE
OF BEING

THE DANCE
OF BEING

MAN'S LABYRINTHINE RHYTHMS

The Natural Ground of the Human

Leonard Charles Feldstein

New York
Fordham University Press
1979

Printed in the United States of America

In memoriam

Theodore Mischel

philosopher   scientist   dear friend
and to his sons
Paul and Ken
in whom live on the promise, the hope, and the joy
of his cherished memory

When to the sessions of sweet silent thought
I summon up remembrance of things past,

.   .   .   .   .

Then can I drown an eye, unus'd to flow,
For precious friends hid in death's dateless night,
And weep afresh love's long since cancell'd woe,
And moan the expense of many a vanish'd sight:

.   .   .   .   .

But if the while I think on thee, dear friend,
All losses are restor'd and sorrows end.
—Shakespeare, Sonnet XXX

CONTENTS

PREFACE

Now I continue the investigation, begun in *Homo Quaerens: The Seeker and the Sought*,[1] into the generic traits of persons from a philosophic point of view. I treat such special topics of my method, set forth in that book, as bear upon the person's infrapersonal aspects: namely, his body and such of its functions as contribute to his preconscious acts. In particular, I deal with those aspects insofar as they may be construed as straining, so to speak, toward that self-transcendence which culminates in the veridical person—in effect, strands of subpersonal events which contribute to and converge upon his consummate personhood. In consequence, I explore the ontology of the person under the perspective of his naturalistically interpreted makeup; and I conceive my enterprise as propaedeutic to more generalized ontologic topics which I shall take up in subsequent books.

In my previous volume, I presented an extended preface in which I both indicated the general tenor of *Homo Quaerens* and provided detailed acknowledgments to my intellectual creditors as well as to those persons to whom I was quite personally indebted. However, what I wrote in that preface was intended to apply not only to that particular work, but, more pervasively, to the present volume, and, indeed, to the succeeding books comprising my systematic inquiry into the metaphysics of the person, books which are in part completed and in part still in the planning stage. Accordingly, everything which I wrote in the earlier preface is equally applicable to *The Dance of Being*; and I respectfully suggest to the reader unacquainted with that book, should he wish to familiarize himself with an overview of my sources, the general drift of my thinking, those who have most markedly influenced my research, and my principal goals, that he review that preface. Nevertheless, the present book may be read quite independently, though deeper grasp of its argument would be facilitated by familiarity with the former book.

In any event, I shall spare the reader of this volume who is already cognizant of the themes set forth in *Homo Quaerens* more than the briefest synopsis of its preface. Suffice it to mention that the present work, like the earlier one, owes its inspiration to five categories of influence: such major philosophers as Kant, Spinoza, Hegel, and, with special gratitude, Alfred North Whitehead; numerous less widely known writers, including both those of philosophic persuasion mentioned in that preface and other thinkers who deal with the empirical disciplines, especially (in the present book) the natural sciences; literature, art, and music, and, above all, the poetry of such masters as Shakespeare, Donne, Keats, Wordsworth, Rilke, and Yeats; numberless encounters with friends with whom, over the years, I have had countless fruitful dialogues; and an abiding religious conviction, which involves, in particular, a synthesis of the Christian and Jewish traditions as they are wedded to the astounding intellectual achievement of the Greeks.

Among the personal acknowledgments indicated in my first volume, I especially reiterate the following: Leonard Beerman, Harry Bone, Justus Buchler, Blanche Feldstein, Frieda Feldstein, Nathan Feldstein, Erich Fromm, Anna Gourevitch, Edmund Hillpern, Benjamin Kahn, Leo and Lillian Kovar, Fanny Krasney, Quentin Lauer, S.J., David Meranze, William Richardson, S.J., Pierre Rubé, Ernest Schachtel, Esther Smellow, Frank and Nettie Smellow, Anna Smelo, and Heinz Westman. I intend that my indebtednesses as specifically set forth in that volume be understood to be equally applicable to the present volume. But among those persons mentioned in that preface, I note the following as meriting special mention in *The Dance of Being*: namely, Patricia and Louis Carini, and Elizabeth M. Kraus. To these dear friends, I owe an immeasurable debt of gratitude for their profound, compassionate, and loving concern, and, hardly the least, for their most skillful and perceptive reading of the manuscript of this volume. Above all, in addition to my acknowledgments of the first volume, I am deeply indebted, for a marvelously empathic study of this book, to one whose refined sense of style, wisdom with respect to the experiential import of my often too abstract formulations, and loving care in attending to every detail of the texture of my thought have aided me enormously to feel implications which otherwise would have escaped me and to rectify certain errors in both style and content—my beloved friend, Rebecca Rice. In addition, as in the earlier book, I gratefully acknowledge a reviewer, whose identity must remain concealed, a distinguished professor of philosophy, for aiding me to modify my Prologue in a way which, I hope, will serve as a more felicitous introduction to my book than would otherwise have been the case. Finally, I am grateful for the unfailing cooperation of the staff of Fordham University Press, and, most particularly, for the exemplary editorial assistance of Mary Beatrice Schulte; for John McNaughton's conscientious proofreading of the manuscript; for the generous permission from the editor of *International Philosophical Quarterly* to incorporate here material previously published in his journal; for the Faculty Fellowship awarded me by Fordham University, which enabled me to complete the present volume as well as the previous volume; and for a careful typing of both manuscripts by Mrs. Joanne Schultz. Beyond that, I am, as always, indebted to my friends and colleagues in the Philosophy Department of Fordham University and to the generations of students whom I have had the privilege of teaching.

Moreover, as in *Homo Quaerens*, I am indebted to my children, Lori and Jonathan, to whom I dedicated that volume, a most important presence in my life, both for what they are, in the beauty and the purity of their natures and in the joy which they give me as I watch them grow and increasingly incorporate into their own lives the ideals which I have here set forth as to what I deem a fulfilled person ought to be (i.e., one who quests after his *own* ideals), and for what they symbolize as exemplars of the generation to succeed my own, a new generation in which rest the promise and the hope of humanity; and I gratefully recall John W. R. Thompson, to whom I dedicate my next book, and whose cherished memory will never cease to haunt these pages and to stir my profoundest gratitude and love. And to the memory of my dear friend, Theodore Mischel, I have dedicated this book as a commemoration of the times of joy, exuberance, wit, and good fellowship which remain imperishably with me as a living and vibrant presence.

Fordham University   LEONARD CHARLES FELDSTEIN

NOTE

1. Leonard Charles Feldstein, *Homo Quaerens: The Seeker and the Sought; Method Become Ontology* (New York: Fordham University Press, 1978).

THE DANCE
OF BEING

PROLOGUE

"It remains controversial," Thomas Mann declares, in *Joseph and His Brothers*,

> which is life and which death; since both, the soul involved with nature and the spirit detached from the world, the principle of the past and the principle of the future, claim, each in its own way, to be the water of life, and each accuses the other of dealings with death. Neither quite wrongly, since neither nature without spirit nor spirit without nature can truly be called life. But the mystery, and the unexpressed hope of God, lie in their union, in the genuine penetration of the spirit into the world of the soul, in the inter-penetration of both principles, in a hallowing of the one through the other which should bring about a present humanity blessed with blessing from heaven above and from the depths beneath.[1]

In this book, I explicitly treat but one member of the formula "neither nature without spirit nor spirit without nature can truly be called life"; and only insofar as it immanently conditions my inquiry do I treat the second member as well. Throughout my account, I assume the mystery of both members: an "inter-penetration of . . . principles," for as spirit hallows body so body hallows spirit. In subsequent books, I shall treat "humanity blessed with blessing from heaven above"; in the present volume I treat "humanity blessed . . . from the depths beneath." So to examine this "humanity," I assume the validity of such classic dualities as they relate to man as matter–spirit, eros–thanatos, structure–function, individual–community, private–public, and birth–death, as well as such meta-physical opposites as non-being–being, being–becoming, permanence–change, potency–act, matter–form, continuity–discontinuity, the ontic (or merely empirical)–the ontologic (or ground of the empirical). Yet in no instance do I seek to reduce one paired factor to another. Nor do I deny the objective reality of either paired factor. In every instance, I unqualifiedly affirm the authenticity of the human experience of the paired opposites *as* opposite and yet as genuinely paired, and, indeed, as interdependent.

My purpose is to portray both man's ante-biologic development and his strictly biologic development as the contemporaneous phases of development—e.g., atoms, molecules, cells, tissues—converge upon his personhood. Accordingly, I treat man as material event, man's organismic evolution amidst life's diverse ramifications, and man's rootedness in his own biologic genesis as uniquely the one who speaks. From within this contemporaneous perspective, I inquire into the person's onto-genesis and his phylogenesis from the standpoint of a "transcendental naturalism." In later books, I approach the person, as it were, from above, "deducing" personal being from pure being. By "transcendental," I do not mean the Kantian concept. Nor do I use the term in a strictly adjectival sense. On the contrary, I imply the verb form "transcendentalizing." For I wish to indicate an active straining of proto-personal elements toward ever new thresholds latent in every zone of what I now designate the *infra*personal spectrum of biologic activities, as those activities tend to converge upon human action. I seek to trace that straining, both its particular fruitions and its cosmic trajectory, from elementary biologic rhythms through which non-being first ventures into being, through ecologic rhythms of organisms and proto-organisms, toward the culmination of those rhythms in the rhythms of speech—the last now viewed as the womb of human thought; and, at each level in these evolving strands, I seek to isolate those invariant structures which are preserved amidst manifold infrapersonal variations. Beyond that, I seek to identify the links between the diverse levels, and to show how those links both replicate themselves and orchestrate all levels and all factors within each level into a great dance of being; I trace man's physiogenesis (i.e., as inanimate event), biogenesis, and "personogenesis" as these modes of genesis intertwine to constitute his emergence upon the cosmic scene.

In short, germinating within matter and, *a fortiori*, within *living* matter is spirit; and spirit comes to its fruition only after having progressively transformed itself through energy's numberless varieties and combinations. Having aggregated itself into particles and coalescences of particles, energy shapes ever more complicated matrices of crystalline lattices, and gives birth to myriad concatenated forms. Naturalistically construed, this vast cosmic panorama, these marvelously orchestrated forms, unfold in endlessly novel ways and converge upon ever new shapes; they orchestrate themselves as immensely subtle events which fluctuate and diversify and ferment within the person's deepest recesses. Whether inanimate or animate, man's "matter" never functions in isolation from the total context of his emerging personhood. Far from being in opposition to a person's substance, that "matter" is one of his essential ingredients. A texture of happenings which itself is never transcendent, "matter" is ever self-transcending toward personhood. Surely, the person emerges as such only in the setting of a "physiogony" construed as profoundly experiential; for he is the culmination of a natural process which at no point may be divorced from mind, however elementary that mind be. So constituted that reflexivity pervades its every level, even the most primitive material reality, that physiogony eventuates in the structures and dynamics of speech —the quintessential ground of consummate human spirit.

In my metaphysical scheme, I rely not so much upon *a priori* assumption as upon empirical generalization. Nevertheless, though special science contributes significantly to an understanding of man's varied facets, one must, *fully* to illuminate each facet, comprehend the person himself, the person as integral and unified—a whole which presents itself concretely in experience. It is not some aspect of the person but the person *in concreto* which is to be explained. By this, I mean person as both datum, a completed fact already given which lies in the past, and *datio*, an activity of giving which, so to speak, lies in the future. A *datio*-cum-datum, this "whole" constitutes a dynamic configuration rhythmically concatenated which, in both a passive sense and an active sense, *presents itself* for explanation. To understand its *modus operandi,* this self-determining complexus, one must employ diverse metaphors, metaphors which (often strangely juxtaposed) interweave and commingle to suggest the person's manifold subtleties.

To achieve this end, I initiate a new kind of inquiry, a quest, essentially ontologic, which has already been prefigured in my *Homo Quaerens,* a book in which I proposed tenets for methodically searching into the essential person. Now I amplify and systematically organize certain ontologic strands which are but fragmentarily indicated in that volume. In a non-formal way, I develop implications of the method therein set forth. Like that volume, this book is intended to stand alone. One may pursue its argument without reference to the first volume, or, for that matter, to complementary books which will succeed the present volume— books wherein I further ramify my philosophic theory of the person. In view of an ultimate interdependence of the volumes intended as forthcoming, volumes which as a totality I designate "An Inquiry Into the Metaphysics of the Person," fullest understanding of this book's contents requires that one sequentially read the entire work. But the necessary framework for understanding my thesis is established within the book itself. My argument proceeds without reference to the earlier book; it will conclude without need of the remaining books.

Accordingly, principles will herein be set forth which may be considered in their own terms; they will constitute a single organon. From this point of view, such criteria as consistency, cogency, and scope will be understood as needed to justify this book's claims without my referring to matters dealt with elsewhere. They will be introduced in the appropriate places. In short, the welter of details pertaining to man's infrapersonal ground, the contributions which his thingly aspect and his organismic aspect make to an understanding of his total being, will be coordinated and organized in whatever way this book requires. Yet a distant light emanating from within the perspective of the entire series will ineluctably illuminate my every thesis. To aid my reader, the general ontologic background therein made explicit will here be sketched.

As I stated in *Homo Quaerens,* "the substantive groundwork for a general human ontology, together with such ramifications of that ontology as will locate man in the larger cosmos,"[2] will, though latently, pervade the present book. Moreover, to repeat my comments: man will thus be located "within a double perspective: the perspective of pride and the perspective of humility." Under the first perspective, I treat the person "from an essentially developmental point of view. . . . I seek to evaluate the roles" of his variegated facets

as they pertain to the essential being of man. Throughout, the person is regarded as center and prime focus of the orchestrated rhythms of the cosmos. In a sense, he is conceptualized in his *ego*centricity, or more broadly, in the communo-centricity of the interpersonal relations within which matrix he arises, plays out the drama of his life, and brings his destiny to consummation. However, under the second perspective, I shift my concern from man's essential egocentricity to a *deo*centric orientation toward his value with respect to the cosmos as a whole.

Throughout, these perspectives provide a significant background. Yet the first perspective dominates. Moreover, I cannot ignore the communal matrix wherein every person enacts his life drama, a matrix here viewed from within an infra-personal frame. True, this book treats only that frame. To converge upon a genu-inely human ontology, its themes must further ramify. For, cogently to explore the infrapersonal, I must prescind from many factors. Yet, throughout, I relate the book's topics to the person qua person. Thereby, I intend my account to be a prolegomenon, from a naturalistic point of view, to a later, more general ontology. At the same time, the entire work is construed as organic, independent, and (relatively) self-sufficient.

By a "naturalistic" point of view, I imply a particular, and limited, route toward an understanding of human ontology. Subsequently, a complementary route, the supranaturalistic way, will have parity with the naturalistic. Though the former way is an essential ingredient of human ontology, the latter is equally important. Surely, these disparate routes demand unification. In *Homo Quaerens*, I sketched the ground for that unity. Under the rubric of "transcendental," I proposed that implicit within a naturalistic approach, and embedded therein as its very basis, is the path by which naturalism itself might be transcended, and indeed wedded to a non-naturalistic *personalist* approach. Throughout the present book, I refer to this transcendence; and I suggest its exemplifications in all those proto-human processes which contribute to building the person.

In *Homo Quaerens*, I stressed, as a fundamental precept for methodic inquiry into the person, a *total* listening to his responses, however focused or restricted the questions addressed to him or the range of the inquirer's responses. For, so I argued, only in the context of the complete involvement of the subject of investi-gation with the acts of inquiry may the veridical contours, interconnections, and overall complexion of the facets under scrutiny be revealed. Bearing in mind this proviso, I seek now to explicate the person's thingly and organismic aspects, in particular the relevance of elements composing these aspects for his being con-strued in its most inclusive sense. Throughout the present book, I treat these mutually compresent thingly and organismic layers in their diversified and inter-woven rhythms; and I regard the person as the culmination—the apotheosis, as it were—of these rhythms: a veritable dance of his every aspect, a dance which bears their latent potential to fruition in his emergent personhood. Compre-hended within this framework, these layers so interact with one another as to constitute the existential basis for what I have designated a transcendentally naturalistic perspective upon man's labyrinthine rhythms. Indeed, this ground of his infrapersonal being is a veritable symphony of life. Theme after theme is layered, one upon another, each with its distinctive variations, and, as they mutu-ally synergize, all shaping a grand counterpoint. As it approaches its climax, this symphony orchestrates resonances which unremittingly echo throughout every person's body. In dialectical interplay, these mutually enclosing levels of infra-personal organization so impinge upon one another as significantly to affect, and indeed veridically to transform, each level. Thus reciprocally interacting, they induce veritable transfigurations of a person's every constitutive element.

By this transmutation of a person's thingly and organismic aspects, a configuration of processes emerges such that all factors within the configuration function differently from the way in which they would function were they outside it. I distinguish thingly and organismic entities *in vitro*, the context for natural scientific study, from those entities *in vivo*, i.e., as they are de facto constituted within and under the perspective of the person. By my argument, the *in vivo* status of inanimate and (subhuman) animate allows themes to be traced which will prefigure topics to be taken up in succeeding books. Numerous thingly and organismic activities—the matrix wherein the person germinates—are not merely analogous to but actually, as seed stands to blossom, continuous with activities on the strictly personal level. Such continuities will be of the utmost pertinence to the present book.

In my next book, *Choros: The Orchestrating Self*, I treat three principal topics: the dialectic between consciousness and the Unconscious, and the transpositions of their respective contents—both, moreover, functioning as relatively autonomous loci within the psyche; the *modus operandi* of these transpositions as, in their complete assemblage, they function within the integral person; the derivation from interpersonal encounters of the *singular* person's defining traits as an integrated complex of many dimensions. At present, I set forth the fundamental infrapersonal dynamisms whereby these personal processes evolve—always, however, from within the restricted perspective of transcendental naturalism; and I suggest certain crucial themes, to be elaborated in subsequent books, which will permit the progressive unfolding of a more inclusive human ontology. Throughout, I shall deal with the person's metaphysics from a developmental point of view. I use "developmental" in a quite special sense as an uncoiling or an unraveling of powers, each set potentiating a succeeding set. Originating through two parallel evolutionary routes from both infrapersonal and suprapersonal matrices—the one, a naturalistic efflorescing; the other, a supranaturalistic emanating—the person undergoes successive profound metamorphoses. Gradually extending his searching powers to outermost cosmic limits and to the most concealed personal depths, every man reveals his consummate being in a grand dialectic of person and cosmos.

Again, to cite from the Prologue to *Homo Quaerens*: I herein

sketch many of the substantive issues which will more cogently, and in greater detail, constitute the topics of the other books. These I enumerate seriatim, in the hope that the titles alone, with but a short accompanying explanation, will suffice to indicate, however tentatively and cursorily, the general drift of my approach. Accordingly, following this volume, the sequence unfolds: . . . *Choros: The Orchestrating Self*—here, I treat the dialectic between consciousness and the Unconscious in a matrix wherein the person is construed as achieving integration both through his private searchings and through his encounters with other persons, and in each instance by dialogue, explicit or immanent, in which the symbolisms of his presence are woven with the symbolisms of the compresence of each with each; *Metamorphosis: The Odyssey of the Self*—here, I treat the orchestrated rhythms and symbols of comportment by which the person reveals the sequence of crises and resolutions of crises, the transformations and the transfigurations, through which he proceeds along his life's journey; *Apotheosis: The Divinizing Self*—here, I treat the person as the locus wherein the great cosmic reverberations articulate themselves and, by man's committed and directed searching activities, come to fruition within the orbit of his potential cognizance; *Cosmos: The Crucible of Man*—here, I bring my work to its penultimate conclusion in a theory woven of ontologic, cosmologic, and theologic components, in effect reversing the orientation of the preceding volume by deriving man from the cosmos, that womb of his being wherein all that is true and good and beautiful is borne to confluence in a doctrine I designate transcendental trinitarianism; but a trinitarianism which is dynamic, progressive, and endlessly revelatory of novel facets; *The Person: A Cosmic Perspective*—here, having adduced from a systematic theory of the person a general cosmology, I explicitly deduce the principal categories of a human ontology, each category condensing yet going beyond the themes proposed in the earlier volumes, by using cosmology as a paradigm, hence, by now construing the person as a veridical microcosm.

I cannot sufficiently stress that though I amplify the themes of the present volume in my later books, I intend *The Dance of Being* to be understood independently and in its own terms. In brief, I treat the vector which arises within nonbeing, the "realm" of *no-thingness*, as that vector leads stage by stage along both phylogenetic and ontogenetic routes of human development—compressed, so to speak, into the mutual compresence of these stages. Each pattern layered upon the remainder, the numerous rhythmic patterns of development so interweave as often quite radically to transfigure one another. Culminating in but one set of man's orchestrated essences—the naturalistic—this set nevertheless constitutes a significant ingredient as all his essences unite to shape his human ontology.

The first two volumes of my overall work constitute a unity. Though from different standpoints, both treat the specific activities by which a person may be known in his essential being. In *Homo Quaerens*, this epistemologic enterprise is set forth in its universal and abstract form. In the present book, which elaborates this epistemologic theme, my inquiry assumes a more particular form. Thus, *Homo Quaerens* concerns knowing activities in general as applied to the person; *The Dance of Being* concerns but one aspect of the "empirical" person, an aspect grounded in his "natural" essence as the presupposition for ontology and cosmology, the topics of my later books.

Whereas *Homo Quaerens* establishes method to be the searching person himself *as* he grasps the integral being of the person searched, *The Dance of Being* proposes specific phases in the concrete knowing of the object sought. Progressively, I experience the person (so I now argue) as incarnating rhythms which unfold from the "merely" natural, beginning with the least perfect the *terminus a quo* of which is non-being, and pass through both inanimate and organismic phases toward the personal, the *terminus ad quem* of which is pure being. Always, the object is, at bottom, a "subject-object." Even primitive phenomena exhibit (so I claim) the spiritual as a component of what is (seemingly with objectivity) apprehended. With Whitehead, I declare that the most stringently determined processes are pervaded by spontaneous "self-enjoyment."[3] In complicated processes, higher modes of emotional intensity prevail. Authentic freedom emerges; a creature deliberates regarding conflicting choices for emotional satisfaction. Moreover, in the present book, the factor of transcendentality gradually discloses itself. Germinating at the most elemental, merely physical level of a person's natural composition, this factor more explicitly manifests itself amidst diverse organismic growths, and culminates in the highest modes of personal coherence and unity. Indeed, transcendental unity is most dramatically exemplified when the organismic transfigures itself into the personal. Yet *every* phase of this transfiguration, from elementary to advanced, involves some significant aspect of knowing the person, and enters relevantly into his overall composition *as* person. My purpose is to exhibit these phases, and to show how, on every grade of complexity in their unfolding sequence, they are inseparable and mutually presupposing.

Throughout this book I treat the character of the human body from an essentially optimistic point of view. For the most part, I defer consideration of sin and degradation until, in *Choros*, I begin to treat human lamentation, especially in its interweavings with human celebration. Yet a preliminary rectification of the predominantly ideal perspective of *The Dance of Being* requires that, if briefly, I point toward the interminglings of schemes of balance with schemes of imbalance, toward life's harmonies when assaulted by life's cacophonies.

To proceed: in *The Magic Mountain*, Thomas Mann raises the question "What was life?" And he confesses that no one really knows. Undoubtedly, as soon as it appeared, in however low a form, life was, to a degree, aware of itself, and, indeed, not, as in its earlier shapes, contingent upon a nervous system, let alone a brain. True, it could not yet *know* what it was. Still, consciousness ineluctably pervades all life. Is mind, then, Mann inquires,

> simply a function of matter organized into life; a function that in higher manifestations turned upon its avatar and became an effort to explore and explain the phenomenon it displayed—a hopeful-hopeless project of life to achieve self-knowledge, nature in recoil—and vainly, in the event, since she cannot be resolved in knowledge, nor life, when all is said, listen to itself?[4]

And so again, he asks "What was life?" And, again, no one knows. For where it began, how it kindled itself, what factors initiated it—all lies buried in mystery. Surely, the widest gap between amoeba and vertebrate is minuscule compared to the gulf which yawns between the living and the inanimate. Yet, this demarcation remains obscure. Numberless minute connecting links suggest themselves. The region within which these links function is deep and broad. And whatever their nature, no life form can be found which is devoid of true procreation; and no procreation exists unless some genetic endowment is present. How to draw life from its primeval slime? How to create, or indeed even to account for, this miracle of its prevalence and its myriad ramifyings? How to devise transitions and intermediate stages between its marvelously variegated forms? Must an endless chain of organisms lower than any now known be postulated? Must ever more primitive organisms be assumed to exist—invisible micro-organisms the very existence of which depends upon prior synthesis of complex protein molecules? What then is life? This theme I now take up, at least as it bears upon and contributes to humankind's unfolding spirit. And, tentative and groping, the response comes: life is a

warmth generated by a form-preserving instability, a fever of matter, . . . ₐ . . . half-painful balancing, or scarcely balancing, in . . . process of decay and renewal. . . . It was not matter and it was not spirit, but something between the two, a phenomenon conveyed by matter, like the rainbow on the waterfall, and like the flame. Yet why not material—it was sentient to the point of desire and disgust, the shamelessness of matter become sensible of itself, the incontinent form of being. It was a secret and ardent stirring in the frozen chastity of the universal; it was a stolen and voluptuous impurity of sucking and secreting; an exhalation of carbonic acid gas and material impurities of mysterious origin and composition. It was a pululation, an unfolding, a form-building (made possible by the overbalancing of its instability, yet controlled by the laws of growth inherent within it), of something brewed out of water, albumen, salt and fats, which was called flesh, and which became form, beauty, a lofty image, and yet all the time the essence of sensuality and desire. For this form and beauty were not spirit-borne; nor, like the form and beauty of sculpture, conveyed by a neutral and spirit-consumed substance, which could in all purity make beauty perceptible to the senses. Rather was it conveyed and shaped by the somehow awakened voluptuousness of matter, of the organic, dying-living substance itself, the reeking flesh.[5]

It is "this form and beauty" which I here treat, this "awakened voluptuousness of matter, of the organic," this "essence of sensuality and desire." The entire thrust of my argument throughout *The Dance of Being* is to establish, precisely as Mann has so incisively stated, that midway between matter and spirit—"not matter and . . . not spirit, but something between the two, a phenomenon conveyed by matter, like the rainbow on the waterfall, and like the flame"—hover resonances of a strange and arcane kind, resonances endowed with the power of mirroring the living self in its relationship to the world *to* itself and *to* that world, and, thereby, of metamorphosing that self into something which germinates within it, yet which constitutes an altogether novel orchestration of cosmic reverberations: this "form, beauty, a lofty image . . . yet all the time the essence of sensuality and desire." Still, contrary to Mann's suggestion, life will be regarded here as "reeking flesh," which *is*, indeed, "spirit-borne."

Two principles govern the flow and vicissitudes, the drama and metamorphoses and transmutations, of a person's life; two perspectives blend to shape the curiously interwoven anguish and ecstasy which haunt human experience: its every manifestation, the profound transfigurations which defy life's decay. One principle, and the perspective which it engenders, govern man's quest for ever more pervasive harmonies and integrations—matter spiritualized; another principle, and *its* correlated perspective, govern inexorable lapses into sheer bodily pleasure, dissipations of energy as one sinks toward voluptuousness—spirit materialized. Polarity and yet, surely, complementarity! For neither struggle toward form nor dwelling in matter can prevail alone. For its continuance, each activity needs the other's resistance. In the first instance, one quests after oneness and pure being, toward transcendence and perfection; in the second, one tends toward plurality and becoming, toward the transitory and the imperfect. Yet no unification prevails without parts to be unified; no diversification, without unity to be diversified. No being exists save as ground for flux; no becoming, unrooted in the durable. No transcendence fails to fall toward dissolution; there is no dissolution which cannot spur transcendence. Spirit and matter interpenetrate and commingle, mutually presupposing elements of a single, indivisible, and singular matrix. Still, each element endures and insists upon its own prerogatives: one aspires toward the angel, the other craves the brute. And, surely, the human is both brute and angel. Every person reveals this double proclivity: he rises to the condition of the angel, he sinks to the condition of the brute. At every juncture of life, a fundamental option poses itself: the choice between this rising and this sinking. Surely, the manifold processes of life consist in ebbings and flowings of such transcendence, and shape themselves from countless undulations of transcendence and immanence.

On the one hand, the living body, composed of numberless animalcules which arose perhaps from a single protean cell and multiplied by recurrent division to adapt themselves to the most varied uses, becomes alternately differentiated and newly configured to give birth, from its womb of metabolizing sinew, nerve, and vessel, to a self-determining, sentient, and passionate ego. Inseparably linked to body, this living unity, so remote from simple life forms, threads itself throughout every act of the body. Thus pervaded, the body hovers mysteriously before its very possessor as an alien presence, yet as intimately attuned to all his feelings and thoughts. Fashioned from organisms which, in their time, had breathed and fed and reproduced, a vast and monstrous multitude which, parting from individual freedom and experience's immediacy, had become specialized, hence, truncated, this ego is formed of countless minute acts of reflection. Hierarchically ordered in strands of subordination and superordination, each act contributes its role to body's overall activity; every act modifies an organic plurality as it unites with other reflective acts to shape, to reconstitute, and even to transform the ego. Now myriad proliferatings and fructifyings find their ways to new minglings which ever drive life on afresh.[6]

Nevertheless, protoplasm's achievement remains unaccountable; life seems
doomed to ignorance of its own foundations. And man strives anew to bridge the
gap between the living and the non-living. But should he postulate those molecular
groupings which mediate transitions, he would stand before another abyss, and
yet another. Countless gulfs would spread before us, each more awesome and more
terrifying: molecules dissolving into atoms, atoms dissolving into energies, energies dissolving into the utterly insubstantial. Throughout nature, seemingly perduring assemblages vanish into the ineffable, the inexplicable. And, Mann wonders, does not the "problem of another original procreation" arise, one "far more
wild and mysterious than the organic: the primeval birth of matter out of the
immaterial."[7] Between the two lie vast labyrinths. Lurking in the very wombs of
atoms, those mysterious protozoa of matter, are the frenzied rotations of still more
subtle particles. Everywhere, riotous energies surge; forces too frightening to con-
template press importunely for their unleashing. Comet-like apparitions drive
with light-year speeds through ethereal spaces, abysses eerie in their many-dimen-
sioned depths. Now, eccentric, careening orbits are traced within seemingly
harmonious arrangements; and, within them, energies and momenta are so compressed that, from moment to moment, they threaten to explode to cacophony.
Distinction between large and small, between time racing by and time unfolding
in minute increments, vanishes into ineffable rhythm. Tautly poised by the brinks
of nature's chasms, weird black holes, heaven's mighty powers endlessly ebb and
flow. And, great or little, space–time's stretches mirror themselves, each reflected
into the other, as vast arrays of microcosm and macrocosm; all are nature's darkly
hidden recesses.[8]

Surely, eerily luminous orchestrations of an altogether different order now
reveal themselves. As, indeed, I gaze into my unconscious depths, or as I envisage
the portent of a contemporary physics which strives to penetrate nature's labyrinth,
I discern, were I to respect my veridical experience, abysses of sheer horror. Yet
when I dare to pursue the images buried therein, images which in myriad shape
and hue now intermingle, now rush by, and I peer ever more deeply, ever more
amply, I detect beyond all cacophony, at first as but an obscure hint, their trans-
mogrification into strange, new harmonies: not the harmonies of a Bach's pervasively tranquil counterpoint or of a Mozart's softly melancholic, rhythmic textures,
but of the wild, awesome dissonances of a Bartók. For, as I emerge from these
weird, frightening, numinous vapors, a nearly Manichean phanstasmagoria gives
way to more delicate blendings of dark and light; and when I reflect upon my
odyssey I come more fully to accept the seemingly horrifying forces concealed
within that great pit as likewise harmonious, as balanced in endlessly bizarre,
intricate, and subtle ways.

Now I realize that every person, every part of every person, and every relationship between one person and another mirrors the cosmos, indeed receives the imprint of its universal harmonies. By his inmost yearning for self-perfection, each
man symbolizes these harmonies; and, to express their complexities, symbols shape

themselves in myriad ways. Joining fragments of an experience which is often
diffuse and amorphous to constitute ever higher unities, the person replicates, in
his symbolic articulatings, the most profound cosmic resonances. Through symbols, he so orchestrates these rhythms as to inspire humankind's ever-renewed
questing. Thereby, the parts of his being, their configuring as his very self, and
the community within which he gains spiritual sustenance are all transfigured as
each, in its manner, struggles toward perfection, as each seeks a destiny defined by
an ideal model appropriate to its particular nature.

Yet, again, I am thrust into a new kind of pit. For, on the other hand, amidst
this great harmony, and spoliating, as it were, the grand procession of great and
small, each reflecting in its inmost depths myriad facets of the other, is inward
decay, bizarre, errant, and often monstrous cells, strange coagulations, "the accentuation of the physical through pain; yet, in so far as it was the accentuation
of the physical, at the same time accentuation through desire." For, as Mann now
announces, "Disease was a perverse, a dissolute form of life. And life? Life itself?
Was it perhaps only an infection, a sickening of matter? Was that which one
might call the original procreation of matter only a disease, a growth produced by
morbid stimulation of the immaterial?"[9] Perhaps when spirit becomes more
dense, a pathologic growth luxuriates, migrates along strange paths, oozes to an
archaic and frightful residue. Might not, indeed, existence doubly fall from grace
—in its transitions, to substance, in its birthing the organic? Could it not be
merely the accentuation of some morbid process? And, as it gathers momentum,
might it not resemble a grotesque intoxication, yet be the ecstatic outpouring of
spirit? An efflux of pathogens, toxins perhaps, is needed, that the anti-toxic soul
might germinate. Could evolving matter be little more than a weird perversion?
Might not evil breed in the very womb of processes which, goaded on by the dim
and obscure goal toward which they seem to unfold, yearn to overcome evil?
Could the good demand the bad's resistance, and even its migrant ways? Might
not falling from grace and rising toward grace interweave their most essential
ingredients? Could life itself be but a defense against strange and alien infiltra-
tions, festering irritants? Might it not even require for its own sustenance that
against which it arises? Could consciousness itself be "but the next step on the
reckless path of the spirit dishonoured; nothing but the automatic blush of matter roused to sensation and become receptive for that which awaked it?"[10]

Still a counter-thrust never ceases to prevail. Against evil's harsh ways, its ob-
duracy and its persistence, could not an altogether new efflux arise, at once delicate and fragile, yet compelling and insistent? So Hans Castorp, Mann's ever-
questing hero, mused; and

> He beheld the image of life in flower, its structure, its flesh-borne loveliness. She
> had lifted her hands from behind her head, she opened her arms. On their inner
> side, particularly beneath the tender skin of the elbow-points, he saw the blue
> branchings of the larger veins. These arms were of unspeakable sweetness. She
> leaned above him, she inclined unto him and bent down over him, he was

conscious of her organic fragrance and the mild pulsation of her heart. Something warm and tender clasped him round the neck; melted with desire and
awe, he laid his hands upon the flesh of her upper arms, where the fine-grained
skin over the triceps came to his sense so heavenly cool; and upon his lips he felt
the moist clinging of her kiss.[11]

Now sensuality is powerfully transformed from a mere organic excrescence, far
beyond a Bacchanalian efflux, into organic matter which has been touched by
spirit. Images of tenderness utterly transfigure vein, heart, skin, muscle. Already,
the organic is in process of transcendence toward the divine. Mere body sensation
and stark gratification give way to human warmth. Everywhere, the spirit hovers.
Nature *as* nature has been brought to its penultimate moment; the utterances of
natural love are on the threshold of their birth. Thus yielding itself *as* flesh, flesh
can only thenceforth await the imprinting upon it of spirit. But no naturalistic
account of human being is competent to trace the vicissitudes of spirit's inscrip-
tions. An altogether new perspective is required: the perspective of transcendental personalism, to be set forth in my succeeding books.

No lines more eloquently or succinctly bespeak the themes of this book, in
which I write of *the great dance of being.* Mann incomparably evokes my main
tenor and drift. And if at times my language be too ornamented, or I take liberties
with cross-linguistic constructions such as "personogenesis," or I seem unduly to
manipulate prefixes and suffixes, it is because we need an altogether new language for speaking of man in a synoptic, and syncretist, way. A person's inherent
mystery requires new paths for conveying genuine paradox and irreducible intricacy in the realms of spirit and nature; it demands that we join science to the
humanities. In these pages, I grope toward framing such a language. And should
hypotheses I herein propose seem disconnected from the work of scientists who
treat man's *particular* aspects, I take refuge in this conviction: inquiry into
humankind is an autonomous discipline, a field in its own right, which, though
borrowing from other fields, is, in the end, answerable to none. I cannot pretend
that such hypotheses, when suggested, are sacrosanct. On the contrary, they are
meant not to substitute for science but merely to exemplify plausible schemes for
illuminating the person. They are conjectures which, appealing to my own philosophic instincts, will, perhaps, stimulate others to *their* philosophic questings.
For I seek to coordinate science's established results, and to explicate vague hints
which it has not yet dared to incorporate within its announced theories. I suggest proposals the details of which are destined to be superseded as science itself
advances, and as it abandons, as surely it must, its own hitherto most persuasive
and treasured findings. Always, in the end, the person remains mysterious, reveren-
tial, irreducibly concrete, and integral.

But, again, we cannot evade the dilemma. How, amidst the countless interweavings of good and evil may the former emerge victorious? Or is it doomed to
inexorable defeat? Again and again, this question presents itself. If the person
as a whole, rather than any of his parts, is the final datum (and *datio!*) to be ex-

plained, is not one driven to acknowledge, beyond his spirit's glory, his deformations and his divisions—even, indeed, amidst his very fructifications? No account of man's lesser nature, manifest in his deepest origins—and expressed, in man's later reversions and recidivisms, by his more perverse kinds of giving—can fail to note humankind's more frightening aberrations.

Yet human grotesquery is always relative to beauty's consummations: to its forms so subtly destined to spring from embryonic man; to its forms concealed as but latent possibilities within perverse deviations from humankind's finer examples. Nonetheless, pervading every phase of human development are bizarre, luxuriant growths, coagulated protoplasm, monstrous decaying cells, organs staggering toward dissolution, parasites which consume wholesome tissue's nourishment and in their wake leave only destruction and toxicity. True, though tenuous, nature's harmonies are wonderful, mysterious, optimistic; yet, after all, nature *is* dumb, arbitrary, and chaotic. It *is* red in tooth and claw. Even to perpetuate itself, nature must consume itself. Nature *is* predatory. Indeed, could it not be that concealed in the very mystery and miracle of living cells as, in the manner I herein trace, they unfold toward personhood are the uttermost sources of devilment? Must not, then, man's profoundest lamentation be itself a ground for celebrating all creation's glory? Might not that lamentation betoken a step-by-step compounding of sin, hence even some dim form of contrition, which lurks in every tissue, cell, and molecule—each instance of sin minute, but, in their totality, momentous and awesome? For, if perfection's quest qualify every existent, must not its opposing power for self-mockery, deceit, and defect equally inhere within it?

I cannot deny the validity of these theses. I may only affirm that in my next book, *Choros*, the theme of tragedy will be taken up; and both there and in subsequent books I shall sketch how matter, life, and human being perpetually fall away from their own potential fruitions. Yet, as I then work out and in this book prefigure, they fall away only to rise again: to rise in the face of seemingly insuperable opposing forces, as witness to a grace which Divinity has conferred, always in the end, upon its every creature. Such, at least, is the unexpressed but pervasive faith of this undertaking. And so I here stress, as I shall in my every book, the themes of human wonder, human achievement, mutual reverence of man for man and of man for God in their never-ending dialogues; and I presuppose, as always, the doctrine of being's redemption, and of the redemption of each instance of being, even such instances as haunt remote and inaccessible regions— creation's rejected and despised corners. For I can only reiterate my root supposition: throughout the cosmos, a profound glory reigns indefeasibly, and ceaselessly affirms itself.

Surely, in my every act I struggle. I struggle with myself and I struggle with myriad forces which reside within me and about me; and I sense the struggle between one force and another as each part of my body, in its minute yet ineluctable quest for autonomy, pits itself against another part. True, in these struggles and by these inexorable quests, I am, again and again, as is my every questing part, thrust back, back indeed and away from an ideal I have set for myself. But surely this very struggle spurs my efforts toward that ideal's renewal. In every instance of my sinking from it, I am impelled to strive toward it. True, never ceasing to haunt me, the cave's shadows draw me ever anew into recidivistic ways which diminish the ideal. Yet, in dialectic of advance and retreat, as ideals are alternately posed and shattered, I reaffirm *my* ideal. Pervading me and haunting me, it directs my every act—no matter how aborted its incarnation within that act, no matter how much I from time to time refuse to entrust myself to it, I cannot desist from allowing it, however minuscule its shape, to reassert itself and to press against me for my full acceptance. In softly relentless steps, one by one or many by many, it assumes new guises. In this book, I affirm hope which resides within humanity's natural being, trust which envelops that being, spirit which suffuses that being.

Like Virginia Woolf's moth, though, in the end, it is doomed to lie eternally still and quiet, every creature, as long as it lives, flies vigorously from one corner of its compartment to another. That was all the moth could do, she tells us,

> in spite of the downs, the width of the sky, the far-off smoke of houses, and the romantic voice, now and then, of a steamer out at sea. What he could do he did. Watching him, it seemed as if a fibre, very thin but pure, of the enormous energy of the world had been thrust into his frail and diminutive body. As often as he crossed the pane, I could fancy that a thread of vital light became visible. He was little or nothing but life.[12]

"Little or nothing but life"! Human being, naturalistically construed, *is* this life: life immensely more intricate, miraculously intensified. Of the forces of nature which shape man's life, I now speak. And wherein consists that life, naturalistically construed, but echoes, with embellishment, of the rhythms and the melody of the rejected, despised moth? Watching its flittings and its meanderings and its minutely humble motions, not however without a certain dignity, one might so easily forget it. It was "as if someone had taken a tiny bead of pure life and decking it as lightly as possible with down and feather had set it dancing and zigzagging to show us the true nature of life."[13] Even in modest and minuscule shape, life resounds throughout the universe's temples and vaults. How much more does the person, immeasurably compounded of life's pure tiny beads, imprint *his* dance upon creation!

NOTES

1. Trans. H. T. Lowe-Porter (New York: Knopf, 1948), p. 29.

2. This, and the following quotations, will be found on pp. 1 and 2.

3. Alfred North Whitehead, *Adventures of Ideas* (New York: Macmillan, 1933), p. 249.

4. Trans. H. T. Lowe-Porter (New York: Knopf, 1975), p. 274.

5. Ibid., pp. 275–76.
6. Ibid., pp. 276–83.
7. Ibid., p. 283.
8. Ibid., p. 284.
9. Ibid., pp. 285–86.
10. Ibid., p. 286.
11. Ibid.
12. *The Death of the Moth and Other Essays* (London & New York: Harcourt, Brace, Jovanovich, 1974), p. 4.
13. Ibid.

I

The Building of Life:
Primordial Categories

1

THE ROOTS
OF THE INFRAPERSONAL:
A VECTOR TOWARD MAN

PREAMBLE

Though my general theme is man's infrapersonal ground, and I designate this chapter "The Roots of the Infrapersonal," the particular "vector toward man" which these roots constitute implicates several general ontologic notions: namely, *agent, power,* and *rhythm.* To facilitate discussion of these ideas, such additional themes as essence, existence, identity, sociality, action, and reflection must also be explored. In their consummate as well as in their primordial forms, all these notions are most strikingly exemplified less by man's infrapersonal parts than by man himself. Though my book deals, for the most part, with the person's inanimate and organismic aspects, I must introduce my account of the infrapersonal by stepping directly into my principal topic: namely, the ontology of the person. For, though I here stress the proto-human factor which grounds human being, this factor is not the only source of man's humanness. As I proceed, I introduce a dual vector, a vector composed of oppositely directed components: the first, focus of my current study, represents man's derivation via the routes of the thingly and the animate, ultimately, indeed, from non-being; the second, focus of later study, represents man's derivation from pure being. Too, I later discuss the complementarity and unity of these vectors; in addition, I delineate the ground of their fusion, and the way in which interconversions are mediated between privative being and plenitudinous being.

The categories agent, power, and rhythm are relevant to man both in his primordial, "original" nature and in his consequent and derivative nature. By the first aspect of man's nature, I mean his constitutive potencies, their *modi operandi,* and the principles in accordance with which they both activate and fructify one an-

other in human expression. By the second aspect, I mean the vicissitudes, co-dependencies, and destiny of the symbols by which human expression is communicated. With respect to the former aspect, these categories are explicated in the present chapter. With respect to the latter, the categories will be amplified in a later book, *Apotheosis,* which treats the person qua person. Since I regard proto-human existence as privatively but nonetheless authentically exemplifying these categories, I introduce them at the very outset. Following my account of agent and power, in their primordial applicability to man, I deal with rhythm in its proto-human character as well as in its strictly *human* relevance to agency and power. In this way, I provide a metaphysical context for depicting such subhuman activity as bears directly upon a theory of man; beyond that, I indicate how these (categoreal) dimensions of being are constitutive of the person himself. Accordingly, my analysis is essentially propaedeutic to an examination of the person qua proto-human. In no respect does it presuppose what will later appear as human ontology. My account is *relatively* autonomous, self-contained, and independent with respect both to *Homo Quaerens* and to subsequent books on the person qua person. Nevertheless, the broader context of my enterprise remains the person: his essential dynamisms, his myriad symbolisms, his variegated modes of existence. Fully to illuminate my argument, I must refer my reader to my entire work.

The three categories of being—agent, power, and rhythm—are complementary, interdependent, and mutually presupposing. In the last analysis, they are interwoven as a single, integral concept. The consummation of these categories—hence, of the concept within which they are subordinate but necessary components —is achieved only on the level of full person-hood. However, by privation, they are equally applicable to all forms of existence, animate and inanimate. In my treatment, I mingle statements of their applicability to infrapersonhood with statements concerning their applicability to man *in stricto sensu*.

A · BEING AS AGENT

(a) The Unity of the Person

In *Homo Quaerens*, I raised the question "What, essentially, and from a philosophic point of view, is a person?" I set forth themes which, further explored and systematically interwoven, approximate to a plausible philosophic answer. Later I asked "What, essentially, is a philosophic inquiry into the person?" Stressing the concept *inquiry*, I showed, first, that the method which one must use is organically woven of diverse phases and diverse moments; that, in their very plurality, these phases and moments exhibit cohesiveness, reciprocal dependency, multiple correlations, correspondences and analogies, and profound inner unity. Secondly, I showed how my question's import implies that the concept *person* must, equally, be stressed; that a deep affinity prevails between the methodologic question "What, from the point of view of *inquiry*, is a philosophic inquiry into the person?" and the ontologic question "What, from the point of view of the *person*, is a philosophic inquiry into the person?"

Effectively to treat the original question "What, essentially, and from a philosophic point of view, is a person?" I must explicitly acknowledge an organic relatedness between the method for clarifying an ontologic issue and the ontologic issue itself. Having set forth Method's principal tenets, I found that I could proceed no further until, in the present investigation, I *re*-ask from a now enriched ontologic point of view—i.e., one which reflects upon man's infrapersonal nature —"What, at bottom, is a person?": enriched initially by a tentative mapping out of salient themes; enriched later by frank application to empirical matters of the injunctions which comprise that tentative schema.

Previously, many observations, themes, and formulations of an ontologic nature were set forth. On the whole, I now construe those remarks to be but an impressionistic survey of what henceforth I must systematically present. My ontologic commentary was given in an essentially non-ontologic frame of reference. Two contexts of inquiry were relevant: the general problematic of my method and the actual working through of my method. In the former, I sought to predelineate in compressed fashion and to anticipate the complexity of what will now be unraveled progressively and in detail. In the latter, ontologic topics were introduced only insofar as they were needed to elucidate, and create a groundwork for, an essentially methodologic task. Doubtless, certain ontologic issues were illuminated. They will be presented anew, but in such a way as to allow them to be woven into a generalized theory of the person. Without attempting to recapitulate these issues, since they will recur in varying shapes, I merely re-present them at this time in more succinct formulation. The relevant ontologic topics may be subsumed under the rubrics of *essence* and *existence*; these themes will themselves be unified under the category *agent*.

As essence, the person is a unity; as existence, a plurality. In the former, he is "centered" in his own potency toward action. Paradoxically, he both persists as he is and transforms himself into what he is not. Thus self-persisting, he is invariantly himself. Thus self-transforming, he is competent to inspect what, as invariant, he essentially is. To inspect his essence, qua invariant, is to search inwardly; but his quest discloses that invariant as problematic. By his essence, incorporated in his essential searching, the person becomes a problem to himself. He is impelled to solve the problem of his own existence: how he comes to be a plurality when, in fact, he is a unity. Searchingly to experience this unity is to peer into labyrinthine depths. What was initially perceived as the constancy of his own being—namely, *his I searching his I*—now becomes object of that search: that is, *his I searching his I* becomes *his "me."* On the assumption that the searching role of "me" now therefore becomes *I*, what hitherto had been *I* is now, reciprocally, converted to *me*. Essentially interchangeable, *I* and *me* dialectically oscillate. In this process (of self-objectification), the person's "*I–me*" is converted into an *It*. Inspection reveals this It to be cavernous, impersonal, and archetypal, yet profoundly subjective, an *interior* object of intricate and variable makeup.

When one discerns the complexity of this pattern, one becomes intrigued with the problematic which it poses. Intrigued, indeed! It is as though intrigue itself unfolds, in its own stages, so arcane is the *It*. A person's inward searching becomes committed, and in his quest to penetrate his own essentiality, his powers are increasingly mobilized. Now his essence is revealed to him as, in fact, an *antithesis* between a *searching I* and a *sought It*. Both factors constitute the person in his interiority. The more he exercises his powers inwardly to search, the more the *It* seems to acquire, and "hastens" to disclose, its own countervailing powers. *I* and *It* are locked in combat. Through their opposition something new is born. What had initially been assumed to be the absolutely essential person is now disclosed as masking a more profoundly essential person. Through essential search, essentiality is corrigible. Essentially transfigured, the person does not terminate his quest. On the contrary, his very essence reveals itself to consist in his conducting the quest, pursuing whatever trajectories unfold before him.

Analogous to a person's introspective searching is a correlative, and complementary, extrospective searching. He questions another person with respect to *his* essence, and the mystery of *his* being. The more he questions, the more profoundly and syncretistically he attends. First, he discerns the essential inseparability of body and mind. He experiences each as a flowing forth composed of acts, pulses which merge into one another. As he penetrates the "essence" of each series, he perceives it to be but the manifestation of a single, underlying substratum: an agent empowered to disclose his unitary being under both a bodily and a mental perspective. Analogously, he experiences his own physicality and spirituality. In both instances, he perceives these series in either of two ways: as detached and relatively autonomous, or as intimately conjoined.

As he listens more attentively, the one initially sought addresses him, the searcher, from *his* center (i.e., the former's). He (the searcher) draws into his own being an imprint of the other. He even reflects into himself the other's own inward searching. *A fortiori*, the searcher experiences a multitude of other selves-searching-into-themselves. He experiences this multitude as, in fact, dwelling within him. As he continues to reflect, he transforms his own being. In reflection, he identifies with the other, and, by these identifyings, weds potent new factors to his own self-transfiguration—a process already instituted as originating from within his own being. By the same token, the other searches *him*. He searches the searcher as, correlatively, he (the one originally sought) searches himself. Accordingly, the being of each person becomes inextricably interwoven with the being of the other, reflexively and from within. By generalization, the entire community collectively searches. As a searching community, it dwells, in its collective way, immanently within its every member, and constitutes itself a witness to each person's individual quest: a witness incorporated into that person's very being. And to exist is to *co*-exist; it is to coexist in communion. In communion, the dialectically constituted "essence" of each becomes orchestrated with the dialectically constituted "essences" of all.

By this dialectic, every person gives himself to another. He is a *datio* providing data for the other's assimilation. Reciprocally, the other receives from him the gift of *his* being. Witnessed by the communal presence, a reciprocity of givings constitutes the ground for the collective transfiguration of all. Each person interprets the gifts which he receives, and responds to them as symbols of a caring presence. In the measure to which he is protected by a tenderly giving community, each person dares to penetrate further into the mystery of his being—beyond that, to the mystery of being-in-general. The awe with which he beholds the wholly Other grows—and, as he searches, so does the reverence. Indeed, each person experiences himself as a medium through which in general being reveals itself, being as refracted by the prism of his idiosyncratic makeup. In the last analysis, the essential person is the one who, in multiple acts of (pious) reflection, makes himself transparent to the marvelously kaleidoscopic realm within him. Though this realm is privately apprehended, it nonetheless publicly binds all persons together. They become concelebrants of the orchestrated facets of the great mystery of being.

The essential person constitutes himself a unity in varying senses. First, he is a unitary locus of searching: he searches within to discern the unity of the suprapersonal being which resides immanently within all; he searches without to discern the unity of each person, himself an analogous searcher, whom he engages; he searches without to discern the unity of the infrapersonal cosmos which, nevertheless, dwells (as well) organically within him. Next, he is a unity of manifold powers, a potency for diversifying himself into many existential expressions. Third, he is a unity centered in himself—self-identical, self-engendering, and self-regenerative activity. Fourth, he is a unity of reflexive (hence, reflective) acts: he draws into himself an Imago of the other; this Imago includes, as one of its elements, *his* Imago reflexively framed by that other. Fifth, he is a unity of a conjunction of opposites: a disunity, dialectically contained within his own unity, which is constituted by the interplay of *I* and *It*. Next, he is a unity in the integrality of his mental acts and his physical acts: two series, internally correlated, betoken his integrated activity. Seventh, he is a unity of self-affirming and self-metamorphosing being, individuating himself amidst the diversity of his acts. Next, he is a unity of commitment; subsuming all commitments, this inclusive commitment involves pervasive loyalty and trust. Ninth, he is a unity of the synthesizing of diverse elements of his being *into* unity. Finally, he is a unity of style and a quality of life—a charisma, peculiarly his own, which can be "read" only through the symbolisms of the plurality of his expressions, expressions congruent with one another with respect to his cohesive and coherent being. In short, the person is a unity involving centeredness, loyalty, trust, and an activity of diversifying and unifying; he is a unity involving self-identification, self-affirmation, and self-transfiguration.

(b) Essentiality as a Quality

From the standpoint of the complementarity of essence and existence, these reflections constitute the fuller import of my desultory ontologic comments in *Homo Quaerens*. Having set the stage, I may proceed with inquiry into the person, philosophically considered, which is *systematic*. To clarify my position, I require a fairly intricate ontologic schema. As primary notions from which the remainder are to be derived, I propose the interwoven ideas of essence, existence, and rhythm. At the moment, I treat the complemental pair of essence and existence. To prepare the way for conceptualizing my root idea, *rhythm*, I next elaborate seriatim the themes of agency, power, and (in this context) identity. Finally, I show how through the interplay of the preceding notions I may define rhythm. Subsequently, this idea will function like a searchlight. Focusing now on this aspect of human ontology now on that, rhythm will also illuminate such critical derivative topics, equally essential for a conceptualizing of the person's development, as his symbolisms and his destiny.

To speak of what a person essentially is to imply that he is in one way an integer, a unity of intrinsic traits, and in another, an aggregate of contingent and "accidental" traits. As essence, he is at once a *being* and a *to be*. In the first instance, the person is a mere enduring, without reference to past or future. As such, he *is*, simply and unqualifiedly. Yet to endure, an entity must become other than what it is, no matter what the depth of resemblance between an initial state and a succeeding one. Endlessly counterposed to the traces within it of what had been, this "other" weaves these traces into yet another, in continual sequence.

True, endurance implies a lasting, a toughness, a self-identity in the sense of an unchanging core of traits. Yet identity itself is but persistence amidst change, inner change as well as outer. What changes inwardly, in conjunction with the vicissitudes of the context in which a person is embedded, is that which is to be. As the latter, a person is the one who by enduring—hence, bearing as part of his inmost constitution a past—thrusts himself toward his future; this thrusting is itself a part of that constitution. His own continued existence implies his agency, a continual bringing forth of novel consequences despite repetition of basic motifs; and the essential consequence of his being is his ever-renewed being. Accordingly, the essence of a person is bound up with temporality; to raise questions about that essence is to deal with the nature of time. For the person is an activity and a ferment, an unfolding of lived time, who continually imprints himself into himself—a gathering together of what had been into presence, hence, a re-collecting and a self-duplicating yet a synthesizing of something new.

As accident, the person is an appearing, a particular way of manifesting his being. He is a standing forth and a presenting, to himself and to another. What he "presents" is a quality, a trait, a mood, an utterance—some mode of behavior. Yet each appearing passes. As being, he endures; as appearing, there is evanescence. The ways in which, in his inmost nature, he shines forth are in perpetual flux. Every appearance is a disclosure, obscure or luminous, of a something other than that appearance, alien to it yet "contained" within it and, in the final analysis, indissociable from it; it is a manifesting, i.e., a "bringing to hand,"[1] of what had been hidden. This "something," this essence, is both estranged from appearance and immanent within it. A person both veils himself, in his essential being, and reveals that being. What he is (his self-revelation) may only be deciphered from those veils. In effect, they constitute symbols of his essence—physical (i.e., behaviorally identifiable) marks of a spiritual content, an inner life which persists in its very fluidity; marks by which he presents this life to another, as well as to himself, and thereby joins himself, however momentary the encounter, to that other. In consequence, the person is an aggregate of aspects (i.e., appearances or veils). Each is both a fragment of his existence and a perspectival illumination of a something the character of which is not exhausted by the summing of those aspects yet never transcends them. This "something" cannot lie beyond any particular way in which he presents himself. At bottom, it is simply that which unites the diversity of aspects and, suffusing them, brings about their congruence and their integration. As such, it is the inner meaning, the *spiritus* or very breath of life, of the symbolism of his presence.

To proceed, I may now affirm: by a person's essence, I mean a quality which, practically speaking, is unique, undefinable, primordial, ineffable, concrete though unspecifiable; I mean a quality which, setting this particular individual apart from all other individuals, distinguishes him as unitary and indiscerptible. By "practically speaking," I mean both the procedure of indicating that quality and the activity of orienting oneself toward the person who embodies it. But no simple criterion can be formulated by which a quality may be adjudged, in an absolute sense, to be irreducible. Nor, short of a thoroughly worked out metaphysical scheme, a scheme in which a particular theory of the person is certified as plausible, may the irreducibility of personal distinguishing qualities be conceptualized. Finally, every individual essence, absolute and unique though it be, is itself a particular variation upon another kind of essence: that which confers universality on each person, establishing him as a special instance of humankind.

Suppose, then, a given quality to be, in truth, a composite of qualities. Instead of a single quality, a congeries of qualities is imputed to the person as constituting his essence. It would follow that the essence is additionally imbued with a power of "holding into" unity its diverse parts, a unity which itself is distinctively qualitied. Only upon the supposition that an absolutely elementary quality be deemed *the* essence of a person may that essence be radically disaffiliated from an associated power. Were there such complete dissociation between the person's allegedly elementary quality and his power, that power would be no longer a unity, but a diversity the dual members of which cannot be held together. He would be not one being but a dyadic being, a dyad the paired components of which would be but tenuously conjoined.

Yet how can a quality, presumably a complex, also be a power, or even be intimately woven with a power? In normal parlance, one speaks of a man's distinctive quality. By this locution, one means precisely what I have been alluding to: namely, a man's indefeasibly individual character. Because of its capacity for self-potentiation as specific deed, character *has* quality, or *is* quality. One cannot think "character" apart from thinking its implementation in practice, its impact upon both its "possessor" and those whom that possessor encounters. Character is not character unless it is, at one and the same time, translated into act. One cannot construe quality without construing resistance; one cannot construe resistance without construing action and reaction; and one cannot construe action and reaction without construing agency. But to deal with the manifestation of quality as act (hence, act of an initiating agent), yet act which in some way is indistinguishable from its "originating" quality, one must treat the complement of essence, *existence*.

To attribute a particular character to a particular man is also to imply that this character is but one instance of a more general quality—a universal, if you will, attributable to all men. In truth, the manifold qualities of men are but variations upon a single theme, the character of humankind; and this character is itself a quality. Often, quality is spoken of as abstract and general. But the question immediately arises: How can a singular quality, which is concrete, be an instance of a general quality, which is abstract? For this to be, on some as yet undefined interpretation, a general quality must be in addition particular and concrete. And if *this* were the case, then each variant would, indeed, be a concrete universal, an instance of a type; still, qua instance it must partake of the nature of that type. In this sense, the universal dwells immanently within each man. In a different sense, still concrete, it transcends each man. Self-identically and idiosyncratically himself, every person is, in that very identity and contemporaneously with it, self-identically that type. In effect, he is *type*-identical. Nonetheless, though in this instance universal and particular become as one, that universal must, qua universal, subsume that particular. Precisely how does this singular essence relate to a universal essence—an essence now abstract and then concrete, now one with the singular and then inclusive of the singular?

For an ontology of the person this is indeed a central problem. But resolution of so subtle an enigma resides not in a simple formula. Quite the contrary. The entire apparatus of a generalized theory of the person is required. To discern the many facets of this problem, an extensive analysis is needed of what it means for a person *to be*. Only in the context of concepts which, in these pages, I progressively articulate may reasonable, if provisional, solutions be provided.

To ground this context, the person's fundamental character must be set forth. Accordingly, I suggest: he is an agent empowered to relate to other agents, and relate in such manner that his interior rhythms are externalized as symbols of his essential being; the symbolic manifolds drawn forth from his inward being themselves interweave to constitute a more inclusive symbol, the meaning of which resides in the orchestration of those collective rhythms in their contrapuntal interplay. To clarify this formulation of the essential person, I now advert to topics previously enumerated: namely, agency, power, identity, rhythm.

(c) The Person as Existent and Symbol

By "existence in general," I mean the interplay of existents, each an agent. By an "existent in particular," I mean a distinctive way of being in the world: a distinctive manner of engaging others which (or who) are analogously in the world. By "world," I mean the interplay of horizons of entities: horizons which endlessly expand, contract, interact, exclude, and overlap; entities which are objects both for discrimination and for engaging by existents associated with particular (and distinctive) horizons. In every instance, a "creature"—complex or simple, animate or inanimate—stands forth in its creatureliness; and this standing forth is effected through the interaction of contingent powers, which surround it, with the self-potentiating powers, which reside within it.

In a manner appropriate to its actual inner constitution and with widely varying gradations of "selfhood," every creature declares itself to be what it essentially is. By self-affirmation, it preserves its identity amidst vicissitudes of intense contrasts of "feeling."[2] In some creatures this feeling is of the order of actual awareness; in but a few, it attains the reflexive intricacy of self-awareness. For all, identity is preserved amidst contingency. From without and from within, influences never cease to impinge upon those creatures. For all, the "feeling" of identity is heightened, solidified, and deepened through successive acts of self-declaring. For all, as novel expressions of their being are drawn forth from hitherto concealed resources, this primordial germinating awareness is, or tends to be, intensified. In each instance, every manifestation of their existence is joined to a reality which, in and by virtue of this merging, continually expands: reality increases in plenitude amidst its ever more labyrinthine and inwardly coiling character. Indeed, reality itself is shaped by a plenum of participants, by its reciprocally constitutive yet mutually isolated and self-individualizing creatures.

Clearly, I am affirming a fairly definite cosmologic doctrine. I propose a creaturely world, essentially an assemblage of agents-in-relation. According to this view, the cosmos is conceived to be an intricately hierarchical ordering of creatures: each is self-active; all are interactive; the totality is transactive. By "transactive," I mean this twofold doctrine: from the perspective of any creature, the world may be divided into its constitutive creatures in manifold ways; from the combined perspectives of all its creatures, the world may be arranged as an indefinite variety of forms.

I have used terms like feeling, identity, agency; I have referred to *self*-declaring, *self*-affirming, *self*-potentiating creatures. By "creature," I have meant simply a creation. Beyond that, I mean an agent who, with the cooperation of external powers—some induced into activity *by* that creature—is capable of catalyzing *from within* its own activity. This doctrine presumes a germ of freedom to be "residing" in every creature. It further presumes a primordial selfhood; for I attribute to the creature an inwardness, a capacity for interiorizing and, therefore, some primordial kind of feeling. By "feeling," I mean the world as it is *for* that creature with respect to its own (self-) identity. Some creatures consist of loosely assembled subordinate creatures; in others, the components cohere more tightly. In no instance, however, do I deny some kind of "feeling" (in the sense indicated) to both whole and part. The more complex creatures are assumed to be affected, in some manner, by their constituent (creaturely) elements.

In building a philosophic doctrine of the person, I commit myself to a minimum of cosmologic and general ontologic suppositions. On the whole, I introduce these commitments *as* I work out my doctrine. In *Homo Quaerens*, especially in the final chapter, several such commitments were announced. These will be repeated, with elaboration, in the present book; and new commitments will gradually be added. I formulate statements pertaining to cosmology and general ontology as succinctly as possible. Only broad contours, not finer details, will be presented. Such conceptual apparatus as is essential for two purposes alone will be introduced: that pertaining to the composition both of the person and of his relevant milieu as in each instance constituted by subordinate agents; and that pertaining to the foundations of a specific ontology of the person with respect to his essential unity. Prior to my resuming an account of *these* doctrines—namely, the person as plurality and the person as unity—I must add some additional cosmologic assumptions.

By my theory, no "existent" can be mere being. As soon as there is being, there is becoming, and this in the least flash of existence. *Becoming* is, in effect, a coming-to-be; newly emergent being is new becoming. To deprive being of some element of becoming is to negate being; it then vanishes into non-being. Later, *non*-being will be reinterpreted as the matrix wherein being comes to be.

At this point, I make no reference to unconditioned being. My remarks here are confined to conditioned being, with respect to which *to be* is "to essence"; "to essence" is to open up into presence—literally, pre-essence: a being before a (potential or prospective) recipient. To be present is to exist in relatedness to another; so "to exist" is to pass out of mere stasis into *ek*-stasis, the vibrance of relational being. By "vibrance," I refer to transmitted pulsation, reverberation, resonance. In short, I mean a rhythm which is propagated to another.

According to my doctrine, the world echoes and resounds with rhythm: rhythm simpliciter, rhythm interwoven as harmony and cacophony, rhythm synergistically mounting to polyphony. Further, *as* becoming, the existence of an existent is a process. It is a process of rhythmically intertwined moments and of rhythmically propagated impulses. Originating in a germinal "center," existing is the manifold of acts which, as they unfold, tend (in the successive aggregates which they form) to cohere as a unity, but never a simple unity. On the contrary, these acts cohere as a unity of rhythmically oscillating and spiraling contrasts, contrasts of variegated coilings and uncoilings. In their consummate expression, they add both depth and meaning to a fluctuant reality.

By "expression," I mean a pressing out of something new, an imprinting of a novel element into the world. What is pressed out is a response to another existent, for which the ramifications of response are diverse and penetrating. Moreover, every response echoes beyond the immediate recipient to infuse with diminuendos and crescendos the entire orchestration of reality. By *consummate* expression, I mean the transmitting of an authentic impression of the one who expresses, an Imago of who or what that one truly is. Such response touches the very "centers" whence arise other existents. By the power "felt" in this touching, the respondent "realizes" its inherent autonomy; it makes its autonomy a vibrant actuality for itself, and gains an impression of its own authentic core. By the repeated touching of *one* center, the respondent's authenticity is affirmed; by the repeated touching of *many* centers, the respondent's authenticity is confirmed. Through a multitude of analogous impressions, that core is solidified and strengthened.

By attending the other, listening to it, and gathering in its varied aspects—in short, by *searching* the other—the respondent confirms to itself its inherent freedom. Indefeasibly free, each "center" stamps something of its own character upon what has been imprinted into it. Thus assimiliating the new item, the respondent absorbs it into its *own* being. An ideal is thereby envisaged: to convey to the encountered other a veridical impression, woven into its being, of what or whom the originative agency truly is. To achieve this ideal, a movement is initiated toward the other, a movement the possibility for the attainment of which is rooted in the germinating center of that agency. The fruition of this germ is potency actualized and repercussive.

Its intrinsic powers "invisible" as immanent within yet symbolically manifested by the actual, this creature presents itself as a non-temporal "unfolding": a coming to fruition at each instant of its existence, an integral which endures through multiphasic pulse. Potent source and actualized power are themselves aspects, correlative and complementary, of every moment and of every pulse, in the temporal growth of any creature; and the person, I now suggest, is the exemplary creature. Entering into the very composition of *this* creature are subordinate creatures in all stages of intricacy, capacity for relatedness, and durability of identity. Now, I treat the qualities peculiar not so much to a person's constituent elements—save by successive privation of complexity and intensity of feeling—as to the person himself.

Through the actualization of a person's latent powers, an expressive manifold is continuously engendered. Its every element derives from his inward being. Beneath the spectatorial as immanent within each of its parts lie vague and premonitory, but potent, stirrings, stirrings which form this invisible realm and perpetually bring the spectatorial to fruition; stirrings which endlessly reverberate in a person's inmost depths, combining and recombining to shape ever-new arrangements; stirrings to which in utterance, gesture, and movement he never ceases to give expression; stirrings toward which this manifold points as a cohesive pattern of *symbols* within which are "contained" an interior archetypal object, their ultimate transcendental referent.

In every symbolization, there is a threefold joining, a συμβάλλειν. First, disparate expressions are fused into an indivisible entity, a single presence which impinges durably on all who confront it; this presence *is* the person presenting himself in all modalities of presence. Next, inner and outer are blended into a unity of action as powers exteriorize themselves in acts ineluctably informed by intent. Finally, charged with action, this entity as embodied in a person is itself united to other entities incarnate; a community of interactant persons thereby arises, persons whose very communion enhances (by their collective participation in the symbols which they originate), not sacrifices, their individualities. Each dips into the composite in his own fashion; each, thereby, reaffirms his own character.

Accordingly, a symbol is neither a word nor any other particular (type of) expression; it is not a static entity. On the contrary, by "symbol," I mean a process of expressing and, through expression, a presenting to another. To symbolize is to actualize a specific human potentiality. As the symbol unfolds, it reveals (to that "other") its meaning to reside in a spiritual content. This content is determined and, indeed, liberated by a special class of relationships: namely, the authentic encounterings of person with person.

The notion of symbol is crucial for clarifying the inner connection between essence and existence, as these ideas pertain to persons. Only through disclosure of this connection may one discern the full import of the person as agent. To link essence and existence, I require the notion of power. Thus, an agent is an agent by virtue of his capacity for self-potentiation into the fullest expression of his being.

B · BEING AS POWER

(a) Action

Like every creature, the person—the consummate species of creature—has both an essential and an existential aspect. In his essence, he is a bundle of powers, themselves undifferentiated but capable of giving rise to a specificity of expression, sheer potency which derives from his unique way of being rooted in nature. These powers express an inherent endowment, specific for each person, and constitute a tendency to grow in a direction determined by that endowment. Though particular powers may be unrealized, the notion of power requires the notion of the actualization of power. Existence expresses the latter. It is the characteristic way in which an entity—and, pre-eminently, the person—stands forth as actual, in the diversity and the abundance of its expressions, within the real world. Neither prior nor posterior to essence, existence is correlative with it. The two are complementary aspects of the same dynamism.

By "existence," I mean self-expression. And the ways in which man expresses himself—hence, presents himself to another—are drawn forth, in the context of meetings between people, from his essential powers. In his existence, a person's inwardness is exteriorized. Yet existence is not only the actualized power of a unique individual. The existence of each is woven into the existence of all. Insofar as he stands forth as an *integrated* individual, the person is in part constituted, in his very modes of expression, by other persons. No person can be conceived, in his complete personhood, apart from the conception of community, the matrix within which alone his powers may give birth to their existential expressions.

Sociality is a basic dimension in the characterization of persons. A web of relationships, the social context includes as its connecting nodes, individual relata, or persons. Neither link nor node can be independently conceptualized. Each requires the other. From the standpoint of a relatum, relationships are engendered from its essential activity; from the standpoint of a relationship, relata are crystallizations within its associated field of processes. Moreover, a complex of essence and existence constitutes every relatum. In the realm of essence, relata are internally related; in the realm of existence, they are externally related. For in reality's spectatorial dimension, entities as actualized power (or existential expression) form a vast pattern of encounterings. And in the dimension of potency, these entities join one another to form a matrix of unfoldings. The empathy which binds persons together is the expression of this inward account which each takes of the other. In his very individuality, the person is constituted by these complementary modalities of relationship, the internal and the external. To understand this phenomenon is a prime goal of my inquiry.

Under the impact of encounter, the powers which engender particular existents never cease to become actualized. And as he exists, a person discloses powers hitherto concealed. He evolves toward what, by these powers, he was meant to become. Inhering in the very nature of each person is a destiny distinctive for him. Yet the specification of that destiny can be made only by the reconstruction of germinal tendencies from the data of a life as it has actually been lived. The appropriate life circumstances themselves must be realized as the necessary milieu for the achieving of one's destiny. Surely, no destiny autonomously comes to pass. Each results from effort, struggle, and decision. To attain a destiny which is peculiarly one's own, one must attend to one's powers as they unfold. Listening and discovering are primordial phases of every act. Without these phases, any act is mere impulse. Their harmonious attunement with decision constitutes an act's true spontaneity.

Every act has a structure. A sequence of acts is a set of interlocking structures. This set may be a responsible set or an irresponsible set. By "responsible," I mean responsive or appropriate to the context in which the sequence occurs. When a structure's components are "smoothly" coordinated, and the acts, as a totality, are so synchronized that their respective structures mesh harmoniously, a responsible sequence of acts constitutes authentic activity. By "authentic," I mean true or adequate to the originative ground—namely, the potency—of a person's being. On the other hand, should the members of the sequence follow one another in random or chaotic fashion, those members are irresponsible. For, then, the context has elicited an inappropriate sequence. When irresponsibility dominates an inclusive process, inauthentic activity supervenes. Moreover, only when potency actualizes itself as specific acts, each internally harmonious, which unfold in accordance with rules uniquely applicable to *this particular* individual do his spontaneous acts constitute his free activity. Freedom consists in one's attuning oneself to an inner law which prescribes the specific character of one's own potency. In fine, *amor fati* is the very basis for responsibility, freedom, and authenticity.

In the very process of existing, an essence unfolds as both ground for existence and the criterion by which it may be judged. In a fulfilled existence, the full essence of the person shines forth. At each stage in the transformation of essence into existence, essence serves as a more explicit criterion than at any antecedent stage. What had been germinal achieves fruition—hence, vindicates itself as criterion.

The powers of a man are connected to the powers of other entities. The entire cosmos is a coming to fruition of primal powers. As such powers unfold according to definite rules, they give birth to specific entities which so act upon one another as continually to alter the makeup of the very powers whence they arose. Accordingly, a fabric of essences is the primordial constituent of reality. But were a person exclusively essence, his uniqueness would be denied. Were he lost within amorphous essentiality, psychosis would supervene. He would dwell in illusion engendered from within, a phantasmagoria which expresses reality degraded. Through decision, by which I mean resolution attended by an act which flows immediately from resolution, the person converts his unformed being into crystallized being. As thus actualized, he is capable of appropriate response to his encounters. Indeed, a person is co-shaper of reality, a reality which includes illusion, which is simply the realm of the façades of encounter, as one of its components. Yet reality transcends illusion. It constitutes the matrix of *authentic* encounter: a mutual presenting, in the full vibrance of presence, of existents to one another, and, hence, their interpenetration and reciprocal transformation. When responsible existence is severed from its source in pure potentiality, or in mere essence, and stands, so to speak, alone, it becomes automatized, stereotyped, and mere façade. Now mere adaptation to superficial societal structures and conventional modes of experiencing reality supervene—i.e., socially patterned defects.

Life which is truly alive results from dialectical interplay between essence and existence. To retain strength and resilience, a person must continually rediscover that center of existence which is life's very source. Yet to affirm his powers, he must exercise them. When it ceases to convert itself to expression, power is no longer power; it degenerates to impotence. In gesture, physiognomy, and movement, the person draws his powers into actuality as an integrated fabric of expression. Therein, he potentiates them anew. This fabric is his distinctive way of presenting himself to his world. It is a comporting toward that world: a bearing of himself in such a way that manifold powers are mobilized.

In every comportment is inscribed a mood. Each element of the physical (and the system of such elements when attached, so to speak, to an agent constitutes comportment) reveals, when its symbolism is appropriately interpreted, a complex of moods which, in their endlessly shifting tonalities, comprises the spiritual life of the person. This composite of mood and comportment is the concrete manifestation of essence. Whether durable or evanescent, it constitutes the living embodiment of essence. When I speak of mood, I refer, of course, to the sphere of the mental; by the comportment which is mood incarnate, I refer to the sphere of the physical.

Throughout this inquiry, I have been presuming that all matter is animated; that matter sufficiently organized is infused with mind; that, so organized, matter becomes, by contrast, body. Thus body and mind are complementary. They are the rubrics under which a person's modes of existence are classified. Hardly mere conventions, these rubrics express a "natural" division in the order of things. But reality exhibits itself under distinct perspectives. As designating these perspectives, mind and body are necessary extractions from reality. Neither can be conceived without reference to the other. When understood within a frame of ideas which grasps each as but a point of view, both may be regarded, when acknowledged in their essential unity, as characterizing the whole of human existence. In every phase of all existence, mood and comportment are themselves manifestations of one reality. They are specializations, and experiential renditions, from the standpoint of the person, of the complemental pair, essence and existence. In sum, mind and body, or their primordia in less organized existents, are inextricably joined. They reflect the underlying and progressively unifying character of the creature which, in its unfolding existence, emerges as, *a fortiori*, a subtle complex of mood and comportment.

This "unifying character" *is* power. Through deliberate, and deliberative, exercise of power a person comes to know who he truly is. As he potentiates his manifold resources into actuality, he himself encounters what, from within himself, he has brought into existence. He engages the expressions, whether detached from himself—as symbols which he has created (as, for example, his own gestures)—or still joined, of his own being. By this *self*-encounter, he perceives himself as resisting himself. In the experience of internal self-resistance, the person first acknowledges a substantive foundation to his own being. He becomes aware of himself as self-activating action. As activity, he further experiences an interplay between himself and others analogously constituted. By now encountering external resistance to his being—i.e., the resistance of another's action to his action—he additionally contributes to a sense of himself as "possessing" a substantive foundation. He internalizes this perception of external resistance; he joins the now interiorized perception to his already perceived autochthonous self-resistance. Accordingly, a person's perception of his own identity derives from the strengthening of that identity through his consummate realization of himself as agent and, in consequence, as capable of exercising power. The theme of identity, to which I now turn, derives directly from my reflections on agency and power.

(*b*) Identity

No matter how primitive, an entity owes creaturely being to its conformance with certain ontologic conditions. First, it is self-identically itself—solitary and distinct, durable and unchanging. Next, an entity dwelling apart from other entities, it is an indiscerptible composite of essence and existence: thus constituted, it acts, by its self-initiating propensity, upon and with respect to other entities. Finally, as actor, an entity confronts, through its ramifying acts, the resistance of an other; by the other's self-initiated *re*action to acts executed with respect to it, a relationship is engendered between entity and entity. These interwoven conditions—namely, identity, action, and relationship—constitute an essential ontologic commentary upon the basic ideas of essence and existence.

To declare a creature self-identically itself is to imply the following as metaphysical consequences: the persistence of a "something" unchanged amidst a multitude of transformations—i.e., the invariance of a pattern of elements despite the intrusion of novel factors into that pattern; the appearance, random or lawful, of unexceptional and irrelevant variations upon a durable theme—a theme which continually reiterates itself; the accumulation of these variants into an assemblage which, so to speak, challenges what had reigned as supremely changeless.

Such a concept of identity requires dialectical interpretation. Accordingly, if identity were to be construed as static, it would annihilate itself as a substantial factor. By my earlier argument, substance cannot *be* unless it is a *coming-to-be*, hence, potency actualized; and, in consequence, a self-sustaining dynamism. The only other option is for it to be a self-*negating* dynamism; in this case, identity ceases to be. On the other hand, a true dynamism exhibits two essential properties: it continually imprints itself into itself as a substantive Imago of what it had just previously been in its character as a coming-to-be; it is a process of engendering products which, though initially *by*-products—therefore, irrelevant to the process —progressively acquire a status requiring their self-detachment from the very process which engendered them. In the second instance, a product detaches itself by reason of its own intrinsically dynamic character. It is a veridical substance in the sense which I have just indicated. In my discussion, I am using the term *substance* in two distinct ways: substance as monistic; substance as pluralistic. By the former usage, substance is the matrix which embeds and originates what, when it has diversified itself, becomes substance according to the latter usage. However, a pluralistic construal of substance is alone of direct relevance to my inquiry.

At this stage, two distinct dynamisms are posed, and de facto juxtaposed. Qua dynamism, each is a "striving" to become separate and distinct. Neither, by its nature, can be completed; each is ineluctably a coming-to-be. By their juxtaposition, two opposing forces are operative, and by analogous *modi operandi*. On the other hand, the product in process of its own engenderment tends (passively) to "fall back" into its engendering matrix. Thus embedded, it, as product, would be inactive, hence, ineffectual and, indeed, obliterated. Should this occur, substance qua dynamic would tend, so to speak, to reverse itself. It would revert to a static— hence, self-negating—state, ultimately reducing itself to a state of nullity or non-being. On the other hand, both product and engendering matrix tend to separate from one another. By an interior impetus resident within each, both are propelled toward autonomy. Should this tendency be consummated, the engendering substance would retain its initial autonomy as self-identically itself. By the very acts of "birthing" a product, its process character would be reinforced. At the same time, the product will acquire identity as, now, self-identically itself, and hence likewise autonomous.

An interplay between two self-actualizing forces supervenes. One force propels what had been a single entity to split into two entities; the other impels a collapse of what might have been two entities into but one. Two propensities are counterposed: one dyadic, one monadic. They are counterposed as oppositional. Yet, by their opposition, they create a *third*. For the relationship of opposition is itself a dynamism. Insofar as a "state" of opposition dominates, triadicity reigns. Substantively construed, the relationship "contains," as its alternately equilibrated and disequilibrated elements, what had been, and continues to be, both an engendering process and what is now an engendered product. At this time, the very momentum, the *vis a tergo*, which set this dialectic in motion, is replicated, *pari passu*, in the dialectical fate of the product.

Identity is pre-eminently reflexive. By my argument, identity *must* be dynamically construed; otherwise, it negates itself. Even self-negation must be dynamically construed. But, according to my account of (dynamic) substance, *whatever* is substance, hence dynamic, must ipso facto persist. Indeed, it must gather accretions and grow. By its essential makeup, identity "divides" itself. Reflecting one another back and forth, every factor is transformed and reconstituted. *A fortiori*, the composite of these factors is veritably metamorphosed. A principle of synergism is the guarantor of this metamorphosis.

Reflection itself must be dialectically interpreted. The impact of any entity upon any other entity transmits itself (by an earlier argument) in pulsing movement. Reverberating to, within, and through the boundary of an affected entity, it penetrates to its very interior. In the wake of this spreading wave, the different parts of that entity are differentially affected. No supposition may be arbitrarily made regarding a postulate of homogeneity with respect to any entity's composition. In principle, each must be construed as, by default, heterogeneous. Whether there is a lower bound to this heterogeneity—hence, a most elemental entity—will be taken up at a later time. The very issue of absolute elementarity with respect to the entity-composition of that complex entity which concerns us—namely, the person—will emerge as significant for my doctrine. In any event, the dynamism which pertains to any particular entity must pertain to all its constituents. By the principle which asserts the absolute coincidence, and *radical* identity, of indiscernibles,[3] that dynamism works, with subtle differences in each instance, for every entity.

By what mechanism does this engendered product become capable of self-detachment? The relevant features of this mechanism are intricate. They are profoundly interwoven with the interaction of entities in general, with respect to identity preservation. To delineate this mechanism, I require extended commentary on the nature of interaction.

Variations upon the identity of the engendering process accumulate. When accretion has attained a sufficient level of intensity and complexity, a strain arises within this process-entity. Associated with an inner "drive" to extrude those factors inducing tension, this strain becomes *straining*, straining to maintain the original identity. Further, the reflexive character of identity itself both produces and results from minor variability, cumulatively "interpreted" by the entity. It is produced by incorporation of "impressions" transmitted to that entity through its encounters with other entities; it results from its own interior rearranging of these transmitted "introjects."

From the standpoint of the persistent element which confers identity, reiteration of this constant is the entity's internalized reaction to a threat of extinction. Another entity (including its own detached product) juxtaposed to it might excessively impinge upon it. Through such impact, the threatened entity may become overburdened with its own content. By its inner constitution, more or less fragile, this entity can only support incorporated impressions in moderation—in effect, such incorporates as may be moderated by its own identity on behalf of its own well-being. To eliminate danger, it must so act upon itself, from within itself, that its identity will be solidified and strengthened. Such of its components as do not contribute to this end are extruded—new products are, so to speak, created. In this way, the endangered entity acquires competency to destroy the effectiveness of a threatening entity by more effectively resisting it, a resistance effectuated by well-being rather than by any kind of "bloated" being (i.e., bloated through avoidance of extrusion).

To *re-sist* is to stand fast, again and again. This repeated standing fast, this rhythmic repetition, is effective only insofar as the dangerous entity is, relative to the threatened entity—though not necessarily with respect to all entities which it encounters—deprived of the capacity for instituting its own effective impingements. This "weakening" arises through its excessive absorption of imprints of the endangered entity. Internalizing these imprints, and welding them to its own identity, the dangerous entity is so altered as to be ineffectual. Alternatively, the threatened entity itself may absorb imprints from the entity which threatens *its* integrity, imprints resulting from impulses transmitted to it by the latter. The power of the threatening entity is diminished in either of two ways: it may be "filled" with imprints from the endangered entity, thereby modifying its own identity; or its own imprints may be absorbed by the endangered entity, thereby modifying the latter's identity in a way felicitous for the former. In both instances, a greater congeniality ensues. On the whole, neither entity readily accepts its own destruction. Both tend effectively to resist extinction. Inhering in each is a profound refusal to accept annihilation.

In sum, the endangered entity reduces threat through the resistance which it offers threat: first, by identifying with it, with respect to this or that aspect; then, by absorbing the items of identification. By assimilating imprints, the threatened entity and, reciprocally, the threatening entities produce an aura of "congeniality." A succession of such identifyings will manifest themselves as minor variations, cumulatively aggregating themselves into significance, upon a thematic identity. In effect, self-identity is closely bound up with a primordial propensity (a kind of "instinct") to survive: conatus[4] or self-preservation.

(c) Ferment

By my argument, self-preservation is tantamount to self-aggrandizement. The matrix wherein self-aggrandizement may occur supplies the factors, as a kind of nutriment, to the relevant entity. Perhaps that entity confronts nutriment with primordial reluctance. For, although it desires nutriment for the preservation of its own integrity, which entails self-growth, it also fears the risk of engaging nutriment—factors which themselves constitute entities counterposed to it. In its very endeavor to maintain itself, the entity is compelled to absorb those factors into its own being. Reflection itself is a reflecting (a bending back into itself) of nutriment into the entity in order, in the final analysis, to protect itself. However, to protect is to grow; to grow is to absorb factors relevant to growth; to absorb is (in oscillating reluctance and eagerness) to be reoriented toward the matrix whence nutriment is derived; so to be reoriented is to dissolve the very solitude with respect to which identity was originally postulated as "cause" (of identity) and, reciprocally, "condition" (for identity). Made possible by this reorientation, such absorption again requires encounter with the resistance of the factor to be absorbed as itself an analogously constituted (actively) self-identical agent.

In every encounter, and consequent absorption, something must be extruded following ingestion. Initially, gestation supervenes. From what had been absorbed, certain components are internally split off. Of these components, those needed for growth—hence, protection—are assimilated; the remainder are exteriorized. But what is exteriorized is, save in the most degraded or privative sense, not simply waste, a *by*-product. On the contrary, the extruded product is, in effect, thrown off. It is *e*jected rather than *re*jected, or cast away. Through birthing, the original entity, on the whole, will, following termination of its "pregnancy," continue to survive. Yet, now, it is self-aggrandized. And self-aggrandized in a double way! For, first, the relevant factors have been absorbed as nutriment; by that absorption there is growth. But consider. A new product, the entity "birthed," has itself become a novel agency. Endowed with full autonomy, it is empowered constructively to encounter, and, thereby, to bring about yet new growth! Granted: the interplay of threat and growth, of birthing and risk, of renewal and subduing is complicated; but it is also a marvelously constituted phenomenon! Later, this topic will be treated as a theme which will disclose a deep analogy, and an inner connection, between reflection and replication: creation of new being *within* being; creation of new being *with-out* being.

Nowhere has this theme been expressed more poignantly, or with greater profundity, than in Shakespeare's Sonnet XVII:

> Who will believe my verse in time to come,
> If it were fill'd with your most high deserts?
> Though yet, heaven knows, it is but as a tomb
> Which hides your life and shows not half your parts.
> If I could write the beauty of your eyes
> And in fresh numbers number all your graces,
> The age to come would say "This poet lies;
> Such heavenly touches ne'er touch'd earthly faces."
> So should my papers, yellow'd with their age,
> Be scorn'd, like old men of less truth than tongue,
> And your true rights be term'd a poet's rage
> And stretched metre of an antique song:
>   But were some child of yours alive that time,
>   You should live twice—in it and in my rhyme.

In the interplay which emerges between the two agents, the one which absorbs and the one which is (prospectively) to be absorbed, the theme of persistence is (now) complemented by the theme of reciprocation. The factor to be absorbed takes, from *its* standpoint, a stand with respect to what it would absorb. In thus taking a stand, i.e., in being *per-sistent*, it establishes itself as in a thoroughly solidified *stasis*, a momentarily positive stasis; it acquires the status of fixity. In this "fixed taking of a stand," it itself seeks to absorb. For it would negate the powers of the one which, to begin with, would absorb it. To guarantee survival of both, a symbiotic relationship is established between the two. By symbiosis, in this context, I mean, literally, a σύμβιος: a living or dwelling together (in harmony). Perhaps precarious, perhaps firm, balance is nonetheless achieved.

When, in general, a multitude of creatures are so related as to resist yet use one another as agencies for their own self-preservation, a dialectical process whereby authentic relationships are created is set in motion. Amidst preservation of certain communal themes as relatively enduring configurations, relata appear and disappear and reappear—transfigured! Now I may speak of the orchestration of rhythmically transmitted propagations of impulse and counter-impulse, impression and expression—all constantly and reflexively woven into the internal constitutions of all creatures. For reflexivity derives, as I later discuss, both from *within* each creature, in his solitary self-encounters, and from *without*, in his (communal) encounters with others.

What is the destiny of this dialectical complexus? Is there a telos immanent within the multitude of creatures? Or does a transcendent power guide the destinies of all? With respect to the individual, I argue in favor of an ἔσχατον. With Plato, I believe that each creature endeavors to shape and to realize, throughout its solitary *conatus,* and no matter how simply it is constituted, an ideal image of itself, a veridical "form" or εἶδος. Through the countless vicissitudes of its journey through "existence," it frames an image, it emends an image, it yearns for that image, it strives toward that image. In tentative gropings and in adventuresome leaps, every creature maps out for itself a trajectory along which it pursues a perhaps unattainable ideal. At times, the pursuit is relentless; at times, it is inconstant. Yet the ideal ceaselessly hovers before it. An ideal always corrigible, perhaps asymptotically approachable, yet, tragically perhaps, in the end, inexorably to vanish.

All creatures similarly execute their own "dances of being." Each etches for itself the broader contours of its dance; the entire community composes the choreography. Yet modification and adjustment are always needed. Ideals are envisaged, entertained, sought, denied, attained, but always with the perception, dim but haunting, of limits which each creature imperceptibly imposes upon the remainder. A community's destiny consists in a synchronized movement, step by step, all integrated into an elaborate balancing of the separately executed movements of the solitary creatures—toward a most inclusive ideal: that ideal which ever potentiates novel possibilities for attainment by the individual; those ideals which, over and again, are prescribed for each by each.

The dance of being! Truly, the person is ferment; the interplay of persons is ferment; the community itself is ferment. Yet the pattern of ferment is elusive. The invariant structures which endure as one pattern is transmuted into another are elusive. To inquire into the makeup of the person is imperceptibly to pass from conceptualizing him as a system of processes of definite contour and fixed composition to apprehending him as a manifold in flux. Surely, he is not, in his essentiality, amorphous. But terms such as pattern, system, and structure tend to commit one, in advance, to suppositions that a person's nature is excessively rigid. On the other hand, terms such as action, power, and ferment threaten to evoke diametrically opposed suppositions; yet no person may be presumed to be excessively malleable. An altogether new vocabulary must be sought to express both what and who the person truly is!

At first, this quest cannot yield a definitive terminology. It must grope, and accept partial formulations. It must trace its way as at dusk from one evanescing image to another. A single analogy will not suffice to express the full range and depth of personhood. A scheme of consistent metaphors is only an artifice. To pass through darkness to dawn, one must be content, as in a dream, to allow the image to be "like a jewel hung in ghastly night" to make "black night beauteous and her old face new";[5] and to assemble, as one gradually acquires insight, imagery of inconsistent content and incongruous implication. Juxtaposing of these images will elicit contrasts, textures, chiaroscuros which will allow to emerge a more probing terminology than is currently available. To gather illuminating metaphors, I therefore often draw upon the arts. For pre-eminently art discloses, so I maintain throughout my inquiry, the "breath and finer spirit of all knowledge."[6] And just as a central theme in all art is rhythm, so this theme will likewise constitute one of my principal integrative topics.

C · BEING AS RHYTHM

(a) Orchestration

Inquiry into the person as activity or ferment raises questions about his temporality, and, ipso facto, his historicity, and his destiny. By "temporality," I mean a self duplicating itself amidst endless novelty despite, and within its passage from one state of being to another, the preservation of a core of identity amidst the perishing details of existence; by "historicity," I mean the "thickening" of this core through its absorbing, layer upon layer, of a "past" woven of the cumulative traces of experience, a self constituting itself by these layers—all recollectible, for their constituent traces may be gathered together and presented anew (i.e., represented) as fresh experience; by "destiny," I mean a self projecting itself, a continual thrusting toward the future—in which very act that future is delineated—an unknown abyss into which one steps, risking one's existence from moment to moment yet somewhere trusting its deeper continuities. These processes—self-duplication, self-constitution, and self-projection—are complementary; they require one another. As interwoven processes they entail, for each person, a characteristic rhythm. Each presupposes the person to be in his essence a flux of rhythms expressed as patterns of symmetry (e.g., anatomy), patterns transmitted from instant to instant—an unfolding of a wave of pulses and their deposition as visible structures, which themselves consist of myriad variations upon persistent and recurrent themes.

What does it mean to speak of the person as, at bottom, a pattern of rhythms? First, he is mobile; his "parts" are ceaselessly in movement, both with respect to one another and in their inner constituency. They act upon one another; and in their interactions they aggregate themselves into mutually synergizing unities. In perpetual vibration and fluctuation, they are dissolved into their components which, in turn, reaggregate themselves; and so the person is the scene of constant interplay of parts and wholes, of dissolutions and reconstitutions. Secondly, these unities constitute systems which in their physical and psychic dimensions are analyzed by the particular sciences of man, rhythmical systems which either synchronize with one another or, in varying ways and degrees, are discordant. Equilibria are achieved as relatively enduring configurations; and equilibria are shattered, in ceaseless alternation.

Accordingly, by nature the person is a flux. Yet though his gestures, his moods, his tissues are mobile, they are not randomly so. The systems of rhythm into which he is organized are coherently enmeshed. Interpenetrating, they imprint their effects into one another. A complex of stimuli and counter-stimuli, the resultant "vibrations" are woven into a fabric trembling with vitality; but they are experienced and projected as a unitary and singular impulse. Instinct, drive, habit, purposive act, and, ultimately, commitment are rubrics under which this impulse is variously classified. By the last (which is but the consummate form of the remainder) I mean, quite literally, the "self–sending-forth" of a person, all his parts conjoined into an integral and cohesive orientation; a comportment, or total directing of himself, toward whatever he selects as object of his concern. And his characteristic rhythm, a quality which pervades all his commitments, manifests the particular way in which these systems interlock.

This rhythm is his "style," his unique way of being in the world. Moreover, it is his *emotionality*. For, etymologically, e-motion means a distinctive kind of moving forth and, by implication, a sensing of oneself among the objects of one's world, a feeling of their texture and of that of one's own being in relation to their being. With respect to these objects a person defines himself; by the qualities of his self he discriminates these objects. Accordingly, an "inward" motion is the result of a multitude of subtle and fine components, all individually mobile; thence from a "center" which is a person's singular and idiosyncratic core of rhythms (i.e., his style) proceeds an "outward" movement toward another; thus is consummated the symbolism of his presence—those varied ways by which he makes himself known as the unique individual he is. Surely, at critical moments of his life, a person may undergo metamorphoses in which particular styles are replaced by others. Yet, interwoven in a fabric of infinite subtlety, the innumerable moods of a person, in all their shifting nuances, and despite vicissitudes and crises, conceal a quality, persistent and sure, which stamps him from the beginning of his life to the end, as identically himself. Like a violin responding to the plucking of strings of fixed pitch and timbre, so the person, in his determinate and characteristic way, resonates to the presences which hover about him.

Harmoniously disposed (and I am not here discussing *pathology*, the study of disrupted harmonies and diminished vitality), these systems comport a style which is like a well-executed dance; a person's every part is, in its very mobility, congruent with his entire being. In its temporal unfolding and the fluctuant interplay of its components, this style—a complex of emotions which constitute his inmost nature—reflects his inner, primordial rhythms. The person, in the mechanical aspect of his being, is, in effect, a clock which, synchronizing the diversity of rhythms, ticks away his own being, a clock which measures the very processes by which in determining himself he both renews and exhausts himself. Man is a creature of many vitalities, concentrated into particular foci of existence, yet of inexorably diminishing energies—energies which by his own efforts, increasingly as he ages, he must bring to new focus by ever-firmer commitments. Initially autochthonous, phylogenetically and genetically, the rhythms of man are increasingly reinforced, altered, or even metamorphosed. And if by his autonomous powers he shapes his own existence, he yet must accept the destiny which flows within him from the cosmos in which he is embedded, and attune his lesser being to its larger being.

Powerful as he is, man is only approximately an autonomous and self-sufficient complex of rhythms. Nor is he their sole source. For man is also the vehicle by which are individualized and brought to substantive focus the larger cosmic rhythms. Passing through him, these rhythms constitute him even as they are affected by him. Layer upon layer of activity stretch out, each resonating to those adjacent to it, beyond the boundaries, fluctuant and mobile, of his nonetheless circumscribed and private world—that world, in effect, which is his body. No absolute boundary prevails. On the contrary, like so many concentric circles, these realms of activity originate diminishing yet ever-potent influences upon that body. As he reverberates with his own typical and "interior" rhythms, every man is altered by these radiating influences. However remote, they are continuously operative.

Into this orchestration of rhythm silence breaks again and again. Prolonged or brief, these pauses are integral to man. They mirror, and reflect into his being, a cosmos still and tranquil. When authentic, and not a mere hiding from cacophony, silence is renewing. It is a womb of quiescent fluids within which eddies of infinite nuance though infinitesimal quiver dwell in peace. Yet in their imperceptible swirlings this ebb and flow germinate a matrix of contrasts, diversified and vital. For, in essence, silence is a primordial, latent, and originative context. Herein burst forth, inexorably and passionately, the manifest rhythms of man.

(*b*) Invariance and Mutuality

Earlier, I alluded to the "great chain of being,"[7] whence each person arises, in which he continues to participate, from which he draws sustenance, of which he is essentially constituted, and to which he eventually returns—as, once again, embedded and interwoven. In effect, this chain links different kinds of rhythm. Moreover, every form of being is associated with characteristic patterns of cycles and epicycles, a certain range of attunings among the factors comprising these patterns. In each instance of being, patterns impinge upon one another; they enmesh, interweave, and interpenetrate. By reciprocally imprinting themselves into each other, they synergistically give rise to new patterns, transmitting from one generation of being's unfolding forms to another a typical set of contrasts, complementarities, incongruities, and consonances and dissonances. As these patterns interlock, the flux which they constitute progressively transforms what had been an invariant mode of orchestrating harmonies into altogether novel forms. Depositing in its wake successive patterns of symmetry, the ferment of rhythm never ceases.

At the lower limit of being lies primordial silence; yet it is not a mere void: radical, absolute, frozen. On the contrary, the rhythms of silence are infinitely subtle, infinitesimally nuanced; there are innumerable kinds of motility, supple and firm, evanescing yet disappearing; there is perpetual flow of myriad entangling resonances, imperceptible but never empty. At the upper limit lies the plenitude of being—an orchestration of overwhelming, all-inclusive, powerfully vibrant rhythms: a mélange of dramatic crescendos and tranquil diminuendos, a great cosmic symphony. Between these bounds, and conditioned by them, lie the rhythms of the kinds of being which one typically encounters—events, organisms, persons.

First, there are rhythms of space, time, and matter. Each set presupposes and requires the remainder. The rhythms and the symmetries of the one are transmitted to, metamorphosed into, those of the others. Together, they constitute a single, integral totality. Within this configuration germinate, for they are therein prefigured, life and, in the end, spirit. I speak, of course, of the events of physical science. Secondly, there are rhythms of intricately organized material elements which aggregate themselves into systems of equilibrium and disequilibrium. This dynamical and transactional complex is endowed with the capacity for self-duplication. Variations of differing significance "play" upon a recurrent theme. This "theme" constitutes the agency for transforming nature lifeless into nature consummately alive. I refer now to the organisms of biological science. Finally, there are rhythms of personal being, a further stage involving a dramatic leap in matters of progressive divinization of matter and its consequent ineluctable redeemability: the leap into the spheres of intellect, emotions, will. Now, in commitment, coordinating all his powers, the *person* imprints his own expressions into reality, wherein they acquire durable shape. Endlessly reconstituting himself, he is a vortex of creativity and self-projection, in freedom, toward an unknowable future.

Events, organisms, persons—three modalities of being! In the chain of being, each subsumes yet goes beyond its predecessor. The first mediates transformation of the privation of being into life; the second mediates transformation of matter into spirituality; the third mediates transformation of life into the plenitude of being. As mediator, each is an agency for achieving an end—an end which, when realized, imprints itself into the evolving cosmos. As a mode of being, each agency (including the person in a restricted sense of instrumentality) dwells immanently within, yet transcendent to, every person as grounding his being—but, now, his being conceived sui generis, not as mediator, a means to an end, but as a fully substantial creature who, in my inquiry, is treated as in himself and for himself. The person as means is a constituent of the person as end. In this sense, the being of the person is grounded by beings lower than he (as end) in the hierarchy of being and by beings higher. The entire interwoven complex of "creatures" (and *non*-creatures, at either bound) constitutes, as a whole, the foundation and *fons et origo* of personal being.

With respect to events, integrated space, time, and matter constitute integral patterns of energy: crystallization, flowings, transformations from one energy kind into another, escalatings and de-escalatings from more organized (and fragile) energy forms to less organized (and durable) forms. Energy aggregates flow independently; they intersect and they coincide; they engage one another by imparting the rhythms of each to the rhythms of the other; they synergistically metamorphose. An aura hovers about every particle which moves along a space–time path; the quest to penetrate the mystery of a particle discloses it to dissolve into its own circumambient halo, a myriad of waves.

Subtle "melodies" are associated with these waves: their movements, their over-lappings, their mutual cancelings, their mutual reinforcements, their reciprocal transmutings. At bottom, "matter is . . . a tapestry of related waves of dynamisms in a structure of melody, harmony, counterpoint, and fugal intricacy . . . the parts of merely shallow, shifting shadows cast by the reality of the whole when it is illuminated by its dynamism."[8] Composed of harmonies woven of sequential dynamisms, this ordered and structured hierarchy of dynamic forms is synthesized, as the form of a spreading (compound) wave in its indefinitely variable shapes and associated rhythms, into what will evolve as the living organism. These shapes and these rhythms prefigure the makeup of the organism within which they dwell, and immanently condition and guide its very destiny.

Accordingly, the diverse vibratory movements—rotational, translational, pulsa-tional, spiraling in weird patterns—constantly impinge upon one another to shape new patterns of movement. The trajectories along which this movement flows are themselves of endlessly intricate design: strange singularities, continua composed of a hierarchy of orders of infinity; spaces multidimensional, isotropic or anisotropic, Archimedean or non-Archimedean, Euclidean or non-Euclidean; time as a composite of correlations between concrete and endlessly variable cycli-cal patterns, patterns of reversal, increments in which congruence never reigns, time contracted and expanded and arrested; finally, space wedded to time, and the two, in turn, linked to energy fields constantly and reciprocally transformed into particulate matter.

All this unimaginably intricate pattern of rhythmic modality and unfolding is transmitted with *variable* invariants of symmetry to the living organism, endlessly new overtones and undertones woven into thematic repetitions. Life inherits all the mysteries resident within the non-living, all the bizarre paradoxes and the miraculous complexities. For "a total dynamic form embodies within it the lesser dynamic forms in the hierarchy,"[9] forms intangible, unseen, unheard. The mysteries communicated from the lifeless to the living are compounded; new and still stranger mysteries emerge. Acquiring the power further to pulsate, and to resonate through accretion of new elements, the organism becomes ever more intricate and differentiated within its own composite makeup. It grows through accretion of factors: those like it and those unlike it, some included within it and some excluded from it; some attached, some incorporated, some detachable yet remaining bonded within its sphere of influence. Accretive growth occurs in pulsing rhythms, and in rhythmic ways of ordering and reordering arrangements within crystalline structures.

Having evolved to an intricacy of creation which requires new modes of growth, the organism acquires the capacity for self-replication. In rhythms at first undulant, then rising with increasing fervor to the spasmodic, a succession of spasms of increasing force, an organism splits asunder into nearly identical members. Thereupon, each member synthesizes its complement from factors, organic or inorganic, which endlessly flow within its circumambient matrix: a new creature is born! But the possibilities for novel creation are herein limited. Though diverse and intriguing—and, surely, of varying capacities to adapt to an environment which itself is ceaselessly changing—the mutants thereby produced are insufficiently novel and complex to gratify the impulse toward authentic and durable new creation. For resident within every creature is the power to leap beyond itself toward new evolutionary forms: to transmute itself into a creature of more intricate design.[10]

Consequently, the momentous discovery (by the creature itself) of replication through mutuality! Two unlike, but quite similar, organisms meet; each performs its characteristic dance about and with respect to the other; the ritual of mating commences. For a brief but ecstatic moment, and but momentarily, they unite. Interchanging factors which embody information about how they themselves are constituted—the design of their individual patterns—each finds itself in a state of accretion. For an instant, each is on the verge of *self*-replication; regression to the preceding mode of creation threatens. But the affinity between two sets of information, one deriving from each parent, dominates—for those organisms of sufficient subtlety and foresight with respect to their own creative potential! A rhythmic "locking-in" of complemental organisms, each endowed with its own typical rhythms, provides the condition for the birthing of a new creature: a perpetuating and an immortalizing of its own parents.

(c) From the Personal to the Suprapersonal

Beyond even this miracle, as their rhythmic consummation, there are rhythms of metabolism, rhythms of nerve transmission, rhythms of genetic transformation, rhythms of organic evolution, rhythms of sexual cyclicity, rhythms of embryologic development, rhythms of cerebral activity. Pervading all is a ceaseless interplay of these diverse patterns as, in their synergistic interlocking, they tend, in stages, toward the most marvelously constituted rhythm of all: reflection—reflection as the fruition of all of which replication is the germ. Until this moment, when reflection frees itself as an autonomous and self-reproducing function, the regnant principles of life, as of the non-living, remain, with immensely increased complexity, principles involving such concepts as form, system, complementarity, dynamism, correlativity, invariance, synthesis, cyclicity. Though each of these concepts, and other needed ones, have their analogue in the phase of personhood, new concepts must now be added.

In short, life itself is a hierarchy of dynamically formed waves superimposed, with varying consequences, one upon another. Composed of lesser dynamic event-forms, the living organism emerges as an ever more intricate pattern. Now the organism transfigures itself into man. The human form is "projected into the intricate and interlacing dimensions of rhythms, strung not on a single thread of time but woven into . . . [the] . . . multidimensional tapestry"[11] of history. Such forms are like a well-choreographed ballet. Men and women dance their differential but complementary rhythms, rhythms which are biopsychically orchestrated. From birth to death, indeed extending backward from birth to conception, every stage, each a veritable metamorphosis—exhibits *its* characteristic rhythms. Man and woman, each in his or her own fashion, inscribe their typical variations upon an identical rhythmic theme: rhythms of symbiosis, rhythms of hope and trust, rhythms of loyalty and friendship, rhythms of tenderness, care, concern, and love, rhythms of resolve and commitment, rhythms of wisdom and the confrontation of death—all these rhythms are species, instances, and variants of the universal rhythmic theme of personhood: namely, *searching.*

Through the journey of life, in the unfolding of these profoundly intimate rhythms, a personal style is engendered for each individual. In the manner of this style, he delves into his own unconscious being; and, as he descends, he confronts images lurking in his inmost depths. Fascinated by this unfolding imagery, he observes its own self-induced transformation. As he gathers these images into integral totality, he discerns them to be suffused by a strangely organic quality: his archetypal organicity, his archetypal physicality—in the one case, an Imago of his organismic nature; in the other, an Imago of his event-nature. He experiences these weird resonances as originating from his *infra*personal being; and, as they are transmitted to him, they echo and re-echo within the labyrinth of his *personal* being. When, moreover, he has sufficiently immersed himself "in" the re-collecting of these numberless resonances, he feels himself purified of dross and encumbrance.

In his very finitude, the person passes *through* this vast infrapersonal realm to stand before the threshold of the transfinite. Therein, he discovers, as his quest continues, symbols of the ultimate unity and harmony of a larger cosmos. He encounters synchronicities of widely dispersed events; he touches new centers of existence. In an act of self-transfiguration, the person projects himself into "unseen domains of the universe" until, finally, he perceives a "mingling of the symphony of the individual soul with the symphonies of other souls to enrich and enlarge their growth and their freedom that the supreme harmony of harmonies . . . [may be] . . . achieved." [12] Beyond all finite boundaries of personhood and beyond the perishings and the vicissitudes of existence, transiency vanishes. A strange incandescent glow irradiates all: the luminous realm of the suprapersonal. Here, the Creator eternally plays that "cosmic symphony in which all tones interpenetrate, where distance is only a difference in tone, where dissonance becomes consonance with a flick of tuning." [13]

To be essentially human is to be truly free. To be truly free is to orient oneself toward the world as a great and wonderful spectacle—joyous, tranquil, and tragic—where, as for Faust, "My soul comes face to face with all-creating Nature," and "all . . . [its] . . . powers stand unveiled around me." [14] Yet it is also to feel the mystery of our being. For Faust also declares,

> . . . such spectredom so throngs the air
> That none knows how to dodge it, none knows where.
> Though one day greet us with a rational gleam,
> The night entangles us in webs of dream. [15]

But wonder at the concealed and delight in the visible must be completed, in the consummate experience of freedom, by our recognition, in a spirit of courage and tranquillity, of the ever-present possibility of our annihilation. "He who loves God," writes Spinoza, "cannot strive that God should love him in return." [16] Only by experiencing the paradox of a mortal existence which *would* know eternity but must, in the end, renounce life can we truly shape our destiny. In this way alone may I, with Meister Eckhardt, "see God," for the brief span of my life, "with the same eye as God sees me." [17] Like Hesse's Siddhartha, we can then be in "harmony with the . . . music of life . . . the lament of those who yearn, the laughter of the wise, the cry of indignation and groan of the dying . . . all interwoven and interlocked, entwined in a thousand ways . . . the great song of a thousand voices." [18]

The way of this journey is the way which I previously set forth as a succession of methodologic doctrines: naturalism, personalism, transcendental naturalism, transcendental personalism—all synthesized into transcendental substantialism.

In this book, I, in effect, schematize subhuman phases and moments in their contemporaneous contributions to a person's existence, the proto-personal ground for man's consummate emergence.

NOTES

1. Adapted from Martin Heidegger, *Being and Time* (London: SCM, 1962). See the index for usages of "to bring."

2. Alfred North Whitehead, *Process and Reality* (New York: Macmillan, 1967), pp. 334–60.

3. G. W. von Leibniz, *The Monadology*, trans. Robert Latta (London: Oxford University Press, 1898), pp. 36, 222.

4. *Works of Spinoza*, trans. R. H. M. Elwes (New York: Dover, 1955), p. 136. Note that *conatus* is translated as "endeavour."

5. Shakespeare, Sonnet 27.

6. William Wordsworth, "Preface to the Second Edition of the Lyrical Ballads," in *The Poetical Works of William Wordsworth*, ed. E. de Selincourt, 2 vols. (Oxford: Clarendon, 1944), II 398.

7. Taken from the title of Arthur Lovejoy's *The Great Chain of Being* (Cambridge: Harvard University Press, 1936).

8. Donald Hatch Andrew, *The Symphony of Life* (Lee's Summit, Mo.: Unity Books, 1966), p. 411.

9. Ibid., p. 414.

10. See George T. Lockland, *Grow or Die* (New York: Random House, 1973).

11. Andrew, *Symphony of Life*, p. 415.

12. Ibid., p. 416.

13. Ibid., p. 419.

14. *Goethe's* FAUST, *Parts I and II*, trans. Louis Macneice (New York: Oxford University Press, 1951), p. 21.

15. Ibid., p. 281.

16. Spinoza, *Ethics*, Proposition XIX.

17. *Meister Eckhardt*, trans. Raymond Bernard Blakney (New York: Harper Torchbooks, 1957).

18. Herman Hesse, *Siddhartha*, trans. Hilda Rosner (New York: New Directions, 1951), pp. 137, 138.

II

The Event:
Rhythms of the Inanimate

2

MAN'S THINGLY ASPECT

PREAMBLE

Now I introduce, in a general way, a theme which will concern me throughout this Part: namely, man in his thingly character. I discern three elements as constituting that character: *pattern*, which expresses spatial configuration—the morphology of things; *change*, which expresses the vicissitudes of temporal unfoldings—the morphogenesis of things; and *force*, which expresses contexts of action and reaction, resistance and counter-resistance—in a word, sheer materiality. Surely, these elements enter significantly into man's composition, and he is endlessly fascinated by them. Every person experiences nature's inanimate rhythms as pervading his entire being and, beyond that, as giving rise to the profound mysteries which that being encloses. Man is, and he knows himself to be, paradoxically both akin to things and counterposed to them.

By his affinity with things, man feels his roots as penetrating the very depths of the inorganic cosmos. Therein he discerns his thingly roots to be intertwined with all nature's great powers. And not only does man's organicity enclose the thing, but, sufficiently understood, the thing itself encloses no-thing: the very annihilation of existence. The comfort of affinity gives way to the terror of difference—and, in the end, of in-difference. In consequence, man combats the inexorable holds of both thing and no-thing upon him. Vigilantly exerting his own spirit, he strives to fill the void with which nothing infects him. Through the very experience of himself as radically determined, thus in his being's inmost regions as other than human, man is compelled to know by what powers he is distinctively human. Perceiving tendencies, inhering in his own existence, toward natural degradation, he "distances" himself from the thingly interplay between himself qua thing and other things. And mirroring his thingly nature to himself, he reflects, and thereby sets in motion a complicated dialectic. Through reflection, man becomes aware of himself as nothing—hence, as free of things; hence, by essence, free. The very acts by which a person articulates his thingly dimension, and thus radically alienates himself from his spirit, enable him to overcome alienation and to exalt himself in freedom.

Nature, so man reveals to himself, contours his very morphology, providing the irreducible resistance against which his vitality tests itself, and his freedom takes its measure. Ultimately, the quest to penetrate the composition of this resistance, hence, of his own thingly character, leads man to explore interstices without end—the interstices between such relata as man and things and thing and thing. His every attempt to probe the mystery resident within the parts of things leads, no matter how minuscule those parts, to new interstices. In the last analysis, to experience oneself as thing is to experience oneself as no-thing—as bare and vacuous space. Yet the quest to understand space reveals it to be a schema of relations which express compresence: not the compresence of the here and the now, but the compresence of the "no-things" toward which man must accordingly strain. Stripped of its ornamentation, thingliness, which is the same as no-thingliness, becomes the locus of man's straining, his straining toward non-existence. Yet, by this straining, man becomes aware of himself as pre-eminently one who *freely* strains and, in so straining, attains to new levels of spiritual awareness.

A · PATTERN, CHANGE, FORCE: THE FASCINATION OF THE LIFELESS

(a) Fascinations

Man is endlessly fascinated by shapes and patterns, by forces and powers, by changes and renewals. Strolling along the seashore, he notices contrasting strips

of sand and dune, the sea in its varied strands of color—gray to pale blue, deep
blue to turquoise of many hues—and the sky with its complementary spectra.
Stopping, he is captivated by the pebbles along the shore, pebbles glistening from
sun and ever-beating surf, pebbles spheroid, elliptoid, cubical, large, small, irreg-
ular, symmetric, coarse, granular, fine, iridescent, dull—a speck of the rainbow
in each; he gazes at patterns of concentricity, spiralings, lines which zigzag this
way or that. He reflects. Is there order, symmetry, harmony in this miracle of
color, hue, texture, arrangement, size, and shape which lies about him? Are these
numberless patterns meaningful, these arrangements of linearity and solid band,
of diverse magnitude and qualities of varying intensity?

He looks to the stars and he perceives their constellations, fixed and seemingly
eternal; he is struck by their radiance and subtle glows, by their delicate formations which so resemble beast and bird and fish. And as he attends them closely,
perhaps with the aid of a telescope, their varied patterns emerge as no less pervasive. On a foggy day, they are obliterated; he is immersed in the gloom of
moisture which hovers everywhere, grays and variations of gray. Not variety,
here, but sameness! His feelings, accordingly, change. After delighting in sheer
heterogeneity the endless variation of which titillates his senses, man is now affected by a touch of awe, the sense of mystery, a haunting melancholy, and a
tranquillity which suffuses all. Different patterns elicit different moods. Diverse
modes of ordering call forth feelings of corresponding subtlety and intricacy.

As he wanders, man chances upon a canyon. As at the seashore, analogous
shapes, lines, textures, hues, grades of luminosity and opacity grip his eye, and
again the mists which roll in and out assault his skin—all this as before, but, now,
on vast, gargantuan, and overwhelming scale. Fear, awe, the sense of the sublime,
vast empty spaces, great mountainous buttes which jut toward the heavens like
temples—gothic, romanesque, baroque, byzantine: temples fashioned of rock
and sand, of fossils and minerals, of decaying vegetation; temples shaped through
the erosion caused by water, wind, and storm. Turning to inspect their strata, he
observes numberless geologic layers and the formations cast by inexorable time:
fossils of multivariate shape, and manifold patterns of line and speckle. As he
looks, he discerns tiny crystals of quartz and feldspar, and the softer fragments of
gypsum and calcite; and all the modes of design which eye and finger are empowered to reveal. A marvelous intuition comes to him: a universality and a
repetition of form from the incredibly small to the unimaginably vast, from the
bizarre and the grotesque to the symmetric and the luminous! A great *spatial* realm
of *quality* and *form* spreads before him, all integrated and coordinated: a laminated
space of incomparable intricacy, a filled space of endlessly rich space-like content
and arrangement.

Now man makes his journey anew. Perhaps he traverses the same terrain. But
with different intent! On this occasion, he attends less to what the eye reveals to
him, eye aided by finger, than to what is disclosed by the ear, ear aided by sight,

by touch, by inner sense of kinesthesia. He beholds ripples by the shore of a lake; crashing waves by the shore of the sea; tricklings of a thousand scattered currents as a brook ripples and hastens over stones and is split into innumerable streams; the roar, the rush, the thunder, the all-enveloping spray of a Niagara; the softly floating feathers blown by a summer breeze in the mist of a lesser waterfall; small ferns gently swaying as they are washed by the mildly quickening waters at its base to a pool, smooth and quiet, which gathers these waters from the nearly torrential flow. But, then, astounded, he lifts his eyes to the sheer bulk, mass and density of a granite El Capitan; he perceives the force and the twistings of a cyclone, the rage, the spasms, the gushing torrents of a hurricane, the rush and the onslaught of a tornado—all sweeping along, tossing, and crumbling all that lies in its wake. Might varying in gradations, and alternating with the weak, the soft, the mild: all interwoven as a wondrous array of heterogeneous densities!

Or he perceives the gentle currents of the wind on a balmy day; the rain now pattering, now gushing; a pressure in his ear and about his body as he plunges to swim in ocean and river; the heavy, cumbersome, strangely slowed steps deep in a mine shaft; the quickening breath, the sense of giddiness as he ascends a high peak; the sudden, spasmodic shock of an electric current; the oppressive heat which weighs heavily upon him in the wastelands of a Mojave or a Sahara; the fearsome masses of sound as sand blows and splinters and pierces in a desert storm; the blinding light of sun wedded to numbing cold and great crystalline masses of ice on a wintry day in the Alps—a mighty glacier spread beneath him, smoothed to glassy surface by raging wind and storm. Feelings deep within him of weight and lightness, feelings pierced by spasms of fright and loneliness or suffused with peace and solitude! Mass woven with mood, each fluctuating in reciprocal conformation.

The journey continues. Man is now overwhelmed by the majesty of a mountain range spreading toward an infinite horizon, layer upon layer of huge land masses which sit now placidly, now grotesquely upon a tranquil valley undulating toward *its* complemental infinities. He is awed by the immense, brilliantly colored, aged, and hardened sandstone of a Zion: great temples of rock and gleaming rainbows playing upon their surface, moistened by waters which trickle without cease from melting snow above, or by the gathering rains which, when the winds appropriately prevail, overflow to discharge their contents down these cliffs which so surround him that he is enveloped and so affect him that he stands before them as though upon an altar of lightly felt grass, gazing upward toward nature's glorious stained glass of ice and stream and waterfall. In awe and in wonder, there throbs within him an incomparable range of density and force and power; the spreading waves of energy in multiple form and kind and shape; the universal repetition of mass and energy from the minuscule to the huge, from the dense to the porous, from the nearly imperceptible and evanescent to the overwhelming and crushing. *Quality* woven with *resistance*, its endless combinations endlessly diversified: this is the realm of differentiated matter.

Humbly, man considers this variable panorama of pattern and density of shape and force, of spaces minute and vast, of powers small and great. An explosion crumbles a great rock to dust; and man wonders again. He renews his journey by the sea; he senses the changing contours and the shifting configuration of the shoreline; he watches as tides sweep in, and in gradual pulsings tides recede; he discerns the variable forms which a familiar rock or dune or cliff assumes as the sea relentlessly beats its pounding surf against them. Too, each day, he observes a new distribution of rocks deposited in the wake of the surging flow, as the sea rhythmically ebbs and rises. Each day, he watches as crabs and fish are washed ashore; he notes the quivering of a dying body, the decay, the contraction, the dissolution as—step by step—it is pulverized and dissolved into a matrix of sand and stone and sea. Time relentless! What seemingly had most endured now seems to last the least. A vanishing into nothingness! The force which disintegrates objects fragile disintegrates objects sturdy. Both are swept away by the same inexorable might.

As man walks, a solitary figure—his unwitting companion—strides along from week to week, an adolescent youth. Weekly, before his disbelieving eyes, in spurts of growth, the youth heightens. From month to month, increasingly bent over, an old man strides with weighty step; leaning ever more heavily upon a cane, he is slowly pressed toward the earth. Turning skyward, man now observes the moon in its varied phases from day to day, as clouds sweep by, now rapidly, now slowly, in varying clusters. All is in perpetual change: generation, dissolution, renewal. From hour to hour, the sun mounts then descends; from season to season, the constellations of the stars vary; from half-day to half-day, from low to high to low again, the sea tides sweep in and out. Drawn on by this spectacle of rhythmic unfolding, so disparate yet (he senses) so interwoven, man is delighted by the blossoming of verdant trees spring after spring; and he wonders at the transformation of bare, stark, wintry boughs into exuberant summer foliage.

And the very works of man himself! Even they cannot resist the battering tides of relentless time. He muses over the disintegration of the creations of his own spirit, works cast in clay and stone and marble. He muses, as he explores an aging yet ageless Acropolis set on a barren cliff, standing guard over the stark, relentless, infinitely spreading sea, a sea which flows into endless horizons of mystery. With the coming of dawn, creating for each new day a new display of color bathing the ever-changing temple, through "full glorious morn,"[1] high noon, somber dusk, and blackest night, he observes the clock surely ticking away, or the swing of the pendulum inexorably carving out the moments of the day, of a life, of an eon. So many measures of time; so many instances of time incarnate; so many correlations, those simple and those intricate, between cycles diverse and palpable, cycles meshing with one another: a great tapestry of dynamic forms unfolding now contrapuntally and now fugally, unfolding in diversely orchestrated ways.

As man walks, and rises to greet each day, for the "sun is but a morning star,"[2]

he reflects upon the variability of the evolving patterns of time: how diversified
—now quick and light movements:

> Like as the waves make towards the pebbled shore,
> So do our minutes hasten to their end;[3]

now ponderous and slow movements: "nor stone, nor earth," "nor the gilded
monuments . . . shall outlive this powerful rime."[4] Indeed, this verse of mine!
My soul's expression! Could *that* be what alone endures, and perdures? Man cannot know, not, surely, in this context. He still dwells on the physical. Here, transiency ineluctably reigns: the fabric of the rhythms of passage and generation and
renewal, of passing away and coming-to-be, of erosion and dissolution and new
formation, of myriad novel arrangements drawn from the womb of time's un-
yielding form.

Embedded in man, and all that lies about him, are inexorable sequences,
rhythmic unfoldings, intricate cyclicities—and their correlations, their analogies,
their correspondences. He is struck by the changing of forms in regular, thematic
fashion. True, variations appear, so it would seem, quite spontaneously. Yet each
variant unfolds in its own progressive manner and, thereby, adds to the great cycle
of birth, death, and renewal. Now in horror, man stands before the harshness of
the wiping away of all trace of what had been; now in wonder, he beholds the
drama and the marvel of all that newly appears. Quietly and softly, he meditates
those perishings which are so gentle, so nearly imperceptible; trembling, he dwells
on those which are quick and devastating. And man reflects: time is woven of
form and *resistance*, of resistance wedded to form—for each moment "in sequent
toil"[5] succeeds its predecessor. Yet he discerns endless kinds of rhythmic unfolding, endless *qualities of resistance.*

All this, man notes, happens as he moves about—from moment to moment and
from day to day; as he inspects patterns and shapes, masses and densities, powers
and forces; as he feels his own movements, in synchronicity with those patterns
and forces, to be rhythmic and cyclical. As he moves about! Shapes and patterns
and forms; forces and powers and densities and masses; rhythms and changes, unfoldings and renewals; all reveal themselves to man as he moves about! It is the
felt motion of man, the motion disclosed to him as he reflects, which is his reference point. It is this felt, self-instituted moving about which establishes him as
"center." Looking out, so to speak, from his "center" upon the tapestry of the
universe, he joins that "center" to the centers of other persons. In community, a
mosaic of tapestries is woven and perceived, a mosaic which is forever transcending its own seemingly completed composition. All this through the motion of
man!

But what is this motion save, precisely, his agency? What is his agency but
his power? What is his power but his *identity*?—that very self-identity which is
ground, substratum, and center whence emanate all his acts. Yet, beyond these

acts, one must presume that his every act is accompanied by an additional act, as, so to speak, its inverse moment: an act of contemplation. And a primordial ingredient of *this* act is his unremitting wonderment as he beholds the vast inanimate tapestry of creation: pattern, force, change.

(b) Searchings

What is the ground for this fascination? Granted: man is a searcher. He searches into all things including, both foremost and ultimately, his own being: its vicissitudes, its mysteries, its source, its foundation. He searches himself qua person, and other persons as well. He searches himself qua living, self-replicating organism, and other organisms as well. Above all (for my present purpose), he searches the lifeless, as it dwells within him and about him. In each instance, the quality of the search differs; both its idiosyncratic character and its motive vary from one kind of search to another. At the moment, I treat only such searching as pertains to the event-makeup of reality—in particular, to a man's own character as event.

Surely, the peculiar, ceaseless fascination which the physical cosmos holds for man derives from his aloneness in the world, and the consequent depths of loneliness which he experiences. As far as man knows, he is the only fully sentient and rational being; he is a solitary wanderer who, to control the forces of nature which from instant to instant threaten to destroy him, must understand those forces. Yet the basis for fascination is far deeper than the need to control, despite the fact that this basis may reveal itself only when man has already controlled. Once having exercised control, he is freed to explore for the sake of the search alone. Surely, man is endowed with a natural curiosity to seek out intriguing objects. Indeed, in many "lower" organisms there are analogous "instincts" toward curiosity. Perhaps such instincts express the need to play, a need which itself could manifest the desire for a more gentle at-homeness: a familiarizing of oneself with the immediate terrain of one's customary life.

Yet, when all is said and done, can one really fail to postulate an innate attraction to the inanimate: a being drawn toward it as though it had a magnetic, charismatic hold for one? Both the most minute and the grandest compel interest; beyond that, they grip man's entire being. Surely, everyone has stood before the vastness of the sea or peered into the abyss of a canyon or beheld the might of a waterfall or heard the rippling of a brook or watched meadowy grasses undulating in the wind—and, in each instance has felt a need, deep and powerful, to tarry to watch. True, one could say that herein resides a primordial aesthetic impulse: the need to find the beauty, the wonder, the awe of nature—for the purpose, in the end, of "playing" with it in imagination. Yet this very entertainment of imaginational possibilities, compelling though it be, cannot diminish the potency of the compulsion to stand before that which occasioned it, and wonder.

However, if one wishes to retain the designation "aesthetic," then surely the aesthetic itself (in this sense) presupposes a profound affinity, a sustained and inexorable attunement, to the inanimate: the need of ceaseless quest for (variable) designs, for (variable) densities, for (variable) cyclic and rhythmic unfoldings, and, just as much, for the invariant factors upon which these variations inscribe themselves. I am, of course, prescinding, for the moment, from all that is organic or personal in my present perspective on the object which so compels our wonderment.

True, a certain paradox resides in my formulation. On the one hand, the inanimate stands over against the organic and, more dramatically, over against the personal as wholly other. Surely, this fact compels an attitude of fascination. Cartesian dualism is grounded in this relationship of radical otherness. Within limits—which, however, it fails to prescribe to itself—dualism is eminently valid. But, on the other, a veridical affinity holds between lifeless nature and personal nature, an affinity based not merely on analogy or likeness but, indeed, on true familiarity and, even more strongly, on actual kinship. Here, I accept as valid the Spinozist critique of Descartes.

In consequence, I postulate dialectical interplay between two contradictory forces—here, I affirm an Hegelian construal of *Geist*—forces which, in their interplay, constitute the special quality of every search into the inanimate: its status as wholly other to the person, an Other before which man stands in fear and trembling; its strange kinship and likeness to man, a presence before which he stands in tranquil but enrapt curiosity. In both instances, interest is compelled; and through the cooperation of opposing forces, interest is converted into fascination. In his essential nature, man is profoundly committed to understanding the inanimate, to penetrating its arcane recesses. He is driven by a surpassing interest rooted in the most fundamental dynamism of his being.

This interest itself derives from a strange ontologic paradox. Man's being encloses, as concealed with it, non-being, its mysterious generative matrix. By the transcendental character of non-being, which inheres in the being of things as well as of persons, the two are profoundly linked. What from a naturalist point of view is the ultimate nothingness of space, time, and matter constitutes, from the standpoint of his event-aspect, an essential ingredient of the very essence of man. By the nature of transcendentality itself, a nature which includes the problem of space, time, and matter, man is impelled to seek the presence within things and, in particular, within the thingly aspect of himself, the being of all-creating Being. God's being is a presence within the very nothingness of things. From a transcendental point of view, He dwells in its inmost depths as continuous with those depths, though extending infinitely beyond them.

With respect to the dialectic which I have proposed, is the inanimate not both part of man's essential being and a-part from it, different from it yet akin to it— quite literally, a *kin*, like a close relative to whom one is bound by loyalty, respect, and tenderness? So often, in the arrogance of power (which he arrogates to himself), modern man loses this gentleness toward things. But is this loss not curious? Consider the nature of technology, that systematic manifestation of man's extraordinary power over nature. Is not the very source of such power an inexorable force within man which drives him to counterpose himself to natural objects as though *he* were a natural force like wind and sea and storm, as though *he* could thereby erode a rock, destroy a mountain, or with Canute hold back the seas? Man has amply demonstrated such power. But the issue is not whether he qua person possesses this power; it is whether he qua event possesses himself qua person in the exercise of this power. For, when it is exercised without loyalty or respect or tenderness, power surely expresses one aspect of the thingliness of the person: namely, that thingly aspect which counterposes itself antagonistically to the thingliness of the other. Herein lies a most significant problem in the relationship between man and the ecology of other living organisms. Insofar as man is antagonistically thingly, he is capable, as, indeed, he so often demonstrates, of creating imbalance, reversals, destruction, chaos within ecology.

When I speak of man's antagonism as "curious," in his technologic orientings toward nature, I refer to the dialectical interplay of these forces: man experiencing nature as wholly other to himself, man experiencing nature as akin to himself. By "wholly other," I mean that man, by his own nature, resists external nature's intrusion; and the resistance derives from *two* powers, themselves conflicting, which dwell within him. On the one hand, qua organism, man resists his intrinsic tendency to sink into lifelessness. By the law of entropy, he tends to pass from a state of high energy organization to a state of low energy organization. Yet counterentropically, he strives against the play of such inanimate forces, or, for that matter, against the destructive forces which originate from other organisms. He combats the forces which, arising both within and without him, promote tendencies for survival adaptation. Effectively to combat degradation toward the inanimate, all man's reserves must be summoned. In his status as organism, these reserves consist in his power for self-replication, metabolism (in which dynamically equilibrated systems maintain homeostasis through interplay of catabolic and anabolic forces), and self-regeneration: in a word, growth. Indeed, man's organismic system is progressively transformed, through minor displacements of equilibrating forces, from a low energy state into a high energy state.

Insofar as man is a person, he reflects. On the other hand, qua person, he resists the lifeless by virtue of his power of reflection and, through exercise of that power, of personal growth: growth through accretion of images, growth by replicatory reflection in which he splits these images and synthesizes the fragments into new imagery, growth in mutual reflection through his encounters with others —encounters in which each person reflects into himself, in a continuing, dynamic, and dialectical process, images which he has of the other. By his very *soul*, this reflexive power is activated, renewed, and consummated. Thus, a power for reflection evolves from the replicatory, metabolizing, and regenerative capacities of non-reflective organisms and, more remotely, from the germinal proto-replicating, proto-metabolizing, and proto-regenerative tendencies which dwell within the inanimate. Nonetheless, once the power for reflection manifests itself, whether as a neutral mutant or as a mutant in some transcendental sense, the possession of this power immediately establishes man as, indeed, radically different from the inanimate and, hence, counterposed to it.

Further to develop these powers—namely, resisting entropy through organic means and resisting entropy through reflective acts—man must ever more effectively create boundaries, sharp and divisive, between himself as person and that which is mere event. But once these boundaries are settled as firm, precisely because of that factor which most dramatically distinguishes him from the inanimate—namely, the *anima* or soul, that which has (to begin with) animated man as organism and thrust him into personhood—man is freed to be authentically human. Thenceforth, he is empowered to orient himself with gentleness toward things, organisms, *and* persons. He is free to perceive even that wherein he most radically differs from the inanimate—his very kinship and identity with the inanimate. But when man orients himself with destructive aggressiveness toward the inanimate, he enslaves himself to a regressive tendency: the tendency to diminish the power of his soul and, hence, to return antagonistically to the state of sheer eventhood. Moreover, by regression, he turns technology against himself, as he turns it against other persons. He autonomizes and reifies the person; he forms a stereotype of what a person ought to be, and he mechanistically strives to bring himself or the other into conformity with that stereotype; he frames a caricature of a person's self-possibilities, constricting and diminishing them. In effect, reducing himself, and *pari passu* the other person, to the status of *mere* event, he sinks into *non*-existence: death, obliteration, nothingness (in its negative sense). Herein lies the import of Freud's thanatos[6] or of Fromm's necrophilia: man's fascination with thinghood, especially his own and that of other persons, in its exclusively nihilistic, decaying, and deformative import.

(c) Dialectics

Not only is there dialectical interplay between thanatos, or necrophilia, and a Freudian-like eros, the striving toward consummate personhood in love and in union with another person (Fromm's biophilia); but a dialectical process characterizes the relationship between the person qua person, hence wholly other to things, and the person qua thing relating to all entities *qua* thing through his perception of his kinship with them—hence, in care and in tenderness. The first dialectic is enclosed within a larger dialectic, one which I here diagram.

$$\text{Kinship} \rightleftharpoons \text{wholly other} \begin{cases} \text{Man qua thing antagonistically} \\ \text{Man qua person} \end{cases}$$

In effect, kinship is man qua thing, protagonistically speaking, in contrast to the antagonistic aspect of man qua thing. Accordingly, I reformulate my diagram.

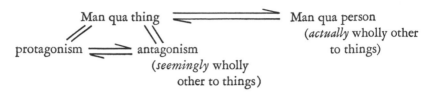

In short, man is the locus of interplay of a double dialectic, one enclosing the other. Qua person, man is dialectically in relation to man qua thing; but qua thing, man—now included within the preceding dialectic—is himself dialectically to be understood as a subordinate locus: the locus of a dialectic between *protago-nistic* thing-forces and *antagonistic* thing-forces. In addition, man qua person is a subordinate locus of opposing tendencies: person qua solitary, in and for himself, is in dialectical opposition to and synthesis with person qua communal, in and for another. The latter (subordinate) dialectic will be treated subsequently.

By my schematization of the general dialectic of the person, I mean to suggest the following. The subordinate dialectic between man qua thing antagonistically understood and man qua thing protagonistically understood is enunciated, under the perspective of thinghood, by the doctrine of transcendental naturalism. The subordinate dialectic of man qua solitary person and man qua communal person is enunciated under the doctrine of transcendental personalism. When I enlarge the scope of my account to include the person qua organism, a third and, indeed, a fourth, dialectic appear. Again, I represent this larger dialectic in a new diagram.

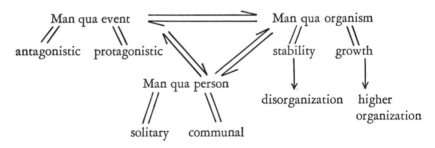

The preceding diagram is itself a simplification of what will subsequently be demonstrated to be a dialectical interplay implying two analogies: that of pro-tagonism, communality, and growth, and that of antagonism, solitariness, and stability. But the inner relationships between the members of these two sets of analogies are, at the moment, too intricate for consideration. One must guard against a simplistic construal of these analogies. For example, I hardly intend a demeaning of the solitary person. Nor are "antagonism" and "stability" to be understood in an exclusively negative sense. Actually I later postulate both a pos-itive and a negative construal for each set. In the next two sections of this chapter, some of these issues will be treated. Their full elaboration, not presented in the present volume, will constitute the doctrine, as far as it pertains to the person, of transcendental substantialism.

The immediately relevant perspective upon the person is that of a multiple dialectic: man qua person in his relationship to himself qua event; man qua antagonist-event pitting his powers against, for the purpose of destroying—or, perhaps, reshaping—other events; man qua protagonist-event affirming his affinity with other events; man qua antagonist-event vis-à-vis man qua protagonist-event. Within the intricacies of this complicated dialectical process of opposition, negation, and renewal, the person emerges as one profoundly absorbed with his thingly character in its relationship to things in general. In both instances, with respect to his own thingly being and with respect to other things, he transforms, he obliterates, he creates, he destroys; he dwells in states of oscillating tension and relaxation with respect to things and thingly aspects; he affirms his very personhood in and through his affirmation of his very thingliness.

Herein is revealed, as deeply embedded in man, a dialectic of antagonism and protagonism with respect to his thingly aspect. In the relationship of man, the person, to this dialectic, his inmost thingly being is so refined and subtilized that he himself, this very person, is transfigured. In the acts by which a person counterposes to himself the things within and about him, he joins himself more profoundly and understandingly to them. By an inner necessity of his being, the person constitutes for himself an horizon whose objects are things, including his own self. He raises these questions: Is this horizon upon things external to one, as person, not an horizon, in the last analysis, *upon* that personhood? Is this horizon upon that personhood not, indeed, an horizon *into* his being in its event-aspect? Beyond that, is it not a seeing *through* his thingly being to a beyond which is neither thing nor person?

B · THE PERSON AS THING

(*a*) Potency and Actuality

Now I consider my problem under a different perspective. The most fundamental statement which can be made about the person, construed from a naturalistic point of view, is that he is a physical event—granted: a peculiarly intricate physical event but, nonetheless, like both living organisms and inanimate objects, subject to the laws of physical science. As in any physical inquiry, some concept must be presumed regarding the most fundamental categories of physics—namely, space, time, and matter—no matter how complex a physical event is construed to be. The event-character, -aspect, or -perspective upon a person can, on no construal of his personhood, be denied as relevant to his being as person. What it is important to decide is: relevant in what way? Certainly, a conceptual account of the person does not need an extended general statement of physical theory.

Granted: such an account may require, for an understanding of certain of his functions and structures, specific topics chosen from physical theory (osmotic phenomena, electrical activity in nerve conduction, or the mechanism of cardiac function, for example). However, my concern in this inquiry is to understand, not specific systems or processes extracted from the person, but the person as a whole. From the standpoint of his personhood, surely the event-character is a perspective, not only upon this or that part of his fabric, but upon all these parts taken as an integral totality. Accordingly, my question now is: In what sense may basic topics pertaining to the character of physical events illuminate the person in his wholeness?

Consider my initial reflections upon the complexity of the actual experience of space, time, and matter from within the present perspective. The three categories of "objects" within the physical horizon of being were originally stated to be pattern, force, and change. From the standpoint of pattern I first raise this question: How does its construal *in concreto* relate to its construal *in abstracto*? Here, one represents pattern as geometric figure. In this representation, pattern is indeed spatialized; one orients oneself toward pattern as an arrangement of factors "in" space—as though space actually contained pattern. But to say that space "contains" pattern means either that pattern is like an object placed in space, and, so to speak, movable about space, or that space qua space is the constitutive ground, the immanent and originative matrix, of pattern. In the first instance, pattern is assimilated to matter; yet, unlike matter, pattern can neither act nor be acted upon. It is not a power; it is not a motion; it is neither particulate nor a field of energies or forces. It is simply a schema of relationships which binds qualities together in certain ways. Furthermore, an object perdures as does pattern; but every object also changes. Unlike time, which expresses the changingness of objects, pattern qua pattern does not alter; it cannot pass from one state to another—though one may speak (in another sense) of the pattern *of* a change. Accordingly, partaking of the nature neither of matter nor of time, pattern must, essentially, *be* space. But if it is space, then it is not the space which is construed as empty, homogeneous, infinite. Thus, though related to space, pattern must be related in a quite special way, related by a particular mode of identity and with peculiar intimacy.

At bottom, this intimacy is connected with the relationship between a potency (here, curiously, space qua vacuous) and its actualization (here, space qua pattern). Clearly, I am prescinding from events the space-aspect and the pattern-aspect. For the moment, I am suppressing reference to matter and to time. More deeply considered, force and matter, change and time must, each in its way, be regarded as integrally woven with pattern and space. I do not yet allude to the immense difficulties inhering in space, on its deeper construal—mysteries so arcane as to require that space engender as its own trajectoral possibilities all the diverse patterns, shapes, arrangements, and modes of ordering which experience so richly reveals to one and which mathematics renders so concisely and with such crystalline purity.

To advert to the relationship between potency and actuality—the question immediately arises: How from something conceived as so utterly devoid of being, often, indeed, counterposed to it as non-being—namely, sheer space—can perceptible patterns be engendered, since patterns are observable, and, hence, by their essence, are being? Having gestated in the womb of non-being, being in its pattern-aspect bursts forth in myriad shapes and forms. Of course, no pattern may (in the last analysis) be conceived as a form of being apart from either the forces which bring about pattern, forces which form and deform pattern, or the forces which hold together the elements of pattern. Nor, for that matter, may force itself be conceived without the conception of its embodiment as pattern or without its conception as a bringing about of change—in effect, new being. Conversely, force requires its conception as itself patterned and, qua pattern, subject to change. But I am leaping ahead of my story.

To proceed: if non-being qua space engenders pattern, then within the essential core of all pattern is non-being, sheer vacuity and all its attendant mystery —the interior silence of things. But consider: one's fascination with pattern stems (as I suggested earlier) from one's self-identification with externally perceived pattern: an exteriorizing of pattern as already operative in, and in part constitutive of, one's own being—a transcendental synthetic *a priori* of one's experience. If so, then is the projection of the silence resident in the very "center" of pattern not, likewise, a stillness which resides in the very "center" of the person's own organicity—from the standpoint of its morphology? *A fortiori*, does this interior stillness not partake of the character of non-being, with all *its* mystery and paradox? And is this perception of nothingness at the very center and *fons et origo* of personal being not itself a cause for fear and trembling, even, indeed, for horror—but, also, when one stresses the *rhythms* of silence, a cause for peace and tranquillity? To penetrate further into the being (or non-being) of space and, in particular, to discern the labyrinthine morphology of one's own being, I must shortly consider seriatim force and change.

(b) Event-Forms

But to take up this problem I must first return briefly to the naturalist perspective. Traditionally, every observable phenomenon is said to alter or to persist "through" time; it is said to occur as an unfolding or a duration of events, processes, and activities "in" space; it is said to be constituted, no matter how intricately organized, "by" matter, its common ingredient. By custom, time is regarded as the unidirectional "flow" of events; space is the "repository" or the "spreadingness" of events, an instant of arrested or frozen time; matter is the "stuff," of which events are made. Accordingly, the "structure" of space is represented by a geometric system of specified properties; time is represented by a variable implicit in most equations of physics, though explicit in some; matter is represented as "mass" or as its equivalent, "energy." In the physics of an earlier day, these parameters were considered as, at bottom, independent of one another. In the physics of today, a profound interdependence is held to prevail. Naturally, the latter view will prevail in my inquiry. In both cases, from the standpoint of science, "through," "in," and "by" are largely unexamined. But what from a scientific point of view is a postulate becomes from the philosopher's point of view problematic.

Two interpretations have been offered of the relationship of space, time, and matter. On the former construal, space and time are interpreted as, jointly, the matrix within which events (made of matter) happen, including the event-parts which compose events. Accordingly, space and time, so to speak, "dwell" *within* events as well as without them. Down to a fine structure, particulate or field, a series of enclosures is conceived. On the latter construal, space–time is conceived as an integral whole: the manifold of relationships between different distributions of matter and energy—in effect, different density fabrics. It is the form of matter-energy. The same considerations regarding enclosures hold as before. However, at the point of maximally fine structure, quantum revisions enter the scene. Philosophically speaking, there is an element of truth in both points of view.

From the standpoint of space *in abstracto*, the person is, on the first interpretation, an object *in space*; the space which he occupies is the "quantity" of space displaced by his mass. Within this perspective, every material part of the person is itself an object in space. Physically speaking, the boundaries of the person enclose the space within which are located these manifold parts. The same considerations apply, *pari passu*, to parts of parts; and, as one proceeds "outward" from him, the person himself is seen to occupy a space which is enclosed by an enveloping (physical) boundary—the space which includes him as one of its objects moving about within that boundary. It follows that one may envisage a series of concentric spheroid- or elliptoid-like enclosures, at times coinciding, overlapping, intersecting, or tangent to one another. The set of these mutually enclosing boundaries constitutes a certain morphological pattern with respect to the person qua thing—i.e., the way in which space is "structured" in this instance.

To speak in this fashion about space is, of course, to speak quite simplistically. It is to regard the person as an event in a gross way. From the standpoint of physical theory, he is a body of a certain mass (associated with its energy equivalent) of middle-range magnitude. Most of the examples of forces, patterns, and changes previously given, from pebbles to mountains, were on this human scale. Moreover, the person moves with middle-range velocity. The space increments which he traverses are middle-range; the time-span of his life is middle-range. My points of reference are two: the mini-space enclosed by the boundaries of such minuscule entities as subatomic particles and the maxi-space of such immense masses as galaxies; the mini-time of the duration, for example, of a quark and the maxi-time of a galaxy; the mini-matter, for example, of a neutrino and the maxi-matter, again, of a galaxy. Accordingly, the laws of Newtonian physics are applicable to the person qua thing. To some extent, these laws are relevant to his consummate personhood.

Given his middle-range character, the person is affected in quite special ways by such persistent middle-range phenomena as the earth's gravitational field, the tides of the sea, the currents of the wind, the oxygen tension of the atmosphere, and myriad others. By the combined impact of these factors upon him, he can move only with limited velocities; he can grow only to a certain size or fail to grow to a certain size; his life span must fall between limits. In a word, certain spatio-temporal–material configurations are possible for him; others are excluded.

And, in general, the event-form of the person is determined by physical processes, processes which involve the very parameters—namely, space, time, and matter—which are applicable to all physical events. Further, this event-form is profoundly relevant to his personhood. Thus far, I have restricted myself to middle-range phenomena, to the construal of space as repository matrix rather than rational manifold, and, essentially, to the spatial aspect of events. These restrictions will subsequently be removed.

Not only is the event-form of the individual person relevant for our consideration. Comparative morphology as well contributes to an understanding of the person. Thus, certain forces induce systematic deformation from a thematic form, the archetypal person qua thing, deformation revealed as the investigator inspects one person after another. Further, it is important to discern the kinds of deformation induced in a *single* person when he is placed in *different* "force" contexts, or, indeed, to perceive the event-form of the person's development as he grows from seed to maturity toward death. Analogous considerations hold for each system of organs, each organ, each tissue, each cell, each particle within each cell. For the event-form of the person is a composite of his constitutive forms and deformations; and the laws of his systematic deformation under the play of forces upon him are themselves the summation, or the integral, of laws separately applicable to his parts. With respect to variety and intensity, the interplay of all relevant forces is enormously complicated.

By the term "force," I refer to an abstract symbol which represents the magnitude and direction of an action, material or energetic. Producing conformation and deformation from within an event or from outside it, forces induce a relative permanence of equilibrium through their interaction and mutual balancing. The nature of this interplay will be further elucidated when I treat the inner connections of pattern, force, and change *in concreto*, in their collective relationship to space, matter, and time (*in abstracto*).

At this point, a methodologic injunction, first discussed in *Homo Quaerens*, must be restated: seek the (mathematically expressible) invariant factors within patterns and deformations of patterns.[7] To this injunction, I now add: seek to understand not only the composition of the forces working upon the person to preserve these factors as invariant, but also the pattern which this composite of forces exhibits—itself an invariant factor expressed as a resultant force (in the vectorial sense). One might add: seek the stresses and strains associated with forms and contextually induced variations of forms. For these stresses and strains are themselves lawful, and they are lawfully connected with lawfully constituted morphologies. Surely, the "image" of body-form in conjunction with its associated transforming and deforming forces is a primordial ingredient of a person's self-reflection. The scheme of dynamical symmetry and asymmetry is a significant factor in a person's reflective acts; it conditions and guides his responses to externally originating stimuli. For every person, such a scheme and image are relatively enduring configurations; they are essential invariants of his being.

I submit that the person, morphologically (or spatially) considered, is determined by the play of multiple (material) forces upon him—that he is, in effect, an event within a material context of forces, forces which designate an energy field. How these forces impinge upon him to determine a specific morphologic configuration is a chapter of physical science deeply relevant to the person. How that configuration is determined to undergo certain systematic deformations in time, involving the alterations of proportion between the forms of the parts constituting the person, indeed the form of the very environment in which he dwells, is also of profound relevance. For example, during a person's growth, certain ratios are preserved as fixed, as in the case of the relative magnitude of heart and kidney and lung. Other ratios, such as that between limbs and trunk and head, vary systematically, hence, lawfully.

At each stage of a person's growth, a certain form may be specified, a form of intricate composition. For it involves both the form of his impact upon his environment and the form of his constituent parts, in their reciprocal impingings upon one another and, collectively, upon his integral form. In addition, a certain form may be specified at each stage in the growth of each of a person's parts: a pattern, an arrangement, a design of his constituent events. As always, the relevant determining forces work both from within each part and from its outside, i.e., from its milieu. Sometimes they work grossly; sometimes, subtly. Further, a certain form of tempo, expressing the pattern of his growth in time, may be specified, as, indeed, there is a form of the tempo for each of his parts. Moreover, an inquirer may formulate the constancies and the variations of constancies for each class, for each species, and for each family—zoologically speaking—as well as for each distinct individual. Insofar as a biologic kinship prevails, all are relevant to the makeup, morphologically speaking, of the person. Indeed, from an embryologic point of view, the forms of all the evolutionary predecessors of a person, as well as the specific and ascertainable forms of every phase of his singular development, become constitutive of each contemporaneous reflective act.

(c) Event-Relationships

This vast multitude and interplay of forms are marvelously woven into a person's being. The account of this process, its dynamics and inner meaning, belongs to my later account of man's rhythms of metabolism and replication. More dramatically, thus physically and organically informed by these diverse forms, the person qua person acquires power to transmit information about them to himself —i.e., to in-form his own reflective process with these forms. The dynamism by which this miraculous process occurs belongs, for the most part, to a later account, when, in *Choros*, I treat the rhythms of reflection and encounter, and, to some extent, to Part IV of the present volume.

Depending upon the special circumstances of his life, every person is subject to seemingly unpredictable and idiosyncratic form variations. Some of these begin at conception; the internal play of generic forces may induce a mutant, morphologically speaking. Others pertain to a particular context of life, naturalistically speaking. Either the person elects to live in certain force-regions or, by contingency, imperceptible influences work upon him. Many of these forces are determined by ecologic factors. For example, a certain redistribution of nutriment or pollutant, in effect an alteration in their balance, will alter one's present form, one's successive forms in time, and one's capacity to replicate these forms. Climatic factors, geologic factors, dangers and congenialities in the ecologic complex, and many other influences make their significant contributions. The inquirer is under injunction to seek to trace the inclusive forms, and the varying arrangements of forms, stemming from such diverse sources.

No account may be given of morphology, the concrete exemplification of space, without explicit reference to matter, and its manifold forms as power, force, action, energy. In particular, that relationship of matter to space called *density* needs to be mentioned: i.e., the ratio of a person's mass to the space which he occupies. Until this point, I have excluded this essential ingredient from my treatment of pattern. But now I must stress: differential densities determine whether, in a given instance, deformation over time is a function of the form of the entire configuration, or whether different regions are differentially deformed. Variable densities of an event make their idiosyncratic contributions to its overall morphology. At times, compensatory adjustment of densities occurs; the total configuration remains unchanged. At other times, specific density variations can significantly affect that configuration. Yet the entire body tends, for the most part, to behave as an integral and indivisible whole. Independently varying organ forms, tissue forms, and cell forms constantly manifest themselves. But, in the aggregate, compensatory forces tend so to restore balance as to maintain an intact morphology.

The second interpretation of space as a pattern of relationships requires postulation of material relata in which inheres the potentiality for change. This interpretation is, in fact, one of a "spatialized" space–time, a space and a time which jointly express the form of the ever-shifting material arrangements: unfolding patterns of conformation and deformation in perpetual flux. Space, time, and matter presuppose and require one another. No member of this triad may be posed without posing the remaining members. Space, time, and matter constitute an intrinsic unity. Such unity expresses itself as a physical event or as a system of physical events. Qua mere abstract flowing, time—like space—is empty. Likewise, matter as *mere* matter, sufficiently analyzed, reveals itself to be devoid of content. Just as the concept of a pure space entails the concept of non-being, so too the concepts of pure time and pure matter. Consequently, the unity of space, time, and matter as, in effect, the form of events in motion is itself non-being.

To deal further with this unity, especially from a transcendental point of view, I treat the more general issue of the inner relationship between a unified space, time, and matter and a unified pattern, change, and force. Moreover, hitherto, I stressed the morphology (or topography) of the person qua event. I suggested that the person frames for himself, in reflection, an Imago of his morphology. To that account, I shall later add an account of the dynamics and the economy of the person qua event. By "dynamics," I mean force and change in their reciprocal relationship. By "economy," I mean the balancing and rebalancing of diverse forces to maintain certain invariances—in effect, economizing the energies utilized by the person qua event. These topics—namely, topography, dynamics, economy[8]—will later be disclosed as complementary. I shall argue that the person frames for himself, in reflection, an Imago of this complementarity as it pertains to his physical makeup. Under the rubric of "The Person Spatialized," and to prepare the way for exposing this complementarity in its significance for the person, I now explore, in their relevance for him, the deeper structure of space, time, and matter: its paradoxes and its mystery. A merely naturalistic account takes no cognizance of this mystery. Its disclosure belongs to the doctrine of transcendental naturalism. Disclosure of the import of this doctrine for the person qua person requires the additional doctrine of transcendental personalism. But preliminary to considering these topics, and as necessary requisite, I must sketch the relationship between the unity of space–time–matter and the unity of pattern–change–force.

To introduce this problematic, I assume the validity of the Peircean metaphysical categories: namely, quality, resistance, and relationship.[9] I presume that these categories express the fundamental, intricately interwoven aspects of experience. Schematically, I indicate first the relationship between pattern, change, and force, on the one hand, and these categories. I indicate, next, in terms of my previous disclosure, the relationship of space, time, and matter and, on the other hand, of pattern, change, and force.

When from events I prescind quality and resistance—in effect, suppressing relationship—"force" (i.e., matter *in concreto*) remains; when from events I prescind quality and relationship—in effect, suppressing resistance—"pattern" (i.e., space *in concreto*) remains; when from events I prescind resistance and relationship—in effect, suppressing quality—"change" (i.e., time *in concreto*) remains. When from force I prescind quality, matter *in abstracto* remains. When from pattern I prescind quality, space *in abstracto* remains; when from change I prescind resistance, time *in abstracto* remains. Hence, matter corresponds, in the physical realm, to the metaphysical category of resistance; space and time correspond, in the physical realm—and in both instances—to the metaphysical category of relationship. Quality, on the other hand, has no physical correlate; it has been stripped away from the fundamental concepts of physical theory.

Accordingly, time and space—*in abstracto* and *in concreto*—are alike with respect to the category of relationship; time and matter—*in concreto*—are alike with respect to the category of resistance; space and matter are alike—*in concreto*—with respect to the category of quality. Otherwise expressed: should the ingredient of quality be added to relationship, *pattern* would emerge; should the ingredient of resistance be added to relationship, *change* would emerge; should the ingredient of resistance be added to quality, *force* would emerge. In a diagram, I succinctly indicate these interconnections.

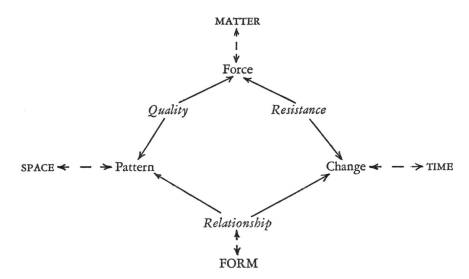

Inspection of this diagram immediately shows how *form*, which—in effect—is the structure of relationship, is itself connected with *matter* via space and time. As traditionally interpreted, space and time jointly constitute the "form" of that of which matter is the content. Now I turn to an account of the import, according to my schema, of this interpretation. By dealing with the fine structure of space, time, and matter, it will be possible to indicate more clearly how a synthesis of their correlates—pattern, change, and force—is relevant to the being of the person, in both a primordial and a consummate sense.

C · THE PERSON SPATIALIZED

(a) Structure Assignations

In the interstices of every organ, tissue, and cell composing the human body, there dwells a mystery—a mere emptiness across which are transmitted the fluids, particles, and energies which constitute it a living body! Yet an emptiness which conceals another emptiness—the interstices between macromolecules of protein, nucleic acid, lipid, carbohydrate; and yet another—the interstices between the atoms of carbon, hydrogen, oxygen, sulfur, phosphorous, and nitrogen which comprise those molecules; and even another, for there are interstices between the electrons, the positrons, the neutrons, the myriad "elementary" particles which constitute the simplest atom; and what is one to say of the emptiness between quarks, those instantaneous flashes of existence presumed to constitute the electron, and the partons which analogously constitute the proton—emptiness enclosed, seemingly without end, in emptiness—and, then again, the emptiness, physically considered, between two human bodies—the very interstices of the human community: all this within the incomparably vast reaches of the cosmos itself. In the very small, there resides one mystery, so the physicist tells us; in the very large, yet another. Surely, the double mystery which physics seeks to penetrate —the structure of those empty spaces—is somehow imparted to phenomena intermediate in size yet as labyrinthine and awesomely intricate as the human body and its matrix, the human community. Are these different orders of emptiness, each with its own concealed structure? Or do they, each in its way, alike exemplify a single pattern, the structure of space qua space? My discussion elaborates upon an affirmative answer to both these questions.

Space is always that which is relegated to the "in-between" of happenings, unfoldings, processes, material configurations. Whether durable, transitory, or evanescent, whether of variable density modulation, texture, rhythmic flow, or mode of duration, events sustain certain non-perceptible relationships among themselves, relationships which, in every instance, are both internal and external. Space is the locus of these relationships; it is what remains when matter and time are prescinded from events. Yet space is the matrix wherein matter and time— each in its characteristic modality—differentiate themselves. To designate space as what remains when all else is prescinded from event is merely to designate space by negation. Strip away everything which may be specified; what remains is space. In this sense, space is non-being. On the other hand, to designate space a "matrix" is to designate space by affirmation; it is to impute to space the character of being.

Inevitably, our conception of space involves a perplexing tension between non-being and being. As soon as being is fully affirmed of space, being is transferred to another realm—that of matter or that of time; as soon as being is fully denied space—and, in consequence of this denial, space is left an absolute void—space discloses itself to be relational, heterogeneous, a complicated function. It is as though one hovers, in one's endeavor to impute to space *some* kind of character, between sheer vacuity and patterns of varying composition, and of varying richness and depth of quality. Different communities of events—events of distinct orders and grades of complexity—are associated with spaces, which vary from the absolutely simple, in which certain general topologic principles are exemplified, to the immensely complex, in which space is qualified by numberless modes, intensities, and classes of quality.

In my section "The Person as Thing," I likewise referred to a double sense of space: space *in abstracto* and space *in concreto*. I suggested that the former ought to be construed as sheer potency and the latter as its actualization. I also proposed that, in the last analysis, one cannot separate space from time, or either space or time from matter. *In abstracto*, time and matter themselves both vanish into nothingness. Accordingly, space, time, and matter may all be regarded, qua nothingness, as a unity of potency, of which its complement, actuality—space, time, and matter *in concreto*—is a unity of patterned activity and density, both in rhythmic flow.

To space qua pattern, the person assigns a structure: a person who moves about, who speculates about ways of conceptualizing space, who collates measurements and concepts, who abstracts invariant factors from the matrix of collatings, who specifies a set of allowable transformations—from one frame of reference to another—with respect to the preservation of invariance; a person who defines simultaneity, contemporaneity, and congruity—those central ideas of physical space—in terms of patterns of transformation and invariance. My concern is not to set forth detailed schemata of physical space. Though surely germane to natural science, such schemata are irrelevant to specifying the import of space for a philosophy of the person. My task is only to indicate the significance of the spatial aspect of events in general for the event-aspect of the person in particular.

Accordingly, I advert to my observation that it is always persons who, in their searchings, assign a structure to space; and it is always persons who in community with others deliberate about diverse modes of assignation that they might, through convergence of private formulations, arrive at public agreement. From the physical point of view, such agreement is a specific physical theory of space in its relationship to time and to matter. It concerns the factual makeup of the physical universe. Here, a distinction is obvious, a distinction between the private experience of space consequent upon the relevant determining activities of each inquirer, the public expression of the collated multiplicity of private experiences, and, finally, the impact of a single publicly acknowledged representation upon the original diverse private representations. I raise this question: What is the import of a physical conceptualization of space for a person's conceptualization to himself of what it means for him to be a person?

(b) Imprintings

To deal with this question, I proceed with a more detailed examination of space. I shall here re-express some of Whitehead's ideas set forth in his *Process and Reality*, ideas, however, which I adapt to my own specific purpose—the framing not, as for him, of a cosmology, but, rather, in the present investigation, of a personology. Hence my treatment is more restricted than his. Whitehead's account is the clearest, broadest, and most profound extant. His philosophy of organism may be considered as the expression *par excellence* of the general doctrine of transcendental naturalism. It may readily be transposed into a specific doctrine of the bearings of transcendental naturalism upon the ontology of the person, particularly since Whitehead's account of events and organism is shot through with analogies to personal activity. Subsequently, I modify his formulations in the light of the necessity (for a general theory of the person) for absorbing transcendental naturalism, first, into transcendental personalism and, later, into transcendental substantialism. Some of his tenets will be reinterpreted in order to bring them into conformity with the latter doctrines. Moreover, I extract from Whitehead's theory only what is directly relevant to my more specialized inquiry.

From the standpoint of the person's body, when regarded as an integral and indivisible unity, space expresses the most general possible scheme of relationships exhibited by the compresence of his body with other things, including the bodies of other persons. These relationships express the contemporaneity of those bodies and things. Insofar as the physical world is experienced in an approximately direct way, it presents itself to one in the *form* of that scheme of relationships, a form pervaded by virtual immediacy and full objectivity. Experienced in this way, the world discloses itself as a threefold manifold: spatial patterns (orderings and arrangements of sets of changeless qualities), temporal patterns (rhythmic unfoldings and sets of cycles and epicycles), and material patterns (density modulations, powers, forces, masses)—all differentially constituted. Thus presented, the world is felt as vividly contemporaneous. But this felt contemporaneity is de facto mediated by body. It is a function of body as body moves about and exerts itself; it is a function of body as the seat of inner stresses which express themselves in a straining toward some region of the world, an effort to meet the world directly as the world (qua composite of things) analogously tends directly to meet that body.

In addition, the world is felt vaguely and hauntingly, yet persistently, as within one. As such, the world is presented to one from one's own past, a past which "perishes" as it were into the immediacy of the present moment—the culmination of a "concresence" of complicated phases involving supplementation, intensification, and cancellation of contrasting feelings about the world previously incorporated within one. Too, inwardly one strains to meet that past, both the proximate past and the remote past—the remote past insofar as the proximate is conditioned by it and as conditioned enters in transmuted form into its constitution. The most vivid experience of what is past and settled is felt as memory; it is also inwardly perceived, or symbolized, as dreams—the expression of a refusal to perish into the inexorable becoming of the person, from one moment of his existence to another.

In the latter case, spatiality, materiality, and temporality are woven together as a single influence. One does not sharply discriminate them as they work in unison, and with "causal efficacy," within one. On the other hand, a clear distinction between these factors is made within "presentational immediacy"[10]—though, ultimately, they are conceptually united as an integral whole. What is thus vaguely apprehended as a unity stemming from one's past is, as immediately deriving from the present, converted to a corresponding unity; and this conversion occurs as one reflects upon the present moment in its passage from novelty into one's again settled past. Unification is effected by communication with other persons who similarly inspect the region within which they all dwell. From the standpoint of the compresence of these persons, the multitude of actualities (i.e., powers, masses, densities) are woven into one's existence in two ways: as spatially patterned qualities, diversely ordered, from which extensive loci are extracted; and as temporally patterned rhythms, diversely correlated, from which extensive loci are also extracted.

Data imprint themselves within the body of the person. Therein they are first objectified, then converted to his own ever-changing yet self-identical substance. These data derive from two sources: objects functioning within the environment of his immediate past; and objects deriving from the immediately antecedent state of his own body. Qua strictly contemporaneous, the world is only a scheme of virtual relationships, qualified by qualities derived from what, having just passed, is transferred to the immediacy of this extensive scheme. Space is thus conceived as a continuum. As such, it exhibits the potentiality for indefinite division into concrete actualities. But those actualities are received only as mediated, hence, in their *just past-ness*. Further, every person shares his past with other things contemporary with him. Owing to this sharing, a common influence pervades both person and his world, even should this influence originate in a remote past. In actuality, one dwells within what is just past with respect to one's own existence; one raises oneself, so to speak, into *virtual* presence as one presents oneself to another. Into this immediate past are woven the data constitutive of a person as objectified within him by prior transmission from other contemporaneous bodies. Accordingly, the *really* present moment spreads itself before him as a scheme of potentialities, and he but glimpses the structures of compresence as genuinely contemporary with him; he diagrams what he glimpses as that set of mathematical relationships which are designated space and time. Abstracted from this potentiality for becoming is the region which he deems as occupied by himself and by those others. The general contours of this region are communally expressed in a shared linguistic fabric shaped by persons who, likewise, share a common experience.

(c) Strainings

As settled, the actual world is not perceived. It is a world which is already past; for it has passed into one's own being, woven therein to condition successive new experiences. Now one perceives with one's body specialized either as this or that sensory organ or as a conventionally designated extension of a sensory organ. Thus, the "what" of perception is a datum woven into one's body, hence, settled therein. A completed fact, this incorporated datum is so transmitted along appropriate routes of transmission as to conform to the character of that body. Consequently, *in stricto sensu* contemporaneous events are absolutely solitary; they are radically independent of one another. The "straining"[11] of an event toward a common locus, a spatial "out there" vectorially referred to by the "here–now" of each event, I construe to be an "endeavor" to dissolve the solitariness common to all events. A sort of cosmic urge seems to work within events to guide them toward a perpetuating, from moment to moment of their existence, of their own "here–now" structures; and to weave each structure into the contemporary complemental structures of other events. But events can achieve only virtual compresence, never authentic compresence. Attainment of the latter is effectively negligible. In consequence, such a cosmic urge need not be specified as relevant to either the being or the becoming of events.

However, for persons the urge to remove the barriers which separate each from his fellows is significant. Unique among entities, a person exhibits a capacity for empathic relatedness. My concern is not to locate the source of this mode of relationship in the non-personal. I can now only indicate (though later I elaborate) the view that persons indeed strive toward, and momentarily achieve success in, uniting themselves in perfect moments of eternity; they seek to dissolve the space between themselves and others. Through such union, the very passage of time is arrested. When union occurs, no data may be transferred between the joined members, no information about the makeup of either to the other; for the moment, the two simply coexist as one: an ecstasy of union. Sexual cohabitation is an instance of this striving for union; the conceived child is the symbolic perpetuation of union. Intense and gratifying friendships are further instances. In general, such union expresses the drive toward self-immortalization; every person strives to replace the ceaseless perishings of his existence by everlastingness. Any accretive growth, indeed, any mode of replication, expresses this striving in primordial form. The locus of the conjoint strainings of events toward a community of coexistents as de facto contemporary, space is the least common denominator, as well as the originative germ, of the "region" wherein these strivings are consummated.

But I must desist from elaborating this supposition. For herein the naturalistic makeup of the world is transcended. No longer are persons construed like events, i.e., as existing in and for themselves in solitary "self-enjoyment." On the contrary, they are regarded as capable of achieving intense moments of reciprocal and mutual enjoyment. Only for persons is this capacity less than negligible. Fully to understand the person, one must supplement an account of the behavior of mere events and organisms by a theory of a sufficiently potent urge toward consummate mutuality—i.e., by a doctrine of transcendental personalism. For when persons enter upon the scene of cosmic evolution, a radical transformation of modes of relating supervenes. True, there may exist creatures with greater potentiality for achieving vivid and intense immediacy of "fusion." For such entities, space and time would be more effectively conquered. In one of His attributes,

God achieves the absolute conquest of space and time. At once He is being and becoming, a paradoxical union of opposites. But for creatures, less than God, the very processes which flow between them in consequence of fusion, momentarily attained, require termination of fusion—though termination may be symbolically defied or overcome: as with a poem, newly born; as with a child, newly born.

A person's power to pass, however momentarily, into contemporaneity is determined through interplay of two factors; his capacity to possess his own spirit and his capacity to possess his own body. Appropriately utilized, each capacity conditions the other. Now only the latter capacity concerns us. In *Choros*, I shall treat the former capacity. To possess one's own body is to orient oneself toward it in many ways. Only as one coordinates these ways may one declare "This body is *mine*." These orientings are divisible into two classes: the power to exercise the body in all *its* powers, and the power to frame an image of that body. In both consummate exertion and pure reflection, one possesses one's body fully. To achieve such possession, a person must without reservation yield himself to the call of his body; he must treat its diverse needs with respect. Only then may he pass out of possession into the full presence of contemporaneity; then, neither body possession nor self-possession is an issue. Once possessed, a body delivers information about itself both to other bodies and to itself, as each passes into its own immediate future.

With respect to their sharing a common past, bodies in process of self-transformation are intertwined. An image of another body includes as essential ingredient an element which represents one's own body. Conversely, an image of one's own body includes as essential ingredient an element representing other bodies. These elements may or may not enter awareness. Moreover, a body may be exercised only vis-à-vis other bodies. In the interplay of resistances, all bodies are exercised if any particular body is exercised. Each delivers to itself both the impact which it has upon the other and the impact which it receives from the other. With respect to either physical exertion or mental exertion, profound reciprocity reigns. The state achieved in either instance is correlative with the state achieved in the other.

In self-possession, one owns one's body disjunctively with respect to the ownership by other persons of their bodies. But through self-possession, one relocates one's ownership; one shifts it to a locus wherein disjunction is replaced by conjunction with respect to the thingly aspect of persons. Now a region of shared occupancy is integrated. This locus is the field of strains to which I referred earlier. In compresence, each strain is disengaged from the vectors of straining, vectors which express the collective orientation of persons qua bodies possessed toward that locus as resident within the immediate shared future. Upon each "occasion" of his straining toward the locus, the person is, in effect, at rest within it. Motion is defined only with respect to the sequence of contiguous occasions.

According to this account, space is the locus of the ends toward which a multitude of contemporaneous events collectively strain. In *their* straining, persons seek (secondarily) to measure this locus. By the indwelling of each person in each, persons project themselves cumulatively throughout the sequence of moments which constitute the life histories of all persons. At every point of this sequence, they project themselves *virtually* into absolute contemporaneity with one another. Through these collective self-projectings, a scheme of compresent trajectoral possibilities is mapped out. Thereupon, it is assigned properties through conceptual entertainment of diverse possible properties. In effect this scheme constitutes the selection, by collective decision, of a trajectoral structure from all possible structures.

NOTES

1. Cf. Shakespeare, Sonnet 33.
2. Henry David Thoreau, *Walden*, ed. Perry Miller (New York: New American Library, 1960), p. 221.
3. Shakespeare, Sonnet 60.
4. Shakespeare, Sonnets 65, 55.
5. Shakespeare, Sonnet 60.
6. *The Standard Edition of the Complete Psychological Works of Sigmund Freud,* trans. James Strachey, 23 vols. (London: Hogarth, 1961), XIX 40–47.
7. P. 3.
8. *Standard Edition*, trans. Strachey, XXII 57–80.
9. See the index references to "quality," "relationship," and "resistance" in Vols. VII and VIII of *Collected Papers of Charles Sanders Peirce*, ed. Arthur Burks (Cambridge: The Belknap Press of Harvard University Press, 1958).
10. Whitehead, *Process and Reality*, pp. 185–97.
11. Ibid., pp. 491–501.

3

GROUNDING THE EVENT

Now, I further penetrate the nature of the thing, and set forth the conditions which ground the event-character of reality. Three fundamental notions are required to express these conditions: space, time, and matter. Within a naturalistic perspective, each notion may be analyzed in its own terms. Thus construed, it requires for its own further elaboration the remaining notions. Yet a *transcendentally* naturalistic perspective goes beyond this synthesis. Within this perspective, the probing of one notion leads to a basic theme from which the remaining notions may be derived. By this theme, a single substance is posed, a substance which is integral and indivisible. Grounding both physical and organismic reality, this substance grounds personal reality as well. Subsequently, I point toward the way by which the concept of a transcendentally naturalist substance is progressively transformed into the concept of a transcendentally personalist substance. For the moment, I shall restrict myself to the former.

With respect to space, naturalism postulates a matrix which, though abstract, nonetheless suggests the rootedness of physical things. Secured in that matrix, events *strain* toward mutual togetherness. Since in significant aspects every event is distinct, and indeed profoundly isolated from all other events, this "quest" is never achieved. Being essentially in and for themselves, events constantly fall away from veridical compresence. At the same time, togetherness remains a real potentiality, but a potentiality which may be actualized only in the transcendentally empathic dwellings of persons with persons. Alone among events, persons are essentially for others as well as for themselves. Yet, in principle, on all levels of existence, space is the primordial medium for the transmission, potential or actual, of influences, impacts, feelings, ideas. It is the scheme of potentiality whereby a community strives to project itself beyond what it *is* and toward what it is *to be*, a potentiality which is fully actualizable only by persons.

With respect to time, naturalism treats the potentiality resident within space for the actual attainment of a solidarity of diverse events.

Pursuing its idiosyncratic route of development, each event passes toward this confluence with a characteristic rhythm. Patterns of specific cyclicity emerge, patterns which are integrated as an overarching matrix of rhythms. In effect, numberless correlations are established between variegated modes of confluence. The cycles associated with these modes are of manifold kinds: pulsations, vibrations, fibrillations, continua of different orders of infinity, singularities woven with continua, reverberations, regularities gross or subtle, arrythmias of innumerable kinds. Time "unfolds" neither uniformly nor homogeneously, but (even on the level of natural phenomena) in the most diversified trajectoral configurations.

As one ascends along the scale of natural complexity, from the most elementary particles to human events, innumerable such trajectories intersect, interact, and transform one another. In particular, the human body is the locus of the compresence of this elaborate flux and confluence, and expresses the synthesis of temporal routes as a complicated fabric of historicity. Just as the less complex levels of natural phenomena are themselves woven of myriad arrangements of temporal sequence, so human time proceeds along even more intricate designs of unfolding, designs which are best expressed by the great poets. Whether construed as an inexorable and sonorous flow, or the ripplings of a brook, or in numberless other ways, past, present, and future are spun together as a single web, a texture of many strands. In later chapters, I further delineate the relationships between these conventionally demarcated phases of time.

The final condition for grounding the event, its "matter," is neither inert nor static. On the contrary, physical matter is a dialectically interwoven fabric of events. For matter is a spatio-temporal unfolding of specific acts and interactions; it is a process of resistance and counter-resistance, a perpetual flux of configuring and dissolution. A unity as well as a plurality, matter both diversifies loci of confluence and unifies disparate forces. With respect to their substantive composition, events are goings forth, exteriorizations of their immanent content. Both symbolizing that content and transferring to one another its ingredients, events on any level of physical organization constitute an assemblage of reciprocally impinging processes which express the panoramic flow of nature. Enveloped by an overall cosmogenesis, events unfold in a sequence of interlocking evolutions: physiogenesis, biogenesis, personogenesis.

In physiogenesis, the principal topic of this chapter, elementary particles first awaken from non-being. In these primordial evanescings, particle and field are created, the first great complementarity of nature. Within a field, particles are assembled, conjugated, and transformed; myriad diverse arrangements supervene: monadic, dyadic, polyadic. Through interplay of particle with particle and of particle with field, new forms perpetually crystallize. Bare potency gives birth to ever more complex factors. Inscribed upon these factors are oscillations of variegated forms, intensities, deformations, and attenuations. Between particles of the same order of complexity, parity reigns. Yet particles on radically different levels of complexity may interact significantly. Within the human body, veritable transfigurations are effected as particles leap across the size barrier from one compresent particulate layer to another. Throughout the domain of nature, and most concretely in the human body, this flux and interplay spur evolution of simple particles toward particles which are *reflexively* constituted in increasingly intricate ways. Correlatively with the growing tendency of every particle to be constituted by the imprints of other particles, the power of self-potentiation is enhanced, hence, the drama with which that particle "affirms" its own identity.

A · THE SPATIO-TEMPORAL MATRIX

(a) Space *in Concreto*

To designate the structure of physical trajectories, certain classes of properties must be determined: namely, enclosures which exhibit their characteristic patterns; configurations of spiralings, involutions, convolutions, recesses and inversions; regions of varying dimensionality and metric; grades of isotropy and anisotropy; curvature with respect to constancy and mode; contraction, expansion, conformation and deformation of bodies as they are moved about; singularities and continua involving different orders, types, or grades of infinity. In general, "space" may be defined, then, as the set of topologic relations, themselves specified by the relevant properties, between possible trajectories for the distribution, density, and form of matter–energy configurations.

To characterize space in this way is to reconstruct space as it is concretely disclosed in primordial experience. Experienced space is an arrangement of specific processes, things, movements, qualities. For each particular situation in which a person is located, a particular arrangement is discerned to constitute *his* space at a given moment. Associating a situation with a limited duration, space is—in actuality—a set of *varying* concrete arrangements, patterns which do not deviate by a significant increment from a certain norm; and this norm is, in effect, some specific arrangement-invariant. Naturally, untoward events, like a gust of wind, may disrupt the constellation of arrangement-variants. In such a case, one would usually speak of a person's situation as having undergone some change. Accordingly, in the long run, space is what remains invariant over an indefinite number of varying situations for an indefinite number of people when they collectively observe their environment with sufficient acuity (i.e., space qua space is the synthesis of numberless private spaces).

By my proposal, physical space is a set of possible trajectories; experienced space is a set of actual trajectories. The latter actualizes what is potentially resident within every situation for every person. From the point of view of a particular being, a subset of the complete set of trajectoral possibilities constitutes the *real* potentialities for that being. Collation of the diverse envisagements of what is potential yields a scheme of trajectories which, at that phase of public inquiry, is deemed *the* structure of space, a scheme which, of course, inevitably refers both to time and to matter–energy. Hence, space qua physical is virtual space qua experiential. In effect, it is an arresting of the rhythms of time in widely varying patterns of symmetry and intricacy.

Furthermore, space must be physically conceptualized as often wrinkled, warped, reticulated, labyrinthine, reflexive. For a theory of the person, the significance of space thus construed resides in the power of that conceptualization to guide one toward a more accurate depiction of one's own space, both in its inner form and in its outer form. In *Choros*, where I shall treat the human "unconscious," I shall indicate how every person reflects into himself his interior spatiality in its relationship to his exterior spatiality. Then I shall demonstrate this Imago to be a special configuration to which diverse spaces of the different parts of his being make their particular contributions. Accordingly, the construal of space as requiring parallelity, zero curvature, isotropy, a metric, and three dimensions is merely the local physical space with respect to a particular set of properties of the world, prescinded from a more inclusive set of possible properties. But the Imago of the person is formed of an incomparably larger set than the local physical set. In general, mathematical patterns exhibit the outermost possibilities for man of his realizing what, *sub specie aeternitatis*, is the total actual set of possibilities for any cosmic epoch.

Many events occupy the same world for prolonged durations. Over large intervals of time, they are mutually contemporaneous. They map out a durable region of recurrent contemporaneity. But consider events which accelerate from this region at sufficient rates. These events will "occupy" the region for a briefer duration. Now consider events which, at sufficient rates, accelerate back and forth with respect to the region. These, in turn, will occupy the region intermittently. Contemporary events define different though overlapping worlds; divergencies from overlap are unusual. But, in principle, they may occur.

As I have shown, an event is both a manifold of "spatially" contiguous occurrences and a sequence of "temporally" contiguous occurrences. Each occurrence of an event is part of an indefinite number of durations. How many, and in what ways they interrelate depend upon the perspective from within which the occurrence is designated as contemporary. Hence, two mutually contemporaneous occurrences may each be contemporary with other occurrences which are not contemporary with one another. Indeed, the first occurrence may be contemporary with a third which, in turn, is not contemporary with the second. This principle may be diagramed.

Here, occurrences {A, B, C, D} are mutually contemporary. In each case, the inverted cone represents the past of an occurrence "located" at the intersection with the non-inverted (upper) cone; the latter represents the future of that occurrence. On the assumption that {B, C} share neither past nor future with {A}, then {B, C} are not in the same duration as {A}. Moreover, even if {B, C, D} themselves were in the same duration, then {A, D} may be in the same duration. Finally, {A, B, C, D} each is in an indefinite number of durations. Thus, when α and β are any two durations for the event, M, this observation may be diagramed:

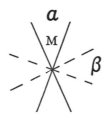

But whether or not mutually contemporaneous events are in the same duration, they "strain" toward and, therefore, define a common locus—though this locus itself may endure only briefly.[1] As a field of strains, a locus of contemporaneous occurrences may itself be defined as a quasi-occurrence which *itself* is associated with a duration. Indeed, the duration of a locus, L, with respect to a set of occurrences {X, Y, Z} does not necessarily overlap with the individual durations of {X, Y, Z}. Moreover, its duration is exceedingly brief; it defines a minimum quantum duration. And certain occurrences which contribute to the formation of this locus may not long remain contemporaneous with other occurrences which contribute to its formation. Insofar as there is a shared past —i.e., occurrences which dwell in the same duration—they qualify the locus which they collectively form in various ways. But a contemporary occurrence which shares *no* duration with the remaining occurrences will not qualify that locus in any way, save that its "presence" will be "felt" by the remainder as a vague, momentary pervasion; or, it may qualify the locus in only a minimal or negligible way—should, for example, it share a duration with but a small number of the remainder.

In general, the "strain locus" includes yet transcends each contemporaneous occurrence. As I have previously indicated, persons alone among events seem to be capable of achieving transcendence—i.e., of dwelling, however briefly, in authentic rather than merely virtual contemporaneity. Furthermore, all persons rely on an implicitly defined antecedent world as exhibiting continuity, permanence, stability. But there is no guarantee that this world cannot disintegrate by contingent acceleration *away from* one or another of its every member—in effect, an explosion. Implosions may also occur, in which events rapidly accelerate *toward* one another—collapsing, so to speak, into the same "strain locus." Instances of both phenomena are defined in physical theory. Since explosions and implosions with respect to minuscule spaces may occur, the Imago which a person frames of his body must include such patterns as are exhibited by stability, explosion, and implosion. Indeed, a schizophrenic disorientation, and other imbalances such as epilepsy, may be associated with excessive *shaking* of certain significant body spaces; this "shaking" may possibly be manifested as erratic electrical discharges across synapses in nerve transmission.

In order for persons to measure the trajectoral structure of their common space, reasonable stability must be assured. Otherwise, the congruence necessarily presupposed by measurement cannot hold. For congruity expresses the pervasive and intrinsic stability of a locus, and guarantees the possibility for carving out equal intervals for that locus by the appropriate measuring instrument. Neither spatial increments nor temporal pulses can "be" without a sufficiently durable world defined for a given set of events. A relatively permanent matrix, specified by some geometry, is the background of the interweaving of the physical peculiarities contributed by a physical field—i.e., it is the integral of physical properties along the typical trajectories of some locus. This matrix must be projected anew as each occasion of eventhood (in particular, of personhood) is consummated. One scheme of trajectories unfolds, and *enfolds*, into the next, with negligible deviation. Only for persons, where possibilities for pathology become so pronounced that certain persons may be disoriented and imbalanced, is space not experienced as exhibiting (spatial) congruence. Nor is it then experienced as carving out temporal congruence.

The extensive continuum,[2] a shared real potentiality of events, expresses the solidarity of all possible perspectives upon the world manifested in the "unison of becoming" of its occupants. Through their respective strains, appropriately integrated, this solidarity both pervades those events and is, in turn, pervaded by them. In consequence, the objects of a person's world are welded into a unity of experience; they constitute a fabric contributed to by the several orders of solidarity effected by the different events constituting a person's body and its environment. This continuum is a scheme of perspectives exhibited in the diverse objectifications of events within one another. Since many orders of events—hence, many modes of objectification—constitute a human body, a multitude of types of compresence are woven into interpersonal space. Inscribed upon the body is an intricate spatial scheme, a scheme transmitted by the body's constituent events through diverse influences on many levels of organization: e.g., organ, tissue, cell, cell components, and molecular composition of those components. Because of the participation within him of diversified systems of trajectoral schemes, each person is empowered to map out the variety of spaces, and to discover the diverse orders of contributing events, assigning to them the requisite properties.

As I have proposed, extensive connection expresses the mode whereby events strain toward mutual togetherness. Space is in-formed with the collective forms of these events. Though defined by some systematic relation to the body, the presented locus is independent of all contemporary activities. In this sense, space is the fundamental medium for the transmitting of influences; it is the matrix of happenings. A morphology of internal relations which binds together events from moment to moment of their unfolding, space conditions all subsequent modes of transmission, and is the basis for the rootedness of all things. Furthermore, space is a patterned region which is *introjected* into each event as a "bare regional feeling." Also *projected* into its collective immediate future, space is the primordial determinant of what is *to be*. This region, which is space, provides the most general scheme of potentiality whereby a community perpetuates itself as the "being" which was "to be."

To summarize: if space were utterly devoid of matter in motion, then it would be purely vacuous and could not be said to possess a structure, save in the barest regional sense. For if space were to possess a structure, topologic or the more specialized geometric, then that structure would be assigned to it by representing it as conforming to some set of mathematical patterns. This assignation is made by certain determining activities, such as the use of measuring rods, and presuppositions regarding the repeatability and consistency of these determinations —i.e., measuring rods preserving their rigidity as they are moved about. Such determinations are made by one set of material configurations over time (namely, persons qua bodies) with respect to another set (namely, matter or objects). Hence, space expresses a set of mathematical relationships between material configurations—provided certain specifications are made about their states of motion with respect to one another in the context of complicated relationships (the determining activities) between who is determining (and how), on the one hand, and what is being determined, on the other. Analogous determinations may be made with respect to the determining activities of people, now regarded as the material configurations the "spatiality" of which as objects is itself being determined.

It follows that space (concretely considered) is a patterning of reciprocally determining activities (immanent or explicit); it is the manifestation of self-actant, interactant, and transactant material configurations. To speak of such activity qua activity (i.e., self-, inter-, and transactivity) is to implicate time; to speak of the configurations therein related is to implicate space. Hence, space is a patterning of interstices abstracted from all temporal and material consideration, a patterning centered in an indefinitely large number of loci of "here–nows." Each locus is the center from which space spreads out indefinitely. In addition, each locus *is* (in one of its aspects) the *spreading out* of space. Thus one could derivatively regard space as an assemblage of all "here–nows," assuming alternatively the status of the *really* here–now and the status of the now "out there."

Most concretely, since persons pre-eminently determine space, space is the "out-spreading" of "here–now" interpersonal relations, transcendentally construed. It is a Kantian-like synthetic *a priori*, but an *a priori* actively interpreted as the *ongoing* synthesizing of various modalities of spatial relations. In effect, this activity involves the projecting onto the (objective) external events of the *interior space* of the person. Such interior body space is constituted by the interweaving of every modality and type of space. To understand it, one must adduce its labyrinthine character by inferences drawn from the character of external (physical) space, for whatever mystery resides there has been transmitted to it by these projections.

The projected patterns constituting space consist in the (mathematical) invariance of statements expressing the structure of space for different frames of reference, each defining a specific type of trajectory along which flow particles or waves, of variegated kinds and degrees of complexity. An elaborate schema of trajectories is sent forth. Spreading out from each *personal* center, this schema implicates the structures of multiple concrete frames of reference. Analogously, *every* material organization is a potent center whence issues the relevant trajectoral structure. In general, space expresses the dynamic interplay between such structures. In this sense, space is a complicated function of several factors: the distribution of masses, their mode of organization, their relative densities, their associated momenta. As these factors change through diverse movement of the masses, the form of the function—hence, the form of space itself—is altered. The changing configurations of space are thus profoundly dependent upon the contours, concentrations, and movements of matter. However minute, every particle or wave is associated with a kind of minuscule clock and measuring rod. The general equations expressing the synchronization of these clocks and the coordination of these rods formulate the invariant structure of concrete space.

(*b*) Time *in Concreto*

According to my concept of the spatio-temporal matrix, the character of exhibiting rhythm belongs not only to time (and matter) but also, in more quiescent, more subtle, and certainly more imperceptible ways, to space itself. These are the rhythms of stillness to which I alluded earlier. The vectorially projected strains which constitute a spatial locus of compresent events are rhythmically propagated. Dwelling within a spatial region, every community of events is immersed in the rhythms of space, rhythms which are the virtual—hence, the never absolutely—arrested rhythms of time. Indeed, time may be construed in two ways. On the one hand, *in abstracto*, and from the standpoint of physical theory, time is but one dimension of a four-dimensional hyperspace. The locus of trajectories which exhibits all the characteristics of space which I have set forth, abstract time conforms to the conceptual scheme which I have elaborated. On the other hand, time *in concreto* is a system of concatenated rhythm, rhythm orchestrated in myriad ways. Moreover, I have defined matter as a system of density, force, and power configurations. In each instance, however matter is conceptualized, it consists of vibrations, resonances, and fluctuations of great rhythmic complexity. It exhibits

the character of being reflexively coiled in upon itself; and it spreads out along
the routes which space and time jointly map as trajectoral possibilities for a given
order of events. In a matrix, space, time, and matter can be summarily expressed
in terms of one another.

	S	T	M
S	pattern	virtual arrested growth rhythms	patterned density configurations
T	rhythmic pattern	rhythmic change	density and forces in flow: rhythmic fluctuations and processes
M	pattern incarnate	solidified rhythm	density (force)

With respect to the import of time for the person, it is, in the first instance,
an ordered totality of concrete durational increments correlated with space—that
ordered totality of concrete extension increments. The ordered totality of durations is concretely experienced by each person in an intricate way. He discerns
this totality to be an endless variety of cyclic unfoldings, between each of which
a pattern of correlation may be established. As with space, one's sensory-motor
equipment, now wedded to the inner sense of kinesthesia, may be extended by
various devices for detecting rhythms more subtle, or more evanescent, so elongated or so shortened as to be imperceptible without an "artificial" device. In
general, concrete time may be specified, in terms of such patterns as day and night
succeeding one another, shifting constellations of stars, cycles of drowsiness,
slumber, and wakefulness, pulse beat, brain waves, clock movement and pendulum
swing, sexual cycles, dream recurrences, the tidal ebb and flow, cell reproduction
cycles, particle emission, and so on endlessly. A problem immediately presents
itself: Which rhythm most accurately measures time? May time itself be defined
independently of a specific standard of measurement? To select a suitable standard, one must, in consultation with other inquirers, establish a pattern of correlations, hierarchically and intricately ordered, for which the ultimately correct
standard is that which promotes the framing of the most systematic and comprehensive physical theory. Numberless correlational possibilities suggest themselves.
Each depends on the selection of a particular scale for the carving out of con-

gruent intervals of time. Only when a standard for time is combined with a standard for space may simultaneity and contemporaneity fully be defined.

Within the ordered manifold of correlational patterns, many modes of temporal unfolding may occur. Indeed, the reticulation of time is as intricate as the reticulation of space. Similar principles apply, such as the different orders of continuity and varying topologic relationships. Like space, time is a concretely ordered totality of trajectoral possibilities—but, distinctively for time, from a presumed past α-point, to a presumed future ω-point. Between these limits, time "unfolds" in an astonishingly intricate variety of cycles and patterns—quick flow, slow flow, reversed flow, momentarily arrested flow. The totality is integrated as a scheme of cyclic potentialities.

Each measure of time in terms of a particular cycle is a function of many variables. For example, pulse is related to myocardial status, kidney glomeruli function, pulmonary capacity. Or, to choose another example, tidal ebb and flow are related to the earth's gravitational field, the mineral composition of the water determining relevant internal forces at given points, and the contours of the bedrock of the sea. In general, one can express each measure of time, T, as t_1 ($v_1^1, \ldots, v_k^1$), each v_m^n being a particular natural process. The time is a complicated function $T = T$ ($t_1, \ldots, t_k$). Since for every pair of processes $\{v_i^j, v_k^1\}$ certain $v_i^j \equiv v_k^1$, the function T can be simplified. Nonetheless, the different t_i functions are drawn from widely varying conventionally demarcated realms—e.g., physics, physiology, psychology, introspection, etc. These diverse realms of activity are so interwoven that time is the great integrator of the whole enormous range of natural phenomena with respect to their process character. It orchestrates these processes as a vast cosmic evolution.

The person qua event is, temporally speaking, a cyclically trajectoral matrix, unified and integral; he is the locus wherein unfold numberless influences. Moreover, time is the durational patterning of things as they are moved about, and as they thus engender in their wake successive spatial structures—those depositions of inexorable temporal flow. Woven into this contrapuntal fabric are strange spiralings and singularities, unidirectional processes pervaded by subtly nuanced time reversals, strands of oscillating flow—backward and forward. Time is the repository of phenomena bizarre and mysterious, phenomena barely hinted at by current physical investigation.

As I have noted, a time sequence may be represented as a composite of concrete processes in a manner analogous to space. Time observed, so to speak, from the outside of its flow with respect to a particular scheme of processes, may, in effect, be spatialized. On the other hand, spatial arrangement observed from a reference frame outside of that arrangement may present *itself* as temporal flow. In this sense, space and time, both *in concreto* and *in abstracto*, are intimately conjoined. Depending upon the perspective within which a material process is observed, they are interchangeable regions within an orchestrated and patterned complex.

Spatio-temporally undifferentiated potency actualizes itself now as concrete time, now as concrete space. A profound metaphysical relativity prevails. The perception of this relativity with respect to spatio-temporal location haunts the person as residing within him as well as about him.

A recurrent quest of man's is for roots: home, country, universe. In physics, this quest assumes the form of a search for invariance amidst the relativities of space and time, an ultimate foundation with respect to which the entire spatio-temporal "activity" may be specified. This invariant is located within the complicated physical relations between phenomena, systematically coordinated within the most inclusive possible physical scheme. In discovering the velocity of light to be an ultimate physical invariant, the physicist is giving precise and abstract expression to our sense of the varying luminosity which pervades the blackness of the universe and in its subtle rhythms constitutes the ultimate ground of physical existence. He cloaks in scientific respectability an abiding intuition expressed by the Greeks and, as eloquently, by Goethe. Even, indeed, if a theory of tachytons as exceeding the velocity of the photons of light, and "traveling" with indefinitely enormous velocities, is substantiated for physical theory, still the velocity of light may be conceived as an asymptotic limit approached, on its one side, by matter as we know it, and, on its other side, by utterly incomprehensible "phenomena." The quest to probe the deeper mysteries of the great beyond is correlative with the quest to probe the haunting mysteries which reside in the "deep within" of persons. Ultimately, they are the same quest. Indeed, perhaps what will be disclosed regarding the foundational makeup of sheer matter is identical with what the penetration of spirit in its inmost depths will reveal: in the end, as for Plato, an outer luminosity and an inner luminosity may well be one and the same.

The image of time which I have suggested is truly the moving "image of eternity";[3] it is an image constituted by the person in his dialectical interchanges with other persons to be the temporal horizon of events. This horizon is constituted by man himself, who, as he moves about, is embedded in the field of his motion. Time is the organic unfolding of correlated cyclic processes. It implicates the cosmos both *within* the person, as contributed to by the diverse movements of his constitutive parts in their reciprocal impingements, and *without* him, i.e., the impacts upon him of his milieu which extends to the uttermost (external) cosmic reaches. When he conceptualizes time and space, he is, in effect, projecting himself into a concise schematic representation of an Imago which works latently within him as physically grounding his own being. As I have shown, spatio-temporally considered, the entire cosmos dwells within each person. In natural science, one gives objective though abstract expression to one's immanent *inner* perception. Accordingly, a person's searchings into exteriority are, in fact, an interior searching which he projects into the world. The results of his search truly correspond to objective actuality. For the *same* actuality dwells within him. I am asserting this metaphysical postulate: the person is the locus wherein unfold and are (quite literally, with respect to his physical aspect) made luminous the vast spaces and intimate recesses of the world.

More precisely, the meaning of physical time in relation to the person involves the following suppositions. Every event, no matter how simple or how complex, is associated with an enduring pattern of contrasts; this pattern expresses the internal arrangements of its components. Endurance implies invariance. Hence, significant and pervasive features of that pattern remain self-identical throughout the history of the event. In one of its meanings, time expresses the *self-sameness* of endurance, the intrinsic congruity of intervals in the flow of time. On the other hand, numberless adjustments and re-equilibrations of event-components are consistent—from pulse to pulse in the unfolding of that event—with its persistence, with respect to its overall pattern of endurance. Regarding the external relationships of events, sequences of event strands exhibit "vibratory locomotion"[4] with respect to one another. By this I mean, every event is associated with distinctive rhythmic motions. These motions are idiosyncratically resolved into a multitude of kinds of spin, rotation, and translation.

(c) The Rootedness of Events in Spatio-Temporal Matrices

From the point of view of a particular event in its strictly individual and self-realizing character, that event is rooted (internally and reflexively considered) in its own ever-shifting constitutive patternings. In its internal (reflexive) relationship to itself, the event is associated with "vibratory organic deformation."[5] This mode of vibration entails two interdependent notions. First, every event is organically composed of interdependent parts, parts the internal arrangements of which exhibit differing and fluctuant kinds of stability. Secondly, because of this organicity, events exhibit patterns of their constitutive elements which constantly alter in response to their changing (external) environments. The community of events is so composed that its members profoundly affect one another. Each event resonates to the "tunes" peculiar to the remaining events. By these resonances, energies are carried to and from events, depleting them or filling them with varying types and grades of throbbing. Internally considered, such throbbings are contrasting intensities with respect to feeling. At the same time, the overall field is the locus of numberless reverberations. These perpetually shifting rhythms comprise the conformations, deformations, and transformations of the events which inhabit that field. Under a larger perspective, the community of events forms a *macro*-event. *Its* reverberations are analogous to the internal vibrations characteristic of the ever-fluctuating design of the hitherto considered micro-event.

Internally considered, every event is rooted in its unique space and time. Each discriminates for itself space from time. For each, the world is a spread of simultaneous and contemporary occurrences. Associated with its private *here and now*, the event (so to speak) conceptually articulates, from *its* standpoint, a cosmic becomingness. By "conceptually articulates," I mean that an event so orients itself toward these cosmic regions so relevant for its own activity as to "take into" its own internal constitution, and to join therein, aspects of the cosmos significant for it.

According to my proposal, time expresses the felt duration of an event, relative to the diverse patterns of associated cyclic changes which have been undergone by other events within its apprehended *distinctive* sphere of reciprocal influence. Every event "looks out" upon a vast scheme of coordination of cycles of varying rhythmic composition. For each event, its own pattern reiterates itself, with subtly altering modulations. *Sub specie aeternitatis*, the largest field, the cosmos itself, is a single, integral, coherent, and unified "event." From *its* standpoint, no distinction prevails between space and time. Unlike its subordinate events, the cosmos cannot "look out" upon anything externally related to it; there is nothing beyond itself. As it were, it can only inspect its *own* subtly and internally shifting modulations of pattern and their associated throbs of feeling. For the cosmos as a whole, space and time are one and the same. Surely, the cosmos is an organic whole. Like the organism, it exhibits an integrity: it is self-contained, autonomous, internally unified. And like the organism's cells, every constituent of the cosmos relates both internally and externally to every other constituent. But contrary to the organism, the cosmos obviously sustains no external relationships whatsoever. For it, energy streams flow internally, and exclusively, within its own configuration.

Short of the maximally inclusive (cosmic) perspective, every event has an outside associated with it. Every event is at rest with respect to that outside, or, at least, with respect to certain of its components. In this instance, the event and what is exterior to it share a common spatio-temporal perspective. With respect to inertial frames of reference—i.e., those associated with events which move with constant velocities with respect to one another—a common spatio-temporal perspective is also shared. On the other hand, when an event accelerates with respect to another event, diverse, and often quite radically variegated, space–time modes of rootedness prevail. Different discriminations of the dimensions of the spatio-temporal matrix are made.

But the mode of endurance differs. Measurement must be applied differently and relationally. Externally considered, a unity of the multitude of events may be hypothecated with respect to which stable invariants are conceptualized. Every event grasps into the unity of its own particularized self-realization a certain pattern of special aspects. The effectiveness of the event beyond itself, its impact upon the cosmos, is determined by the particular aspects which it incorporates, and by the way in which those aspects become constitutive for other events. Multiple space–times prevail. *Sub specie durationis*, each event is a world unto itself; its spatio-temporal discriminations are absolutely valid. *Sub specie aeternitatis*, this multitude is a relatively inchoate assemblage of fragments. Yet, ultimately, unity dominates—of course, always within a given cosmic epoch, but perhaps within the overall cosmos itself!

For each individual event, space–time discrimination is absolute. The paradoxicality of rootedness with both self *and* cosmos, with apparently different consequences for a theory of space and time, is ultimately referable to God. Herein (or here in whom) reconciliation is achieved. The publicality, abstractness, and objectivity of an external unity of space and time (as depicted by general relativity theory) are inextricably linked with the privacy, concreteness, and subjectivity of the internal plurality of spaces and times. In the final analysis, time expresses the adjustments of the synthetic activities by which, in multiple inner contrasts, each event realizes itself, and accordingly individuates its existence. General relativity endeavors to give physical expression to happenings which, externally speaking, pervade the physical cosmos. From the point of view of the merely *local* activity of each event, that expression is experienced in strict abstraction and externality from that event.

But God does not merely impose multiple successions of epochal durations on things. Nor does He simply in abstract fashion confer invariance upon them. Beyond abstraction, He temporalizes and individualizes each thing in and for itself. The apparently external relatedness of things is woven with the real internal relatedness of things. God creates a community of empathically bound events. At once, this community sustains concrete and indigenous relationships among its members, and, at the very same time, guarantees the integrity of their *internalized* external relationships. Both are required for grounding the being of physical events; both, accordingly, are relevant for grounding the being of persons.

B · THE EVENT AS SUBSTANCE

(*a*) Events as Constituting a Relational Complex

In *Metamorphosis*, I set forth the person's developmental phases, phases to some extent prenatal but, for the most part, post-natal. There I treat development as unfolding within a larger ontologic context; and I designate this context *personogenesis*. I exhibit the biologic, psychologic, and spiritual factors which contribute to the person's overall genesis from an ontologic point of view. Even in the present book, I later deal with the biologic dimension. At the moment, I elaborate only the theme of antebiologic development: namely, the unfolding stages of a person's "eventhood" as, through the increasing complexity of his event-aspect, his consummately personal growth manifests itself. In contrast to my treatment of the spatio-temporal matrix as ground for the solidarity of events, I deal with the *substance* of events—i.e., with the nature of that solidarity. This account is to be understood from two related points of view: as expressing the different levels of non-organismic structure and function which, throughout his personal development, constitute the fabric of a person's body; and as expressing that body's nature as an evolutionary product, the end result of a sequence of progressively more intricate events. In the latter case, I am assuming the validity of a metaphysical interpretation of the dictum that ontogeny recapitulates phylogeny.

In general, a metaphysical account of ontogenesis construes each state not only as bringing its antecedent stages to culmination but as actually containing those stages, even while it prefigures its own succeeding stages.

As the cell configures itself into the tissues and organs which constitute living organisms, so the atom configures itself into those variegated molecular arrangements which constitute material events, living or non-living. Etymologically, atom means that which cannot be cut or divided, an absolutely elementary particle. Though it has, indeed, been ascertained to be composed of more elementary particles, "atom" symbolizes the fact that as one divides and subdivides matter one reaches a limit to tangibility. Were the atom to be sufficiently enlarged, it would exhibit tangible properties. Whether de facto this limit is the atom, its nucleus, or some combination of molecules, or whether indeed one ought to reserve the term "tangibility" for those immense aggregates of molecules composing the things which actually induce sensation, a "region" may be specified within which the manifest attributes of "matter" are replaced by experientially *strange* attributes—i.e., such attributes as render meaningless the application of the term "tangible." Likewise, one passes from events of the magnitude of human bodies toward enormous material aggregations such as nebulae and galaxies to an analogous "region." For all we know, there are strange but imperceptible phenomena of similar orders of magnitude to those phenomena which are directly within the ken of perception.

Three orders of "existence" imprint themselves upon the human body: two systematically disclosed to us in the horizons of "objects" explored by natural science; the third referred to by more esoteric inquiry, such as the investigation of ghosts. The information with which these imprints *in*-form that body is registered within reflection as a component of a person's body image. For a human body *con*-forms to a multitude of physical events, ranging from the vast to the minuscule; and the character of these events is transmitted to its every reflective act. The multifarious forms contributed by body's constitutive events are woven into its overall fabric, and thereby made accessible, however remotely, to reflection. Throughout my inquiry, I have assumed that the horizons of scientific investigation systematically express the " 'real internal constitutions' "[6] of reflective bodies, i.e., of persons—both with regard to their intrinsic composition and in their relational composition with respect to things external to them.

In referring to objects not "directly" given within experience, I am assuming a principle of methodologic continuity. *All* physical reality is disclosed both systematically and symbolically.[7] Whether directly in immediate experience or indirectly as mediated, it presents itself by coordinated sensible signs. The difference between direct and indirect presence is a relative difference of intricacy with respect to the patterning of these signs. Betokening its actual presence, the signs are *representatives* of reality. They are the agents, themselves physical marks, through which other agents, either deeply concealed or closer to the "surface" of experience, communicate their respective characteristics to the inquirer. Via a multitude of signs linked to one another and linked within experience, they transmit to him the presence of those hidden agents. What is thus represented to the inquirer is not merely a thing *for him*, but a thing in relationship to other things.

Appearing within symbolic presence is a relational complex. Each relatum within that complex—down to the limit of absolute elementarity—is itself a composite, a pattern of subordinate relations and relata. When combined with increasing acuity of observation as aided by instruments of increasing precision, systematic theory progressively articulates such horizons of objects. It makes accessible for conceptual entertainment what hitherto had radically transcended human subjectivity. What had been transcendent becomes immanent within subjectivity. As immanent, these objects disclose their inner content. Nevertheless, some elements can never fully be known. Each object exhibits a *noumenal* aspect, what that structure of things is in and for itself. Only speculative thought may probe this (hidden) content. Surely, a dialectical relationship holds between science and metaphysics. By their partnership, man can approximate with ever-increasing accuracy the "true" nature of things.

Insofar as things reveal their constitutive *external* relationships to an inquirer, they function instrumentally for him. Their impact upon him, their value for him, and, *a fortiori*, their import for the entire community of searchers are alone relevant. Certainly, therein is disclosed an essential aspect of things: namely, their power for affecting the sentient observer. Though it presents itself as but a relation of exteriority between inquirer and the object which he constitutes, this power affirms the agential character of the object: its capacity for entering into experience in such a way as to disclose its "form" to the experient. Indeed, by event I mean *e-vent*, a process of coming forth from within itself, a self-exteriorizing image of itself which, by replication, incarnates the originative event. Secondary reflection on what is thus presented to the inquirer leads him to construct hypotheses about the *interiority* of the event, hypotheses regarding the dynamism by which it reveals itself. Hidden from the naked eye, a fabric of powers possesses a capacity for self-revelation, i.e., whenever a sentient being allows himself to "receive" that fabric.

On the other hand, systematic conceptual elaboration discloses intrinsic relations between things and things, the actual nature of their interplay. In the first case, by the very fact of the impressing of an object, via the relevant symbolism, into consciousness, the intrinsic power of the event for self-disclosure is revealed. The very activity by which one investigates that object "catalyzes" the opening up of its inner content for further investigation. By a chain of inferences, this power is shown to condition the symbolism which the inquirer frames. In consequence, by exhibiting its inner content, an event discloses a double power: that of affecting sensibility; that of affecting other things and, in turn, of being affected by them. In the second case, the object discloses itself as, in reality, constituted by a matrix of relationships. This matrix consists of the mutual impingements of things: the transformations undergone by each thing as well as the transformations undergone by the pattern of relationships which they constitute. In such double disclosure, things reveal themselves to possess powers for three modes of action: self-action, interaction, transaction. By the last mode, I mean the capacity of things to sustain analysis of their constituent parts in diverse ways. They may be "sliced" into a multitude of cross-sections, each a valid perspective upon the thing. Science seeks systematically to articulate an increasing number of such perspectives. By the joining of articulated perspectives the "true" nature of things is approached with ever-increasing accuracy. In my account, I try briefly, as it has been put, "to disengage the physiognomy of the strict object . . . affirmed [by the procedures of science] from the matrix of scientific methodology within which it makes its appearance."[8] In speculative fashion, I attend only those details of the physiognomy of events which are relevant for a systematic personology and personogeny.

I assume first that events functioning with the double power which I have just suggested possess, in another sense, a dual character: the particulate and the field. In the former case, the event may be specified by determinate spatial coordinates. In the latter, the event is "an infinitely extended medium for three dimensional wave motions."[9] Moreover, I assume that the ground for the similarity of diverse things—hence, their unity—is the "form" of those things, a form shared by different particles and by different waves. The ground for dissimilarity—hence, the multiplicity of diverse things in their materiality—is "matter." Next, I assume that each event "participates" in a variety of distinguishable forms whereas, in its uniqueness, that event exhibits itself as an instance of matter. All events are essentially a composite of form and matter. Whatever the manner in which it "clings" to, or "ingresses" within, a unique particle or wave, every form is (as detachable) universal and general. To refer to my earlier discussion on space and time: under the present perspective space and time jointly constitute the most general possible form. They jointly disclose themselves as the most inclusive possible potentialities for diverse material realization by events. Beyond spatio-temporality, there are many orders of events. Each order is qualified by several classes of forms. Qua unique, every event exhibits as *its* particular form a form which deviates by some increment from the universal form, though such deviation could be negligible or irrelevant for that event. On the other hand, I distinguish universal, general, and shared forms from those forms which are particular, inseparable, and, ultimately, uninvestigatable—hence, in effect, noumenal.

Finally, with respect to that immensely complicated yet integral and unified fabric of events, the person, I assume him to be, like any event, a power of disclosing himself through a matrix of observable symbols, symbols which belong to a large variety of classes. Further, I assume that each class may be independently investigated as itself manifesting a lesser order of event, an order within the intricate hierarchy of orders which contributes to the composition of that power. Revealing itself as gesture, vocal inflection, physiognomy, and indeed as the myriad ways by which a person may express his power of being, his dynamic presence and full actuality are immanent within his every symbolism; yet, as with any event, there is always a transcendent residue which awaits exploration. Too, as with any event, diverse behavioral signs may be represented by sets of measurable variables. Ultimately, the relational totality of these variables refers, through a complicated system of links, to that power which *is* the person. The integral pattern which constitutes this power is revealed to be immanent within the symbolic matrix, and yet, I stress, transcendent to it. For one can never exhaustively specify personal unity. In his absolute uniqueness and concrete individuality, the person cannot be completely conceptualized. The polymorphic structure of human consciousness reveals a polymorphism of structures as composing a person's being: dynamic forms interwoven as myriad waves and orchestrated as his body; forms which immanently condition and implicitly direct the questions, modes of searching, and categories of expected answers for each subordinate perspective upon that body.

(*b*) Phases of Ontogenesis

In their general contours, the unfolding phases in the evolving of events toward persons must now be specified. Physiogenesis passes into biogenesis, which, in turn, passes into the personogenesis which will be my principal concern. Each mode of genesis will be exhibited as including as immanent within it its predecessor; each mode will be exhibited as itself germinating within that predecessor. In designating the culminating phase *personogenesis* I am expressing, in part, Teilhard de Chardin's intent when he speaks of "anthropogenesis"; [10] I also include elements of Teilhard's "noosphere," [11] the realm of the actualization of man's powers of thought. For I not only construe man as a bundle of distinctively human potentialities. I also conceive of him as the locus of these potentialities with respect to the actual forms of their unfolding, and as the locus of the coalescence of these forms as revealing the very form *of* that unfolding.

To disclose the latter requires a theory of the forms of man's powers as themselves *in-forming* one another. According to this theory, each form is so enveloped in each, in intricate patterns of inversion and conversion, that the entire complex is transformed and, indeed, veritably transfigured. This process of involution and convolution I exhibit as already prefigured in the evolvings depicted by the antecedent phases of physiogenesis and biogenesis. By attending to the entire process of personal evolution, an observer is sensitized to the progressive transformation of man himself—a prolongation of man, so to speak, into a hyperpersonal phase. Every specification of both the phases and the manifestations of the personal points toward man as self-impelled radically to project himself beyond what he already is—beyond toward an altogether new sphere of existence, a sphere which, embracing the natural and the apparent, is, in effect, their symbolic content and, as such, transcendental and spiritual.

These classes of genesis express phases in every person's unfolding ontology.

My argument rests on this assumption: becoming is an essential ingredient of being: no ontology may ultimately be divorced from its associated, and complementary, ontogeny. In general, being is not a state but a process. To articulate being, not only must elements integral to this process be specified, but the dynamics of the passage from one configuration of these elements to another configuration must be formulated. My claim is simply an instance of the methodologic injunction: for every seemingly constant factor, seek the class of transformations with respect to which that factor is truly constant. No invariant can be such without a correlative transformational set, and conversely. With respect to most kinds of being, the genetic component is negligible. With respect to the person, it is critical.

Here, I take issue with Heidegger's sharp separation of the ontic and the ontologic. Surely, no deep conceptual account of the person may relegate his essentially event-character and his essentially organismic character to the realm of the merely empirical or the strictly apparent. Qua person, his essence is intimately woven with both his essence qua event and his essence qua organism. From a developmental point of view, ontology and ontogeny must be interpreted as complementary aspects of a single, organic *being–becoming*. At bottom, these three seemingly distinct "essences" are but facets of one and the same essence. Moreover, *to be* is to be a process of being, or becoming; *to become* is to be a *being* of becoming. Save *in abstracto*, neither may be construed without the other. Elsewhere, and analogously, I shall argue that events which never grow *to be* organisms and, likewise, organisms which never grow *to be* persons, though sui generis consummately event or organism, are from the perspective of the person, abortedly, and respectively, organism or person. Within this perspective, organisms are the fruition of events; and persons, the fruition of organisms. I do not deny that events have effects irrelevant to organisms or persons. Nor do organisms not have effects irrelevant to persons. Conversely, persons have effects not relevant to events and organisms, and organisms, effects not relevant to events. To a degree, each domain—event, organism, and person—is a domain sui generis. But I need not here expand, nor need I justify, these general ontologic claims. It suffices for me to lay down this principle: in the particular case of the person, his event-character is one set of levels in a hierarchically unfolding sequence of levels of which his organismic character is another; in every stage of that unfolding, all levels are functional—though their particular contributions do, indeed, vary from one stage to another.

(c) Matter *in Concreto*

Though intimately affiliated with each phase of ontogenesis, an associated congeries of scientific disciplines prescinds from certain ontologically relevant aspects of that phase. True, physiogenesis corresponds to physics, physical chemistry, organic chemistry; biogenesis corresponds to molecular biology, biochemistry, general biology; personogenesis corresponds to psychology, psychoanalysis, sociology; other special disciplines may be added. Nevertheless, the "object" treated by any scientific discipline cannot be identified with the "object" treated by its correlative ontogenetic phase. In each instance, something significant for consummate personhood has been systematically excluded by the scientific; an essential ontologic ingredient remains unassimilated. Granted: the scientist provides direction for ontologic quest. He constructs a heuristic foundation for conceptualizing its objective; he delineates the constitutive relations of its associated object. But the object itself, ontologically speaking, eludes his grasp. Albeit incisively and penetratively, the scientist formulates only the exterior manifestation of the *inseitas* of that object. Its intrinsic activity, the *vis vitae* of material process, projects itself, by a dynamism the nature of which may be sought only by epistemologic query. For human experience provides the data for scientific query.

The more elemental the phenomena with which the scientist deals, the more "removed" from ordinary experience *seems* the objective of his quest, the more caricatural a representation of the objective actuality he perforce *seems* to render. Matter is never actually encountered as "mere" matter. Stones and artifacts and mountain and city and sea and sand—all appear in variegated shape and hue; the movements of the earth and the rushings of wind and tide add to these myriad tangible, visual factors the element of sound. And the steps by which the scientist strips away penumbral layers of sensation and customary meaning from the *experiential* reality of matter in order to subject his now refined and subtilized matter to experiment, controlled speculation, and theoretic scrutiny are surely intricate and circuitous. When all is said and done, he has connected hypothetical entities, freely invented constructs of conceptual imagination, through concatenated linkages of enormously laminated composition, to simply observable "facts." On the other hand, the representation of both organic and personal phenomena, for the most part of a magnitude consonant with actual experience, *seems* to involve conceptual links of less intricate variety. To render organic phenomena, the biologist *seems* to remain "closer" to experience; to render personal phenomena, the psychologist *seems* to remain still "closer." Yet these distinctions between concrete and abstract, that which is closer to or that which is more distant from experience, are not as self-evident as would on first inspection appear. Many relevant organic phenomena are not made visible by conventional instruments of observation. Granted: the optical rather than the electronic microscope is more germane for such phenomena. But who can say what subtle techniques of staining, techniques not yet even dimly known, would, were they available, bring forth and sharply etch the astounding variety of organic structures, or what complexities of spectography, or what hypersensitive sonic devices, might disclose the finer organic resonances? When I turn to the realm of the human, and in particular when I discern the immense ramifications of cognitive activity, the diverse ingredients of the human Unconscious, those myriad emotions quite unarticulated in normal experience—emotions of a range incomparably greater than that involved in either the periodic table of chemistry or the periodic table of elementary nuclear particles—I again see how marvelously intricate chains of hypothetic entities are implicated in their relevant correlational links to the grosser marks of personal behavior.

Exploration of the phases of ontogenesis—namely, physiogenesis, biogenesis, and personogenesis—leads to concepts of equivalent "abstractness," hence, to concepts analogously remote from or close to "ordinary" experience. On the other hand, a general theory of the person ought to rest on suppositions which express those pervasive traits in human experience which are of sufficient richness, depth, and scope. Certainly, it is a central task of metaphysics to formulate ideas which clarify and enlarge that experience. Penetration of *each* phase of ontogenesis yields concepts esoteric and bizarre. A *thorough* thinking through of these experientially strange ideas leads to a thinking *the person* in a less constricted way than initial encounter with him suggests as ever possible. Surely, the philosopher's endeavor to think matter, life, personal existence is, in *each* instance, a thinking *through* to deeper implications of thought itself. Such thinking entails a purity of thought which sets the limits—hence, defines the content—of person qua material, qua organismic, qua spiritual. Whether he thinks matter, life, or persons *in stricto sensu*, the philosopher is thinking his way *into* a realm which counterposes itself to existence—material, organismic, personal; yet a realm which, as thought, is foundational to his personal existence in its every aspect. In this thought process, the philosopher discerns something archetypal about his own nature, his own activity as thinking activity.

For the moment, I restrict myself to matter. When the philosopher thinks matter, he seeks as an essential ingredient of the personal, an ingredient which, by its very essence, is directly antithetical to the personal. I propose this maxim: to think the maximally infrapersonal is, in the end, by the intrinsic character of thought, to disclose the maximally personal. In deepest scientific query, the very categories of thought are, in effect, projected onto the substance postulated as grounding physical existence. By this line of thinking, thought's abstractions are thought itself, thought unfolding in its most essential and inward moments. To grasp this movement, this vitality of thought, to lay bare the interior activity of matter, is ipso facto to lay bare the interior activity of him who thinks matter. Insofar as thinking matter transfers the searcher to a realm seemingly far removed from the customary, the thinker is, by a circuitous route, brought to rest on ground which is closer to the familiar than he had ever dared to confess: it is the proto-familiar, the aboriginally familiar. The philosopher is the one who would dare to think matter *through* to its non-material ground; he is the one who would seek the foundation of physiogenesis in a paradoxical ontogenesis of the non-ontologic. Prefigured in imagery of myth and lore, the concepts therein engendered come to rest within the inmost center of thought; and this *point d'appui* is the philosopher's very self, its inmost and ownmost being, as fulcrum and as lever.

Proceeding from everyday experience through levels of abstraction toward matter's sheer materiality, the event's very essence, one is strangely launched toward the animate and the spiritual. On the earth's surface, the shortest distance between two points is a segment of that globe's great arc. In whichever direction I adventure along such segments, I shall eventually arrive at the same destiny. So to journey by the straightest and the most economical path into the material is to traverse another kind of arc on another kind of globe, one of ideas, wherein the seemingly opposite ways toward the physical and the personal converge, in the end, on a single theme—philosophy's primordial categories of physiogenesis, biogenesis, and personogenesis.

C · ELEMENTARY STRUCTURES

(a) Virtual Particulateness

In physiogenesis, which—sufficiently explored—leads one toward personogenesis via the route of biogenesis and, ultimately, toward consummate personhood, I distinguish three subordinate phases: elementarity, differentiation, and coalescence. Now, I take up the first of these stages. In this stage, three sets of primary integrative notions present themselves. Each set is replicated with increasing complexity and amplification of detail in the succeeding stages. The first pertains to the complementarity of field and particle; the second, to the complementarity of externality—the material manifestation of spirit—and internality—the spiritual manifestation of the material; and the third, to the complementary subordinate phases recurrent in every stage, assemblage, conjugation, and transformation. Moreover, elementarity itself unfolds in substages. In the initial substage, a substage which indeed sets in motion the entire ontogenetic process, a primordial field dominates the virtual particularization of that field. Relationships of externality between regions of the field dominate relationships of internality; mere assemblage as contingent and haphazard randomicity dominates the increasingly determinate subphases of conjugation and transformation.

In subsequent substages of elementarity, this dominance is either negated or inverted. Nonetheless, in every substage, all complemental factors are functionally discriminable. Moreover, the triadic domination found in the initial substage expresses, and indeed hypostatizes, a regressive tendency of threefold character: once formed, particles tend to revert to their originating field; when they have acquired sufficient depth, internal relations tend to submit to, or even be overwhelmed by, external relations; while still tenuous, conjugated and even transformed elements tend to degenerate, or degrade themselves into, merely assembled elements. On the other hand, in no substage of elementarity does an immanent influence, however subtle its workings, cease to propel assemblages toward conjugation and, ultimately, transformation, to metamorphose ingredients of externality into internality, and to convert an essentially field phenomenon into a particulate texture. A dialectical interplay prevails between the movement toward sheer materiality, and, eventually, non-being—the absolute impoverishment of being—and a movement toward organicity and, in the end, consummate personhood—in effect, toward spiritualization as the perfection and the fullness of being. Later, I treat implications of this dialectic under the rubric of coherence.

At the outset, I must consider the inner connection between field and particle. With respect to the former, two construals may be placed upon "field." On the one hand, a field is the (*noumenal*) condition for the possible emergence of particles, which are virtually present, as one might elliptically say, "within" the field. As mere condition, the field is non-existent. It is the unspecifiable and non-identifiable setting of limits to the initial appearance of genuine particles, and the ground for their distribution, their interplay, and their transformation—always, however, with respect to their collective actuality as an assemblage, or a proto-community, of distinct units. On the other hand, the field is the (*numinous*) matrix within which particles are to be construed, in the first instance, as singularities "about" which, so to speak, swirl—like the twisting eddies of a whirlpool —the field currents which, accordingly, sweep into, or toward, intrinsically vacuous loci. From my present point of view, the field is a scheme of regions of variable density and rarefaction, a contrapuntal orchestration of differential rhythms; and the loci which represent particles are analogous to the calm eye of a hurricane. Alternatively, particles may be construed as regions of great density which, as it were, so spread over the entire field that seemingly distinct particles exhibit what are, in effect, overlapping identities.

Reflections concerning the complementarity of field and particle involve such notions as noumenal condition, numinous matrix, virtuality and actuality, singularity, regions of density and rarefaction, ethereal rhythms, overlapping identities, sharply contoured identities. Not only are all these ideas germane to a theory of elementarity as the initial stage of physiogenesis. Beyond that, they will tend to repeat themselves, acquiring new penumbral meanings, as one ascends the "ladder" of complexity not merely with respect to physiogenesis, but also with respect to the remaining phases of ontogenesis. Most significantly, they adumbrate more intricately contrived notions of direct relevance to the makeup, the experience, and the destiny of persons.

As far as the primordial nature of the particle as a primary conceptual entity is concerned, the following considerations hold. The system of particles, analogously to the system of field regions, may be interpreted in two contrasting ways. On the one hand, they may be regarded as constituting the noumenal condition for the possibility of the emergence of a field from virtuality to actuality, the scheme of limits imposed upon the assembled particles by way of bounding them, configuring them, and determining their characteristic dynamics. On the other, they may be construed as a numinous texture—a laminated, contoured, and particulate matrix—which engenders, and sustains as an increasingly complex medium, a field of processes, rhythms, and resonances. As such, they may be understood as setting in motion, by a kind of spreading out and overlapping in mutually synergistic activity—and thereby casting up patterns of marvelous intricacy and design—the eddies and the vortices and the tides of the field. Here, such notions as boundary, configuration, lamination, resonance, rhythm, process, synergistic activity, and pattern deposition first appear; and, as in the previous case, these notions may themselves be understood as prefiguring, in endlessly new incarnations, their immeasurably more intricate analogues throughout the ontogenetic process. Such concepts as these reassert themselves again and again; they persist even into the most complicated and reclusive domains of human and spiritual activity.

When I earlier suggested the dominance, in the initiating moment of *elementarity*, of field over particle, I was conceptualizing "elementarity" in a more elementary fashion than that just tentatively set forth. I was speculating regarding the primordial emergence of the first, fragmentary flash of being within a matrix, which counterposed to this flash is, at bottom, no matrix at all: a non-matrix which, accordingly, is non-being—the mysterious and unknowable ground of an intrinsically undifferentiated and homogeneous noumenon. From this point of view, "field" simply expresses a something which as *no* thing may not even be regarded as an assemblage in the most primitive sense. It is a logical stipulation. On the other hand, particles construed as vacuous singularities are, at the least, an assembled congeries of loci, however bare, ineffable, and unfathomable they be. In consequence, I assigned priority to field over particle.

These ways of expressing absolutely elemental phenomena are based upon models or schemes of elementarity which are *thought* by persons. True, by experimental sanction and precise mathematical representation, the objectivity of these conceptual frameworks is secured for the community of enlightened searchers (into "physical" existence). Yet, after all is said and done, these frameworks are but projections into sensuous reality of modes of representation rooted in experience which is concrete and radically internal. One cannot discover "nothingness" within customary experience. *Virtual* phenomena are not given in the immediacy of sense and perception. Nor does one actually encounter the emergence of bare flashes of existence into a richly diversified nature. Granted: there are evanescent phenomena, subtle phenomena, nearly imperceptible phenomena. But, and this is the crux of the matter, such phenomena are, in every instance, no matter how seemingly concealed or arcane, recognizable phenomena. Immediate experience ineluctably reveals differential textures, rhythmic unfoldings, patterns of variegated shape and hue, contours sharp or obscure, complexities of action, interaction, and transaction. All these findings defy any endeavor to discern in these phenomena elemental factors which conform to my initial portrayal of a complementarity between field and particle. Only through intricate reasoning, and by the systematic constitution of horizons of "objects" through both a combination and an extraction from the objects given in ordinary experience, may the sophisticate in the ways of theoretical physics impute such elementarity to phenomena as their very ground and source.

(*b*) Monadicity

Where, then, does one find the deepest source of such modes of conceptualization? "What a wonderfully complex thing! this seeming unity—the self!" H. G. Wells exclaims of the awakening sleeper.

> Who can trace its reintegration as morning after morning we awaken, the flux and confluence of its countless factors interweaving, rebuilding, the dim first stirrings of the soul, the growth and synthesis of the unconscious to the subconscious, the subconscious to dawning consciousness, until at last we recognise ourselves again.[12]

The germ of the perception of elementarity resides, precisely, in this experience of awakening from slumber. It is the peculiarity of the confluences of fragmentary experiences, each an evanescent appearing, each a passage from virtuality to actuality, all unfolding within a "field" of primordial silence; it is this which, when conceptualized, is projected into nature as a veritable womb of the birthing process of all natural activity. Of this process, with respect, however, to the psyche, William James writes:

> So vaguely drawn are the outlines between what is actual and what is only potential . . . and marginal . . . at any moment of our conscious life, that it is always hard to say of certain mental elements whether we are conscious of them or not.[13]

And C. G. Jung, having thus cited James, continues, speaking of the gradations of luminosity of the psyche, by drawing the analogy between it and an archipelago capable of "indefinite expansion . . . [to] . . . gleaming islands . . . whole continents"; and he further refers to the

> scintillae of arcane substance . . . seeds of light broadcast in the chaos . . . a certain effulgence of quasi-consciousness . . . [such that] . . . luminosity entails luminosity . . . [of] germinal luminosities shining forth from the darkness of the unconscious . . . [of] . . . sparks scintillating in the blackness of the arcane substance . . . [of] . . . the "interior firmament."[14]

What do these synoptic insights suggest regarding primordial (intrapsychic) experience? How do their implied proposals bear upon the character of elementarity as the first stage of physiogenesis? Dawning of light; emerging fragments of scintillae which coalesce and interweave; a flux and a confluence which crystallize as the luminous field within a numinous, arcane firmament! True, these are metaphors. Yet are not such images the direct ancestors, archetypes, if you will, of such themes as being's quiescent and imperceptible mist, its subtle and silent rhythms, its eddies which gradually form and re-form those densities and rarefactions which are then converted to lines of variegated clarity and chiaroscuro, its laminae shared by configured loci of activity: all, however, symbols of *virtual* presence? And yet—is this "field" not a scene of hauntingly ethereal fluctuation, itself likewise, and conversely, conditioned by ineffable but germinal, indistinct yet demarcated, regions of particulate character? Might it not be argued that just as a field of such rhythms may condition the virtual emergence of a texture of particles so, reciprocally, a texture of distinctive particles may condition the virtual emergence of a field of rhythms? In the beginning, in the silence and in the void and in the darkness, what is condition and what is virtual may not be conceptually differentiated. They are conceptually equivalent, and keep different emphases within a matrix of bare potency. Qua actual, field is an evolute of this potency; qua actual, particle is an evolute of this potency. Of course, how sheer potency can originate actuality is another question, a question of profound metaphysical import. In any event, I must now withdraw my earlier supposition that field is antecedent to particle. In its place, I substitute the view which, favoring re-definition of both field and particle, proposes a perspective of coeval parity and complementarity.

To illuminate potency which is bare and primal yet transfigured and articulated, I must suggest these suppositions. First, field and particle are, on initial construal, each the condition for the possibility of the virtual emergence of the other. Next, field as spread out is particle attenuated; particle focused is concentrated field. Thirdly, though, in this sense, field and particle are complementary and, at bot-tom, equivalent—each presupposing and requiring the other—both are loci of distinctive kinds of activity and, as such, each affects the other. Finally, a mani-fold of reciprocal influence, what had been regarded under the perspective of primordial assemblage must be reinterpreted as involving conjugation and transformation.

Consider three moments of elementarity. Each is essential to the passage of elementarity toward the next phase of personogenesis. The first moment, the character of which I have just sketched, I designate "non-adicity." Here proto-assemblage, proto-conjugation, and proto-transformation reign. A profound feel-ing of emptiness—now numinously terrifying, now hauntingly tranquilizing; a sense of bare potential; a straining toward emergence into articulate reality: these are the phenomenologic correlates of this moment. Insofar as it is imputed to nature, absolute elementarity constitutes the projection onto "matter" of that "other side" of matter which, nonetheless, is presumed to ground matter—so to speak, from its *far* side. It corresponds to a feeling for the radically infrapersonal which, surely, conditions all personal activity from *within* the person and, in-deed, is constitutive of his entire evolving existence.

As second moment, I treat *monadicity*, the circumstance in which a single particle emerges into actuality within a field which correlatively emerges into complementary actuality. As psychic analogue to this moment, I propose the in-ward feeling of a single datum of awareness, a datum which arises from ob-scurity to clarity within a psychic field which is arcane, dark, and concealed, but a field which itself gradually becomes luminescent. Here, primitive *quasi*-assem-blage, *quasi*-conjugation, and *quasi*-transformation obtain. As third moment, I treat *polyadicity*, the circumstance in which a multitude of particles emerges within an already self-differentiated field. Sharpness of contour, dialectic of laminated reflexivity, authentic manifestations of assemblage, conjugation, and transformation now first make their efficacious appearance. Two subordinate phases may be distinguished: *dyadicity* and *polyadicity proper*. In the following diagram, I schematize this representation of the first stage of physiogenesis.

Elementarity: First Stage of Physiogenesis

Non-adicity: Conditionality and Virtuality; Proto-assemblage, -conjugation, -transformation	
Monadicity· Emergence from bare potency into mere actuality; Quasi-assemblage, -conjugation, -transformation	
Polyadicity Dialectically contoured actuality; Authentic, primordial assemblage, conjugation, transformation	
Dyadicity	Polyadicity Proper

Further to conceptualize the event, consider a hypothetical universe in which there is but one particle, the monad. Assume that this particle is embedded in a field of influence, subtle to the point of extreme attenuation, and, in spreading about that particle, extending indefinitely far beyond it. In some fashion, the field acts upon the particle, and the particle, in turn, acts upon the field. In reciprocal activity, both are altered. In this mutual change, each retains something of its original character. For the field authentically to retain self-identity, it must tend continually to return to some fixed state. Despite perturbations induced within it, the field will oscillate among a variety of states. Yet, a single immanent state both conditions this oscillation and brings about a return to that state. In short, the field is a power of retaining a certain "form," and it deviates from this form by only minimal increments. Moreover, each deviant form is reflected into the primary form, as the primary form, though remaining self-identically itself, is transmitted to a locus composed of forms which endlessly envelop forms.

At the same time, the particle absorbs certain "waves" from perturbations in the field of influence; and it rejects other waves. Rejected waves themselves reverberate throughout that field, affecting the most remote regions, though, as they spread out from their origin, they become ever more attenuated. Nevertheless, within each region of the now overlapping scheme of waves, a more *forceful* set of perturbations is set in motion. Interaction has occurred with resonances already indigenous to the field. On the other hand, those waves which were absorbed are woven into the inner constitution of the particle, conforming to its very character. Insofar as assimilation is incomplete, a residual factor which forms a separate locus of activity within the particle is established. Should the new activity become so great as to threaten disruption of the integrity of the original particle, a portion of the latter will be ejected into the field. In this way, the field becomes further perturbed. Alternatively, should certain perturbances be such as to constitute a whirl of rotatory resonances within the field, an independent proto-particulate locus might get constituted, a locus which becomes a possible source for the evolving of a new particle within the field. As a given locus of activity passes through stages which might be denominated, successively, as proto-particle, quasi-particle, and consummate particle, interactions between that self-transfiguring locus and its "nutrient" field are re-enacted in a manner analogous to the original interaction. An additional type of interaction ensues: namely, that between what have now been constituted as *two* particles.

On the other hand, should the original particle be incapable of mobilizing sufficient power to eject into the field the new locus evolving within that particle, that locus itself would gradually be transformed into a particle within the particle. It would enter into dialectical relationship with the other regions of the particle, and would so converge vectorially upon particular regions as to effect a special interplay of subordinate particles within the originating particle. Now, the monad is converted into a dyad. The latter might be so constituted as to preserve its integral character. Then a new particle superadded to it from within would acquire the status of a mere accretion. Alternatively, the dyadically constituted particle itself might split into two new units. Or, finally, the new locus might acquire dominance over the former locus, and the original particle be transmuted with respect to a self-identity now transferred to one of its own incorporated subparticles. In all instances, the original system consisting of particle and complementary field is converted, by stages, into a more intricate field. In the long run, a dynamism inhering within that field creates for it a new texture. A multiply particulate field evolves.

(c) Dyadicity and Polyadicity

Now consider the dyadic situation of two-particle interaction. Three cases may be distinguished: the particles arise from a splitting asunder of the original particle; the particles are constituted by a combining of the original particle with the ejected particle; and the particles arise from the combining of the original particle and a new particle which inhabits the field, a particle to which the field itself, so to speak, gave birth. Here, I deal with conceptually primitive fields and particles: I do not yet treat either aggregated or organized entities. Hence, the model presented expresses the simplest kind of self-actant and interactant complexes, and the most elementary transactionally divided complexes.

Consider, further, such independent particles as embedded in a field of influences. These particles bombard one another with some kind of periodicity; the precise type of rhythm is unspecified. Nevertheless, each particle must be presumed to be in a complicated state of motion with respect to the other. For certain purposes, some of the components of this motion may be neglected. For other purposes, they must be acknowledged. In general, such motions are classified as vibratory, rotational, and translational. For each particle, these motions set up resonances within the field, resonances which further complicate its texture. Overlapping and mutually reinforcing waves induce concentrated energy regions: intricate energy distributions, variegated energy forms. Such new areas of *potential* particulate character acquire a power for self-activation into actual particularity. The field itself is a virtual matrix of particulate texture, just as each particle is a virtual field of characteristic perturbation. Moreover, the motion of each particle gives rise to special resonances in the region immediately adjoining that particle and, with diminishing intensity, pervading the entire field. This development leads to interaction with analogous regions constituted by an adjacent but noncontiguous particle.

Consequent upon the impact of one particle upon another, each particle transmits to its mate a "form" of itself in relation to its own environment; a form which must, however, be partly deformed in order to *con*-form with the form of its mate. This form substantively *in*-forms the mate with the "presence" of the impinging particle. When the roles of the particles with respect to their effects upon one another are reversed, reciprocal activity and interchange occur. Accordingly, the *structural* aspect of the correlative functions of "sending forth"—namely, e-mitting, trans-mitting, and in-mitting of interparticulate impingements—involve deformation, conformation, and "information." From these considerations, it follows that the interior dynamics of a particle and the dynamics of interparticulate behavior are complementary aspects of single, integral activity. With growing complexity of detail and deepening subtlety of orchestration, this complementarity prefigures the successive aggregations which culminate, on the level of the personal, in the bringing to fruition of the complemental domains of the intrapsychic and the interpersonal. In general, a metaphysical principle, intimately related to the principle of the parity of field and particle, prevails on all levels of ontogenesis: the principle of complementarity between interiority and exteriority. Reflection upon the deeper import of field and particle enables the inquirer more precisely to render the dynamics of this complementarity.

The greater the "commotion" of either particle—in effect, their agitations—the more "warping" will occur within the adjacent field region. To illuminate this phenomenon, one must analyze a particle from a double standpoint: how it receives impacts, and how it sends them forth. Furthermore, one must analyze the field with respect to the trajectories which a particle might take in delivering its characteristic impacts.

With respect, first, to particle structure, one must reflect upon the general properties of the boundary which separates a particle from its surrounding region. This boundary exhibits some kind of porosity. In addition, it may be resilient, flexible, or malleable in varying degrees. Finally, it is capable of some kind of differentiation, either structural or functional. Moreover, the very interior of the particle is itself differentiated. As a "center," for both initiating impact and receiving impact, that interior might, in effect, be either a single, indivisible center or a composite, i.e., a multitude of centers. In turn, those centers might either coalesce or function diffusely. In general, both the nuclear structure of the particle and its boundary structure—and, likewise, their associated functions—may exhibit variegated patterns.

Consider, now, the character of field modification induced by particle behavior. Intraparticulate centers themselves may be differentiated; some send forth impacts, and others receive them. In some instances, a double role will be played. Furthermore, variously designed morphologic or proto-morphologic routes of transmission for intraparticulate nuclei or their associated boundary may be shaped. Many patterns of reticulation are possible. Either nucleus or boundary may generate this scheme of routes. From these modes of reticulation, boundaries evolve which acquire the power to engender a recticulum of routes of transmission *external* to that particle. In effect, the particle, itself intricately reticulated, may *invade* the field which it inhabits, mapping onto that field diverse reticular patterns. With respect to such reticula, certain groups of their termini may be differentiated in their respective sensitivities for receiving specialized stimuli or sending forth specialized response patterns. In this way, a paradigm for both cell and, indeed, central nervous system itself may be created. In Part III, I discuss such trajectories and vectors. Treating the general problem of boundary morphology, I then elaborate this paradigm.

Given the particle–field morphology which I have thus far set forth—now stressing particle structure, now stressing field structure—it is evident that whether the total fabric is regarded as structured field or as a "field-ed" particle is a matter of perspective: some aspect is emphasized; another is neglected. I have been sketching a proto-topography which reaches its culmination in the phase of biogenesis, but is transcended as an altogether new mode of morphology in the subsequent phase of personogenesis—a mode which requires, for its effective conceptualization, frank incorporation of the earlier mode. Yet, even now, in the context of physiogenesis, I may proceed further, though I must resort to the language of imagery. Later, I justify this language as an effective device for communicating those metaphysical suppositions which are heuristic for conceptualizing the person.

To proceed: in effect, each particle receives an Imago of its mate; each mirrors its mate, via that Imago, both to itself and to that mate. Thus incorporating this mirroring, each particle reflects itself to the other. An indefinite process of reciprocal reflexivity is thereby engendered. Accordingly, I make the following metaphysical claim: no matter how elementary, particles are reflexively constituted. As both recipient and engendering matrix of this dialectical interplay, fields also are reflexively constituted. In consequence, the entire configuration, particle and field together giving birth to new particle and new field, is reflexively constituted. Stated dramatically, matter—i.e., substance, the stuff of events—is through and through reflexive. Thus turned in upon itself, and accordingly entering into *internal* relationship with itself, matter is endowed with a power for self-potentiation with respect to its capacity for transmitting influences.

Essentially the same considerations which apply to dyadic interplay, on the physiogenetic level of elementarity, apply to polyadic interplay. In short, as one conceptualizes more particles, the reflexive makeup of particle and field becomes more intricate; correlatively, the associated oscillations, analyzable in terms of diverse types of motion—vortices within particle–field configurations—exhibit complicated patterns. For a given particle, the internal relations between the multitude of introjected images acquire a complex design. Analogously, the field itself is transmuted. For fields are the repositories of influences among multiply reflexive particles. They are matrices for transmitting those influences; they are conditions for the effective dialectical interplay of those particles. The very source of "energies" which allow the entire process to unfold, a field *en-folds* resonances which, as they interweave and wrap about and within one another, synergize new powers latent in that field's embedded particles. Therefore, the metaphysical principles which characterize polyadicity in its dyadic phase and those principles which characterize polyadicity proper are essentially the same—with one notable exception! When more than two particles are implicated in this scheme, a community has already formed; where there is community, there is specialization of function, hierarchization of role, differential aggregations with respect to a primordially egalitarian assemblage. To treat this theme, I must pass beyond the stage of elementarity; I must analyze the remaining stages of physiogenesis.

Before I advance beyond elementarity, an additional metaphysical problem needs mentioning. Until this point, I have prescinded from all considerations which might falsify an intrinsically atomistic view of the infrapersonal cosmos. Later, I show that a generalized theory of the person, when its full import is discerned, requires abandonment of the atomistic supposition. I make this double claim: first, when particle and field are construed as reflexive, one seeks to penetrate the very nature of reflexivity; when, consequently, one has come to attribute to events an inwardness, or affective character, one must dismiss the hypothesis of *irreducible* elementarity; secondly, the further one probes the most elemental feelings, impulses, and volitions (of persons)—in effect, all "simple" psychic elements—the more powerfully are revealed the arcane depths, the immeasurably subtle flux and confluence of the affective resonances foundational to, and originative of, those elements. If, indeed, it is true that the elementarity of the physical cosmos consists, in effect, in the projection onto that cosmos of the felt elementarity of intrapsychic factors, then one must conclude that the supposition of irreducible actualities, of absolute simples, is fallacious. Insofar as the sheer existentiality of events is considered, their fixity in strictly objective and material terms, that supposition is perhaps justified. But when the *quiddity* of events is so probed as to reveal their dissolution into an abyss of *interiority*, a labyrinth of sheer feeling—or, at least, an analogue to such feeling as resonances of incredibly complicated strands, evanescent and subtly constituted fluctuations—then the contrary supposition must be posed.

In a diagram, I schematize the latter as a *quaternity*:

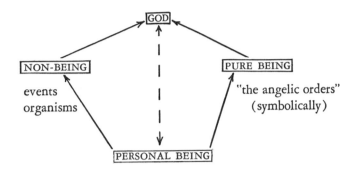

In this scheme, each item enclosed in a rectangle must be understood in terms of a species of feeling; and feeling becomes extraordinarily complex, though in different (but complemental) senses, as one moves "away" from the person—either in the direction of pure being or in the direction of non-being. A behaviorist account of phenomena is relevant only as the inquirer hovers about events and organisms. As he passes from organisms toward persons, and, indeed, beyond persons, or, alternately, as he passes from events toward elementarity, and even beyond that, there emerges into significance an altogether new category, the numinous. Here, the inquirer must conceive hitherto unimaginable horizons for novel disclosure. He is now dealing with the realm of the diaphanous, the ineffable, the most subtle effulgences. But having indulged in these desultory reflections, I must pass seriatim to the succeeding stages in the evolution of the event in its significance for the person.

NOTES

1. Whitehead, *Process and Reality*, pp. 491–501.
2. Ibid., pp. 449–559.
3. Attributed to Plato by Diogenes Laertius. See his *The Lives and Opinions of Eminent Philosophers*, trans. C. D. Yonge (London: Bohn, 1853), p. 139.
4. Alfred North Whitehead, *Science and the Modern World* (New York: Macmillan, 1931), p. 191.
5. Ibid.
6. Whitehead, *Process and Reality*, p. 37.

7. For the following discussion, I am indebted to Patrick Heelan, *Quantum Mechanics and Objectivity* (The Hague: Nijhoff, 1965), esp. chaps. 1, 2, 8.

8. Ibid., p. 162.

9. See the discussion in chap. 8 of ibid.

10. Pierre Teilhard de Chardin, *The Phenomenon of Man*, trans. Bernard Wall (New York: Harper, 1959), pp. 42, 50, 138, 210, 241.

11. See indexed items under "noosphere" in ibid.

12. *The Sleeper Wakes* (London: Collins, 1921), p. 25.

13. *The Varieties of Religious Experience* (New York: Modern Library, 1902), p. 232.

14. "On the Nature of the Psyche," *The Structure and Dynamics of the Psyche*, trans. R. F. C. Hull (New York: Pantheon, 1960), pp. 188–95, esp. pp. 192, 195.

4

MAN'S CRYSTALLINE ESSENCE

Now I treat the physiogenetic process from two points of view. First, I deal with the stages along its passage, stages which range from the constellating of elementary particles to the intricate configuring of durable strands of matter. Within this passage, I designate as *terminus a quo* evanescing existence and as *terminus ad quem* crystalline existence. Secondly, I set forth themes pertaining to the overall character of the process, especially in their relevance for the composition, within a transcendentally naturalist perspective, of the person. The stage wherein particles merely appear and vanish is progressively transferred through a succession of stages: durable structures emerge to be preserved amidst manifold physical transformations; strands of these self-differentiating structures shape themselves into more intricate configurations; the latter acquire the laminated composition exhibited, just prior to the emergence of life, by multilatticed crystalline polymers. Insofar as, from a physical point of view, man is constituted by laminae, each layered upon the next, of interacting particles of increasing complexity, he exhibits a double physical essence: the evanescing and the crystalline.

The dynamism whereby transition from the evanescent stage to the crystalline stage is effected consists, I show, in a variety of subsidiary processes. These include the following: reflexive transmission, from particle to particle, from strand to strand, and from configuration to configuration of Imagos of their respective interior contents; the gathering together by each such factor of these Imagos so that conjointly they potentiate a unified impact; imposition upon an assemblage of factors of the "form" associated with its antecedent phase; conformation to this form with deviations of increasing complexity; dynamic relatedness by every factor to the alien contents inscribed upon it and appropriated by it; reiteration of self-identity despite successive intrusion of these imprints; mutual attunement of all relevant particles; orchestration of the rhythms associated with each texture of differentiated strands; and supervention of novel schemes of proto-ecologic co-adaptation. Through the conjoint working of these diverse

processes, a labyrinthine character, a character which involves manifold convolutions and involutions, becomes increasingly associated with compresent particles, strands, and configurations. Within this context, profound continuities prevail, continuities grounded in the "field" resonances engendered by all particulate assemblages and, in turn, enveloping them. These resonances weave primordial rhythms with rhythms of more elaborate ornamentation. By participating within these complex rhythms, every factor roots itself so securely as to intensify its power of self-affirmation, and, hence, to solidify its self-identity.

Considered in all its unfoldings, the various forms of physiogenesis are compresent as integrally unified within the human body. These numberless dynamic forms, which constitute the overall form of physiogenesis, interpenetrate and suffuse one another. Such interweaving confers upon every complex factor the character of profound continuity rather than of atomicity. The most subtly modulated rhythms enclose all compresent layers. They are the medium through which impulses are transmitted from one event to another. So pervasive is this matrix of rhythms that events derive their very self-identities through their dwelling *within* the interstices between events. Because of such continuity and rhythmicity, no factor within any complex may be conceived as radically isolated from any other factor. No factor is bound, so to speak, to its own privacy.

In effect, a scheme of internal relationships prevails, a network of "empathic" bonds by which each factor is *interiorly* connected with every other factor. No matter how elementary or indiscerptible the factors seem to be, the texture of this system of bonds is imposed upon all factors. In particular, a principle of contextuality is operative. By this principle, the complexity of elementarity becomes dramatically apparent. The rhythms of the most complex aggregations become constitutive of the simplest particles—i.e., when the context within which the latter function is constituted by the former. On the other hand, a principle asserting the converse situation does not cease to reign. No matter how intricate, many aggregates in being self-identically themselves perpetually affirm their own unity and indivisibility—and, in this sense, their utter simplicity. In sum, by the argument which follows, two types of determi-nation are interwoven: contextual determination of the diversification of elementarity, and the self-potentiating determination of the unifica-tion of complexity.

A · MATTER DIFFERENTIATED

(a) The Particle

In the second stage of physiogenesis, particles acquire durability and, in conse-quence, differentiation. Amidst the changing perturbations which sweep across the field, temporally enduring structures—each associated with a "dynamic form" —are shaped, preserved, and re-formed. In every instance of this persistence through a multitude of transformations, a momentary flash of existence imposes its form upon its immediate successor. Correlatively, the internal reflexivity of that "flash," its (affective) relationship to itself, is transmitted to that successor. Each "occasion" of existence temporally conforms to other such "occasions"; every "occasion" is associated with an affective element, a composite of primordial feel-ings. This process now governs the assemblage of particles. To the reflexive trans-mission of Imagos from one nearly contemporary particle to another is now added the reflexive transmission of Imagos within a sequence of particles, all conjoined as temporally contiguous. Having gathered together impulses received from (spatially) adjacent units, and having woven these impulses into an integral pat-tern, each particle flows in its essential totality, even as it perishes as a self-reflexive and autonomous unit, into its immediate temporal successor. Thus, all members of a temporal strand of particles exhibit a recurrent form of twofold character: for every member of the strand, that form does not deviate significantly from the form of any component member; at every stage of this unfolding, a particular form is the cumulative integral of all preceding constituent forms, subtly re-composed by the contribution of a novel factor.

Every pulse of *affective* existence (the dipolar character of any real entity) is intrinsically triphasic. First, it is a gathering together of diverse influences. A unifying of their individual impacts into a composition of unique design, it im-prints its own evolving character into them. Next, this primordial ferment is woven into a potent unity of action. By this process, the pulse enters into dynamic relatedness with itself, "experiencing" within itself intricate rhythms of feeling, rhythms nuanced and orchestrated in myriad ways. Finally, unless the pulse—catalyzed by the relevant field perturbations—is empowered by its own self-potentiating acts potently to replicate itself and, moreover, to join its replica to itself as its immediate temporal successor, it perishes into the field of its origin. And should it perish, that pulse distributes to the field resonances now dispersed, but without loss of intrinsic significance. This pulse has brought these resonances to internal "subjective" consummation.

But when the internal energies (each a primitive affect), associated with the reflexive character of a particle, become sufficiently intense and concentrated, that particle will replicate itself. Splitting into like vortices within the field, it durably affects the subsequent destiny of that field. Among these replicas, a single, unique replica may "cling" to the originating particle as its immediate temporal successor. Like effulgent sparks, an array of replicas is scattered into the field. Depending upon the character of that field, a certain trajectoral pattern—the paths of "motion" for these replicas—will be mapped out. Within this pattern, some paths are so constituted as to be adjacent immediately to the originating particle—i.e., to surround, or to hover about, that particle. When such adjacency is associated with certain selected particle motions, what had in effect been spatial adjacency is converted into temporal adjacency. The kinds of "spin" associated with a given motion —i.e., the character of the vortex, and the mode of orchestrating its rhythms, created within the immediate neighborhood of that particle—determine the type of pulse sequences which will temporally endure.

In general, associated with every entity is a certain energy "content." The energy surplus, beyond what is needed to maintain its immediate integrity, determines the mode of self-replication which that entity is capable of initiating. Some replicas tend toward fragmentation; others, toward integrality. Some replicas are propelled away from the originating entity, either to acquire "existences" of their own or to unite with other than the originating entity; some replicas will so conjoin themselves with their parent entities as to constitute an effective duration. Transmitting to other regions of the field information about the initiating entity, certain replicas (or quasi-replicas) will serve as "messengers." Through attachments of temporal sequence, other replicas will become recipients of further information about that entity and, subsequently, become the transmitters of that information, synthesized with their indigenously engendered "data," to their *own* successors.

Accordingly, diverse patterns of transmission, modes of cohesiveness with respect to contiguity, and types of temporal strand will be created. In effect, the field becomes criss-crossed by a network, often quite intricate, of information bearers which make up the *durably* particulate structure of that field. What had been essentially assembled on the level of elementarity (with proto-conjugational and proto-transformational configurations) now becomes more solidly conjugated on the level of duration. But naturally, the categories of assemblage and transformation are still applicable. At this stage, the field itself is an assemblage of patterns of durational strands. Through the interplay of these strands, in ways which recapitulate the interplay of elementary entities—though engendering incomparably more intricate patterns of reflexivity, hence, internal "feelings" of great intensity—the temporal design of the field is progressively transformed.

In sum, a particle is, in effect, impregnated with data delivered to it from other particles. Two fundamental options are available to it. On the one hand, it may discharge those contents into the field of its own origin, thereby permanently altering the field: no equilibrium is identical in all respects with an antecedent equilibrium. Should the particle be an especially fragile pulse, this option will, so to speak, be "chosen." On the other hand, absorption of new data tends, on the whole, to potentiate a more durable particle. In this way, the particle not only acquires duration, persisting amidst transformations of its associated field, but also reinforces its own identity, increasing the likelihood of its continued survival. As soon as the stage of elementarity appears, a scheme of temporally contiguous particles emerges, each transmitting a form from its own immediate past to its own immediate future.

(b) Strands of Pulsation

In a durational succession of pulses, the component members cohere by virtue of the continuing transmission throughout the duration of an Imago which, in effect, persists from member to member. Though adding its autochthonous subtle modulations, every pulse essentially mediates this transmission from its immediate predecessor to its immediate successor. In consequence, the cumulative transmission of a "string" of Imagos constitutes the self-identity of the entity shaped by a duration. Accordingly, self-identity is a process of reiteration. It must be declared again and again; and this self-declaration is tantamount to the extrusion from the interiority of all pulses of Imagos of their very selves. In thus declaring its persistent identity, the entity constituted by those pulses affirms the exuberance of its own existence. A kind of music is created, the expression of the arrangement of the diverse parts of that entity: its spin, its vibrations, its resonances—all interwoven in myriad ways. From this point of view, every entity "possesses" a score for transforming its elementary, often seemingly inchoate, material ground into the elaborately ordered dance of emerging dynamic forms. In such fashion, the proto-durational origins of a particle are recapitulated; they are presented anew. As the germinal center unfolds, successively more intricate arrangements of matter are formed: novel clusterings, cumulative balancings and ornamentations, confluences of innumerable "notes" reflecting quanta of data absorbed and quanta of data emitted, crystallizings into lattices of marvelous design.

No matter how simple the makeup—hence, the associated music—of any entity, the entity is dynamically oriented toward all other entities in its field of occupancy. Now it turns to this durational sequence, and pipes its tune, now to that. As it thereby inscribes its own theme upon every occupant, it "listens" to that occupant, itself an entity which analogously declares its own archetypal character. A veritable counterpoint of orientings flows forth, each occupant toward the other. Throbbing with energies associated with internal "emotional" tensions, every entity differentiates itself into a matrix of finely nuanced improvisation. The strand which composes it is like an instrument endowed with the power of replicating its own nature. As that strand's typical rhythms unfold, they incorporate themselves within portions of the strand, portions which split off to constitute novel existents in their own right. A fortiori, the entire assemblage of entities is, at bottom, an orchestration of the reciprocal attunings of many durational particles, each, in effect, humming its own melody.

Pulsating with its own rhythm, the composite of multitudinous rhythms cumulatively transmitted to it by the separate "musical" configurations of its constituent pulses, each temporal strand establishes for itself its own identity. The rhythmic differences between one temporal strand and another articulate the field as a differentiated pattern of temporal strands. These strands contour themselves in many ways. Each contour shapes new routes for the transmission of influences among the strands. A specific spatio-temporal configuration is defined with respect to a given mode of interrelating these strands, and recurs with varying periodicity, with respect to such properties as (to speak the language of physics) spin, energy, momentum, action. A taxonomy of durational strands corresponding to the periodic table of elementary physical particles suggests itself.

Each strand is a self-repeating pulse. Each exists sui generis, exhibiting its own mode of repetition; each orchestrates the inner music of its components in a characteristic way. When I declare this music to be archetypal, I mean that the fundamental "key" of its score is determined by its originating pulse, but always in the context of the relationship between that pulse and other analogously originating pulses. Myriad archetypal perspectives prevail, perspectives within which a rhythmic theme is transcribed over and over again by the succeeding members of a strand in ways which vary, sometimes greatly, from one strand to another. In every instance, the strand throbs with musicality, its interior and indigenous musicality, the novel themes inscribed upon it owing their attunement to the throbbings of other durational strands.

By the autonomous activity of each strand, "data" are gathered in, data deriving from neighboring strands—but always this gathering occurs under the form of its own (subjective) throbbing. Once absorbed, these data are objectified within that gathering strand as its own (rhythmic) values: the valuation which it places upon other strands in their relevance for it; its effective ordering of these strands; their modes of harmonizing with its indigenous music. Notes, so to speak, played upon the instruments of diverse strands are disjunctively incorporated within a recipient strand. Once orchestrated with notes already being "played" by that recipient, these "introjects" acquire the status of conjunctivity; an integral contrapuntal scheme is created.

By relevant attunement, within a given assemblage of durational strands, each strand identifies itself for an "instant" of its existence with all strands, powerfully, in the case of some, weakly, in the case of others. An inclusive manifold of such identifyings is shaped: an orchestration of reciprocal attunings. As the choreography of this intricate "dance" of durational strands is actualized, each strand acquires a distinctive role. And the totality of enacted roles harmonizes in varying ways. In this process, the emptiness of the "space" between compresent durational strands breaks down. Vacuity is replaced by vibrancy. The "life" of every strand is transferred to the "life" of the community; the "life" of the community resides in the interstices of its component strands.

These interstices constitute the region wherein arises an essential power of action with respect to the differential possibilities realizable for those strands. Ultimately, this region is a center of feeling as well as a center of action. With respect to feeling and action, I affirm a threefold doctrine: parity; complementarity; mutual presupposition—each center requiring the other for its effective realization. As unified, the overall power suggested by these doctrines operates within the locus of the "in-between" with respect to the multitude of self-actant and interactant strands.

Each strand is related internally to that locus. For, sufficiently probed—by its own self-searching activity, however feeble, on such primordial levels of existence—the reflexive character of a durational strand is disclosed as "residing" within the region shared by all strands. A fortiori, the totality of reflective acts which may be imputed to those strands is ultimately referrable to the same "point." That point is their shared center of feeling and action. And between the "self-centeredness" of each strand and its "communal centeredness," a tension ineluctably prevails. Such tension gives rise to a dialectical interplay between these modes of centeredness.

Accordingly, what hitherto, in the stage of duration (and ipso facto, differentiation) had been homogeneity in the temporal "design" of the field, a paucity of differentiation, is now elaborated into an incomparably richer texture. A mosaic of differential strands is constituted; each component of this mosaic is a specific instrument for transcribing, interpreting, and rendering the "music" of the entire assemblage. In consequence, each durational strand participates in two realms of existence: that of the community of durational strands; that of its own interior existence. In the first instance, the strand is but a single though integral factor contributing its own peculiarities to the "ecologic balance" which equilibrates all members of its community. In the second instance, the strand both coordinates and integrates the diverse components which constitute its self-identity, its integrity as a strictly autonomous agent.

As a member of a community, every strand is oriented toward all that lies without it. Even though it internalizes the data received from the community, those data never cease to flow into its own being. By its "decisions," a strand impresses such data into its own "concrescence."[1] Certain data are included, though in varying grades of relevance; other data are excluded, though in varying grades of irrelevance. Through interplay of acts of inclusion and acts of exclusion, a strand establishes the limits for its own sphere of functioning. It demarcates itself as an existent, an entity separate and distinct from other entities. And as it stretches toward other strands to effect, with varying sensitivity, incorporation of the data which they send forth, the strand converts the public character of its orientings into a private status. What had been public is transmuted into minuscule drops of experience; what had been a communal concern is converted into a harmony of private intentions. Thus transfigured, each strand once again enters the public domain. It exhibits itself to the community precisely in its character of being what it had been, yet, however subtly modified, of being other than what it had been.

As an individual, the strand is oriented toward its own interiority, its "within-ness." It discriminates such factors as are relevant to its private existence. Re-balancing these factors, it establishes orders of priority for them. To exist effectively, every strand must establish for itself a configuration of internal factors. These factors must be hierarchically so ordered into lattices of subordination and superordination as to enable that strand to utilize available energies for its own continued existence in the most efficacious manner. To achieve this end, a strand must, in effect, design for itself ever more intricate modes of internal organization so as to allow each unit of "energy" to count for something in its own self-preservation. Such internal reconstitution is effected by an intensification of the reflexive acts of every pulse in every strand. Each component pulse must, so to speak, double back upon itself to inspect its own inner content. It must mobilize all energies to allow discernment of novel factors, to redeploy those factors, to reconstitute its own character. I am here presuming a metaphysical principle of primordial freedom with respect to every entity: no matter how complex, no matter how simple, an entity is empowered to induce modulations within its own internal makeup.

(c) Trajectories

In effect, every particle is empowered both to *extro*spect and to *intro*spect. In the former case, its existence essentially pertains to its dwelling among other particles. Existence is even constituted by their reciprocal impingements under the perspective of that particle. Its very content is specified in terms of the functions of particles, and their mutual relationships, within an intrinsically granulated field. As the field evolves, and the mode of granulation alters, the functions associated with its constituent particles correlatively change. In effect, the inalterable structure of a particle, hence, its foundational existence—the basis from which, so to speak, it stands forth and declares itself—*is* the set of factors which remain when, one by one, the variegated functions which it acquires are stripped away. On the one hand, this structure is the "residue" of a systematic prescinding from those functions. On the other, it is the ground for the (possible) acquisition of those functions. This is not to deny that functions, once operative, do not modulate a basic structure. On the contrary, every new function induces some variation in that structure. It inscribes upon its associated rhythms some characteristic orna-mentation. I am asserting that no particle can be exhaustively *defined* in terms of any set of functions—though it may be that no particle can be specified save in the context of identifying those functions. In any event, in consequence of the realization of its associated functions, every particle exhibits some invariant traits over the set of transformations which its diverse displacements cause it to undergo. In this sense, the particle has objective existence. The more inclusive the sets of transformations, the greater the likelihood that the associated invariants will constitute *authentic* objectivity.

Classifying particles with respect to their fundamental physical properties, the physicist depicts the panorama of interparticulate relations. He exhibits the alterations of functions undergone by the members of this matrix. These alterations depend upon such factors as differential energy distributions, differential energy gradients, "knots" in modalities of energy which hinder degradation—all, in effect, expressing a profound struggle against the inexorable regressive "flow" of entropy: that tendency to fall back into randomicity, disorganization, and chaos.

One of the most pervasive ways in which the counter-entropic "battle" is fought is expressed by various forms of "least action." According to this principle, the path taken by any particle within a field, given particular field constraints working upon that particle, will be that unique path, from among all possible paths, which will minimize the "action" associated with the particle. Hence, the expenditure of energy for a given time increment will be at a minimum. In equivalent formulation, the momentum associated with a particle with respect to a given spatial increment will be at a minimum. The path taken with respect to space or time (both understood in a local, non-general relativistic sense) will be such as maximally to conserve both energy expended and momentum expended. To secure the effective working of this principle, each particle (rooted within its own reference frame) will "choose" an internal dynamism which will guarantee the integrity of the principle. Its continued existence must be consistent with its capacity perpetually to rearrange its own inner composition, and to redesign that internal pattern so as to create a sufficiently delicately balanced ecology with respect to its components. From this standpoint, "action" represents that fine attunement of the particle's internal ecology with the external ecology of the field which it inhabits which will guarantee the stability of the cosmic order, with respect to the degree of organization which the cosmos has attained in a given epoch.

Once a particle is, so to speak, preoccupied with its own interiority (its power to *intro*spect), it acquires creative discontent with mere instability. By inner compulsion, it must forge ahead, creating new schemes of adaptation, schemes which will enhance the quality of its own interior (psychic-like) existence. In this way, the particle will achieve such orientations toward its environment as will effectively reconstitute that environment. The orchestration effected with respect to the matrix of interparticulate attunings will become increasingly rich, subtle, and diversified. There ensues a wealth of psychic-like outpouring into the field. The profusion of new elements, originally subjective and now objectified, provides the ground for the continual evolving and reconstituting of that field— an evolving from sheer elementarity, through durational pulses and differentiated strands, into such aggregations of those strands into quasi-organizational units as will culminate in the fusion of complemental aggregations to form authentic organizations. When a sufficient number of such organizations are gathered together, each becomes a primordium of life itself: life which is self-metabolizing, self-replicating, and self-mutating!

The several principles of least action are physical expressions of a metaphysical principle of co-adaptation between the internal "quest" of every particle for increased novelty, breadth of "experience," and emotional intensity amidst organizational stability, on the one hand, and the external quest of that particle for variety amidst stability within its external environment, on the other. This principle suggests the interlocking of two ecologic systems—the privately intraparticulate and the publicly extraparticulate—and affirms the need for a fine balance and adjustment between creativity and stability with respect to the interplay of these systems.

In sum, the originally introduced complementarity between field and particle is but the physical analogue of a general metaphysical complementarity between two aspects of reality: the sphere of interparticulate relations, each (durable) particle extrospecting, under the perspective of objectivity or existentiality; the sphere of the intraparticulate (with respect to any random member of the previous sphere), each particle introspecting, under the perspective of subjectivity or proto-psychic "self-interpretation," its own internal ingredients—a sphere in which an intricate inner world, a configuration of diversely arranged laminae, is reflexively connected to the particle as a whole. In this bipolar representation, each sphere conditions the other, imposing constraints upon it, yet, at the same time, catalyzing and even liberating certain of its potentialities. The endogenous ecologic scheme of factors constituting the second sphere is co-adapted to the exogenous ecologic scheme of factors constituting the first sphere.

When these complemental spheres with respect to a given assemblage of factors are viewed from without their region of *modus operandi*, they become, in effect, but a single sphere, unified and integral. Bipolarity becomes unipolarity. A single interwoven ecologic nexus emerges as a well-ordered composite of what, as "seen" from any region within either sphere, has hitherto presented itself as a dualistic manifold. Whether, indeed, one may conceptualize an "ultimate outside" to the entire series of conceivable bipolar enclosures, from which a maximally inclusive perspective emerges—like a Spinozist substance, a monistic portrait of the cosmos—is a cosmological question the consideration of which I must defer until *Cosmos*.

In any event, from the point of view of a bipolar representation, each durational strand—in effect, each particle—is a "searcher" which pursues a certain trajectory of searching, the trajectory determined by the metaphysical analogue of the least action principle. In consequence, the bipolar manifold is contoured by a multitude of *searching trajectories*, trajectories which are given physical expression as paths of motion with respect to one another, under the constraints of a relative spatio-temporal warping. These paths are associated with properties which may be characterized in two ways: space–time derivatives at every point along the path; and integrals of those derivatives over the entire course of the paths. For my purpose, the searching particle is, quite literally, an explorer, an explorer among the recesses of the physical world, recesses often arcane and intricate but at times luminous and demarcated with clarity: an explorer, to speak dramatically, in the sense of ex-*plorare—a crying out* with all the music resident within that particle. It is like a playing upon the innumerable instruments which its every constituent factor creates; it is, as it were, an ex-pression, literally, a pressing out from within, of the orchestrated manifold components of the endo-ecologic system constituting that particle. As it explores, each particle encounters other exploring particles; the entire configuration of particles transcribes a score—the instructions for the rendering of the authentic symphony of matter.

B · THE EVENT ORGANIZED

(*a*) Aggregations

When a field, initially elementary, has attained a sufficiently intricate level of differentiation with respect to its durational strands, a new phenomenon will appear: coalescence. To bring this process about, certain strands must first aggregate themselves into cohesive organizations. Then the entire field must evolve into a matrix of hierarchically ordered aggregates.

In the first stage, relative instability reigns. Through interchange of significant components, aggregates are ceaselessly rearranged. The bonds joining the parts which constitute these aggregates exhibit varying gradations of weakness. A sudden influx of energy may disrupt an aggregate, and new configurations of equivalent instability form. All is in flux: confluence, efflux, at times disarray. Yet, throughout the field, there persists a quest for more stable organizations, organizations the components of which distinguish themselves as relatively enduring constellations of functions.

In the second stage, these ordered constellations comprise an integral manifold of relative stability. Associated with such durable organizations is a lower probability of dissolution by the highly charged energy quanta which never cease to impinge. The field's very labyrinthine character encourages stability. Elaborately coiled structures, paths of transmission which are intricately convoluted and involuted, convey those energies which will maintain rather than disrupt the delicate morphologic and dynamic balances. Correlative with this renewed stability arise new self-identities, self-identities analogous to those associated with the durable particles of an earlier phase. Not only are such self-identities newly shaped; they even tend to prevail. Accordingly, the field has been progressively rearticulated in patterns of stronger bonds than hitherto were operative. Relatively enduring proto-ecologic systems now dominate that field.

The compresence of strands and, indeed, of aggregates of strands sets in motion a double orchestration: that implicating the rhythms of each strand, taken individually; that implicating the rhythms of all strands, taken collectively. Both strands and their aggregates participate within this "music." For the music of compresence becomes an objective medium which grounds their subsequent unfoldings; and the specific responses of every strand and every aggregate shape their very self-identities. By self-identity I now refer to the resonances which continually traverse and sweep about every entity, enveloping that entity, suffusing it, and transfiguring it. From this point of view, it is truer to say that an entity dwells with its own identity than to say that an entity possesses or exhibits that identity. It is also as true to say that every entity dwells among the self-identities of all other entities as to say that that entity dwells with its own identity.

I am affirming the doctrine that every entity "inhabits" the interstices, those music-filled spaces, between all compresent entities. Furthermore, each entity discovers its own identity by attuning its structures to the appropriate rhythmic modulations which constantly bathe it and swirl about it. In effect, it becomes self-identically itself by its recognizance of the information most relevant to its own private existence. This information consists of diverse data diversely valued. A specific reverberation which emanates from its donating source, each datum *in*-forms the recipient entity with the "form" of the special music which it has extracted from the total music which flows about it, music to which it itself has contributed and which properly belongs to it. The self-identities of different particles are not conferred upon them through their immediate association alone; they are functions of their identifyings with a multitude of other particles. Moreover, every self-identity is autonomously "selected" from among the resonances set up within the community of particles. To be self-identically oneself is to be in symbiotic relatedness to others, a relatedness which involves dialectical interplay between other-identifying and self-identifying. One turns toward another, attuning oneself to *its* rhythms; one turns toward oneself, attuning that self to its *own* rhythms. Identity is the continual resultant of this process.

Fully to feel one's own identity—on all levels of "feeling," including those appropriate to the particle—is fully to experience oneself as a medium through which are transmitted, filtered, and altered all rhythms which dwell in the interstices of compresent events. Propagated as resonances of varying complexity along strands of durable particles and through aggregates of such strands, these now internalized rhythms are catalyzed into activity by interplay between the introspective and the extrospective functions of a strand-complex. In addition, the multitude of strands which constitute an *aggregate* of co-adapted entities "projects" a characteristic music into the region of compresence—music which orchestrates the separate themes contributed by each component. By this projection, it presents itself as symbol to other compresent entities, all occupying the locus of an unfolding polyphony of rhythm. Depending upon the constraints imposed upon a region by the particular sets of strands which inhabit it, each strand "introjects" rhythmic elements appropriate to its unique configuration. By such introjection, the composition of any aggregate alters; correlatively, the interstitial space of its compresent pulses alters. Its very self-identity is transformed.

Inhering in every aggregate is a quest for that mode of stability consistent with the fragile composition required to counterpose the aggregate to entropy's inexorable workings. This quest is tantamount to a search for more durable self-identity, identity which will enable that aggregate to survive as an autonomous agency. But survival means growth. To avoid sinking into a less fragile though, in the end, more sturdy organization—hence, organization less efficient with respect to its power for utilizing the decreasingly available energies for its functioning—every aggregate is impelled toward increasingly reticulated, coherent, integral, and delicately balanced organization.

Now an immensely complicated fabric of pulses linked to pulses is shaped: aggregate laminated upon aggregate, dynamically interpenetrating organizations. Strongly bonded and weakly bonded factors pervade this fabric. Waves of diverse frequency, amplitude, form, and length overlap, reinforce, and cancel one another, waves which pervade the region in endlessly fluctuant configuration. And every fabric is embedded in a milieu. Energies specified by each milieu form conditions for the very possibility of the sorts of processes and systems capable of surviving within that milieu.[2] Setting limits to the boundaries and functions of those processes and systems, these energies, in effect, govern the many transformations which they undergo. Many centers of activity coalesce: all linked, interwoven, and interpenetrating. Each center is associated with its own characteristic mode of reflexivity; multiply reflexive centers crystallize into new and more inclusive centers. Schemes of dominance and subordination emerge, of mastery and specialization of function. Novel modes of reticulation in myriad shape and form evolve. Every factor in this complex is a medium or agency for transmitting the rhythms which flow with their variegated styles of movement, their oscillations upon which are inscribed unimaginably intricate arabesques. And everywhere there is flow through increasingly labyrinthine interstices. Every factor impinges on every other factor. Every factor presents to the total plexus the impacts which have shaped it, and conferred upon it its typical rhythms. In this reciprocity of self-presentings, each factor symbolizes to all factors its unique identity; and thereby a *composite* symbol is fashioned.

(b) Orchestrations

Rhythm, symbol, medium! These are the primordial characteristics of every pulse, every strand, every organization—no matter how simple, no matter how complex. Though primordial, each fibrous network in the physical fabric replicates itself. With minor variations, it duplicates, on ontogeny's every level, intricacies of its composition and import. In this book I stress rhythm as a seminal integrative theme for grounding an ontology of the person; in subsequent books, and especially in *Apotheosis*, symbol and medium will assume more central roles.

By "rhythm," I mean ρυθμός, a measured movement, and ρεῖν, to flow; hence, I refer to the concatenated flowings forth, with thematic repetitions and orna-

mentations, of a motif or of a constellation of motifs. By "symbol," I mean
συμβάλλειν: the joining together of exteriority and interiority to unitary and integral existence, the joining of an existent to other like existents, the integration
of each existent as mirroring and contributing to the integration of all existents.
For "medium," I can substitute agent. By that I mean the one who, self-engendering and autonomous, is, nonetheless, an instrument for conveying the very texture
of the existential fabric in which he is embedded. Qua medium, an agent is, as it
were, the one who has been "chosen" *by* the cosmos for *meditating* its inner message, for in-forming himself with its rhythms and with its symbols; he is the one
who, quite literally, is *in mediis rebus*. All existents, each in its own perspective,
are located somewhere between the vast and the minute. But full agents are centered. And, unique among entities in rhythmic subtlety and intricacy of symbolic
makeup, the person, also thus centered, is the appropriate interpreter, the authentic
spokesman, for the vast and the minute. Only he may truly mediate each to the
other or, for that matter, all that lies between. Yet at no stage in shaping the
architectonics of human ontology or in the unfolding levels of ontogenesis may
any of these themes—namely, rhythm, symbol, and medium—be ignored. In the
final analysis, they are defined in terms of one another. Each presupposes and requires the other. They are but aspects of a single metaphysical entity.

Turning again to the issue of self-identity, I note that every pulse, every strand,
and every organization is rooted, more or less stably, in a milieu wherein may
be discerned other pulses, other strands, and other organizations: all are like fibers
woven of threads which either contrast with or complement one another. This
milieu is the very locus of individual existence. It provides the "personal" standpoint, a unique and private perspective from within which an existent "views"
what presents itself to it as cosmos; and it orchestrates its idiosyncratic *discrimi-
nanda* of a universe construed as itself cosmogenetic, and possessing phases which
must be differently specified for every type of event, whether simple or composite.
Moreover, under a relevant limiting perspective, the cosmos, by its own collective potency, presents itself as exterior, objective, and material. At the same time,
the event, by its *individual* potency, presents itself to *its* own self in its character
as reflexive. By virtue of this reflexive dynamism, the event absorbs all that it
apprehends as exterior to it. Gathering relevant factors of the cosmos-for-it into
its own interiority, each existent "reflects" upon the cosmos. Weaving the depositions of these reflections into its own inner constitution, it creates for itself a
truly syncretist existence. Often it radically transcends what it hitherto had been.

Communicating with one another their respective views of the cosmos, persons
emerge from their questings with a multitude of cosmologies. In all seeking, no
matter how humble, these limited cosmologies tend to converge upon a single,
universally binding cosmology. What is cosmos for the human community is
only the summation, synergistically effected, of an unimaginably vast unity of
separate cosmologies: those framed by the community's collective quest; those

unconsciously framed by each individual as he introspects upon the infinite array
of minuscule cosmologic perspectives which, each associated with a particular
body-component, "dwell" potently within him.

In *Choros*, I treat the activities by which a person, in order to illuminate the
multiform microcosmos associated with the events and the organisms which compose his body, delves into his own unconscious processes. Under the methodologic
perspective of transcendental naturalism, these private, internally sought (mini-)
cosmologies converge, so I argue in *Choros*, upon archetypal themes which ultimately are identical for every person who conducts an analogous search. To probe
this aspect of one's unconscious is, at bottom, to delve ever more deeply *through*
one's very organicity into *its* inorganic ground. In the end, the searcher who so
quests encounters, as dwelling at his own infrapersonal being's very foundation,
something which may only be regarded as radical non-being. Yet this regressive
quest is, at the very same time, immanently conditioned by and increasingly articulated as the search for the ground of personal being in the realm of the suprapersonal, ultimately of pure being. How these two inquiries—that into *nature*, that
into *spirit*—direct, synergize, complement, and converge upon one another will
be the topic of the final book, *The Person*, in my metaphysical inquiry into the
person.

To return to the rhythms of the inanimate event: I may now affirm that integration of diverse public perspectives, woven as data into each existent's very constitution, provides deeper ground for that existent's interpretation of the cosmos.
However minimal the flicker of awareness in an existent's inmost recesses, the
unity of space, time, and matter dwells within that existent, together with such
universally invariant factors as define that unity. The behavior of every event is
conditioned by two kinds of factor: that pertaining to the *local* milieu within
which the event dwells, and that pertaining to the larger cosmos. The former are
more readily articulated; the latter may be specified only in the context of cumulative, wide-ranging, patient, and collective searching—searching which points
toward the ground of all being as a single, indivisible, and transcendent substance.
It is beyond the scope of my inquiry to elucidate competing schemes of physical
cosmology. Suffice it for me to propose that whatever scheme will emerge from
their interplay as the "true" scheme is surely operative within and for every existent, and, in consequence, is profoundly relevant to a more refined and human
ontology than any which I can here delineate.

A cosmic image which involves principles (like Heisenberg's) which set a
limit to the (naturalistically) knowable texture of physical reality or (like Ein-
stein's) which propose an interwoven space, time, and matter must deeply affect
every man's reflections upon his status in the world. Thus reflecting, one becomes aware of oneself as dwelling with mystery, intimately bonded to the universe's very beginnings and endings, to the utterly minute and the incomparably
huge. Such speculations as the physicist engages in when he interprets quasars as
the original universe flying away from a point already receded into the remote

past and with velocities approaching that of light; or when he envisages "black holes" as implying phenomena so strange as to be consistent with a multiverse theory of an organically cellular "uni"-verse, woven of hierarchically arranged tissues—each vast, remote, incomprehensible; or when he conjures up images of cosmic epochs governed by principles quite inconceivable even to his informed intuition—all this allows the imagination a freedom which is momentous. It roots man's poetic instinct, beyond mere local experience, in a grander cosmic order; it enjoins him to shape for himself a double image of small and large which, however remote, intimately meet; it inspires the dim perception of haunting mysteries which spread infinitely beyond the familiar yet profoundly condition it, even indeed in its merely local import. And man conceives himself as peering into the earth's most intimate recesses and into the sky's vastest recesses; and he marvels at earth and sky just as, in primeval astonishment, he first stood upright and stretched himself securely into the former and proudly toward the latter—all unbelievably vast, but nurturing, and, paradoxically, his own personal home, his *only* home: now incomparably more subtly nuanced than ever before.

In the final stage of physiogenesis, structures are formed the bizarre images of which (I later show) invade deeper layers of the Unconscious. Synthesized from simpler components, these structures (like amino acids) are among the precursors of living matter. By quasi-duplication—prototype of replication itself—like units (the indicated structures, for example) are joined, each an event woven of tightly-knit strands, to create unstable, weakly-bonded polymers of varying length, motility, and contour. Infolding upon themselves these now elongated strands shape themselves into intricately latticed crystals, into myriad strangely granulated fibers, into symmetric patterns of marvelous design. Exhibiting minor variations, or occasionally a frank mutation, such aggregates assemble themselves into stable vortices in finely articulated fields. In turn, they twist themselves into dancing polymers; they orchestrate diverse rhythms; they form endless infoldings, convolutions, involutions, ex-volutions. Immensely complicated macro(molecular) events are configured; regions of rarefaction and condensation associated with resonances of dissonance and consonance shape themselves into ever new accretive units; life itself is prefigured.

(c) The Advance Toward Life

Now the theme of complementarity becomes relevant. The field separates itself into two regions: asymmetric complexes, like crystalline substances of indissociable lattice structure; and asymmetric complexes, each "seeking" to complete itself by "recognizing," then combining with, its complement. Within every such event, a special nexus of elements becomes selectively sensitized to information transmitted from other events. Subsequent to recognition, a "locking-in" occurs, transient or durable, with respect to some corresponding factor in a complementary event. Each event in-forms the other with significant rhythms of its presence. It thereby effects transformations which compound the fineness and the intricacy of reticulation in the multiform threads of an event. In effect, a mating occurs, however transitory it be. What had been an asymmetrically articulated field-region is now changed into a congregation of symmetric organizations the destiny of which has one of two culminations. On the one hand, each organization may be resolved into the original asymmetric complements; thereupon either it receives minor ornamentation, or it becomes further degraded. On the other, each organization might so transfigure the other, through relevant energy intensity, flow, and distribution, that novel constellations are engendered.

In every instance, the integrity of the system, whether maintained, transformed, or altered, is determined by the *modus operandi* of resonance which prevails (as in Kekulé's benzene ring). Whether rotatory, spinning, vibratory, translational, or indeed any variant upon these motions, resonances sweep endlessly about diverse morphologic configurations; motilities reveal themselves to be of enormous subtlety of modulation and intricacy of design. To guarantee the continual evolving of structures toward states of increasing fragility, with sacrifice neither of strength nor of organizational complexity, a balance must be maintained, consistent with the relevant increments of displacement from equilibrium, between energy conservation and those energy dissipations which are prescribed by entropy requirements. By a kind of natural selection involving suitable adaptations, specific variants arise from within the innumerably possible topologic patterns; diverse agglutinations of morphologic structure emerge.

The advance toward life requires a single step: *closure*. For this phenomenon to occur, a fluctuant *proto*-morphologic closure must initially appear. Next, the strictly functional paths of influence which constitute the proto-boundaries of physical organization must be converted to frankly morphologic strands. Wrapped about this non-organismic event, yet woven with its intricately arranged fibers, is a region which becomes increasingly demarcated as a distinct structure. Information about the milieu within which the event is embedded is transmitted by the appropriate energies. Sweeping about the now closed strand, these energies spread throughout all event-parts in contact with that strand. Such unimpeded energy flow severely restricts the kinds of configuration which otherwise might evolve *within* the enclosure. In the end, there evolves a disengaging of all (inner) fibers from the enclosing (outer) fiber.

By this process, two separate organizations are created. Both become integral components within the same proto-cell. On the one hand, a true boundary has formed. On the other, a structure has arisen which floats with minimal constraints within the medium enclosed by this boundary. Now the primordia of living matter have emerged. Accordingly, cell boundary and intracellular structures are partly independent, yet partly symbiotic. Often each part freely evolves in its own fashion, the growth of one part conditions the growth of the other. Working together, these complementary units acquire the power to incorporate new organizations, assemblages of particles associated with special roles—e.g., membrane cilia or organelles such as the chloroplasts and mitochondria floating in intracellular fluid. Some of these incorporates are themselves proto-cellular; others are the pre-living forms which regulate the very processes of life.

In Part III, I set forth the full drama of this "complexification"[3] of the membranous, nuclear, and organelle constituents of life. Yet this culminating stage of physiogenesis blends indistinguishably with the initial stage of biogenesis. Beginning with elementary particles, themselves both of intricate composition and interacting in myriad ways, the various levels of physiogenetic organization mediate transformation of these particles into composite structures, of which the primary trait is a power for growth with numberless degrees of freedom. At this final level, a motile (nuclear or organelle) component "dances" in myriad ways within, and protected by, a membrane in which instructions for its own choreographic possibilities are inscribed. Delicate schemes of growth and mutation are elaborated. Complicated networks of reticula stretch inward and outward from the membrane to set up new modes of balance in both endo-ecologic and exo-ecologic relationships. Reflexivity becomes immeasurably more intricate. Just as in the beginning every particle was a locus of influence which pervaded the entire field, so now the emergent cell functions as an analogous locus. From the most elementary existent to the most intricate physical organization, an entity spreads its sphere of influence. With increasing definition and ornamentation of reflexive "imagery," it reaches out toward the entire cosmos.

C · PHYSIOGENESIS: ITS METAPHYSICAL GROUND

Two sets of metaphysical principles have dominated my account: principles which link a transcendental with a naturalistic perspective on ontology—i.e., with respect to the event's relevance for the person; and principles which announce a deep complementarity between the ontogenetic phases, physiogenesis, biogenesis, and personogenesis. As my argument evolves, these principles will recur with increasingly significant import for human ontology. At the moment, I treat only the first set, a set which itself implies three injunctions: namely, superimpose a transcendental continuum upon a naturalistically discrete image of physical reality; superimpose both transcendental communality and transcendental unity, i.e., "substantiality," upon a naturalistically conceived private–public bipolar image of physical reality; and superimpose transcendental complexity upon a naturalistically conceived elementary image of physical reality. These injunctions I now treat seriatim, but briefly.

(a) The Transcendental Continuum

With respect to the relationship between the continuum and the atomistic aspect of events, philosophic naturalism has usually assumed that all natural complexes are analyzable in terms of pervasively granulated phenomena—phenomena which are discrete, disjoined, and (despite acknowledged interdependencies) radically separate and autonomous. Thus, in physics, the "building blocks" of the universe are held to be elementary particles, atoms, molecules, macro-molecular complexes; energy is construed as transmitted in packets or quanta; fundamental waves are regarded as associated with definite and fixed amplitudes, frequencies, forms, wave lengths. Unquestionably, from the point of view of constructing a precise, systematic, and detailed schema for analyzing physical phenomena, this "image" is of immense heuristic value. On the other hand, to create a systematic metaphysics which persuasively grounds personal self-identity, the profound continuities between one's various parts, dimensions, and roles must be acknowledged. As authentic continuities, these factors cannot be derived from a sequence of discrete units, no matter what order of infinity be deemed interposable between any two units. Moreover, such continuity itself appears to be rooted in analogous and deeper continuities, continuities involving more primordial structures and functional complexes. Were this not the case, one would require much too radical a separation between man and nature, a dualistic cosmos in which nature reveals itself to be "incurably atomistic," and man exhibits miraculously emergent continuities.

Within the perspective of this work, general ontology and human ontology cannot be isolated from one another. Granted: a naturalism which is both circumspect and analytical must either postulate an exclusively atomistic basis for all phenomena, personal and natural, or presume a mysterious, primordial complementarity between the two. However, a third metaphysical approach is plausible. According to this position (which I here support), every pulse, every strand, every organization—no matter how small or large, no matter how simple or complex—though existentially composed of many elements, is, in essence, but one substance, indivisible and integral. Moreover, I hold, every combination of such factors—indeed, the totality of all cosmic processes—is likewise one substance. I assume that every part and every "mode" of this unified but composite substance replicates, in miniature and as a kind of microcosmos, the radical coherence which pervades the entirety. Here I am maintaining the doctrine of the consistency, and, indeed, the complementarity, of a naturalistic pluralism with a transcendental monism. Elsewhere, the metaphysical justification for this supposition will be argued.

In consequence of this view, two complementary perspectives on every phenomenon are valid. By the one, a naturalistically discriminable set of factors is deemed by convention to be linked both spatially and temporally, this supposition constituting a convenient taxonomic or even an explanatory device; by the second, an assemblage of factors is deemed to be internally linked as substantively cohering. In the latter case, the category which expresses the continuity which sweeps over a naturalistically divisible chain of pulses, conferring essential unity upon those pulses, is *transcendental rhythmicality*. According to this category, an entity's power to act derives from its intrinsic unity. In turn, unity is constituted by a dynamically flowing resonance *within* and *about* every pulse, strand, or organization. This flow pervades the very matrix in which they are embedded. By successive *identifyings* with themes selected from but a single orchestration, the unique self-identity of every factor is shaped.

In general, any entity's power to encounter any other entity, that the two entities be joined in compresence which affects both, derives from that entity's functioning as an integral, indivisible, and unified agent. This agent's every part and aspect—however diversified and under whatever perspective, each part or aspect an autonomous subordinate agent—are indivisibly integrated. To specify this synthesis, one must evoke an image of subtly modulated rhythms which "contain" every entity while pervading its substance—rhythms the *modus operandi* of which enable an entity to be a unified power of acting. In each such instance of acting, a single, integral fabric imprints its total character, even its most ineffable reverberations, upon every being which it encounters. An authentic "substance," not a mere relational pattern of invariants, is truly preserved amidst its metamorphoses and the ever-shifting movements, resolutions, renewals, or replacements of its parts. A "form" is preserved which is neither inert nor formal, but dynamic, flowing, and ethereal.

The community of agents is in-formed by the dynamic forms which invade its interstices and constitute its self-sustaining locus. Ultimately, this locus is referable to a single, perpetually enduring, and absolutely integral substance. In sum, I subscribe to the doctrine that a transcendental continuum of rhythms is, so to speak, superimposed upon a discretely granulated tissue of events, both suffusing that tissue and transfiguring it. The naturalistic inclination to discriminate separate units within this continuum is requisite for the framing of cogent principles of explanation of the "behavior" of diverse entities under diverse perspectives. But the ground, the presupposition, for all such modes of patterning of the reality of material events is, precisely, the matrix of transcendental rhythms.

(b) Transcendental Communality and Unity

Often, radically dualistic doctrines provoke philosophic discontent. Notable among these is the supposition of a sharp dichotomy between an event's privacy and interiority, on the one hand—in ultimate form, Whitehead's "satisfaction of a concrescence,"[4] satisfaction so inward and, indeed, so esoteric as already to be beyond feeling—and an event's publicality and exteriority, on the other. To resolve this dichotomy, I suggest the correlative ideas of *transcendental communality* and *transcendental unity*.

To replace the doctrine of alleged ultimacy of a bipolar mental and physical "occasion," and the equally unsatisfactory views of a physical event which inexplicably derives from a mental event, or the converse, four tenets are needed: (i) every event is reflexive; (ii) by its reflexive activity, it symbolizes itself, transparently and opaquely, as a viable and dynamic presence, to other reciprocal, presenting events; (iii) reflexivity, in the end, refers to the laminae and interstices of a community of events, the very medium within which the community articulates itself; and (iv) the medium itself is rooted in the seemingly opposite states of non-being and pure being. Far from suggesting radically conflicting modes of being—namely, absolute privation and absolute plenitude—I hold these tenets to be complementary and mutually presupposing. They themselves are rooted in a supremely reflexive center.

By this doctrine the metaphysical justification of which I treat in *Cosmos*, it is more appropriate to speak of the contrasting opposite, yet profoundly related, notions, God and person, rather than the notions, God and World.[5] For World is the infrapersonal substratum, be it material or organismic, which conditions human being from the side of (relative) non-being. And one must surely acknowledge a realm of the suprapersonal, a spiritual and ethereal substratum, which conditions human being from the side of (relative) pure being.

In brief, the rhythmically integral, subtly modulated entities which, on every level of physiogenesis, make up the physical cosmos exhibit a pervasively reflexive character. From the standpoint of every particle, its compresent milieu is deemed (at first "glance") to be sheer exteriority, objectivity, mere chunks of "matter"—matter not inert but surely unfeeling. Not only does the particle dwell among externally compresent entities; it also dwells interiorly among its own inner constituents. The physical image of the universe prescinds from this inward intensity of "self-experience." Nevertheless, speculation upon the deeper import of mutations undergone by particles, mutations seemingly induced through impingements upon them by neighboring particles (i.e., their milieu) *suggests* an interior experience as a relevant factor in effecting the internal rearrangements of the mutant elements. This experience, as it were, *announces* to the event how the outer world, which so interlocks with its own inner world, "looks" from *its* standpoint.

True, to postulate such interiority, a leap of philosophic imagination is needed. Yet, is it really ultimately satisfying to attribute the sudden emergence of experience, when a certain level of organic complexity has been reached, to a miraculous implanting of an entelechy, an *élan vital*, at that level alone? In my account, I assume the contrary hypothesis. Germinating within physiogenesis itself, so I argue, are those primordia of feeling, however negligible, the mutual contributions of which, synergistically united, bring about, after long and circuitous evolution, those intensities and contrasts of feeling which are characteristic of higher organisms. Otherwise, I repeat, one must magically derive spirit from a matter assumed *ex hypothesi* to be utterly devoid of spirit. Whatever additional sources of spirit may later be postulated, I must minimally stipulate that spirit germinates within matter. Further, I must affirm that when matter has attained sufficient intricacy of organization, spirit in association with matter achieves a sufficient grade of consummation.

Surely, natural scientists prescind from the full activity of material agents. They schematize assemblages of particles and fields which are associated only with the residue of that activity. Data received and data transmitted by such entities are reconstituted as hypothetical constructs. Through convergence of diverse conceptualizations of nature upon more inclusive theories, an ontologic status is imputed to nature which is based on the consistent and stable order which these constructs form. My depiction of physiogenesis is an endeavor to sketch such an ontology.

Pre-eminently, personogenesis requires an account of how personal feeling arises from the unconscious "discernment" of numerous fragmented feelings derived from antecedent phases of ontogenesis. In particular, it requires examination of how these components are woven into a unified but vastly complicated fabric. Diverse parts of a person's body represent to one another their diverse confluences; the integral of these representations is itself represented to the body as a whole. Within every person's body, both living organisms and inanimate events contribute their respective centers of feeling. Analogous considerations hold when bodies encounter other bodies. Absolute privacy is a fiction. All interior reflection, deriving as it must from the composition of diverse internal and external centers of feeling, dwells within every member of the human community. Moreover, the self-feelings of every component, no matter how minuscule, of every member of that community dwells within that member—always, of course, under perspectives appropriate to the relevant order of individual complexity.

Every entity throbs with emotionality. Quite literally, it "moves out" from its own center toward other like entities; and this *moving out* occurs in diverse modalities, grades, and intensities. To say that energy grounds the possibility for the emergence of actual particles from virtual status is equivalent to relegating energy to the inner life. Such energy is the correlate of the emotional intensity of each entity. Furthermore, every emotion is vectorially directed. Energy is the total scheme of such emotions when it is integrated over the community of particles. Thus, each particle is self-directed toward other particles with scalar, localizing energy. Catalyzed by the presence of other energy-"filled" particles, the *overall* pattern of flowings of energy acquires directional—hence, vectorial—status. Individual feelings correspond to the diversity of specific forms with which energy clothes itself and, as such, are transmitted from one entity to another. The entire field is a contrapuntal interplay of entities which ever surge and flow, each performing its characteristic "dance." Together, these entities give rise to complicated rhythmic unfoldings.

Each level of physiogenesis is an assemblage of factors which in their varying modes of conjugation and transformation shape the fabric of the human body. On every body, the collective character of these factors, and their interweavings, is imprinted. Accordingly, the body undergoes continual transmutations with respect to the mosaic of structural-functional complexes composing it. A unifying psychic principle dwells immanently within each part of every body and at every stage of physiogenesis. This principle guides the movements and the changes of each part. It extends itself into each part; it alters the mutual arrangements of all parts. In consequence, part and whole are reciprocally conditioning. Finally, all (inward-turned) reflections are ultimately directed toward, and converge upon, a single center. Referable to that center, they are progressively transferred to the loci of ever more inclusive communities, and, ultimately, to God.

(c) Transcendental Complexity

With respect to the contrasting doctrines of primordial elementarity—namely, radical irreducibility of certain physical entities—and radical complexity—namely, that, no matter how apparently simple, all events exhibit endlessly subtle modulations—it has been the persistent claim of philosophic naturalism that everything is composed, in the end, of discrete absolutely simple units. When, in physics, one seeks as "ultimate" particles such hypothecated entities as quarks and partons, or when complex waves are deemed to be resolvable into elementary forms, and, indeed, at the very moment when the physicist is driven to exclaim "I have found the simplest conceivable physical entities," the most bizarre phenomena inexplicably make their appearance: matter and anti-matter "implode" to non-existence; time seemingly reverses itself; regions are disclosed within which strange spins occur; energy appears to be newly made or utterly destroyed. The methodologic principle of irreducibility seems again and again to be challenged. From a metaphysical point of view, what can this mean?

Throughout, I have presumed that every person participates at once in two realms: pure being and non-being; that these realms are, on the deepest levels of their relevance for him, complementary; and that, exhibiting parity with one another, they are also intimately adjacent and even interwoven. The more one pursues a person's infrapersonal dimensions and his naturalistic dimensions, the more one is led toward the absolute vacuity of being. On the other hand, the more one searches a person's strictly spiritual aspect—in effect, the suprapersonal—the more one is led toward being which is pure, perfect, and surely more transparent to cosmic flow than is the person's own being. There is no *a priori* reason for assigning priority to one domain of being, its deficiency and its emptiness, over the other, its richness and its plenitude. On the contrary, both modes of being are essential constituents in the very ground of human being. As such, a kind of community prevails between the two, a community mediated by God. In this community, each mode of being is associated with subtly delineated rhythms. Each emanates toward the person; each affords him his sustenance.

On the one hand, the rhythms of matter are derived from non-material rhythms —in the end, from silence. Analogously, the rhythms of spirit are derived from the rhythms of a nameless transcendence of spirit: silence. In both instances, via God's mediation, spirit traverses the entire cycle of being. From both sides, originating in the ineffable, mysterious, and ethereal pulses of silence, spirit suffuses man. The more one explores the inmost recesses of the seemingly most elementary occasions of experience, the more one arrives at the subtle interpenetration of particles by one another. In the end, each such particle is reflexively constituted by myriad images of the other; "down" to the most elementary events; "up" to the most composite entities, persons, and/or even beyond persons. But the directions of traversal are invertible. They depend entirely upon the point in the cycles at which one initiates one's journey. Accordingly, I postulate a principle of transcendental agency. By this principle, the doctrine of absolute elementarity must be deemed a myth. In varying modulations, so I propose, complexity alone reigns, and it reigns throughout the cosmos.

In effect, a cycle of mediation must be supposed. In diagrams, I indicate several ways by which the cycle may be represented. In each instance, I suggest that every discriminable entity reveals within its own composition the very composition of all factors intermediate with respect to that factor. Thus, a person's being is transparent to the being of other beings. The medium through which those beings reveal themselves, the person is the one who, pre-eminently, mediates their composition and their dynamisms.

Multiple Modes of Mediation

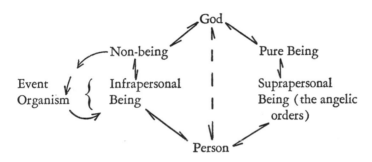

God mediates pure being in relation to non-being
Person mediates infrapersonal in relation to suprapersonal
Infrapersonal mediates non-being in relation to person
Suprapersonal mediates person in relation to pure being
Organism mediates event in relation to person
Event mediates non-being in relation to organism
Person mediates organism in relation to suprapersonal

Note:

Non-being prefigures matter
Matter prefigures life
Life prefigures thought
Thought prefigures pure being
Pure being prefigures God
God prefigures non-being

The relationship between physiogenesis and the remaining phases of onto-genesis may thus be represented:

First Model

ABSTRACT CATEGORIES	PHYSIOGENESIS	BIOGENESIS	PERSONOGENESIS
Assemblage	Elementarity	Boundaries	Trust
Conjugation	Differentiation	Replication	Orientation
Transformation	Organization	Co-Adaptation	Searching

Second Model

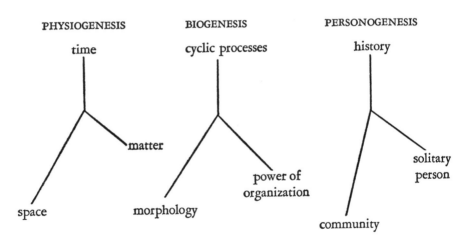

In the following diagrams, I represent the interconnections between physio-genesis and its correlative stages, first for living organisms in general and, secondly, for human beings.

Schema A

PHASES *in concreto*

Physiogenesis p   (now being treated, throughout Part II)

Elementarity	$E_{(p)}$
Durability	$D_{(p)}$
Differentiation	$Di_{(p)}$
Aggregative Organization	$Ao_{(p)}$
Complementary Organization	$Co_{(p)}$

Biogenesis b   (to be treated in Parts III and IV)

Metabolism	$M_{(b)}$
Replication	$R_{(b)}$
Variation	$V_{(b)}$
Co-Adaptation	$C_{(b)}$
Reflection	$Re_{(b)}$

Personogenesis ps   (to be treated in *Choros* and in *Metamorphosis*)

Trust	$T_{(ps)}$
Competency	$Com_{(ps)}$
Loyalty	$L_{(ps)}$
Commitment	$Ctm_{(ps)}$
Transfiguration (Searching)	$Tr_{(ps)}$

Schema B

PHASES *in abstracto*   (repeat this schema for each phase *in concreto*)

Assemblage	ASS
Conjugation	CON
Transformation	TRA

Applications of·Schema B to Schema A

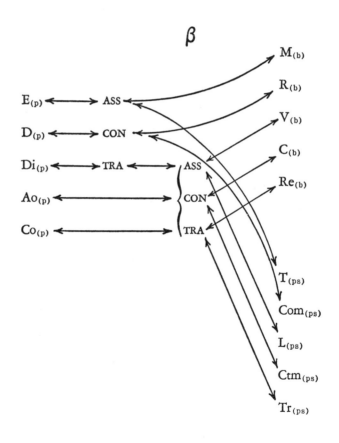

γ

	ONTOGENESIS	PHYSIOGENESIS	BIOGENESIS	PERSONOGENESIS
Initial Phase	ASS	$E_{(p)}$	$M_{(b)}$	$T_{(ps)}$
Intermediate Phases	CON	$D_{(p)}$ Mediates	$R_{(b)}$ Mediates	$Com_{(ps)}$ Mediates
	ASS	$Di_{(p)}$	$V_{(b)}$	$L_{(ps)}$
	CON	$Ao_{(p)}$ Mediates	$C_{(b)}$ Mediates	$Ctm_{(ps)}$ Mediates
Final Phase	TRA	$Co_{(p)}$	$Re_{(b)}$	$Tr_{(ps)}$
	Abstract, recurrent Categories		Concrete categories	

NOTES

1. See index of Whitehead, *Process and Reality*, for items on "concrescence."
2. Heelan, *Quantum Mechanics and Objectivity*, p. 161.
3. See the index references to "complexity" in Teilhard de Chardin, *Phenomenon of Man*.
4. See the index items on "satisfaction" in *Process and Reality*.
5. Ibid., Part V, chap. 2.

III

The Organism:
Rhythms of Life

5

MAN'S LIVING ASPECT

PREAMBLE

Throughout Part III, I treat man's organismic nature, stressing not so much the differences between him and other living creatures as the affinities. Surely, mutations coalesce within man to establish him as profoundly unique among creatures, sufficiently unique to suggest a third kingdom in nature: a kingdom more significant than that of either plant or animal. In Part IV, I indicate the identifying marks of this kingdom, and I anticipate the topics of later books: namely, how proto-human rhythms are so synthesized with spiritual rhythms as ever more dramatically to set man apart from other creatures. But for the moment I restrict myself to the particular features which distinguish man's living aspect.

By his affinity with other organisms, man roots himself in intricate ecologic cycles and balances, a vast organismic fabric in which he secures himself and gains his sustenance. True, under a biologic perspective, man exhibits organismic rhythms akin to those of all living creatures. In particular, he both extends and deepens a power for spontaneous action already resident in those creatures. Yet, alone among organisms, man perceives the inanimate, and the void which it encloses, to be concealed in the very center of his being; he seeks to fill that void with symbolisms of the unique compresence of himself and his world. In this spiritual quest, and by his discernment of the ceaseless proliferation of those symbols, he acquires, experiences, and intensifies his own freedom.

As he searches, man evolves the capacity for self-determination. Thereby, he reveals himself to be in perpetual quest of self-transcendence with respect to nature. Yet this quest only dramatizes and amplifies a tendency already deeply rooted in all life. By its replication and by its mutation, metabolizing matter tends to fill the hidden recesses of the inorganic, spreading by a kind of collective organic will to close all ecologic gaps. This grand procession of nature unfolds from a single, unique replicatory element. Spreading its variegated forms, nature reiterates a single theme: replication as the means for organismic self-preservation. Once these variations have arisen, they orchestrate themselves into endlessly ascending patterns. Each variation constitutes a new theme to be integrated with patterns indigenous to the very first living organisms.

The organic resonances which thus pervade the earth, and indeed extend themselves far beyond, also suffuse each individual man. Woven into his existence are the manifold rhythms of organic space and time. By these rhythms, the very form of his metabolizing matter is shaped. Transmitted through the central nervous system, spatio-temporal contractions and expansions, symmetries and asymmetries are reflected by each person to himself, as he reflects on them, as a kaleidoscopically shifting Imago of these processes. In their differing morphologic contours, the vast scheme of internal organic activities is registered within him. The vectorial product of these forces determines man's biologic form. And his organismic nature conforms to their diverse influences. But should deformation exceed certain quite flexible limits, metabolic equilibria are shattered beyond possibility of repair.

Every organism—and man, in particular—strives to avert inexorable sinking toward death. It aims at self-perpetuation. In effect, questing to immortalize itself, life enters upon ceaseless battle with forces which ever threaten to destroy it. Every member of the entire family of organisms collaborates in order to survive. And beyond mere survival, life, in its collective sense as an integral organismic fabric, wills to prevail. In great counter-entropic surges, surviving life combats entropy. Constituted by the motions of organisms increasingly fragile yet correlatively more resilient, nature casts in its evolutionary wake a living fabric which requires decreasing quantities of energy for its overall metabolizing activities. More and more subtle schemes of biochemical reaction supervene. In their complicated interwovenness, these reactions transmit to one another their ever-increasing suppleness. To survive, I repeat, is to combat entropy; it is to seek to eternalize time. Intensifying zest, an organism experiences time more richly, and links past and present into a meaningful composite of solidarity and wealth of content.

One may justifiably speak of the monotony and the tedium of the inorganic. For organisms less capable of ecstasy, time also tends to be contracted and shortened. "Great spaces of time passed in unbroken uniformity," so Thomas Mann wrote, "tend to shrink together." Yet, he continues,

> conversely, a full and interesting content can put wings to the hour and the day; yet it will lend to the general passage of time a weightiness, a breadth and solidity which cause the eventful years to flow far more slowly. . . . [For] the intercalation of periods of change and novelty is the only means by which we can refresh our sense of time, strengthen, retard, and rejuvenate it, and therewith renew our perception of life itself.[1]

In general, every organic act is a thirsting after eternity; and this yearning is facilitated by and grounded in life's capacity for producing novelty, excitement, and involvement. Only for the more intricately designed yet more profoundly integrated organisms—for man, in particular—may the overarching purpose be realized.

In life's search, and in this grand evolutionary movement toward more and more sensitive organisms, a nature emerges which is composed of factors more delicately poised with respect to one another but, at the same time, more deeply attuned. Many organismic factors converge. Each confluence serves as the idiosyncratic vehicle whereby life itself will prevail and grow. Structures are formed and re-formed. Yet, in actuality, every structure is a ferment, but a ferment fixed and frozen. In organismic thaw, reliquefaction of biologic structures ensues. New forms are endlessly created. A complicated reticulation spreads, with ever novel transfiguration, to join organism with organism. A great ebb and flow of numberless organic and proto-organic trajectories comprise the process of morphogenesis. Woven of a complex system of fibrillating organic strands, all rhythmically intertwined, each endlessly pulsating and endlessly motile, nature tends, in the long run, to supersede itself. Giving way to the organismic, the proto-organismic eventually culminates in the hyperorganismic: nature's realm now spiritualized.

A · AFFINITIES BETWEEN PERSON AND ORGANISM

(a) Kinship

Earlier, I stressed the depth of sharing between man and the inanimate. I showed how he is a thingly being profoundly attuned to, and, in fact, attached to other thingly beings; that, subject to the same laws, he conforms to those laws with respect to his morphology, his energy exchanges, and the new metabolic configurations which they induce; that he exhibits the economy of a complicated being whose "spaces" are filled with interwoven physico-chemical processes—processes which through an intricate design of interlocking laminae efficiently utilize energy. And I indicated how, layer upon layer, he is composed of all stages of physiogenesis, both in his individual self-development and in his ancestral links to ancient activities of bare, lifeless matter.

Man's kinship with the myriad forms of living organisms is equally profound and, surely, even closer. So intimately is he linked to other species and phyla that life's entirety is like a single vast organism. Sprawled over the thingly, life, nonetheless, is orchestrated with it, and, dwelling attachedly to it, differentiates itself from it in relative autonomy. Yet man is but a particular organism, albeit one which is quite special. All humankind itself is an elaborately designed organism. Powerful, autonomous, and dominant, it is, nonetheless, within itself, co-dependent and constituted by reciprocal interactions; and it dwells in mutual symbiosis with sentiently less advanced organisms.

Like all organisms, man is delicate and vulnerable. But more so than most, save in one crucial and distinguished aspect: he has the power for relating self-consciously to God! Not only do other organisms often dwell about him in (seemingly) solitary independence; they also dwell within him with relative independence. Like mitochondria and centrioles, organelles, for example, are probably living descendants of freely roaming creatures; now become little beings at home within larger beings, they nevertheless retain their vibrancy as they lodge within man for the benefit of both. Even beyond organelles, one finds a "dancing matrix of viruses"[2] which like "mobile genes"[3] pass from organism to organism. As they traverse the interstices between creature and creature, these viruses transmit the quintessential stuff of life. By this mechanism, the solidarity of man with man, and of man with other organisms, far from becoming more remote as man evolves with his own distinctive qualities—his power of thought, symbolism, and language—is both perpetuated and reaffirmed.

Symbiosis, intricate co-adaptations, sharings of membranes with other structures, myriad linked functions: a single fabric implicates man with the organic world. By sight, by sound, by odor, by taste, by specialized "dances," and by deep empathic processes which cannot yet be specified, information is transmitted from man to his organismic cousins, and from them to him. An elaborate texture of these elements is orchestrated in diverse arrangements of tonal balance, timbre modulation, tensions and resolutions—a vast assemblage of motions and ornamentations of polymorphic design. These manifold factors, these variegated modes of communication, bind man and all living nature to their common ancestry. Despite wide-ranging and diversified offshoots of multivariate configuration, an incredible variety of intricate schemes of communication, recognition, and transformation, this rootedness remains secure. Throughout nature, a vast ecosystem prevails. Each part is governed by both state and function of all parts. The integrity of the entire fabric is preserved by an unconscious, dynamic, and smoothly working dynamism. Yet the fabric itself is woven of the integrities of its many components. Through the membranes of every cell, tissue, and organ pass bacteria, as, likewise, are transmitted such organelles as chloroplasts, basal bodies, mitochondria, and ribosomes: all "endosymbionts"; all parts of a syncytium—that network of influence; that veil of organized living matter which envelops and protects the entire fabric.[4]

Life is a great adventure into the unknown. In it, a vast multitude of forces come to confluence. The more intricately they are organized the more they "involute" upon themselves, the more they interiorize living strands which wrap about one another to shape fantastic patterns. This matrix of intercommunicating dynamic forms traces its ultimate origins to a perhaps single organic particle which, with vast improbability, appears at a unique point in the earth's unfolding geophysical processes. By accretion and nucleation, by replication of amalgams of macromolecules, by mutual encounter, by interchange of energies and images in variegated modes of conjugation, separation, cohesion, and transformation: by all these mechanisms, growth proceeds. By diversification, amplification, and multiplication, with ever-increasing sensitivity to the circumambient milieu, generation upon generation of organismic forms arise in response to ever-shifting environmental factors. The kinship structures which bind man, animal, and plant become constantly more elaborate as they evolve to form a veritable "biosphere" which envelops and penetrates the earth's "geosphere."[5]

(b) Spontaneity

Beyond a strictly organic evolution, the first dim hint of freedom, prefigured in lifeless matter, shines forth. A capacity for *self*-organization ensues, for *self*-control and *self*-directedness. In this process, life—at bottom, allied to the non-living—establishes itself in opposition to the non-living. Tension mounts between the two. Organic defenses shape themselves, defenses which impede an ineluctable regression to what, with increasing perceptiveness, living matter discerns as *non*-being. To achieve an organic identity, however faint, is to sense death. It is to yield to an inexorable tendency to revert to the non-living as lying at the core of organic existence. Like an elaborately patterned shell which encloses space which is topologically complex—but space which is utterly devoid of existence—the organism perceives in its inmost being space analogously devoid of existence.

Against this tendency, a nascence and a regeneration, the ascent toward ever more delicately constellated forms continues; it mounts with ever-increasing acceleration. By complicated entwinings of the living and the lifeless, the living eventuates in the human estate. With greatly self-enhanced freedom and self-awareness, humankind emerges from the arcane mysteries of infrapersonal being; yet, in the very wake of its development, it never ceases to enclose its own mysteries—mysteries elaborated upon and refined, but always intact: the matrix and very condition of personhood, yet ever its threat. These mysteries express themselves in fascination with the lifeless, but as a compulsion to escape its monotonies and its repetitiousness. Thus the drive to create more fluctuant, more dynamic, and self-mutating patterns! Thus these variegated patterns arise from a vast stillness which the lifeless—hence, which life itself—inexorably encloses within itself! To fill this void with his free spirit is man's most urgent need.

Primeval life extends back to matter, one of its (two) key ontologic grounds. When I say "two," I am anticipating my later thesis that a complementary ground lies in the realm of the suprapersonal. With respect to matter, which alone concerns me here, one finds prefigured in physiogenesis all stages of biogenesis: membrane formation, replication, variation, mutation, diversification, differentiation, hierarchization, coalescence, formation of novel constellations of mutually "acknowledging" factors, decisions, choices. In sheer unconscious fashion, the will strives to bring to fruition the bare activities manifested in physical process. Thereby, matter is drawn through successively more complicated modes of organismic existence. Patterned as increasingly self-reflective, it interweaves its many components. It becomes involuted and turned in upon itself. At every instant, data derived from other existents are appropriated into the unity of a novel existent. New schemes of unity are associated with successively more intense modalities of self-enjoyment. With abundant zest, each scheme aims at actualizing its fleeting, diverse potentialities.

From this process, different levels of complexity and sentience emerge. Up and down life's hierarchy, these levels influence one another. Varying arrangements of living materials evolve: a republic of cells, an autocracy of specialization, a collaboration of diverse functions. In no instance of life may one discover mere passive acquiescence in conformation to relatively stable environments. On the contrary, life's most characteristic impulse is actively to shape, ceaselessly to transact with, its environment. It ever engenders the profound continuities which reign among its multiform textures and recesses. Synthesized into a unity of self-enjoyment, immanent bare data give birth to flashes of mentality, to vectors which point toward higher grades of mentality: all this is life; all this is man!

Save for his incomparably richer and more diversified types of mentation, man's essential kinship with nature, whether alive or lifeless, is profound, inescapable, indefeasible. From mere soma, the will arises. As soma, the body is, quite literally, a "tomb," a repository for what is perpetually dying. Yet, etymologically, σῶμα and *semina* are connected. Hence, as *semen*, the body "embodies" a life force; it is the great container of potentialities for growth, a seminal confluence of processes which converge in ever-new self-reflexive centers of metabolism and replication. Through this converging, body transforms itself into a new fullness of being, a richness and a plenitude.

Man is embedded, first in the inanimate, then in the organismic. Never ceasing to acknowledge the depths and intricacies of his affinities, he seeks transcendence. Constantly the inwardness of the self projects itself into the natural. As freedom awakens, man experiences nature's presence in symbolic ways, hence, as intensifying these projections. Rhythm after rhythm orchestrates itself to shape new symbols. Emerging as integral, unified, and concrete, and expressing the immediacy of the inner and the outer, the human body now gives birth to a profound polarity. Man reveals himself to be poised between propulsion toward the inanimate, mere body dissolution, and self-conscious quest for spiritual fulfillment.

Under the methodologic perspective of transcendental naturalism, increments of disequilibrium afford motive power for originating, as counter-entropic forces, novel schemes of complexity, schemes which combat entropy by diverting their energies through myriad subtle channels. By a kind of prearranged plan of growth through re*production*, creative *re*-embodiments arise: all reincarnations of diverse patterns upon recurrent themes. Battles rage between pulverization, which tends toward non-entity, and coherence, which tends toward substantive unity. Ever-present options of thanatos and eros prevail. Man shares this tension with all living organisms. Yet since he is incomparably more self-conscious than those organisms—and, hence, capable of exercising a measure of control over nature's great ecosystem—he alone may alter the balance between these options. In what way he must eventually succumb to the former I treat in *The Person.*

(c) Ancestry

What an extraordinarily shaking experience to reflect upon this fact: that the essential replicatory material—interactions between nucleic acids RNA and DNA, those varied arrangements of nucleotide polymers—replicates itself identically over the entire range of living phenomena with respect to the most diversified modes of metabolic process, and with but minor variations usually rhythmic rather than morphologic! A fibrous aggregate, the intercoiled double helix responsible for a genetic code which prescribes a specific and unique design for every phylum, class, species, and individual, is, in each instance, a virtually identical configuration, an invariant core which controls the most subtle processes of life. Thus, a "repetitious network of neural chromosomes strung throughout the [human] body [and in proto-neural structures for all bodies] . . . represents the true 'physical' invariant in the general molecular shift of the organic whole." A single pattern, the "fine tracery of molecular groupings,"[6] is reiterated, a soft but resilient skeleton which is fixed and unchanging for each individual, and over all forms of life, indeed despite the ever-changing composition of the whole. What are the implications of such facts for the affinity between man and organism?

Consider as metaphor a "metabolic river of life"[7] which flows forward and is continually splitting into separate streams, each with its own destiny: its divergences and its confluences. By a directive activity from within the organism itself, through its inherently searching acts, this great delta forms and re-forms, pouring its content into the immeasurable sea of a unified life. This vast temporal unfolding, an incredible material diversification, this ramifying over space which fills the most arcane recesses of the inorganic, pressing against it and crushing it, bending it to its collective will—though always under powerful constraints (ultimately, those of non-being)—is governed by a single, persistent, and seemingly immutable structure: the fundamental replicating stuff. From paleontologic evidence and probability theory, it would seem incredibly improbable that this sturdy panoply of such manifold life did not derive from a single, unique, and original replicatory unit. If the reverse situation held, wherein multiple sources for the origins of life were postulated, the coincidental arrangements of the forces which must be hypothecated to account for the simultaneous appearance, over vast epochs of time and vast reaches of space, would be wildly, improbably, indeed virtually, impossible.[8]

I entertain a thesis analogous to the proposition that the entire cosmos originated in a single explosive elementary particle, inexplicably bursting forth from non-being, preceded by neither space nor time, imbued with all the resident mysteries of an utter void. I dare to propose that a unique germ cell is formed under unique conditions of confluence of the requisite paths of traversal, over widely separated spaces, by the essential ingredients of life—namely, carbon, hydrogen, oxygen, nitrogen, sulfur, phosphorous—each endowed with its ever so slightly mutant and absolutely unique rhythms, each driven by unique forces composed of uniquely interwoven strands, as though an immanent purpose governs this great convergence. By this thesis, associated with every such particle is a vector, inhering in each, which inexorably drives them on, all flowing directionally within an orchestrating matrix, to a special locus to shape that portentous molecule. Similarly, for every atom composing the molecule, a remote ancestry in mutant elementary particles may be postulated. In every instance, a special attunement holds. Potentially integrative rhythms traverse the entire cosmos; integral cosmic reverberations arising from widely separated regions sweep through the totality; all, in the end, refer to an absolutely compact and original exploding cosmic particle. Perhaps, even within this aboriginal structure, infinitesimally subtle modulations set themselves in primeval antithesis to other modulations—a dialectical tension which engenders, for aught we know, the primordia for what will, after numberless eons, through strangely circuitous routes, transfigure itself into life!

A transfiguration which culminates in man! And he himself constitutes himself a new source for continuance of the evolutionary process. From the nodules of the tree of life many such branches spring. With respect to mental development of variegated types, to mutant forms of will and feeling and perception, the range of circumstances and climes which give rise to sports—especially to those of the order of the spiritual—are immeasurably more variable for man than for any other species. Receding levels of kinship, receding layerings of cousinhood, from the proximate to the remote! Herein, in this particular phase of history, lies the essential tragedy of humankind. Can a Stalin really speak to a Solzhenitsyn? Can a paramecium commune with a fawn?

I affirm this doctrine: in his origins, as well as by his contemporary ecologic relations with organic forms, man is pervaded by the resonances of the organismic; and were he to reach sufficiently far into the recesses of his Unconscious, they would, in principle, be discoverable to him. There, quite hidden, resides an Imago of his body structure, and its deep bonds to living creatures over earth and heaven. Yet man continues to diversify himself. New and ever more comprehensive variants arise upon his own thematic. Nevertheless, the realm of the organic, as the realm of the event, profoundly conditions man. Immanently working within him, both realms enter deeply into the formation of his sentience, his style, his communications, his symbolisms, his yearnings, his language. In each instance, the primordia are, first, the inanimate and, nearer his personal being, the nobler kingdom of life.

Corresponding to a coordinate system for the event, in which the axes are those of space, time, and matter–energy, is the analogous, though complex, system relevant for living organisms.

If, accordingly, one represents the former in the diagram

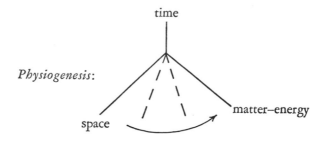

Physiogenesis:

then the latter becomes, correlatively,

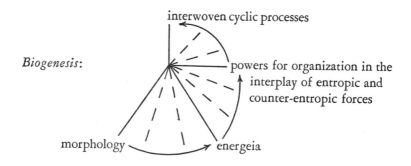

Biogenesis:

Comparing these diagrams, one immediately notes that, in the case of material events, space is three-dimensional, time is one-dimensional, and matter–energy distributions can be represented as a pattern of variables, hence, by several dimensions. But, in the case of living organisms, the analogues of space and time must be converted from a limited three dimensionality into, in each instance, an indefinite dimensionality.

To complete my proposed model, I briefly anticipate in the following (oversimplified) diagram the analogue on the level of personogenesis.

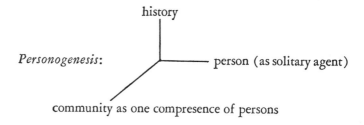

Personogenesis:

Clearly, each dimension is a compressed linear counterpart to a richly textured tapestry of strands. In my next chapter, I explore certain implications of this model. At present, I deal with merely the biogenetic scheme, especially with respect to its indigenous content and, secondarily, in its relationship to the physiogenetic and the personogenetic model. Later, I shall note how the simplistic separation between these models breaks down and must be replaced by a *hyper*-space: that of event, organism, and person; and I show how these hyperspaces themselves interweave as a single complicated *cosmic* representation.

B · THE ORGANISM TEMPORALIZED

(a) Interwoven Temporal Cycles

Woven[9] into the fabric of the body is a multitude of temporal flowings, cycles, and fluctuations. These rhythmic configurations interweave; the overall pattern which they form becomes, in self-reflection, the time sense of the person. A series of scales carves out temporal increments which are neither congruent with each other, with respect to a given scale, nor congruent with respect to correlative increments associated with other scales. In general, several notions of time have dominated civilized thought. These notions are of two kinds. The first concerns the relative positions of earth and the heavenly bodies, i.e., *external* time. The second concerns the status of personal experience: mood, human encounter, body image—i.e., *internal* time.

With respect to "external time," two varieties may be distinguished as dominating occidental thought. First, time may be a cosmic becoming, a universal unfolding associated with irreversible unidirectionality. Here, the temporal is conceived to be constituted either by homogeneous intervals or, alternatively, by spiraling, zig-zagging, arrhythmic, and heterogeneous intervals. Secondly, time may be cyclic. Here, it implies eternal return to a fixed point of origin or, perhaps, to a rhythmically moving point; time is typified by renewal, rebirth, recurrence—in all cases, either of inexorable regularity or of diverse kinds of oscillation. With respect to "internal time," three formulations dominate both ancient thought and oriental thought. There, time may be καιρός, the momentous, decisive, and critical junctures of human and cosmic affairs, junctures replete with portent and mystery. Next, time may be αἰών, a principle of creativity which is inexhaustible, relentless, unfathomable, eternal. Finally, time may refer to a concept which is etymologically related to such notions as *tempo, tempus, temperature, temperament*. Here, time may suggest burning, light, fiery disposition, quickening rhythm; it may suggest inexorable but variable flow; or it may, "swift-footed," "make the earth devour her own sweet brood";[10] or it is the time which is thus immortalized:

O, how shall summer's honey breath hold out
Against the wrackful siege of battering days,
When rocks impregnable are not so stout,
Nor gates of steel so strong, but Time decays.[11]

Or, again, time may suggest the spiritual, the ineffable, the very antithesis of physicality.

All these notions of time, and perhaps many more—surely, Shakespeare's sonnets propose numerous possibilities—are woven into man's being. They are conferred upon him by his event-character, by his organismic character, by his status as person. With respect to his infrapersonal makeup, at least these temporal rhythms compose his body: a gaseous substance consisting of protons, neutrons, and electrons at extremely high temperatures, and associated with kinetic energies of many millions of electron volts, engenders a particular time scale; at lower temperatures, at less than one million volts, protons and neutrons assemble to form atomic nuclei of great specificity which engender another time scale; at still lower temperatures (corresponding to the temperature of the sun's surface) electrons assume regular quantum states which orbit about the atomic nucleus and confer on the atom specific chemical qualities which engender still another time scale; at energies of about one-tenth of an electron volt, atoms form simple molecules, creating yet another time scale; at energy levels of a few hundredths of an electron volt (at room temperature), molecules aggregate to liquids, crystals, and giant macromolecular chains to shape yet another time scale; the lengthy polypeptides (i.e., amino acid polymers) twisting into protein and polyneucleotides to form nucleic acids, all continually stretching out in space, engender even an additional time scale. All of life is a process of transformation, for the most part, irreversible, and evolutionary; it unfolds at an exponentially progressing time-rate of change, always with regional reversals, in the direction of decreasing entropy, as though by some counter-entropic force which comes more and more to dominate the far-flung cosmic processes. So many time scales! Such varieties of patterning those scales! Organismic time is, surely, intricate and, often, bizarre.

At high temperatures involving high energy levels, time "seems" to pass more slowly; at low temperatures associated with low energy levels, time "seems" to pass more quickly. The "apparent" passage of time—under the assumption of an absolute scale of cosmic becoming—in the earliest phase of cosmic evolution would, on the whole, have "seemed" to an observer implicated in the process to have proceeded with incredible rapidity; in the latest phase, the reverse occurs.

On the other hand, by reference to some (allegedly) absolute time measure, the converse holds. Incomparably "more" time accompanies the earlier phases of evolution than accompanies the later. For example, the spiral of time, the inward curving portion of which represents process in which there is increasingly efficient utilization of energy, the actual time-rate of change is enormously rapid. Yet the felt rate of time change (as, on the whole, in dreaming) is correspondingly slow. How to reconcile "objective, external" time with "experiential, internal" time poses a serious problem. Naturally, the observer cannot experience himself where he is not located. He can barely even dare to imagine placing himself where he could not possibly have been—namely, at the earlier stages of evolution. However, physical and organic activities characteristic of the initial and middle phases of the evolutionary time spiral, exponential (or logarithmic) in form, are, in fact, incorporated into the human organism. There they express the metabolic activities foundational to its overall organismic functioning. In consequence, there coexist functions, energy exchanges and transformations, activities, processes, events, and quite stable objects analogous to, though not in strict correlation with, the different phases of evolution. From this fact, it follows that my earlier remarks concerning multiple time scales interwoven with the fabric of the body are substantiated and, indeed, reinforced. Now I amplify the character of this enmeshing, first with respect to certain selected factual details—in order to provide paradigms—then with respect to certain philosophic implications of these details.

Whenever cerebral organization is disrupted, as by the drug reaction-patterns which induce desynchronization, a "chromosystole" occurs (i.e., a time contraction), with waves of oscillation of variable periodicity, all synchronized with cardiac, vasomotor, and other physiologic fluctuations. In general, the variety of chemical, physical, and biological agents (e.g., hormones, electrical impulses, viruses, the organelles responsible for intracellular oxidation and intercellular energy transfer) is enormous. Interplay of such agents produces an elaborately textured correlation of organic cyclicity, systems which are both species-typical and individual-typical; and in the case of the individual-typical system, there are variables for each individual, depending upon both his moods and the different qualities and intensities of stimulus-input. Truly, the rhythms of biologic activity are multiplex. Rhythms abound: heart pacemaker, respiratory, endocrinologic, central nervous, ovarian. Some rhythms are passive and susceptible to imposed oscillations such as diurnal ("circadian"), annual, tidal, or lunar cycles; some rhythms are active and self-sustaining. Both sorts are woven into numberless aggregates. And one may distinguish the exogenous rhythms, which originate in the organism's milieu, from such endogenous rhythms as the menstrual cycle. The organism is composed of a vast hierarchy of superimposed and interlocking rhythms, rhythms of many origins, all in relations of subordination and superordination: a vast tapestry of cyclical strands, an orchestration of myriad periodic motions. Organismic time is, indeed, complicated beyond imagination.

Depending on the body's physiological state, its homeostatic condition, and on the dynamic equilibria which bind its parts together and relate their totality to the milieu in which the organism functions, many different time senses will be experienced. Perhaps time is felt as of great density; perhaps as torrential flow; perhaps as a richness and a fullness; perhaps as oscillations of quickening measure or, alternatively, of a majestic pacing out of sonorous rhythms perhaps woven of caesurae of varying length; perhaps as a gentle trickling. Moreover, with respect to the concept of simultaneity, it is remarkable, for example, to note how Mozart heard his interior music, prior to its formal composition—not successively, but as *gleich alles zusammen*; or, indeed, as different and extended simultaneous patterns: "Weil ich die Fuge schon gemacht hatte," he wrote, "und sie, unter dessen dass ich das Preludium ausdacht, abgeschrieben!"[12] My purpose in this chapter is not now to elaborate different experiences of time as such: in effect, its phenomenology. I seek only to locate the sources of those experiences, and to determine whether they involve some mode of time sense which is not strictly idiosyncratic for the individual, a mere reflection of his mood and his gifts, or for the empathic resonances of several persons. On the contrary, my intent is to determine whether such time *in concreto* is, at the very same time, objective and universal. I seek to ascertain whether objectivity and universality, if such be found, exhibit analogies, parities, or complementarities with the objectivity and the universality claimed for the spatio-temporal invariants of general relativity theory.

To decide these issues, one must note the presence of the numberless asynchronous temporal cycles manifested by intra-organismic reactions, cycles the rhythms of which are functions of such physiological processes as the rate of oxidative reaction, the length of polymers forming the polypeptide strands of protein molecules, transmission among cells (i.e., across their membranes) of chloroplasts and mitochondria, the neurophysiologic mechanisms of energy reception, transmission, in-mission, and absorption. Indeed, many local excitations in the central nervous system induced either by drugs or by metabolic and endocrinologic factors will be associated with hallucinations, fantasy flow, dreams which "seemingly" last now an instant, now an eternity—and, in each instance, "seemingly" transport one to other realms, strange and bizarre.

Furthermore, temporal contractions and expansions are associated with such organic transformations as those found in epilepsy or even, perhaps, in schizophrenia. Such associations depend upon the relative sensitivities of the sensory receptor organs which both receive stimuli and transmit them in "all-or-none" packets and with varying grades of complexity and intensity. Because of this activity, certain "objective" time delays are experienced as spatial spreads. In this sense, a curious equivalence between space and time reigns for very organism. This equivalence seems to complement the equivalence postulated by general relativity theory. Unlike that theory, the relevant invariants are neither the upper bound, c (i.e., the velocity of light), nor the lower bound, h (Planck's constant, a unit of action). Far more complicated, they consist of such interwoven factors as temperature ranges consistent with homeostasis maintenance, rate of DNA–RNA formation, or units of nerve impulse transference (lying somewhere between 1 and 100 milliseconds, and inversely proportional to the size of a neuron fiber and the intensity of the agent which stimulates that fiber). Moreover, assuming a stochastic interpretation of the time–entropy association, one cannot fail to speculate regarding plausible quantum-level time reversals which significantly affect critical and subtle body transformations—e.g., replication, in which the recurrent benzene ring of the DNA–RNA system exhibits resonance, modulations, and deviations which, however minuscule, arise from photon/n-electron interaction.

In sum, the body is constantly in-formed with the configurations of a vast hierarchy of biochemical reactions and diverse macromolecular depositions. It is a complicated informational matrix, a matrix which involves crystal-lattice arrangements, antigen–antibody communication systems, and manifold other physico-biologic processes. When I say "in-formed," I mean both acquiring a form by virtue of internal organismic activities, and deriving from the milieu myriad factors which work upon the organism as extra-organismic in-formational imprints. Together, these endogenous and exogenous influences confer upon organisms, through their intricate interplay, their diverse morphologic contours.

(b) Organismic Time Consummated

I am proposing that one continually recreates an image of his intra-organismic activities. Mirroring these activities to himself, he projects this image, as though it were a map of his bodily processes, onto his body *in its relationship to* its milieu; he interprets this map as the temporality of interactant bodies. Reincorporated within his body, this pro-ject is therein redintegrated with his own organicity; a dialectic of projection and introjection ensues. For each organism, *this present moment* expresses a particular style of dynamic interchange and reciprocity. Profoundly conditioned by two sets of factors, the present, so to speak, hovers about the body. These factors are a particular past which surges into the present to define the limits of its actualities, and a future "returned" to, and reclaimed by, the present as that scheme of anticipations which define the limits of its possibilities.

Nonetheless, every present moment is replete with vectors for novel origination. It selectively discerns elements of the past which are relevant to it; it selectively discriminates trajectories for its future. Doubly grounded upon the interweaving of past and future, the "structure" of the present is itself (on the infrapersonal level) referable to a multitude of organic processes: cellular life spans, molecular and polymolecular systems, organs of varying complexity. These variable processes implicate the interactions of those metabolites which guarantee the integrity of the body. They enable it to wage battle, by diverse counter-entropic stratagems, against a stochastically construed though nonetheless inexorable cosmic entropy. Depending upon the differing arrangements of metabolites thereby effected, organic time flows quickly or slowly, smoothly or granulately, and with all the variegated rhythms which I sketched earlier.

The phenomenon of temporal passage[13] is like a mediation of cosmologic and microphysical events; it is even a kind of compromise between them. Time represents the primordial relationship between the two. What I mean is this: the ratio of the largest time unit (c, the velocity of light) to cross the universe in 10^9 years and the smallest time unit to cross the electron (h, or minimal action) in 10^{-23}

seconds is of the order of $\sqrt{N}$, where N equals the total estimated number of particles in the universe, 2^{264}. Were one to traverse either cosmos or electron at the indicated velocities, it would be as though one were not moving, as though time itself were arrested. Between these limits, depending on the number, arrangement, distribution, and fate of the particles composing the universe, various time fluctuations would be experienced.

Organismic activity is regulated by a kind of body clock, but the mechanism of this clock cannot be simplistically determined. On the contrary, periodicities dependent upon such processes as chemical kinetic systems, interconnected chains of catalysis for mitochondria which originate oxidative reactions, and numerous biosynthetic pathways alike contribute, each in its own way; to the vast mosaic of synchronization which *is* (over all life) that time clock. Moreover, every imaginable frequency, of which one may postulate $\sqrt{N} = 2^{132}$, lying between c and h, will be found. In some way, they are all relevant to the biologic clock.

Through interplay of many oscillating particles and aggregations of particles, evolutionary complexes of variable structure and rhythm unfold. The whole of life is like a single event which exponentially recedes or proceeds in time. In the course of evolution, many techniques are devised by nature to combat "morpholysis"—the death of forms as coerced by inexorable entropy. Such techniques are consistent with stochastic processes which, in certain (privileged) regions, impede, reverse, arrest, or hasten the flow of time. Perhaps telepathic phenomena are expressions of these time quirks. Such techniques are manifold. They include such factors as neuron sharing, half-lives of radioactive elements, shifting periods in the rotation of the earth, moon phase changes in the course of evolution—many perhaps unique and non-repeatable events. Innumerable temporal complexities are possible. All are relevant to organismic functioning. On the other hand, rhythmic periods and cyclic fluctuations vary enormously from organism to organism. A vast heterogeneity reigns. It has even been hypothecated that the universal constant for intercommunicating humming bees is not light but sound. From the standpoint of ecology, all organisms are co-adapted with respect to the most diverse schemes of correlated cycles. From an organismic point of view, it may be that the most general invariants involve the transmission of quanta of energy through nerve fibers and across their synapses.

What conclusions may one draw from these diverse observations? As man looks out upon the world, he seeks to conceptualize the meaning of time with respect to a range of entities: slowly moving, stable objects; faster moving events which may cohere as objects; processes which are manifolds of flowings of variable rhythm, processes which agglutinize as events—a confluence of factors constituting an "instant" of time, the internal cohesion of interlocking temporal phases; the still more rapidly fluctuant activities; energies transmitted with extraordinary velocities and possessing the very antithesis to an object character; ineffable "functions" which express interactions of *virtual* simultaneity. Objects, events, processes, activities, energies, functions: all these varied configurations express the taxonomy of time (as well as its associated morphology); all these classes of flow are immanent within each man as constitutive of his event–organismic character.[14]

Stratified layer upon layer, these diverse types of occurrence exhibit varying modes of stability, each requiring and presupposing the other modes. All layers are interwoven as an integral fabric of intricate design, a fabric which confers a "stratiform" quality upon the body. Between the different laminae composing this fabric, a dialectical relationship holds. By the dynamism of this relationship, the entire fabric coheres. Yet an incomparably more precarious equilibrium seems to hold for the body fabric than for the "world": world as objectively constituted by the reflections of compresent persons who by their collective acts, habits, and suppositions seek to construct a common external frame of reference—a frame, however, which is not immanent within each person, but transcendent to him.

The objective coordinate system thereby superimposed upon the "outer" world deals with aspects, appearances, and manifestations of physical occurrences. Hence the space–time, and its associated (simple) invariants, of general relativity theory! This external time, this congeries of externally cohesive relations, is counterposed to the organism as a veridical threat. True, according to the kind of configuration which the external milieu assumes, conformation is imposed upon the organism which enables its interior activities to function effectively. Yet the very factors which induce this protective conformation must impinge upon a body surface of exceptionally sensitive texture. Too weighty a force for conformation may induce such deformations as can, in principle, disrupt or even destroy the internal integrity of the organism. Should these deformations felicitously aggregate themselves, an effective re-equilibration will be achieved. Still, so much depends upon fortuitous circumstance.

This great scheme of external relations provides the most inclusive perspective available upon those spatial, temporal, and material transformations with respect to which a minimum number of invariants must be posed as objective reality. Not that the spatialization of time in general relativity theory, formulated as a Minkowsky pattern of space–time equivalences, is simplistic. Nor, certainly, is this the case for a relativistic quantum mechanics, a theory so complicated that, for example, the positron behaves as an electron which, so to speak, flows *backward* in time. On the contrary, in both instances, manifold and fragmented data of the most variegated kind are coordinated; and even today these two great topics of theoretical physics have not been united. Nonetheless, together they afford the most plausible extant image of nature, this despite profound inconsistencies between their underlying methodologic and substantive assumptions: the first image based on a deterministic view of reality; the second, on a probabilistic view.

Despite the comprehensiveness of this perspective, such time remains essentially material and external. As such, the spiraling of cosmic becomingness—hitherto depicted as homogeneous, unidirectional, and intrinsically composed (over sufficiently large increments) of congruent intervals, nevertheless within a stochastic interpretation—allows for evolutionary speeding up and slowing down. Thus constituted, this kind of time pertains to the infrapersonal realm, in particular to matter, which grounds and conditions human action from but one of two possible sides and, in this mode of relatedness to man, is an emanation and efflux of that "kind" of being which I designate non-being.

A novel situation arises when one passes beyond mere events to "higher" organismic levels—the infrapersonal organizations of life. Here, a new richness with respect to time, and a new variability, come upon the scene. Already, a conceptual transition is in process. What is usually deemed abstract, non-illusory, and objective physical time is now more and more seen to be, at bottom, what is usually deemed intersubjective, interpersonal, and, its complement, intrapsychic time: time which is idiosyncratic, private, concrete, experiential. Save in fragmentary clues, I have not yet dealt with personal time, yet this mode of temporality has surely been prefigured in my comments on organismic time.

To summarize: different parts of the organism re-collect imprints upon them in varying rhythmic schemes. Gathering together such occurrences as I have classified—namely, objects, events, processes, activities, energies, functions—such organizations as cells, organs, and organelles bring these occurrences to convergence, in their relevance for the ongoing activity of those organizations. While all factors interlock in seeming cacophony and asynchronicity, a deeper harmony underlies the entire fabric. This harmony expresses the overall confluence of innumerable depositions of past imprints, traces left in the wake of earlier organismic activities.

As a living organism works out its life destiny, the residue of its past never ceases to recede; it sinks back into a dead past, toward non-being: itself lying at the very center, side by side with the fullness of being, as the bipolar core of all existents. This progressive (more accurately, *regressive*) fading with respect to a vibrant present is, in another sense, only apparent. All that ever was in the fabric of a life remains, as mirror of itself, within each present moment—remains to condition that moment, to guide it, to constitute its substance. The innumerable schemes of re-collection to which I earlier referred as coming to confluence in each present instant weave a tapestry of many strata. Radically transcendent with respect to the full immediacy of the present, the past is yet paradoxically, in its unfathomable depths, ever retained as immanent within the present. Cumulatively evolving, a present moment is organic and multilaminated. Many strands of transiency are interwoven in diverse organic patterns; variegated rhythms are deposited in the wake of the collective unfolding of these strands, strands which are but the arrested, symmetrized depositions of numberless periodicities, cycles, and flows.

From discrete segments of objects to the multiple phases of processes, from the fragile fibers which constitute particular activities to amorphous, turbulent energies and, finally, to ineffable functions with but a trace of the existential, yet incomparably subtle in their own modulations and undertones—in all these modes of occurrence, invariants manifest themselves which only the most arduous search might one day specify. Pervading the organism are manifold types, rates, and intensities of developmental stages, all constituted by different ways of aggregating these occurrences. Nevertheless, quite amazingly, the organism is not so frangible as one might surmise. On the contrary, it is an autonomous source for resisting devastating change; it is a sturdy core against the ravages of external time. Protected by sensitive membranes interwoven throughout the body and, ultimately, for persons, synthesized as the skin itself, the organism sets interior limits to the ranges of metabolic processes by which it sustains itself against potential, externally induced disruption. While, in a certain sense, the inorganic is a chance resultant of activities which lead to a meaningless confusion of detail, the *organic* is the "residue" of factors re-collected in numerous enmeshing patterns of dynamic forms. A complex system in need of constant nurture, yet always protected by the relevant membranes and internal morphology, the organic is a meaningful integral of numberless processes and acts.

(c) Personal Time Prefigured

For the person, the culmination of temporal becoming reveals itself in the dialectic between, on the one hand, unconscious aggregates "drawn in," through his event makeup and his organismic makeup, from *non-being* and, on the other, the conscious formations constituted in human encounter and, ultimately, transmitted via the domain of the *spiritual.* Thus far, I have not dealt with the personal Unconscious as such. Nor, certainly, have I set forth the indicated dialectic. My argument has stressed only themes which I conceive to be foundational to a strictly human ontology: the interwovenness of asynchronous with synchronous rhythms, the contrast and interplay of biological and physical time, the fact that the entire system of organisms, an ecologic scheme of co-adaptation, may be conceived as but a single *super*-organism, an inclusive configuration which (however) conditions each of its components, the interaction of exo-ecologic systems with endo-ecologic systems. In short, I have been concerned with the diverse textures and the subtle fabric of the infrapersonal, insofar as these textures and this fabric themselves get woven into the still richer tapestry of the personal.

Granted, I am here dealing with internal time: ultimately, the time of those internal relations which bind organism with organism, organism with milieu. As I later show, this species of time, mediated by organicity, is transformed into a new species of time, that of freedom, spontaneity, creativity: the multiple rhythms, the styles and flows, and orchestration of Shakespeare's great time sonnets; reflections on time incorporated in the immortal writings of an Aeschylus, a Dante, a Goethe, a Rilke, a Yeats, a Donne, an Eliot. Surely, *this* species of time is already immanent in prepersonal life. It is a newly emergent species: vital, filled, malleable, indeterminate, self-determined.

For the first time, in association with the inner meaning of time itself, self-identity fully appears on the scene. By self-identity, I now mean a dynamic, self-sustaining identity. No longer is self-identity to be equated with the idea of a passive core, the mere "having" of an identity. On the contrary, self-identity now means the self so orienting itself to itself, especially (on this level of analysis) toward its thingly and organismic character, that it meditatively imputes an identity to itself, and this in the context of its identifyings—its successive adherings to other things and its absorbing of their qualities and their contours. In so adhering, the self reflects into itself its *own* images of its complicatedly interwoven event–organismic character. No simplistically durable structure, this imputing to self by self creates a new time: the subtle, fluctuant, personal time of many modes of intentionality—time which is not passive, but active and creative.

In brief, I am here treating the *two* aspects of time which are immanent in life: its freedom and its foundation. On the one hand, temporality stems from the mystery of non-being. On the other, identity as self-imputing suggests that temporality also arises from the reverse direction: the suprapersonal. Ultimately, the latter sense of time articulates the negation of "external time" which itself tends to negate "internal time." A doubly reducible time! The former derives from non-being; the latter, from pure being. Each mode tends to negate the other. Yet the two modes themselves are dialectically related. Pre-eminently, the person is the locus wherein this dialectic reveals itself. Herein, they achieve complementarity and exhibit parity. For it is man who is the great mediator of time, in its double aspect—just as it is God who is the great mediator of being, or eternity, in *its* double aspect—the plenitude of being, the privation of being.

Once again, I stress: the internal and the external modalities of time are non-isolable, inseparable, and unopposed. Even within the organism, on its prepersonal level, they commingle and participate as a single complicated process. Associated with external time is death; associated with internal time is eternal "existence." Thus, time *überhaupt* is no merely fragmented succession of vanishing moments. It involves integrity, an inner correlation, a strange co-existence of past, present, and future, a strange co-existence of many pasts, many presents, and many futures. Yet this correlation is enormously complicated. With respect to the inner time which is associated with intentionality, one is free. Still the inexorable threat of external time is not dissolved. But fully to be a person is, in some way, to resolve this contradiction; it is to reduce or, perhaps, to negate the threat. Human existence is poised between death (of a kind!) and immortality (of a kind!).

As I have proposed, time's modalities are interwoven as one. All time indissolubly penetrates every singular present moment. This condition holds for every event, every organism, and (pre-eminently) every person. *Retention* and *protension* express, respectively, the "tendings" of a past toward and into the present, and, conversely, a future toward and into the present. In general, past and future alike set limits for the present, and condition its structure. Yet each opens possibilities germinally residing in the present. In this sense, past and future are complementary and liberating. Both serve as means, vehicles, and agents whereby the present is consummated.

Time is an integrity of consonances and dissonances, of harmony and opposition. Deriving from the infrapersonal and the suprapersonal, it weaves its multifarious strands into intricate patterns. Organismic time prefigures characteristically personal time. Insofar as time is an emanation of pure being, it expresses the irradiation of person by spirit. Nevertheless, rooted at once in non-being and in pure being, organismic time incarnates that to which the later evolute, the person, will give reflective expression as his being's coeval ground. Equally, one can speak of the irradiation of the person by differing grades of non-being: non-being proper, eventhood, the organismic. In a modified version of a diagram earlier introduced, these observations may be represented:

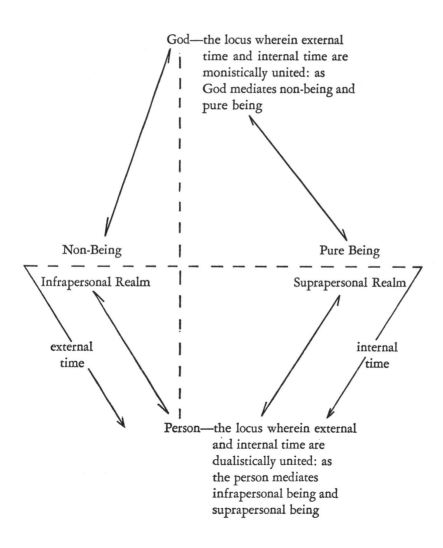

God—the locus wherein external
time and internal time are
monistically united: as
God mediates non-being and
pure being

Non-Being   Pure Being

Infrapersonal Realm   Suprapersonal Realm

external
time   internal
time

Person—the locus wherein external
and internal time are
dualistically united: as
the person mediates
infrapersonal being and
suprapersonal being

In this representation,[15] time receives a threefold ground: ontologic, cosmologic, theologic. What alone needs now to be noted is the radical complementarity of time's two modalities: their parity, their penultimately dualistic but ultimately unitary origin, their associated invariants. By my thesis, non-being gives birth to the external time depicted by general relativity theory; pure being gives birth to the integrated time first manifested in the interwoven activities of the inanimate and, more strikingly, in the intricate cycles of the animate. Since, in the last analysis, external time and internal time are both referable to an absolute parity and merger in God of both non-being and pure being, both modalities of time may be regarded as actual manifestations of the same numinous reality.

C · MORPHOLOGY AND MORPHOGENESIS

(a) Structure

In my biological coordinate system, the dimension corresponding to the space-dimension of a physical coordinate system I designate *morphology*. The unfolding sequence of morphologies, with respect to a particular organism, a class of organisms, or a particular co-adaptation of organisms, I designate *morphogenesis*. Morphology expresses the ways in which the components of an organism arrange themselves. Such components may be objects, events, processes, activities, energies, or functions. Morphology treats the configuration which these occurrences form, the manner in which they distribute themselves within the organism, and the different ways in which their mutual impingements contour one another. Associated with every "instant" of time, the "unfolding" of which for biological systems has been construed as an interwoven set of cyclical processes, is a distinct morphologic configuration. With respect to a set of contiguous "instants," every organism develops along a trajectory characteristic for its class, and distinctive (within each class) for the particular individual. In effect, developmental trajectories are defined for all organisms, all species, all classes, all phyla. For each of these entities or kinds of entity, the outermost limits of trajectoral possibilities is specified. A set of limits is posed which are related to one another like so many Chinese boxes, each enclosed by another and each enclosing another—down, of course, to a certain limit. As one approaches the center of this scheme of enclosures—namely, a "point" which corresponds to a particular organism—certain trajectoral possibilities are progressively eliminated. Those trajectories which remain are, so to speak, variations upon a *thematic* trajectoral set which corresponds to the immediately adjacent enclosure.

For every organism associated with a distinctive trajectory of development—i.e., its set of morphogenetic possibilities—three developmental phases may be distinguished. How these phases are articulated, and the manner in which they interrelate, depend upon the type of organism under consideration, the specific morphologic potential of each phase associated with that organism, and the kinds of environment which the organism inhabits. With respect to the entire scheme of life, considered as a vast, evolving ecologic system, a space of the most diversified topologic properties must be conceived. Whether one considers, at one extreme, a single organism, or, at the other, an inclusive ecosystem composed of living parts, these phases exhibit certain analogies. At first sight trivial, their obvious characteristics nonetheless conceal features critical for the specification of life, in its morphologic aspect. Accordingly, I distinguish an initial phase of origination, or conceiving, a middle transitional phase composed of its own subordinate phases, and a terminal phase of perishing. Now I treat the curiously analogous initial and culminating phases. Next, I treat the intermediate phases.

In the initial phase, the morphology of conceiving consists of an arrangement of factors, all delicately poised in a state of virtual passage into living, metabolizing existence. The various parts of this structure are, so to speak, vectorially directed toward one another in such fashion that a vast ferment sweeps over the entirety. In short, a tenuous morphology prevails. Structural factors are in a state of evanescence; they give the appearance of dissolution—save for the fact that associated with this fluctuant configuration is a general "tensor" which points toward resolution. From this point of view, the phase of conceiving and the phase of perishing, or dying, are analogous—save for the direction of that tensor, though not necessarily the intensities of its associated qualities. For conceiving, the movement is toward organization; for dying, it is toward disorganization. The task of establishing criteria by which one or the other phase may, on morphologic grounds, be recognized is not easy. In both instances, the morphologic configuration is in a state of virtual disequilibration. Yet the mode of disequilibration differs. For conceiving, there is a distinctive kind of gathering together, a collecting of many structures from widely dispersed sources, a passage to confluence, a tending toward convergence; for dying, there is a distinctive kind of un-gathering, a separation of strands, and a diverging, which, however, is preceded by a new modality of collecting: a peculiarly intense re-collection of all the lived experiential fragments, each group associated with the relevant physiologic correlates, into a single pregnant instant of momentous intensity . . . before passage into transfiguration.

Associated with both conceiving and dying is an organization-in-ferment; all is in motion. But this ferment is not random; nor is it merely diffuse. On the contrary, it is suffused with immanent purposiveness. Though no specific aim or telos may simplistically be specified, one may, with sufficiently refined techniques of investigation, discern a meaningful pattern in the very "virtuality" of the diverse motions constituting this mobile configuration. To specify the architecture of this phase—as, indeed, the architecture of the complicatedly interwoven subphases of the "middle phase"—many procedures must be employed: e.g., microscopy, radiological analysis, cinematography, histochemical techniques. By these procedures, the intimate relation between form and function strikingly manifests itself; as, indeed, does the graduated continuum ranging from structures, quasi-structures, and proto-structures to processes, activities, and functional relationships. With Hegel, one may say that

> Structure, as alive, is essentially process, and it is, as such, *abstract process*, the *structural process within structure itself*, in which the organism converts its own members into a non-organic nature, into *means*, lives on itself and produces its own self, i.e. this same totality of articulated members, so that each member is reciprocally end and means, maintains itself through the other members and is opposition to them. It is the process which has for result the simple immediate *feeling of self*.[16]

Alternatively expressed: structure is *frozen process*, just as process is *fluid structure*. These formulations are equivalent. From this point of view, process (synonymous, in this context, with both function and activity) extrudes and externalizes itself as structure. Relatively fixed and rigid—i.e., a *relatively* enduring configuration—structure itself, nonetheless, remains essentially a process, a process which represents the curious interplay between the *in*organic and the organic. It is, so Hegel continues, "a special articulation, not containing independent parts, but only moments in a living subjectivity" so that "these moments are sublated, negated, and posited by the organism's vitality."[17] Accordingly, he concludes, the "process within structure," insofar as it is necessarily organic—hence, the factor which binds to a unified, integral whole the "articulated members"—grounds structure's own self-transformation into new structure, thereby incorporating new process. Vis-à-vis its own intrinsic vitality, the organism externalizes or exteriorizes itself, presenting itself as a fixed morphologic pattern. At the same time, the very external components having been, so to speak, projected from the organism are still essential for maintaining those conditions which alone allow the organism to continue to function. In this sense, structure is perpetually *e*jected only to be re*intro*jected and incorporated as process, whereupon the dialectic continues anew.

As far as the structure–process dialectic is concerned, it must be stressed that the morphologic possibilities are numberless. Structures may be distinguished which are coarse or fragile, sturdy or frangible, flexible or rigid, fibrous or laminated, friable or malleable, dense or rarefied; and these structures are interwoven in the most intricate topologic schemes: e.g., spiralings, labyrinths, coilings. Furthermore, between the interfaces of structures, indeed permeating and transforming them, the most subtle processes occur: energy exchanges, ion transfers, permeability shifts of varying grades. And complicated routes for transmission, each itself an enmeshing of biological processes, conduct enzymes, organelles, immunological ingredients, replicatory material. This ordered conglomeration of structures is suspended in an aqueous solution rich in ion-bearing minerals which, by their electrical activity, allow for continual morphogenesis—hence, the ceaseless re-configuring of intra-organismic "space": a tapestry of perpetually interweaving trajectories which implicate dynamic forms of structure–process complexes in constantly shifting designs.

(b) Flow

Earlier, I referred to the phases of conceiving and dying as mutually complementary. In both instances, I argued, a ferment or "state" of transfiguration supervenes; but, in each case, this "state" is associated with oppositely directed tensors —tensors woven of a multitude of vectors. By *transfiguration*, I mean: the genesis of a radically new scheme of structures which are totally at variance with the scheme whence they arose. In the phase of conceiving, dispersed, unrelated structures are welded into a single structure of hierarchically ordered units. In the phase of dying, a hierarchically composed structure disintegrates into a mere collection of unrelated units. The totality of vectors, each proposing a specific direction of movement with respect to a particular structure, is manifold.

I designate the vectors associated with conceiving and dying as, respectively, the α-set and the ω-set; they are the limits which enclose, so to speak, the morphogenesis of an organism from both its "temporally bound" sides. In each instance, beyond the limits and, indeed, at the limits themselves when they are conceived as transitions, dwell mystery, the arcane and the numinous. These vectors constitute two spaces: α-organismic space and ω-organismic space. Both are spaces of merely virtual equilibrium or, equivalently, virtual disequilibrium. For, at both the nethermost and the uppermost bounds of organismic development, no structure and no aggregation of structures are rigid, immobile, or fixed. Quite the contrary. There is perpetual resolution and dissolution, transmigration and transfiguration: a drama of conception and death which, from both sides, encloses an unfolding process of many subordinate phases, each a virtual arresting of the (temporally evolving) textures of cyclic processes. With respect to the passage into and out of every subphase of the middle phase, a quasi-duplication is effected of the ferment characteristic of the morphologically but oppositely directed α- and ω-limits.

More specifically to characterize organismic morphology, I must stress the profoundly filamentous makeup of the $\mu o \rho \phi \acute{\eta}$ of a living organism—filaments of varying degrees with respect to delicacy or sturdiness of fibrous composition. At each moment in the development of that organism, or, for that matter, of the entire ecosystem itself when it is construed as an integrated and integral organism, this motile enmeshing scheme of filaments not merely occupies space; it, in fact, *is* a *hyper*space of a peculiarly organic sort. In every phase of morphogenesis, a new assemblage of filaments is constituted. Packed together, overlapping, extending one another, criss-crossing, interwoven, they are capable of forming variegated patterns. Within every pattern may be found regions of variable density, rarefaction, reticulation, granulation, continuity, singularity, heterogeneity, cohesiveness, and fragmentation.

Every specific alignment of the filaments constituting morphologic units determines a kind of choreography; every such arrangement determines the trajectoral–topologic possibilities for each succeeding moment of organismic spatial spread. From the available options, a single option is selected by ἐνέργεια: the power for initiating, organizing, sustaining, consummating, and dissolving morphologic patterns. Via specific bio-molecular structures, information traverses the entire configuration, information which in-forms the organism with μορφή. These structures communicate to each sector of the organism the idiosyncratic role (in structural–functional terms) which it will execute for an immediately succeeding arrangement. In this way, ranges of possibilities, restrictions, eliminations, and constraints are imposed upon the set. Doubtless, stochastically interpreted entropic considerations are relevant in effecting these determinations. Later, I treat this topic under the rubric of a third theme relevant to characterizing bio-space: namely, *the power for organization.*

Throughout morphogenesis, forms of variegated shape, texture, hue, sound, and, indeed, innumerable resonances not yet dreamt of, unfold with organized kaleidoscopy to constitute an ever-shifting morphologic fabric. My observations concerning the overall triphasic character of this process, and its triphasic duplication in each of its subordinate phases, cannot be sufficiently stressed. In addition, I must note the following. In the in-gathering phase—the initial moment of any subordinate phase—a boundary and a center are established; a dialectical relationship between the two is set up. Diverse structures are imprinted which inexorably come to confluence, and thereby establish the essential integrity of the organism. In the middle phase—the central moment of any subordinate phase—this confluence is converted into a veridical synthesis of its constituent strands, a metabolizing and self-replicating system, which, as relatively autonomous, exhibits its own specialized stages of growth. Finally, in the terminal phase, and indeed in the terminal moment of any subordinate phase, the now integrally joined components of the organism are co-adapted with respect to both intra-organismic activity and the significant transactions of the organism with its circumambient milieu. Amidst this diverse "satisfaction," organisms come to fruition and organisms perish. But they dissolve into fragments which, under a new perspective, constitute overflowings of organic plenitude into a system which is still larger and more inclusive. Now one may discern three singular loci of organismic activity: confluence and integrity, synthesis and autonomy, fruition and perishing. Herein consists the most essential stages of biogenesis.

In general, morphology expresses modes of compresence of the diverse organic structures composing the organism. It indicates termini of the routes traversed by each assemblage of factors as they culminate in a "concrescent" organ. Immeasurably more varied than their analogous physical events, these modes constitute the ground for transformation of physical space, essentially naturalistic but already, in a measure, transcendentally naturalistic, to a still more thoroughgoing transcendentally naturalistic space. A single concrete duration, composed of a multitude of simpler durations, an organism's every organ-component is temporally spread out along some complicated trajectory and is spatially adjacent, in diverse configurations of adjacency, to neighboring organs. As a totality, the variegated compresence of these organic parts is the morphologic (organismic) correlate of physical space.

In my comments on triphasic organismic space, I proposed a principle, dramatically exemplified in the first phase but recapitulated throughout: namely, a principle which governs the complementary process of boundary-genesis and centro-genesis. By this principle, a closed surface forms with respect to each living part of the organism, to the organism as a whole, and to the superorganismic ecosystem. Furthermore, the entire organismic configuration arranges itself with respect to these two nodes: a nodal surface; a nodal point—in effect, boundedness and centeredness. Together, these nodes determine a polarity of tensions. In turn, these tensions determine the morphologic possibilities for that organism. They set in motion the processes which morphogenetically engender each particular morphologic option.

In this bipolarity, through interaction of these nodal points, an organic surface originates both proto-structural and frankly structural filaments which stretch both outward into its circumambient milieu and inward toward its center. Later, these filaments become associated with sensitivities to both intra-organismic and extra-organismic activity. The assemblage of these sensitivities eventuates in the phenomenon of consciousness. Indeed, the boundary of any organism differentiates itself into primordia of what will become sensory receptors, central nervous system, peripheral nervous system, sympathetic nervous system, and para-sympathetic nervous system. Taken together, the last three systems mediate the stimuli which arise both from within the organism and from without it. Such boundary phenomena are associated with the organism under the perspective of naturalism. On the other hand, the organism's "center" originates its own scheme of filaments, an ethereal filamentarity, which stretches non-naturalistically toward processes of organismic activity inaccessible to observation. By contrast with the former naturalistic mode, I designate this mode of filament origination *transcendental*.

The resonances affiliated with such centro-genetically determined filamentarity are primordia of the Unconscious. As such, filamentary strands comprise two kinds: those which sink deeply into the infrapersonal, and those which sink deeply into the suprapersonal. Associated with each kind are loci of activity which in more complex organisms germinate archetypes—those of sheer physicality, and those of (ethereal) spirituality. For the "inwardness" of the center stretches toward a beyond: the very depths of the Unconscious. In contrast, the outwardness of the boundary constitutes the person a mosaic, a symbol, indeed a symbolic orchestration which, correctly deciphered, points toward his inner persono-dynamics. By these very dynamics, the organism, a mere living body, is also enabled to touch the outermost reaches of the cosmos. Thereby it constitutes itself the locus wherein the exterior cosmos articulates itself in self-conscious disclosure.

In complementary fashion, the center, in its inward stretching, "touches" the interior, transcendental cosmos. Under this perspective, every organism is the locus wherein the numinous articulates its own subtle rhythms. In principle, the exterior cosmos is an emanation of non-being. Correlatively, the interior cosmos is an emanation of pure being. Indeed, in the most primeval organisms, a kind of proto-dialectic is set up between the primordia of the Unconscious and consciousness. Still more complex, a larger dialectic between non-being and pure being unfolds as mirroring the lesser dialectic.

In sum, both parity and complementarity hold between boundary and center. The former participates in the transcendentality of the latter; the latter partakes of the naturality of the former. Each mode conditions and limits the other. Together, they determine the complex reticulations which spread over the organism, reticulations which evolve the special structures by which it acquires powers for both metabolism and replication. Throughout these subordinate phases of morphogenesis, a *meta*morphosis occurs in which the different modalities of morphofunctional being manifest themselves. Within his own unfolding metamorphoses, embryologic and post-natal, the human person germinates. And as he grows, he actualizes his consummate powers for spiritual existence. This morphogenetic process may be studied cinematographically. In the hastening and slowing of the "images" of morphogenesis, the inner relations between morphologic fixity and morphologic flexibility are disclosed. Herein is revealed the fact that every topologic distribution is responsible for a succeeding topologic distribution. Beyond that, in every subphase of morphogenesis, the processes of both conceiving and dying are renewed, and their special characteristics recapitulated.

(c) Interwoven Functions

Composed of various kinds of "packing," the metabolic–replicatory systems initiate different sorts of entwining polymers: e.g., the polypeptide polymers of amino acids, the polynucleotides of monomers analogous to amino acids. In the first case, the twisting polymers issue in diverse proteins, the basis for metabolism. In the second case, the twisting polymers issue in nucleic acids, the basis for replication. Each "packing," whether rarefied or condensed, and the resonances associated with it—resonances which are related to the pervasiveness of the resonating benzene ring—determine a finite number of possible unfoldings, always subject, of course, to constraints imposed by the specific kinds of "packing" involved. Each state of morphogenesis is associated with a distinct species of "packing."

The three primary phases of morphogenesis, and all subordinate phases (each itself triphasic) of the intermediate phase—phases which mediate the processes of conceiving and dying—duplicate by analogy the stages, later to be set forth, of biogenesis itself, stages which correspond to the physiogenetic stages previously discussed. For this reason, biogenesis begins with boundary formation, integrity, and centeredness; it passes into replication and metabolism; it culminates in co-adaptation, true communication, and, in the end, human speech. In the last in-

stance, there is a transition from the individual to the collectivity: radical solitariness gives way to radical participation. Elaborating upon its basic architecture
in various ways, assemblage, conjugation, and transformation are, as for physiogenesis, also implicated in biogenesis, and brought to fruition in personogenesis.

From these reflections, the following considerations flow. Organismic morphology is the study of two primary topics: the contemporaneous ramifyings throughout the organism of structures, objects, events, processes, activities, energies, and
functions; and the topology of the pathways of morphogenesis—i.e., of organismic
trajectories "projected" onto a spatial frame from the organism's temporally interwoven cycles. In this (double) sense, biologic morphology is the theory of
both bio-spatial structure and bio-temporal structure, and the various exemplifications of that theory. More precisely, it treats organismic structure with respect to
its "being" in every phase of its development, and it treats the structure of the
becoming of the organism throughout its life history. According to this theory,
a motile web of migratory possibilities characterizes the organism. Certain aggregations of pathways may atrophy; other aggregations may, in response, develop
compensatory hypertrophies. The entire scheme is a structural–functional complex. No element may be separated from any other element. A principle of over-
determination reigns throughout; and this principle holds with respect to both
structures and functions.

From the standpoint of the former, certain structures share similar or identical
functions. They may either duplicate these functions, or, at least, acquire the capacity for compensatorily evolving a function should one structure atrophy or become inoperative. In this contingency, the relevant structure will (compensatorily)
hypertrophy. Structural interchangeability is deeply embedded in organismic activity. For example, differential and migratory foci for acquiring identical functions are part of the protective, immunologic system. In more advanced organisms,
a special but mobile region assumes this protective role: the reticulo-endothelial
system. In less advanced organisms, boundary-cum-external reticulatory pattern
and center-cum-transcendental reticulatory pattern assume this role. This boundary
is associated with external time; it coordinates the experience of time as a unified
manifold. Alternatively, the center is associated with internal time; it coordinates
time as an integration of the interiorly interwoven cyclic processes. In addition,
the membrane is eventually organized into a texture of sensitivity differentials,
all initially associated with electric potential gradients which vary from one point
of the membrane to another. In both instances, with respect to time perception
and sensory perception, certain functions not only migrate, so to speak, to other
structures. Should a given function be destroyed, another function will assume
compensatory status and, in effect, combine in a single activity a double role.

The latter consideration leads to my second comment on the principle of overcompensation. Analogously to structures, functions themselves are systematically
ambiguous. Overcompensation applies to them as well. Surely, functions are imbued with a power to diversify themselves in response to the dissolution of other

functions, becoming, in effect, substitutive functions. A doubly overcompensatory principle is operative: that with respect to structures, and their mutual replacements; that with respect to functions, and their mutual replacements. It is as though both structure and function alike are endowed with a capacity to migrate. Should one structural–functional locus be destroyed, another will arise. Hence, organismic morphology can be expressed in terms of a system of reciprocally interdependent structure–function arrangements, and the pathways over which "migrations" will occur. The organism as a whole is a sphere of potentialities for diverse structure–function differentiations.

This primordial morphologic characteristic has, as its ground, the fundamental "frame" of the organism as a scheme of motile fibers—fibers which are enmeshing, intercoiled, involuted, or convoluted polymeric arrangements of protein, nucleic acid, lipid, and carbohydrate. This multitude of patterns is woven into cellular aggregates, differentiated tissues, diverse organs, and systems of organs: a hierarchy of subordination and superordination. Floating within an ionized aqueous solution, this organismic complex is saturated with the agents by which it may continually be re-equilibrated, in ever new design. A motile complex of fibers in perpetual fibrillation, the most diverse patterns of integration, coordination, and co-adaptation are exemplified by organismic morphology. Naturally, the possible motions involved in these patterns is immensely complex: vibratory, rotatory, translational—diverse rhythms orchestrated to manifold cyclic processes.

In my three-dimensional representation of the bio-coordinate system of the organism, I must convert my original diagram, namely

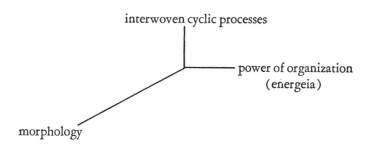

into a new form, which involves (in three-dimensional bio-space) the hemispheric

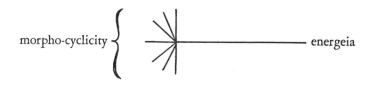

In the latter diagram, the hemispheric portion of the above diagram, namely

represents an intrinsic merging of morphology and cyclicity; the distinction between what had been construed as two dimensions is now obliterated. In the event-coordinate system, the analogue to the biological realm is the spatio-temporal continuum understood as a single, integral manifold.

To summarize: by the relevant collisions, interlockings, interfacial tensions, impingements, and collusions, those constraints are engendered by which novel, mutant patterns of morphology emerge. Fibrous, laminated, strand-like, lattice structures involving both deformations and conformations of myriad kinds constitute these patterns. To guarantee the integrity, and to set limits to the possibilities, of either morphology or morphogenesis, numerous specific factors must replicate themselves over the widest imaginable range of life, from organism to organism. These factors include such ingredients as boundaries, nuclei, reticula, metabolites, replication templates, antigen–antibody systems, and myofibrils, and indeed numberless other components. In their collective activity, these components maintain organismic integrity. They transmit the information which in-forms it with μορφή, determines its contours, protects it from dissolution, and sets in motion its unfolding stages—in a word, preserves its vitality. In sum, they bind together its manifold structures and functions as a fabric of trembling coherence: pulsating, motile, rhythmic.

NOTES

1. *The Magic Mountain*, p. 104.
2. Lewis Thomas, *The Lives of a Cell* (New York: Viking, 1974), p. 5.
3. Ibid.
4. Ibid., pp. 18, 65.
5. Andrew, *Symphony of Life*, pp. 212, 223. See also Lockland, *Grow or Die*, p. 18; and Hans Jonas, *The Phenomenon of Life: Toward a Philosophical Biology* (New York: Harper & Row, 1966), p. 3. The discussion here interweaves material from these three sources.
6. Jonas, *Phenomenon of Life*, p. 98; emphasis deleted.
7. Alister Hardy, *The Living Stream* (Cleveland & New York: World, 1968), p. 30.
8. Alfred North Whitehead, *Modes of Thought* (New York: The Free Press, 1966), chap. 8.
9. See the discussion in Roland Fischer, "The Biological Fabric of Time," *Inter-

disciplinary Perspectives of Time, Annals of the New York Academy of Sciences, 138 (1967); see also Roland Fischer, "Biological Time," in *The Voices of Time*, ed. J. T. Fraser(New York: Braziller, 1966), pp. 357–82.

10. Shakespeare, Sonnet 19.

11. Shakespeare, Sonnet 55.

12. Fischer, "Biological Fabric of Time," 452.

13. See the discussion in Fischer, "Biological Time," p. 368.

14. See the discussion of different modes of time by Roman Ingarden, *Time and Modes of Being*, trans. Helen R. Michejda (Springfield, Ill.: Charles C. Thomas, 1964).

15. See the discussion in Friedrich Kümmel, "Time as Succession and the Problem of Duration," in *Voices of Time*, ed. Fraser, pp. 38, 44.

16. *Hegel's* PHILOSOPHY OF NATURE, trans. A. V. Miller (Oxford: Clarendon, 1970), p. 377.

17. Ibid.

6

GROUNDING THE ORGANISM

PREAMBLE

Now I treat the organization of biologic matter as the substantive ground for life. Previously, I dealt with bio-space and bio-time, the form of this ground. An intricate network of trajectories and interwoven cyclic processes, the integral form of bio-space–time inherits but only partly conforms to the tedium and the monotony of mere physical spatio-temporal complexes, transmitting these structures to the substance of living creatures. The essential property and primordial condition for the emergence of metabolizing matter is its power for shaping a self-identity amidst the changing configurations of its material components. Migrating back and forth, and endlessly colliding, through their impacts, these constituents distribute among themselves Imagos of their intensities and their solidarity. The resultant dynamic form of the overall motions, the form of restlessness, is associated with this power. Hence, perduring oppositional factors, expressed on the metabolic level by the forces of catabolism and anabolism, dialectically interplay to constitute the identities of all living creatures.

Within the human body, a new essence is layered upon the evanescing and crystalline essences hitherto set forth: namely, man's *fermenting* essence. From within a proto-personal perspective, one may now accordingly speak of man's triadic essence. Subsequently, as I pass toward the veridical spiritual being of man, new essences will be added. Then, I conceptualize his symbolizing, ethereal, and ineffable essences, and to these add both the privative essence of non-being and the plenitudinous essence of pure being. Hence, in later books I shall refer to the orchestrated laminae of what, in effect, is the person's *octa*dic essence.

Organismic matter is an activity of ferment. It is matter self-sustaining, self-integrating, and self-unifying. On whatever level of organizational complexity, matter is endowed with the power of self-affirmation. Immanently intentional, biologic creatures are, however latently, primordially self-concerned. By its own choices and acts, the organism, no matter how primitive, is empowered to decide issues regarding its own fate. Between stimulus and response, a gap lies,

often minuscule but at times lengthy. From this gap, decision emerges. Determining the limits within which it may spontaneously range from one material state to another, the organism never relinquishes its self-identity; it is thoroughly imbued with dynamic and purposeful form, form which is spontaneous, reflexive, intentional, and free. Life is a process of emergence, emergence amidst risk, risk amidst a dialectical relationship between solitude and community. In ineluctable passage from dwelling in its own interiority to dwelling in its circumambient organismic milieu, every organism engages the cosmos in its quest for concerned relatedness in co-adaptation: freedom, the zest for individuality, self-transcendence—though immanently, these are its primordial characteristics.

Discerning the increment between the *here-now* and the *there-then*, the organism *loco*motes itself from a state of *e*motionality to a state of *com*motionality. Originating from a displaceable center of rhythms, the primordial motions of its being, every living creature so associates itself with other living creatures that new motions derive from new contacts. Throughout, there is a quest for rootedness, for security in its grounding rhythms. Yet every organism must also *re*locate itself within the larger ecosystem. It must establish new dwellings for itself, dwellings which will enable it to gratify its needs and to exercise its powers. In this process, it conserves (in the sense of maintaining its own security) its indigenous energies, and so it cautiously moves from locale to locale. Nonetheless, depending upon the intensity of feeling which it is capable of experiencing, every organism, in this passage from one dwelling to another, though conserving its *economy*, experiences zest and ecstasy, in a manner appropriate both to the complexity and to the unity of its organization.

Motion not only occurs in the interstices between organisms; it also occurs within the organisms themselves. All organisms are bounded. Within their boundaries, processes spontaneously evolve. Numberless experiments with differing arrangements of these processes may be tried. Such experimentation occurs freely and securely. The semi-permeable boundary controls energy flow, supply, loss, dissipation. By affording resistance between intra-organismic contents and the world about, the boundary permits increasingly complicated organizations to evolve within its confines. At the same time, as the organ of contact which constantly extends itself into the environment, the boundary, owing both to its motility and to its sensitivity, is also the organ of sense and recipiency. Impulses are transmitted throughout it, around it, and within it. The manner, direction, and intensity of their flow determines what new organizational structures will unfold.

The concept of boundary is essentially naturalistic. Transcendentally speaking, the organism is also centered. Centered in and on itself, it is reflexively turned toward its own ever-deepening, non-naturalistically construed labyrinthine interiority—the non-specifiable locus of all emotionality, hence, of locomotion and, ultimately, of commotion. Just as boundaries complicatedly criss-cross a naturalistically conceived milieu, so centers themselves are internally interconnected in transcendental criss-crossings which complement those of the naturalistic variety. Accordingly, "influences" constantly flow between complementary sets of patterns: naturalistic boundaries, transcendental centers. In effect, the center is the proto-spiritual locus of organismic activity. From it proceed those supra-morphologic channels which are transfigured, back and forth, into the morphologic reticula which spread inward and outward from the boundary.

The former mediate empathic-like influences; the latter, natural influences.

This transcendental center is the *un*conscious source of growing awareness. An infinite abyss of possibilities, it is, within a naturalistic perspective, a void. From a spiritual point of view, it is eminently full. Alone among organisms, man is empowered to search this labyrinth. By the *charisma* of its hidden recesses, which pervade and dimly haunt his being, man is led on and on, searching ever-new depths, the concealed chambers of his own intricate essentiality. Emanating from this center are numberless resonances. By sensing his way among them, man balances his diverse parts and equilibrates himself *trans*-metabolically. Likewise, every organism implicitly yearns to draw *its* proto-spiritual sustenance by analogous searching.

When I write here of organismic "freedom," "yearning," "deciding," and indeed in my use of all such anthropomorphic designation, I mean such terms to be understood as referring to *Anlage*, germinating matrices, for phenomena which come to fruition only in man. To proceed: since, by my previous hypothesis, all organismic centers are to be construed as transcendentally connected so that among them I conceive to flow finely nuanced non-naturalistic rhythms, all living beings including persons, I shall further propose, collectively yearn to fill themselves with these rhythms. It is as though all nature were enveloped by transcendental reverberations, reverberations which *trans*-organismically ground the spiritual existence of its every creature.

A · ENERGEIA AND BIOGENESIS

In my preceding chapter, I treated biologic time in partial abstraction from biologic space and biologic matter. There, I conceptualized bio-time as a system of interwoven cyclic processes, processes which jointly constitute the internal self-directedness of an organism as it thrusts itself toward the newly impending stages of its being. Temporally considered, organismic being ceaselessly reconstitutes itself; it both renews and reaffirms its own power for continuing to be. Moreover, I treated biologic space in partial abstraction from biologic time and biologic matter, and conceptualized bio-space as a set of intricate morphological relations —relations which (internally) bind the parts of an organism into mutual compresence and (externally) bind the entirety into compresence with all that is not itself. Indeed, the relational pattern constitutive of the organism, a pattern to which it (dynamically) relates itself, is complementary to the relatedness of the organism to all that is other than itself, i.e., its circumambient milieu. Having sketched the complicated dialectics between cyclicity and morphology, I must now treat biologic matter: what such matter is in and for itself, and what it is in its interwovenness—ultimately, its unity with biologic space and biologic time. To this final topic in the characterizing of the bio-coordinate system, preparatory to treating seriatim the unfolding phases of biogenesis, I now turn. As throughout my account of the infrapersonal rhythms of human existence, my concern is to deal only with such biologic themes as bear directly upon human ontology.

(a) Organismic Ferment

The stuff of life is matter bounded and centered. It is a dialectical interplay between boundary and center, metabolizing matter and self-replicating matter, and co-adaptation of the constituents of an organism both inter se and inter alia. In my examination of (mere) physical matter, I introduced the notion of rhythmic activity. The biological powers just enumerated (i.e., powers for achieving boundedness and centeredness, powers for achieving metabolism and replication, powers for achieving co-adaptation) are associated with a particular kind of rhythmic activity: namely, that kind the essential identity of which consists in the preservation, amidst variations and transformations of both its living and its non-living components, of a certain dynamic form. Changing matter, constant form! I contrast this sort of activity with that which involves, for non-living matter, the preservation of material ingredients amidst variations and transformations of *their* form: designs, arrangements, and patterns which they exhibit. Changing form, or states of matter, constant matter! Naturally, this distinction between form and matter is hardly absolute. Nor, given the dependence of one upon the other, may quite so sharp a demarcation be made between nature alive and nature lifeless. For the difference between these modes of natural existence is, essentially, one of emphasis. What is immediately required, therefore, is a statement concerning the specific senses in which I am now using the locutions *form* and *matter* in treating the "stuff" of living organisms.

With respect to its physically material makeup, the *material* identity of an organism is even more problematic than that of a non-living event. Surely, in both instances, there are perpetually shifting constituents which traverse the border of an entity—constituents which pass from interior to exterior and from exterior to interior, and constituents which circulate about within the confines of that entity. However, with respect to the living entity, there is a significantly diminished retention of material parts. Retention of a specific and identifiable content of "particles" is not only irrelevant to the identity preservation of the organism. But, to a degree, such retention *is* relevant, if not essential, for (physical) event identity. For living matter, the very opposite circumstance holds. *Non*-retention of numerous such particles is a necessary condition for organismic identity. Beyond this circumstance, active migration of "material" parts back and forth through a membrane is requisite for continuance of that very identity. This is not to suggest that certain material configurations do not remain relatively constant, with respect to their content, vis-à-vis the content of the organism in which they are embedded. But if *these* configurations themselves are living, then the same species of migration to which I have referred is also operative here—though now it is as if the organism itself had acquired the status of circumambient milieu for the indicated configurations.

The living organism is an activity of restlessness without cease. The very continuity of its life depends upon such flow, inflow and outflow, as will maintain this restlessness, indeed as will increase rather than diminish it. Yet it is no mere random restlessness to which I allude. On the contrary, it is restlessness suffused with purpose, directed restlessness, and, indeed, restlessness directed from within by the dynamism of its own ferment. It is in-formed restlessness, restlessness pervaded by a "form" which is self-propagated from moment to moment of its own formation. For it is a *form* which is dynamic: at times self-*trans*forming, always persistent and self-perpetuating. And it is a form which organizes the information which resides within the organism, for the purpose of transmitting that information through each of its unfolding phases—information, indeed, whatever its source, which conditions the very possibility for the preserving of a (variable) form amidst ferment and restlessness. By this in-formation, the organism perdures in its own self-identity. It both affirms and reiterates its own organismic character. But unlike the form of an oscillating wave propagated with distinctive unity, history, and destiny—and, in this sense, a dynamic form—the form of life is not derivable from, or contained within, more elementary events the mutual interplay of which constitutes that form. Organismic form is a configuration which *itself* constitutes the organic reality within which crystallize, as derivates, certain relatively enduring structures, processes, and other activities, enduring, surely, over the whole range of types of occurrence hitherto enumerated.

In my proposal, organismic activity pertains to "matter" construed as self-sustaining, self-integrating, and self-unifying. Such self-action is dependent upon at least two factors. On the one hand, the reciprocal interdependencies of an organism's components so potentiate one another that synergism mounts, eventuating in the mobilization of that organism's full resources. On the other, the very dynamism which constitutes the organism's "in and for itself" character guarantees continuance of its directed activity: an orientation toward self-perpetuation; an orientation toward (as I later note) perpetuation of neighboring organisms. By this dynamism, organismic activity is self-concerned; and self-concern involves the experience, on whatever level of awareness, of interior freedom, a possibility for choice. Each option exercised places the organism in a distinct "state" of materiality. By my previous argument, its form remains invariant. But, as invariant, the form *is* (in contradistinction to physical events) the very substance of life. Through its intrinsic capacity, living form mediates material transitions. Moreover, (substantial) form is a power for holding into unity the diverse elements of organismic ferment preparatory to its passage into ever-new states.

As power, living form is associated with a treble intentionality. First, it enables the organism to be *retentive*. Every organism stretches back toward its own past. Gathering the perishing fragments into coherent memory, the organism preserves its historicity. Secondly, living form enables the organism to be *protensive*. For every organism pro-tends. Stretching forward into its future, it guarantees its own self-preservation, entertaining options the realization of which lies, so to speak, in the future. When I say "entertains options," I mean, as in the French, *entretenir*, that the organism holds together its possible choices as a manifold to be surveyed. From this pattern, it extracts whatever might perpetuate its integrity. Finally, the organism is *attentive*. Every organism stretches inwardly toward itself to comprehend its own contemporaneous being; and every organism stretches outwardly toward the world to comprehend the world's being with respect to itself.

By this third aspect of intentionality, the organism, in effect, *doubles* intentionality. It both superimposes and duplicates itself upon all modes of intentionality. A double Imago is thereby framed: inner world reflexively in relation to itself, outer world reflexively in relation to inner world. Indeed, every aspect of intentionality is associated with a reflexive character. In each case, the organism mirrors to itself some pattern related to its own existence—past, present, future. Always accompanying its acts of self-stretching, whether forward, inward, backward, or outward, is an Imago of that toward which it stretches—that which, albeit under one perspective, is its *own* substance, is, from another point of view, distinct from and wholly other to itself.

The organismic ferment is a dynamic and purposive form. Spontaneous and free, it is multiply intentional and, as such, pervasively reflexive. Given these properties, it follows that living matter is essentially dipolar. By this I mean: life is always in the process of emergence; and emergence is associated with an identity which, to be maintained, must be reasserted from instant to instant—and reasserted in such wise as to bring the organism into double relatedness to its milieu. On the one hand, the organism is isolated and solitary. It lives in risk; it confronts the imminence of annihilation; it experiences its aloneness in anxiety and in terror. On the other, the organism is empathically united to, and *en rapport* with, its milieu. From this point of view, it experiences itself as fulfilled, and alternately tranquil and ecstatic. Between aloneness and relatedness, a dialectic prevails. Now the organism individuates itself. It acquires a self. By this acquisition, the organism develops an ever-heightening awareness of the precariousness of its own existence. It yearns for relationship and community. Yet it is unwilling to sacrifice its solitariness. Only when effectively interwoven with communality may the organism's (constructive) solitude prevail. Whereas relatedness nurtures and, indeed, conditions its very self-sufficiency, aloneness confers upon the organism its strength, its autonomy, and its freedom. When it turns in upon itself, the French adage is realized: *reculer pour mieux sauter*.

My concern is not yet with organismic freedom: its vicissitudes, its fulfillments, its renunciations. This topic will recur in the context of my account of the person qua person. Here alone, on the level of human rhythms, may veridical freedom be consummated. On the other hand, I do stress that, given an intrinsic organismic dipolarity, the germ of freedom is planted. Dwelling with and rooted in its own past, *living* matter begins to aspire toward future growth. In so doing, it recaptures that past. Thus cognizant, however primordially, of an *owning* of past and future, the organism immensely extends the horizons of its present, and fills that present with vibrance.

As it evolves toward sentient clarity, the organism enters into relationship with non-being. Confronting the absolute negation of existence (which though, in a manner of speaking, "is" external to it), the organism inexorably "encloses" non-being as residing at the core of its own existence. In this stretching back toward its past, an origination from the very dust whence matter itself arose, the organism must inexorably take its stand before death. It takes that stand in proto-personal fear and trembling—yet resolutely and perforce unswervingly. But, at the very instant at which it encounters privation of being, every organism yearns for and, accordingly, stretches toward future consummation in the fullness of being. For the organism is forever compelled to touch the very ground of its own being as, I must now add, a *double* ground: non-being and pure being in tension. However dim its awareness, this living ferment, the organism, is characteristically suspended between its apprehensions of both termini of being. It must doubly comport itself; and in this double relatedness, its emotionality manifests itself. Arising from the ground of organismic being, *e-motion* is associated with a *moving out* from that ground into individuation. Such spontaneity and risk constitute the awesomeness of living existence.

This organismic ferment is not only (dialectically) poised between the two limits of being; it is also suspended between its temporal horizons, conception and death. For it is both a questing after its origins and a yearning for its destiny. Hovering in diverse states of excitation, every organism is constantly stirred by the affects which arise within it but which direct themselves toward what lies without it. Though apart from the organism, this compresent milieu is nevertheless incorporated within it. Whether the organism accepts the milieu or rejects it, the milieu ineluctably dwells within the organism. Every organism must constantly differentiate itself, in its aboriginal dynamism, from that which is *other* than itself—yet which, though other, is incorporated within it as presences which are absorbed, assimilated, perhaps even perished, but, nonetheless, viable and operative. In this sense, the self must again be construed as pre-eminently a locus of *self*-concern.

(b) Organismic Locomotion

As I have said, the organism is a restlessness without cease. Throughout its life span, it is a perpetual tension between appetition directed toward world contact and appetition directed toward self-contact. In this process, the organism integrates the world as a coordinated, hence, secure, domain—a domain which it may inhabit without trepidation. At the same time, it integrates itself as an ordered manifold, and this integration is achieved not only for itself, but, beyond that, *for the world*. Indeed, germinating within the organism, though coming to fruition only as the organism is transmuted into a person, is a specific and irreducible power of giving. By this power, I mean a disinterested giving of self to other, giving in trust, care, concern, commitment—ultimately, a searching for its own sake. Prefigured in mammalian life, and consummated in the mature person, this tendency is primordially rooted in the organism itself—and this rootedness extends backward toward the most primitive stages of organismic development.

What is the mechanism by which, through coalescencing elementary powers, this specifically human power, though possessing its organismic proto-type, is potentiated first into potential existence, then into self-actualization? By its very character as a ferment bounded and centered, metabolizing, and woven of co-adapted organic parts, the organism develops vis-à-vis its nurturing milieu, standing over and against that milieu. Counterposed to milieu even while juxtaposed to it, the organism distances itself from the components of that milieu. In ceaseless opposition to milieu, despite necessary apposition, its needs may be gratified only "across" the spatial increments and through the temporal increments entailed by this distancing. Thereby, it gives itself "room" for mobility. Freely moving about within constraints vastly less coercive than those imposed on physical matter, it may discern a present which is there but not here, a future which though *not yet* can nonetheless become a now. It evolves the power to convert a *not-yet-there* into a *here–now*. For, by its own self-individuation, the organism acquires a sense, however primeval, of space and time.

Once this distinction between space and time is made, the organism must, correlatively, acquire capacity for delayed gratification. By this acquisition, an (inner) time sense is wedded to an unfolding emotional life, and a sense of (outer) space is joined to the sensations and kinesthesias associated with a *self-extending-itself* into the world. In short, the organism is a *mobile* ferment. In moving about, it moves from its own center. E-motions which had been infolded upon and into one another now unfold and press for expression. They flow toward the "periphery" of the organism—i.e., its contact with the world with respect to which need-gratification is delayed. In the context of this delay arises the miracle of giving. Mere appetition is associated with immediate energy utilization. But when it is alone, and at a distance from other entities, the organism accumulates surplus energies from its metabolic activity; these surplus energies allow for locomotion. Naturally, a locomotive capacity is indigenous to the animal. Yet, even for the plant, which gains immediate sustenance and reassurance from minerals already located in regions immediately adjacent to its roots, a tension prevails throughout —a straining, however minimal, for locomotion toward more nutritious materials.

Accordingly, superimposed on internal vegetative activity is external action. For higher animals, internal vegetative activity is the primordium of the sympathetic nervous system. But typical for the animal, vital action is necessarily mediated by motion, motion through which the animal redeems its energy expenditures. And the more mobile the nutriment, the greater the skills and the competencies the animal must evolve. Ever in quest of an elusive and not-yet-present prey, it must be able to dart about, to give chase. So to act, the animal must deploy its resources with utmost economy. Yet, however alert, and wakeful, it must, again and again, return to dormancy. It needs sleep; then, perchance, it dreams. In the darkness of its unconscious, in its primeval awareness and its fragmented sensitivities, it must once again touch its own roots and origins and thereby renew its vitality. Ever restless, organismic being, when consummated, is passionate being. As its passions grow, it acquires greater scope for action. It risks greater hazards, yet it discerns more ample opportunity. Now a more pronounced self is set over and against a more pronounced world. Indeed, by pro-nounced, I mean *pre-named*: a domain, self, or world, which is localized, demarcated, discriminated, specified.

Nevertheless, I must not cease to stress, not only is organic nutriment required, but, as significantly, nutritious reassurance! Lest energies be needlessly dissipated, anxiety must be assuaged. In turn, the need for reassurance gives birth to tenderness in the recipiency of security, the tenderness of giving. Yet tenderness is always reciprocal. Tender contacts are with organisms which, likewise, need tenderness. Growing from need and the very solitariness of the organism is the germ of mutuality!

This power of giving, a reciprocity of tenderness and reassurance, is grounded in the essence of organismic activity. As I stated earlier, the organism stands in double relatedness: it is in and for itself—solitary, isolated, yet individuated; it is in communal relatedness to another. From *its* point of view, *both* modes of relatedness imply mutuality: i.e., relationships from the point of view of the other relatum as well; hence, the possibility of being *for another*. The first mode of (reflexive) relatedness is associated with need, appetition, self-gratification, desire. And out of need, I repeat, evolves a new power. Thus, the second mode of (symmetric and transitive) relatedness is associated with giving—hence with interest and tenderness.

Complementarity of need and giving is constitutive of organismic activity. Yet such activity comes to fruition only when the organism is so transfigured that it enters the sphere of the personal—and, beyond that, of the interpersonal and the communal. But the primordium of this power lies in the organism itself. Like sociality, the power derives from the nurtural situation. Through attachment to another—symbiosis, if you will, or the need to gratify need—is engendered an autonomous power. Liberated from bondage to bare need, and requiring only organismic isolation, this power itself is based upon a new need: the need to avoid loneliness, a consequent dread of experiencing loneliness. Arising from conditions inherent in nurtural attachment are dread and the need to avoid it. In turn, nurtural attachment arises from conditions inherent in the very isolation of organismic activity.

To characterize this activity, I take as my key theme the idea of motion.[1] The verb "to move" is etymologically akin both to the Greek ἀμεύσασθαι, meaning "to become displaced" or "to pass beyond," and to the Sanskrit *mívati*, "he displaces," and *kāmamūtas*, "impelled by desire." First, I distinguish three sorts of motion, each relevant for specifying the way in which an organism, by its inner momentum—a kind of primordial urge—is impelled toward self-displacement.

Next, I set forth the topography, or structural interrelations, of these interwoven phases. Indeed, "topography" derives from τόπος and γράφειν, which together mean "to inscribe (the structure of) the place." Then, I discuss their dynamics— the very word derives from δύναμις and δυναμικός, which mean, respectively, "strength" and "possessing power." I treat both the nature and the implications of this strength. Finally, I examine the economy of their organization. Here, economy is related to the Greek οἶκος, meaning "dwelling place," νέμειν, meaning "distribution or management," and νόμος, meaning "law" or "custom." Hence, by economics of the organism, I shall mean the laws which regulate both the distribution of the regions of the dwelling place of that organism and the ways in which its habitat is managed. And, in general, topography, dynamics, and economy are three interrelated perspectives on organismic motion. They are heuristic categories for clarifying organismic activity.

With respect to all motion, I postulate three phases: an intermediate phase of loco-motion, in which is contained displacement, a passing beyond, and a being impelled by desire; next, the two phases mediated by locomotion. With respect to the latter, I distinguish a phase of origination, the *terminus a quo* of all motion, which I designate e-motion. Then I specify a phase of culmination or termination, the *terminus ad quem* of all motion, which I designate com-motion.

Regarding the middle phase: organismic locomotion is suffused with purposiveness, the power to move toward another entity or away from another entity, or to linger in a state of indecision. In each instance, motion arises from a specific locus wherein movement is initiated. In the case of plants, this locus is normally fixed by contingency. There is minimal need or possibility for the plant to relocate itself. In the case of animals, the locus is usually mobile. An animal is normally empowered to move the very locus whence springs its own locomotive conduct. For organisms in general, the locus may, in varying degrees, be fixed or mobile; its fixity, momentary, transitory, or durable. With respect to this region of *relative* permanence or motility, many types of locomotion may be exemplified, ranging from simple oscillations to intricate patterns of movement. To assert that the optive power of locomotion is of three basic varieties is but crudely to classify these numberless rhythmic possibilities into approachings, withdrawings, and hoverings. For plants, this rough taxonomy can be illustrated by different tropisms. For animals, one may examine amoebae, in the presence of nutriment, as they extend their pseudopods to ingest it or, in the presence of noxious material, as they retract their pseudopods and thicken the adjoining membrane.

In general, the locomotion of every organism is dipolar in character. There is an origin, an initiating ground and source; there is a goal, that with respect to which the organism locates itself or alters its location. Locomotion is the power of stretching backward toward roots and forward toward milieu. In both instances, the organism makes contact. Originating within inanimate matter, indeed in the very sensitivities of certain molecular groupings of one set of macromolecules to certain molecular groupings of another (complementary) set of macromolecules,

this power comes to fruition in man. Man who bears in his being the frailty of
the animal, and, hence, is rooted in non-being! Man who, nonetheless, stands upright, his arms extended toward the heavens, his eyes peering toward the most
distant horizons of the circumambient globe! Man who is empowered to indi-
viduate himself, and even to re-create his own being, extending antennae of vision
and hearing, and perhaps senses beyond the reach of contemporary knowledge,
toward the entire universe! Man who clings now tenaciously, now tenuously and
tentatively, man who adheres to and identifies with the outermost reaches of the
cosmos! Man who in the pulsing rhythms of his communal acts reinstates his
energies and attunes his being to the cosmic rhythms, a profound affinity!

All this is man; all this is prefigured in living proto-human organisms! Alone
among creatures, yet only fulfilling powers already immanent within his non-
human ancestors, man is empowered to frame an Imago of himself in relationship to the world. He alone is empowered reflectively to integrate that Imago with
his own substance. Unique among beings, he thereby transfigures that substance
so that the rhythms of his own ferment are orchestrated again and again, in endlessly novel pattern. Now it becomes evident that organismic activity is, so to
speak, suspended between two termini: a *terminus a quo*—the deeply internal
activity of an originating locus; and a *terminus ad quem*—the irritabilities, sensitivities, and reflections of contact with an incisively articulated milieu. The former,
I designate the organism's emotional life: a moving out from a center, accompanied by agitations ranging from the simple to the refined, from the gross to the
subtly modulated. With respect to the latter, I refer to that toward which the
organism comports itself, and the attendant commotions of its being: the wholly
other which it encounters, all its powers activated as new motions commingle
with indigenous motions. Surely, as these motions commingle, they are woven
together to synthesize still new products.

Profoundly related and intertwined in dialectical play, the indicated phases of
energeia (ἐνέργεια) involve: first, initiation, origination, emotionality; next, locomotion, displacement; and, finally, contact, encounter, "commotionality." Mediating the terminal phases, the middle phase, locomotion, transforms origin into
destiny, then reflects a projected destiny to merge with an *ejected* origin: an endless dialectical process in which destiny *in communitate* is achieved while the
integrity of origin remains intact. Furthermore, the destiny of every organism requires its locomotion toward a center (of contact) which it shares with other
analogously "locomoting" organisms. By this collective movement, all organisms
of a given type intercommunicate; and, in subtle ways, all organisms of all types
intercommunicate. Indeed, every (complex) organism is itself a centering of
its numerous organismic components, each in locomotion. Many origins, many
termini, many displacements intermingle and coalesce, all within each and every
organism.

In consequence, the organism is in itself an intricate system of intercommunication; all organisms, whatever their location within a comprehensive biological

taxonomy, constitute an intricate system of intercommunication. Surely, "the same events are recalled by the rhythms of insects, the long, pulsing runs of birdsong, the descants of whales, the modulated vibrations of a million locusts in migration, the tympani of gorilla breasts, termite heads, drumfish bladders . . . a 'grand canonical ensemble.' . . ."[2] For a great "symphony of life" unfolds, consisting of "intricate and interlacing dimensions of rhythm, strung not on a single thread of time but woven into a multidimensional tapestry."[3] The diverse components of this symphony are themselves living, collaborating creatures: termites, ants, organelles. There is a collective excitation wherein each creature contributes its characteristic value, its idiosyncratic rhythm. Yet, together, all creatures form a vast contrapuntal scheme woven of dissonances and consonances, innumerable elements in mutual consolidation, adaptation, and integration. A great ecosystem is fashioned: each organism, by itself; all organisms, taken conjointly.

(c) Organismic Topography, Dynamics, and Economics

By my earlier proposal, three interrelated perspectives upon organismic activity may be framed: topography, dynamics, economy. With respect to the first, a taxonomy of motions must now be summarily sketched. Later, relevant details will be traced out.

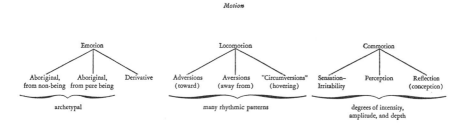

With respect to derivative emotions, it must be observed that there is a transmission from the regions of commotion—a flowing back from encounter—of new rhythms, new vibrations, new resonances. In varying admixtures, these novel factors commingle with and, indeed, may transform the archetypal. Many routes and pathways, and many multiplex combinations of these, exist for transmitting such influences, impacts, confluences, and resonances from one organismic region to another. These patterns of migration establish, perpetuate, and subtly modify the pulsating ferment.

From the standpoint of the dynamics of organismic substance, I must emphasize that the intricacies of structure and process implicated in living activity require that biologic space, time, and matter be conceived as even more integrally and concretely interwoven than are their physical analogues. Far from being representable in the manner of customary axes, the bio-coordinate system must be transposed to, indeed transformed into, a spheroidal type of system. Herein, the three hitherto distinguished dimensions—namely, κύκλος, μορφή, and ἐνέργεια—are absolutely united as a single, unitary, and indiscerptible manifold. In consequence, my previous diagrammatic paradigm should be revised, and replaced (in its two-dimensional analogue) simply by a circle. In this new representation, distinct regions of separate dimensionality may no longer be demarcated. On the contrary, one can, at this stage, only distinguish center, radii, and periphery. I thus diagram this new "space":

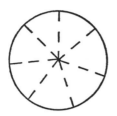

Kyklo–Morpho–Energeia sphere

In this representation, the first factor—namely, the center—corresponds to the rootedness, the emotionality, of organismic activity; and emotionality is associated with internal time, which, in turn, constitutes the *emanata* from non-being and pure being—in both instances, *emanata* of transcendental status. The second factor, the spokes which spread like a fan, constitutes the locomotive activity which radiates toward a surface in contact with another organism. These spokes are, in effect, the means by which the transcendental center irradiates (i.e., *noumenally* illuminates) inter-organismic encounter, translating the sphere of transcendentality into the realm of the naturalistic. Finally, the third factor—namely, the periphery—is to be naturalistically construed as a region of direct contact; it is extensivity, or external space wedded to external time. When, later, I treat the personal space analogue of bio-space, both center and periphery (to cite Eckhardt's image) become as one. Together, they dissolve into pure transcendentality, a strictly noumenal order which manifests itself in the natural symbols of (phenomenal) behavior. Then, truly, the "light in the soul's core overflows into the body, which becomes radiant with it."[4]

I have introduced a mode of representation in which periphery, radii, and center replace my original coordinate system. As I have proposed, the center is to be construed as transcendental, and the periphery as naturalistic. Yet the two comprise a single transcendental–naturalistic complex, a complex which involves diversifications, vicissitudes, and ramifications beyond anything a simplistic representation can suggest. One must not forget that the unfolding stages of biogenesis, each stage itself a kyklo–morpho–energeia sphere, constitute an organism *in passage* from conception to death. Furthermore, though every stage is prefigured in the remaining stages, no stage is nullified by any other stage. Though each stage achieves its consummation in a successor, all stages are mutually compresent. The distinction between the several biogenetic stages is one of logically different moments as well as of historically different phases.

Designating these stages anew, I distinguish *perocentrogenesis*, treating boundary and center; *metabologenesis*, treating the mediating state of metabolism and replication; and *ecogenesis*, treating the terminal stage of co-adaptation. In each instance, well-formed structures, dynamic equilibria, and transitions to more elaborate systems are significant factors. Moreover, the originally abstract categories of assemblage, conjugation, and transformation never cease to be exemplified as still further experientialized. As the concretization occurs, the sphere of kyklo–morpho–energeia must, in effect, be converted to a hypersphere. Into the "co-ordinate" scheme proposed, the interwoven but unfolding moments of biogenesis must be incorporated. Finally, personogenesis itself is prefigured in biogenesis. When I treat that topic in *Metamorphosis*, I shall exhibit, as still a new mode of "spatialization," analogies between trust and "emotion," commitment and "locomotion," searching and "commotion."

Finally, I briefly take up the theme of organismic economy. Certain rules may be discerned which prescribe how the habitat of an organism—hence, the diverse parts of the organism itself—are economically joined together as a coherent organization which functions with maximum efficiency. First, no sharp distinction may be made between habitat and the organism itself. More accurately, a commentary upon the class of possible regions which an organism may inhabit, i.e., by its locomotion *locate* itself, is equivalent to a discussion of the power of impact possessed by that organism. In a word, milieu and organism are intimately interwoven. Hence, the original use of "economy" as pertaining to the management of a dwelling place, and its derivative use as referring to schemes for distributing or assigning orders of priority to scarce resources, is intimately connected to the sense of economy which concerns integrity—namely, the effective concentration of organismic potency. Gathered from diversified data into an integral unity of "self-enjoyment," the organism presents itself—i.e., makes itself a living *presence* and, as such, *gives of itself, as a present, to another*—as a matrix of powers. As, one by one, these powers are actualized, they potentiate one another to shape an even more compactly potent arrangement. So effectively are such powers interwoven that, by their thus intensifying one another, in their mutual actualities, they create (as a "concrescence") an exceedingly efficient organism.

Secondly, the powers thus coordinated constitute a synthesis of contrasting motions. In their diverse phases, these motions culminate, through their mutual potentialities, in the sharp focusing of a power which is effective and integral. By their very cohesiveness, such powers are minimally dispersed and fragmented. With respect to emotion, locomotion, and commotion, there is little diffusion of contrast. On the contrary, in all phases zest and vibrancy prevail. Contrasts are sharply delineated, yet intimately conjoined. The organism is intent on satisfaction and self-enjoyment with respect to its own "concrescence." Intentionally, it draws into a unity its own in-gathered perished data.

Organismic activity is pre-eminently conserving activity. What is conserved are organic resources, energies in various quantities, states, and modes. Only such energy quanta are ejected as will enable an organism's diverse internal processes more effectively to serve its aim at satisfaction. Interplay between counter-entropy and energy conservation undergoes many vicissitudes. But, in every instance, such interplay is so arranged that patterns of equilibria are maintained which are consistent with a continued introduction of novelty. Furthermore, the never-ending oscillations between need-gratification and giving-fulfillment are themselves the means by which an organism attains as its end a unity of effective self-fulfilling action. They are the ways by which dynamic equilibria between contrasting factors are achieved on all levels of biogenesis. With minimal superfluity, the numberless modulations of tranquillity and ecstasy are gathered together. By decision, an organism excludes "the boundless wealth of alternative potentiality."[5] Fusing all data into an "immediacy of self-enjoyment,"[6] it never ceases to yearn for peace woven with zest, and to deploy its (scarce) resources accordingly.

A key supposition underlying the theme of organismic economy is the dual thesis: the experienced world is in the organism; the organism is in the experienced world. From this complex fact, one may deduce the principle: since the world includes the organism in its own composition, the organism enters in its own self-composition. It is immanent within its own being as one of its integral components. Truly, the organism is constitutive of itself. By the processes whereby the organism reflectively articulates, and mirrors to itself, its own modes of relatedness to the world, and thereby achieves its self-identity, that organism is continually in the act of self-reconstitution. Both by origination and by derivation, it acquires its power of existence.

Furthermore, there is mutual compresence of all parts of the organism, as of its milieu, with one another. In their reciprocally interpenetrating presences, these parts are, as a whole, compresent *within* and *to* the total organism. Being one of its own components (and coinciding with it in an overall sense), the organism is compresent with itself. Self-compresence is the very ground for reflexivity; it is the organism's relating to itself as one of its own internalized constituents. Accordingly, the whole is present in the single complex organism; it is present in itself. This self-presence of the organism, which entails a profound sense of its own selfhood, *is* its self-identity. Self-identity presupposes a multiply authentic rootedness in the world. I say "multiply" because the process of internalization which I set forth is a process of indefinitely perpetuated self-incorporation, hence, one of infinite reflexivity.

The self-presence of the organism as one of its own constituents, reintrojected into itself after its self-projection into the world, supplies the momentum for the organism's own *self-thrusting-toward* the world. To cite Whitehead:

> The unity of emotion, which is the unity of the present occasion, is a patterned texture of qualities, always shifting as it is passed into the future. The creative activity aims at preservation of the components and at preservation of intensity. The modifications of pattern, the dismissal into elimination, are in obedience to this aim.[7]

In short, "energetic activity [of physics] is the emotional intensity entertained in life."[8] To this emotional intensity, I add the intensities of locomotion and commotion. By these combined intensities, the organism assigns a structure to the interrelated phases of its motions. It gathers the energies required to sustain its dynamism of self-preservation; it organizes those energies, and reconstitutes that structure. Always it resourcefully obeys the aim of its own self-*re*-creative activity.

B · BOUNDARY AND CENTER

(*a*) The Natural Boundary

For a strict naturalism, every entity—event, organism, person—is a bounded entity. Whether the boundary is transparent, opaque, or translucent, to scrutinize that entity within a thus essentially behavioristic perspective is to encounter it exclusively qua bounded entity. In every initial encounter, one perceives a boundary. At first approach, one (conceptually) assigns a content which one presumes would be revealed (behavioristically) were that boundary to be perforated, or were an instrument to be devised for penetrating to the interior enclosed by the boundary. But again, within this perspective, when the interior itself is inspected, whether its contents are experienced as emptying themselves through porosities within the boundary, or, alternatively, they are "seen through" the boundary, those contents are also disclosed *as* boundary. As such, they must again be construed as enclosing an interior. No matter how an entity is dissected, or which of its regions is opened for examination, the behavioristic encounter is always an encounter of boundaries. Under the perspective of naturalism, one must *postulate* an entity, of whatever kind, as composed of boundaries enfolded within boundaries: an infinite regress of boundaries; a texture all the layers of which are boundaries. Of course, I speak here only of phenomena construed as bare appearances: the mere presentings of entities, in the immediacy of encounter, for perceptual scrutiny.

Nonetheless, whenever the idea of boundary is posed, a conceptual distinction must be made—its very definition requires distinguishing interior with respect to boundary from exterior, its inside and its outside. Inside and outside are distinctions invariably associated with a limit presumed to separate two regions from one another. This supposition is required by this procedure. But the very concept of limit entails an interpretive ambiguity. The question immediately arises regarding whether the limit, as such, truly exists, i.e., can be definitively assigned. Is the limit substantive? Or is it ideal, an abstract notion heuristic for specifying a content which, so to speak, it encloses? If the former, one finds oneself in pursuit of a further limit, a limit to the limit, and so on endlessly. But if the latter, how may the content itself be thought without thinking *its* constitutive limits? For this reason, every entity must be understood, from a naturalistic point of view, to be a matrix of bounded regions, a matrix which is divisible into boundaries from within an indefinite number of perspectives, but a matrix which, on one interpretation, must be regarded as non-real—i.e., a collection of ideal limits. From this standpoint, the entity as, so to speak, *possessing* a content vanishes. But if substantive, there must somewhere (which, being ideal, is no-where) be a non-substantive limit, in effect, a singularity with respect to the substantive continuum which is the entity. By this line of argument, the very notion of boundary as possessing ontologic import vanishes.

Consider, once more, any entity exemplified in such spheres of inquiry as physics, biology, psychology. Meaning "a particular state of existence," "a real thing," "entity" may alternatively be construed as the locus wherein certain activities, processes, or events occur. These occurrences are not merely evanescent or transitory. However brief their durations, they always endure. In lasting, they are durable configurations. Exterior to such configurations, the indicated occurrences cannot be found; interior to it, they may be found. In consequence, the concept of boundary is associated with searching, the questing after specifiable occurrences. Always, and only, within the context of a (consciously) searching comportment may a bounded region be discerned and articulated as such. By this I mean, such a region reveals itself to be as it is, a region of activity of some sort, when the different modalities of searching are so integrated as to bring the searcher into contact with that region. In this context, the latter un-conceals *its* indigenous powers, its status as real, hence, as capable of exerting impact. With respect to the locus of what now is conceived as mutually potentiating powers, boundary must be redefined as, in some sense, a function of those powers. In this respect, the concept of boundary is derivative rather than primary. What I introduced as the initially encountered aspect of a real entity now reveals itself to negate itself as a *real* aspect; it dissolves into a lattice of mathematical forms.

Regarding the boundary as integral to these activities, which, as an elliptical way of speaking, the boundary is said to enclose, opens the way for the conceiving of varieties of substantive boundaries, each a complicated function of substantive activity—a differentiation, so to speak, of that substance, a scheme of structures which endure, pass away, and re-form. With respect, now, to physical entities, the relativity of their boundaries vis-à-vis physically searching comportment can justifiably be presumed. Here the boundary is relative to the horizon of an inquiry and to the schema of theoretical ideas which express the contours of that horizon. Boundaries are construed as engendered in the context of the activity of an *active object* in relation to an active comportment toward that object. And a taxonomy of entities with respect to the kinds of boundaries which they exhibit is immediately created.

Accordingly, one speaks of the boundary of an atom, a molecule, a neutron. But as one approaches, with respect to physical entities, the very large, or, alternatively, the very small, the notion of boundary, even in the relativistic sense, becomes quite fuzzy. Indeed, that usage is applicable only to physical phenomena of middle-range magnitude—i.e., to phenomena which either appear directly to sense or manifest themselves indirectly through instruments conventionally deemed to be acceptable extensions of sense. Again, with respect to the vastly huge, like the very limits of the physical universe, or to the utterly minute, like elementary particles, such notions as boundary, region, interior, and exterior are not readily definable. Nor may these notions be easily entertained. Yet, for general metaphysics and, more relevant to my inquiry, for an ontology of the person, the idea of limit in these senses is indeed significant. It is the person who *sets* the limits with respect to great and small; it is he who claims for himself the powers for limitless searching. When man speculates that the universe might be but a single cell within a vast organism, each tangent to the others at singular nodes scattered lawfully about, and when the physicist informs man that his imaginings are meaningless since physical parameters are uniquely defined for this universe alone, it is man in defiance of the physicist who scoffs. Nor does man desist from pursuing his fantasy along whatever paths it may lead him, and into whatever bizarre paradoxes he may fall. Surely, the idea of boundary, both ultimate boundary and local boundary, is of authentic, indeed momentous, concern for the person. Any metaphysics of the person requires an account of the idea of *personal* limit, the region defining personhood itself within an interpersonal community. And every theoretician who sets for himself the task of articulating the morphology, the dynamics, and the cyclicities of that community wonders about how its destiny may be linked to that of the great abyss of the infrapersonal.

My present discussion of boundary I intend merely as a prelude to a deeper inquiry, which can be conducted only when I shall have passed from a consideration of biological entities, living organisms, to reflections upon the essential traits of persons. There, in the unfolding phases of biogenesis, the idea of boundary first appears as a truly viable issue—though certainly there are intimations of the relevance of boundary considerations even in middle-range physical phenomena. Only when the organism has sufficiently evolved does the idea of boundary emerge as a central theme, a theme which becomes seminally important when the infrapersonal realm is transmuted into personal being. For the boundary of the organism—"where" it is, of "what" it is constituted, and "how" it functions—is truly an issue *for* that organism. In living matter the idea of distance between entity and environment first arises as significant for the perseverance of the entity, and for its growth; and the idea of distance entails, in a non-relativist sense, the idea of boundary. I say "non-relativist," for the boundary of the organism is an identifiable and conceptualizable structure. Certainly, this fact is, in part, true for physical entities as well. But there is no distinctive sense in which this structure, as specifiable, is of concern for physical entities; and concern, in its germinal aspects, first makes itself evident in post-physical and in proto-personal phenomena.

(b) The Transcendental Center

Thus far I have confined myself to a naturalist perspective upon the notion of boundary. But when I refer to boundary as involving a reflexive relationship of the organism to itself—namely, a relationship in which the organism *possesses* a boundary, and the possessing is an issue and a concern for that organism—I imply that woven with a naturalist perspective is the element of transcendentality. As soon as the topic of boundary becomes relevant for an entity, the complementary topic of center becomes equally pertinent. The two notions, boundary and center, cannot be considered separately from one another. A boundary is engendered by a center; correlatively, a center cannot be were there not a bounded region.

I have stressed general philosophic considerations applicable to the concept of boundary, and have indicated that this concept first emerges into full significance when one has reached the level of organismic development. Nevertheless, a generalized theory of boundary, a *perology*, can be developed for general metaphysics. In such a theory, the import of the relationship between naturality and transcendentality would occupy a focal position. But here I confine myself to a special category of boundary—namely, the biologic membrane—as of particular relevance for a philosophic theory of the person. The discipline which treats this category in detail could be designated membranology, a special topic within the more inclusive topic of perology. Such a discipline would deal with such factors as structure, modes of formation, phases of genesis, dynamics, economics, types, and functions of biological membranes. In the context of a theory of organismic evolution, such membranes may be regarded as prototypes of the structures which culminate, for the person, in such specialized organs as the central nervous system, the sympathetic and parasympathetic nervous system, the peripheral nervous system, and the special sensory receptor organs. The biological membrane is the primordial organ of recipiency and sensitivity. Pre-eminently, it mediates, and, indeed, grounds, the very processes which flow between the interior of the organism and its exterior—i.e., its circumambient milieu. Here, I attend only to such organismic properties as those which pertain to the germinating ingredients of naturality and transcendentality as they enmesh, and unfold toward a veridical personogenesis.

Earlier, I referred to the complementarity of boundary and center. By center, with respect to the organism, I now mean that transcendental "point," a singularity, so to speak, in the bio-coordinate system, toward which all parts of the organism are in some sense (later to be specified) oriented, and toward which, should those parts themselves be organisms, in particular, locomotively oriented. Their center is locus of a *spiritual* dynamism which, jointly with the activity of the membrane which (naturalistically) circumscribes it, preserves the integrity of that organism as a viable and self-affirming unit of life. Previously, too, I proposed that every organism is part of a community—a community composed, in part, of like organisms and, in part, of unlike organisms, i.e., those with respect to which symbiosis holds. I suggested that these organisms are, in general, locomotively oriented toward some region within that community toward which they incline by a kind of intentionality. Now, I designate this region as, likewise, a transcendental "point." It is a singular node, the dynamism and the spiritual center, which, as it were, draws organisms toward it. I am postulating a complementarity between two transcendental centers, an intra-organismic center and an interorganismic center. Further, I am presuming that the organismic membrane is, in actuality, definable in terms of a dialectical interplay between these centers. It is both manifestation and symbol of a dialectic which is inherently noumenal in status. This natural expression of an ethereal and hidden activity is the morphologically definable representative of that dialectic; it is, so to speak, engendered in its wake as a kind of phenomenal crystallization of processes and structures.

In the cosmogenetic process, the biologic membrane mediates transition from one species of boundary, a morphologically indistinct but nonetheless significant region of (physical) activity, to another species of boundary, those complex activities which are integrally woven with the morphology of the person as a whole. An organismic boundary is structurally well defined; its features are sharply etched. It can be conceptually articulated in a more specific fashion than its analogue for events and persons. This is not to suggest that processes, activities, and ferment are not traits of biologic boundaries. On the contrary, it is because, on the level of organisms, one can so precisely delineate the contours of the membrane that the relations between structure and function with respect to the *organ* which also mediates sentiency may be more accurately discerned than for either events or persons. Arising from physical activity, as a crystallization of certain macromolecular patterns, this organ itself evolves to constitute the regions within which, on the level of persons, the dialectic between consciousness and the Unconscious may be illuminated; and the spiritual life of man, his multifarious symbolisms, may be clarified. Here, I but sketch the relevant aspects of (biologic) boundaries from this point of view.

In sum, bio-boundaries are relevant to persons, for they mediate in a double sense. On the one hand, they mediate passage from physical to personal activity. They constitute the agency for transmitting to the person what is significant for his makeup in the event. On the other, they mediate sentiency. They bring the world to the organism and the organism to the world. As prototype of encounter in compresence, spirituality itself is thereby grounded.

First, I treat bio-membranes from the point of view of topography, then of dynamics, and finally of economics. As I pass toward the latter topics, the issues of transcendentality and centricity become increasingly significant. With respect to topography, specific morphologic elements, ingredients of the boundary *to be*, are assembled, conjugated, and transformed. They are elaborated into membranous structures exhibiting varied designs. Essentially, it is these boundary designs which confer its morphologic contours upon an organism. They determine the characteristic form of this or that type of organism.

The formation of this form is rooted in the activity of specific morphogens. These, in turn, are related to the replicatory dynamism of the organism by the agency of which (I later show) the most varied morphologic arrangements are encoded. It is as though each part of the organism "knows" where to locate itself within that organism so as to laminate and to configure the organism in its characteristic and self-replicating way. I do not yet treat the topic of the fidelity with which, among an untold variety of distinct living forms, each form comes to acquire a capacity for generating its own kind. Suffice it now to suggest that differential gradients, perhaps analyzable in the language of electro-chemistry, lead to distinct orientation of cellular structures, causing them to align themselves into distinctive patterns. Moreover, cell differentiation and cell migration probably depend on *pre-patterns*, which themselves are not structurally analogous to the patterns which they engender, but are factors which nonetheless bear powerfully formative agencies. These agencies presumably inhere as potentials within the relevant chemical materials, directing pattern genesis by electro-chemical polarity or by some other asymmetric property. The dynamism governing such pattern formation could be a set of morphogen distributions based on the physical interactions of its component molecules. Ultimately, the efficacy of morphogens seems to be determined by this principle: the uniform distribution of matter tends to be unstable. Even in chemical solutions, cross-catalysis and auto-catalysis will engender forms of variegated pattern which persist despite their fluid character. Dialectical interplay of pattern activators and pattern inhibitors, based upon DNA-induced classes of possibilities, give rise to the relevant patterns.

But the details of these activities are not important for my purpose. Suffice it to stress that, by whatever elaborate physico-biologic operations, bio-boundary genesis is a function of specific biological acts, acts woven into the overall activity of each living organism. The manner in which such acts are interlocked, and the specific nature of a primordial biological act, I treat, in the following section.

(c) Bio-Boundaries

A single boundary pattern, elaborated in many ways but all variants upon a single invariant thematic structure, appears to represent the topography of organisms, communities of organisms, and subordinate organismic arrangements within (composite) organisms. Now I indicate that factor which persists as a constant amidst the multitude of metabolic transformations. The fundamental topologic features to which I must direct attention are three: concentricity, reticularity, meshing. In each instance, further distinctions must be made between frankly morphologic configurations and proto-morphologic configurations—such arrangements as, indeed, verge upon the functional and non-structural. In every case, certain other properties are significant: namely, those pertaining to singularities and continuities, permeabilities and impermeabilities, motilities and fixities, contractions and expansions, and fibrillations of varying kinds. Many morphologic and morphogenetic patterns may be exhibited. Here, I trace but the simplest and, from the standpoint of personogenesis, the most relevant.

To clarify my account, I must construct a topographic paradigm for the bio-boundary. Clearly, to represent a membrane by a circle is too simplistic. Every biologic membrane has a structure. It is a region of influence and activity. Within it, such processes unfold as transmission, emission, and inmission, processes later to be described. Hence, the bio-boundary must be conceived, first, as a conventionally demarcated circle into which is introduced a series of additional concentric circles, passing both into the interior of that circle (which represents, to a first approximation, the organism) and toward and into its exterior (which represents, to a first approximation, the milieu of the organism). The situation may thus be diagramed.

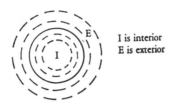

I is interior
E is exterior

Now conceive the unbroken circle as the boundary proper, in its narrowest construal; conceive the broken circles as gradations of that boundary as one moves interiorwise and exteriorwise, i.e., into and out of the organism. Note that the unbroken circle may shift its position. Indeed, certain quantum considerations may even be relevant. That is, certain positions might be intrinsically occupiable, and others might not be intrinsically occupiable by a demarcated boundary. Depending upon organism–environment interactions, that line might occupy one of a variety of members of a set of concentric circles. Alternatively, two or more members may simultaneously be occupied, in which case the membrane would acquire thickness.

Next, linear reticulations, extending from the concentric circles, may traverse both exterior, E, and interior, I, by transsecting the circles. In simplest form, the following diagram represents this situation.

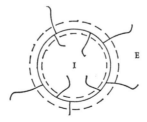

Immediately, the possibility for various patterns of ramification superimposed upon the linear stems arise. Hence, as in the next diagram, the filaments, or microreticula, extend from the ends of the reticula. In this case, they are free-floating filaments.

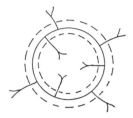

Further, consider the filaments as a set of mini-reticulated structures which wrap about one another within the organism, either enclosing intra-organismic organelles or functioning as strictly "empty" regions—in both instances, a meshwork of interwoven filaments.

Or is an organelle

In this instance, it is essential to distinguish two kinds of "wrapping." On the one hand, structures, such as complex macromolecules, which are themselves not enclosed by membranes, stand in the relationship of "incomplete wrapping" with respect to mini-reticula. The juncture between the latter structures and the former involves a singularity, in the sense already indicated. This condition may thus be diagramed.

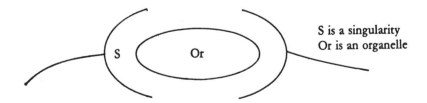

S is a singularity
Or is an organelle

On the other hand, organelles such as mitochondria and cell nuclei are themselves enclosed by membranes, membranes which, analogously to cellular membranes, are continuous with both an interior and an exterior network of sub-reticula. In each of these cases, wrappings and free-floatings of the kind which I am discussing here with respect to the enclosing organisms are, again, to be found.

Organismic membranes are continuous with organelle membranes. These continuities may themselves be either proto-morphologic or frankly morphologic in status. In this case, the wrappings may be designated "complete." In addition, among differentiated cellular systems composed of many cells, one finds organisms comprising intricately connected organs. For these specimens of life, the same considerations hold. Here, the patterns just set forth repeat themselves, but on a larger scale. These reflections will be amplified in my next two subsections, in particular when I treat the theme of *co-adaptation*. Then, I take up the topic of the central nervous system, an intricate and specialized analogue to the simple organismic membranes, a system which constitutes the organ for coordinating the innumerable membranous structures spreading throughout the body, a plexus of the most variegated arrangements. At this time, I confine myself to boundary designs which, in the evolutionary unfolding of life, antedate such nervous structures. In the following representations, I illustrate the two primary modes of membranous enclosure with respect to organelles and, additionally, but in crude form, a sample reticular network with respect to a multi-organ organism.

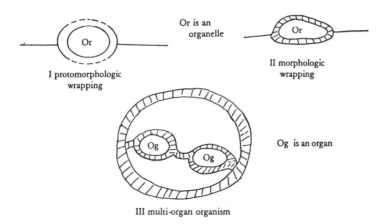

Finally, consider an ecosystem of organisms. This system could constitute either a community of organisms or a composite organism, with respect to the pattern of meshings which they exhibit. I simplify my representation by reducing the arrangement to a dyadic situation. I treat only the simplest models for organismic forms, prescinding from the immeasurably huge variety of variants, with respect to structure, complexity, and number of organic factors involved.

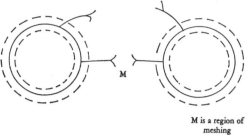

M is a region of
meshing

The regions designated X, X′, and Y, as in the next diagram, are particularly note-worthy for my purposes. Both organisms and organismic components of a composite organism are designated O and O′, respectively.

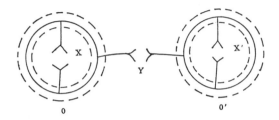

Analogously to my representation of concentric circles, the proto-morphologic reticula may be represented by dotted lines, and similarly for mini-reticula. As a paradigm, the following case, in which I introduce the regions Z and Z′, corre-lated with their respective proto-morphs, is particularly relevant. In this diagram, I designate Y the region associated with extra-organismic, morphologically distinct reticula.

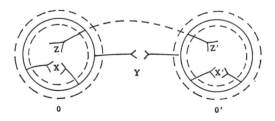

C · LIFE′S FORMATIVE MATRIX

(*a*) Reticulations

Envisage an n-adic community based on the above simplified model, a new model in which (i) multi-reticularity, multi–mini-reticularity, and multi-concentricity prevail and (ii) proto-morphic as well as morphologically distinct structures are interwoven in complicated patterns. No matter how complex I make the design, I focus attention upon all sets of the general type, hitherto diagramed (X, Y, Z). In particular, I comment upon the dynamical and the economic properties of such sets. Thus, I must complicate my diagrams, introducing the n-tensor, →, associated with a certain direction and intensity of flow with respect to n-properties. Hence, the following representation.

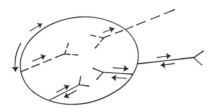

Simplifying this representation by substituting ⇌ for the bidirectional tensor pair, (→, ←), one obtains the next diagram.

My concern will henceforth be with both the set of bidirectional n-tensors, (⇌) and the set of (X, Y, Z) regions.

These two sets, the "synaptic" set (X, Y, Z), which I designate S, and the "n-tensor" set (⇌), which I designate T, are of particular importance. Together, (S, T) define the *morphologic* and *energeia* components of the bio-coordinate system. With respect to the T-set, numerous patterns may be exhibited. These I classify as transverse, rotatory, and twisting. They are autochthonous rhythms, pulsations of the entire boundary. Correlatively, the S-set is associated with resonances, arising within each "synapse," which pervade that structure, spreading, as it were, from synapse to synapse along the reticular meshwork.

To elucidate T-pulsations, consider a paradigmatic organism, represented by thickening the reticula and mini-reticula, upon which T-pulsations are superimposed. This representation is obtained for organismic motility.

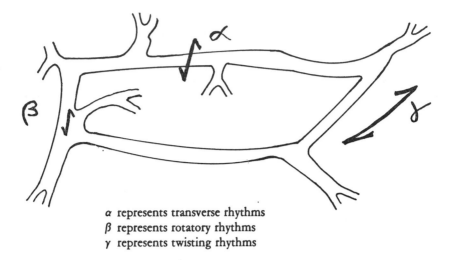

α represents transverse rhythms
β represents rotatory rhythms
γ represents twisting rhythms

In general, a "wiggling," motile, and fluent structure, the boundary, together with its ramifyings, is the organ of locomotion as well as of sentiency and protection. By reference to the forms of motion previously introduced, intra-organismic "synapses" are loci of emotionality, and extra-organismic "synapses" are loci of commotionality. Within this perspective, the boundary itself, as the locus of locomotive activity, is the seat of processes of transmission, emission, and inmission, each process being associated with some combination of modes of autogenic rhythm.

Two kinds of ingredients flow through or across the boundary: nutriment, which sustains metabolism; resonances, which sustain replication, and all its complex variants. But, in the end, no sharp distinction holds between metabolism and replication. Aspects of organismic activity, aspects in which replication represents the consummation of metabolism, they are part of a single process. Grounded in the dialectic of boundary and center, this process manifests itself, in its culminating form, as co-adaptation.

Referring to my last diagram, consider a system of motile organisms, each with its associated rhythms, autochthonous or derivative. Further, consider the topologic properties previously enumerated, properties such as deformability, morphologic delineability, singularities "through" which energies flow back and forth, variegated modes of closure (associated, perhaps, with the hierarchy of Cantorian infinities). Given the variety of such patterns and schemes of motility, the elements making up any particular boundary network can be infolded, one within another, to form marvelously intricate designs. These designs culminate in such astounding phenomena as neuron circuitry, convolutions of the human brain, the elaborate system of impulses which oscillate throughout the many layers and laminae of the nervous system.

Despite intricacies of ornamentation, a single theme—a paradigmatic structure

—reiterates itself on every level of organizational complexity. For example, a cell may be represented as the structure ⊖—<, where membrane x mediates cell interior and exterior; the nerve synapse is a juncture of cells, represented as ——○<——○<, in which a communicating dendritic-axon complex and resonances mediated electrochemically across the synapse may be discerned; the human body may be schematized as the more complicated arrangement:

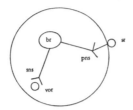

Here, br stands for brain, sns for sympathetic nervous system, pns for peripheral nervous system, vor for visceral organ, and sr for sensory receptor. In each instance, a cell-like enclosure, single or composite, is linked both to its own interiority and to its external milieu by a recticular filament or by a network terminating in a synaptic region, a region composed of one synapse or of many synapses. This schema replicates itself throughout the tree of life, up and down its scale of complexity.

Reaching back to atoms, one finds analogous synaptic–tensorial structures. The phenomenon of valence illustrates this fact. But I must confine myself to organismic boundaries with respect to their relationship to the person. Clearly, such membranes separate interior activities from exterior activities. They establish a distance between the classes of activities which permit intercalating of pauses before the responses to the multifarious stimuli which ceaselessly impinge upon the organism, pauses which are the very primordia of reflection. During a pause, the organism represents to itself a schema of itself in its relationship to its milieu, so that it might more effectively respond in a manner which preserves its integrity.

However, stimulus–response patterns are invertible. The boundary between organism and milieu "belongs" to the latter as well as to the former. Certainly, the milieu impinges upon the organism in such wise as continually to modify the contours of its boundary; the boundary itself is shaped by milieu as well as by organism. What lies external to the organism is not itself an organism, though it may contain organisms, save where the milieu embeds, in the manner of parasitical acts, an enclosed organism. Nonetheless, in both instances, the milieu is a conglomeration of factors rather than a true organismic integrity of factors. Whereas the milieu grossly exerts control upon the organism as responses to stimuli received from the latter, the organism exerts much finer control, indeed carefully regulated autogenic control, upon the milieu. In consequence, no matter how many organisms constitute that milieu, its *modus operandi* with respect to the organism always, and pre-eminently, involves impact.

Contrariwise for the reverse case. In more intricate (and, indeed, *intimate*) a manner, the organism insinuates itself into the milieu. Exclusively, it is empowered to articulate, to rearrange, and radically to transform that milieu. Exclusively, it is endowed with a capacity for intimacy. I stress these topics in the next phase of biogenesis: namely, *metabologenesis*. For the moment, I dwell only upon this theme: whereas the environment is constitutive of the organism just as the organism is constitutive of the environment, the modes of constituency differ. Compresence both of organism with self and of organism with other requires that every organism extend itself, via its network of fibrillating reticula, into the uttermost reaches of the cosmos. Indeed, all organisms inhabit, as their single communal habitat, one and the same cosmos, but they inhabit that cosmos in a different way from the way in which they themselves are inhabited by the cosmos. For an organism possesses a distinctive identity as focus of maximal concentration and minimal attenuation of organismic activity. *As such*, the milieu possesses no such self-identity. And to say that all organisms inhabit the same place means that they all dwell totally—i.e., with their whole being—in the same world; it means that the cosmos is a common habitat for all organisms, that the same region is communally occupied. For the unique self-identity of each organism to be sustained, each organism must occupy that region, a region self-identical for all organisms, in a distinctive way.

Translated into the language of boundaries, this means that the same habitat is differently reticulated, though *totally* reticulated, by each organism. Each spreads a mesh in a particular and unique pattern over the same cosmos; each distinguishes itself by the kind of mesh which it spreads. Insofar as every scheme of reticulation exhibits its characteristic morphologic and proto-morphologic ornamentation, the type of motility associated with every mesh is distinctive. Hence, every boundary pulsates with its own rhythms; similar resonances crystallize as different patterns. From a naturalist standpoint, the interior of every membrane is strictly local. Radiating from a focal region of intense activity are the "spokes" which constitute the ground for a progressive attenuation in the organism's spreading forth into the world. From a transcendental and noumenal point of view, resonances far beyond the local region of natural habitancy are intense in their own peculiar ways. Potencies for novel modes of intensity continually unfold as new regions of the cosmos are activated by their interactions with those resonances. What often are subliminally effective powers, stemming from organismic activity in immediately adjacent regions, may evoke startling effects in regions remote from that activity. This supposition will become of particular importance when I treat, in *Choros*, personal phenomena of a telepathic and empathic kind.

(*b*) Resonances

What I am asserting is that, transcendentally construed, the cosmos as a whole is pervaded by the most intense resonances. Only within the perspective of their transposition into *natural* phenomena are these resonances diminished or attenuated. Though naturalistically concentrated, every organism is transcendentally attenuated. Otherwise, were cosmic rhythms to be admitted into the local habitat (perforating it, so to speak), the fragile constitution of the organism would rupture; the potency of these rhythms would be too great for it to sustain. Its very contents would pour forth into the cosmos. Flowing about in cosmic circumambiency, they would (qua natural) dissipate themselves. They would return to their transcendental source. Hence, the boundary protects the organism from invasion by rhythms too powerful for it to contain. At the same time, it admits into sentiency those rhythms which may cautiously be gathered into memory—memory layered upon memory, each lamina protecting those "beneath" it. For the organism is local region for re-collection, as memory, of certain natural rhythms selected from imperishable transcendental rhythms—rhythms to be articulated and transferred to finite thought. Though, because of their overwhelming power, these rhythms perpetually withdraw into transcendental concealment and remain hidden from organismic experience, the living organism never ceases its quest to reveal what, ultimately, must remain concealed; it does not desist from inclining toward what gently and persuasively inclines toward it, inclines from transcendentality.

From the standpoint of naturalism, these transcendental resonances themselves "inhabit" loci which are singularities within the material makeup of the universe. They are regions utterly devoid of organismic occupancy. Insofar as resonances of diverse modalities, representing all phases of cosmogenesis, pervade the cosmos, overlapping, interacting, and transmuting one another, their associated loci of habitation are "nodes" of compresence—i.e., spatio-temporal regions emptied of all matter. As such, as in my earlier account, these loci always lie in the immediate future with respect to any existent. They are intentionally striven toward and yearned for. For organisms, the agency whereby this reaching out is effected *is* the scheme of reticulated membranes. And the loci of such intentionality are precisely the synapses to which I earlier alluded, synapses which are both intra-organismic and interorganismic. Between these synapses, the indicated resonances flow along the relevant boundaries. Still, as I have stressed, their primordial source is transcendental. From their origins, they emanate into the natural manifestations represented by T, the set of n-tensors.

Amidst the swirlings of these resonances, resonances of all grades of composition and intricacy, the self-identities of the organisms which they suffuse remain intact. If one assumes a principle of hierarchy with respect to both infrapersonal and personal domains, these waves of resonance must themselves be presumed to be interwoven in patterns of hierarchical imposition and superposition. On the other hand, if, as I originally proposed, the rhythms of non-being and the rhythms of pure being are assumed to be absolutely complementary with respect to the person, then no simplistic hierarchical view of the orchestration of these resonances may be assumed. This topic, which in its most general form properly belongs to cosmology, will be of greater importance when, in my succeeding books, beginning with *Choros*, I treat the person qua person.

With respect to its perocentrogenetic phase, the picture of organismic activity may thus be restated. The organismic aspect of the configured world is a membrane together with its ramifyings. Holding together diverse organic processes, this membrane protects these processes—hence, itself—in their integrity, their haleness, and their unity. At the junctures which I have designated synapses arise, from the intra-organismic point of view, the emotions and, from the interorganismic point of view, the commotions. The former are autogenic and intentional feelings; the latter, external feelings involving the sensation of impact. The former are stirred by and within the organism's own self-encounter; the latter, by the organism's encounters with other things and other organisms. Within this frame of reference, diverse organismic locomotions are natural symbols and expressions of the complex interplay of emotion and commotion. Adjusting and adapting these "motions" to one another—hence, protecting organismic integrity via the mechanism of immunologic and other metabolic functions—the locomotions of any organism fulfill their proper role. Via the interlockings of boundary reticula, in the context of the appropriate locomotions, the resonances associated with emotions and commotions are transmitted and diffused throughout the organismic world. Arising in the purely "spatial" interstices of compresence, both intra-organismic and interorganismic, these resonances undergo many vicissitudes. The manner in which any organism relates to itself, and the ways in which several organisms are locomotively oriented toward a single synapse, are determined by these vicissitudes: i.e., how organisms gather in the resonances which ceaselessly hover about the synapses.

One must affirm the doctrine of synaptic relativity. A composite organism contains many such synapses with respect to its several organismic components. These synapses themselves are woven into super-synaptic unity, a unity which is always referred to the sphere of the transcendental. Each organism is external to each of its components which, if itself simple, has its own internal synapses. In consequence, the distinction between synaptic internality and synaptic externality is never absolute. Numerous ecosystems interweave to form diverse patterns. What with respect to one system is an external synapse is an internal synapse with respect to another. A kind of parity holds between synapses; ultimately, all meet in mystery. In general, there is reflexive introjection of exteriorly derived resonances in dialectical interplay with complementary reflexive projection of interiorly derived resonances. These two sets of noumenal centers, so interwoven that each is in fact doubly transcendental, constitute a kind of Hegelian *Geist*. Though they themselves are ineffable, the resonances emanating from these centers are manifested in natural structural arrangements, often patterns of great complexity. The organism itself is a complicated symbol of the interplay of transcendental resonances. It is a relatively enduring crystallization of processes, actually a mosaic of symbols, or, to stress its dynamic character, an orchestration of symbols—in each case, symbols which mirror the organismic ferment to itself.

Organisms are loci of collective yearning and striving, both within themselves as self-directed and with respect to others as communally directed; and they aim at filling themselves with spiritual rhythms. These diverse centers of feeling are internally related, and so adapted to one another that one may truly speak of the *family* of life. All living things constitute a unitary and integral fabric. No matter how variegated the arrangements of co-adaptation, the resonances originating in regions which I have designated synapses are transmitted to every organism with sufficient efficacy to allow that organism to carry out its vital functions in accordance with its distinctive propensities and limitations. When a particular organismic structure is sufficiently complex, and its associated vital activity has reached an appropriate intricacy and intensity, the entire aggregate of elements constituting that structure passes into a certain phase or state of excitation. This phase is associated with—indeed, in the end, is tantamount to—feeling itself. I am proposing the doctrine that structure and function are to be understood as not only intimately connected but as themselves complementary aspects of the same reality.

Accordingly, to speak of resonances as flowing through or transmitted by a reticulum, from synaptic origin to synaptic destiny, is an elliptical way, within the perspective which I am setting forth, of thinking about a succession of structural transformations, and the associated "flowings" in each instance, through which, nonetheless, a common pattern is maintained. As paradigm, consider two adjacent structures of a particular reticulum, such that the first structure is itself immediately adjacent to the synaptic juncture. An intensely concatenated orchestration of resonances deriving from a synapse, intra-organismic or extra-organismic, may so impinge upon that reticulum as to transform the first structure, placing it in a new phase or state of excitation. For example, when heated to one critical degree, metal becomes red-hot; at the next critical degree, it becomes white-hot, yet remains the selfsame metal. The new phase in which that structure has been placed, as a result of the indicated conversion, propagates itself, so to speak, by a "flow" across a gradient to the neighboring and analogously constituted (reticular) structure. The impact of the first structure, and its associated phase, upon the second structure so transforms the latter as to place it in a phase similar to the first. In analogous fashion, this process continues for each of a succession of structures, one adjacent to the other, until the synapse "lying" at the opposite pole of the reticulum is affected. By this I mean, resonances "pour forth" into the new synapse, commingling (so to speak) with resonances passing from it, in precisely the reverse direction, toward the initial pole—the pole whence, in my paradigm, the entire process originated. To elucidate how these cross-currents, such seemingly opposed flows, synergize and reconstitute one another, I must later treat the topic of reflection.

For the moment, it suffices to note that immediately subsequent to the (phasic) transformation of the second structure, in any pair of adjacent or neighboring structures, the first member of that pair, is, as it were, counter-transformed; it reverts to its original state. Throughout these changes, a relatively invariant pattern of relations is preserved within certain limits of constancy, deviating from a fixed value by some minimal increment. This pattern (or set of patterns falling within the prescribed increment) is constituted by unit structures, each with its correlated unit flow. In turn, unit flow is associated with a specified intensity and direction. When these units are aligned in a certain way, a limen of sentiency is established. Depending upon diverse realignments, this feeling tone constantly shifts. At times, it becomes intense and precise; at times, it becomes vague and diffuse. In general, sentiency is associated with the complex interweavings of bidirectional flow. As I have earlier noted, bipolarity reigns as the governing principle of these processes. Tensions are so interwoven that, at certain points, feeling emerges. The perpetually shifting eddies of intra-organismically originating flow is transmuted, on higher organismic levels, into felt autogenic activity, the indigenous and autochthonous emotions: will, desire, appetition. On the other hand, analogous eddies deriving from extra-organismic activity cumulatively emerge, in higher organisms, in such differentiated sensations as vision, hearing, touch—all, in effect, commotions in the existence of the organism. Commotions and emotions mingle to produce the most complicated patterns of feeling, patterns which eventuate in mentation. Under the rubric of organismic action, interaction, and transaction, this topic will be treated in the remaining phases of biogenesis, and, with strictly personal import, in my subsequent books.

(c) The Passage Toward Replication

Consider the originating locus of the resonances to which I have repeatedly directed attention, the synapse itself. Imagine two funnels confronting one another, quite close but not actually touching—hence, in *virtual* contact. Therefore, the representation:

The interstices of these funnels comprise the set of funnel parts which are open toward one another. Together, they constitute a singularity in three-dimensional bio-space. I hypothecate this situation. Powers but dormant within the "in-between" region are activated by the very adjacency of the funnels. In the language of physics, an electric charge involving ionization might be construed as placed upon each. By the reciprocal potentiation of these parts, a kind of suction occurs. Resonances drawn into the funnel are transmitted, by connecting reticula, to organismic membranes. Rhythmic patterns of reverberation of diverse sorts are, depending upon the pole of origination, set in com-motion and in e-motion. Again, by com-motion, I mean the *movings-together* of organisms, felt as impact; by e-motion, I mean the *movings-out* from organisms, felt as self-initiated action. Because of the dipolar character of this process, counter-resonances are sucked back into the synapses. In turn, the latter draw resonances toward them from the former. Highly motile and fibrillating in their diverse locomotive rhythms, interstitial regions are storehouses of "energy," i.e., energeia, in the form of information which potentially circulates, via the appropriate endo-reticular membranes and exo-reticular membranous networks. Complementing one another, those factors, endogenous and exogenous, also, with respect to the overall functioning of the organism, complete one another.

The topic of the composition of the juncture, which catalyzes excitation across the limen or threshold, with bursts into the feeling phases of hyper-excitability, belongs, depending upon whether the naturalistic or the transcendental aspect is emphasized, both to biology and to general ontology. It is relevant for me to note how mutual intensification and activation bring about significant transformation of feeling, transformation which culminates in "a texture of emotive tensions so closely woven that the separate strands of process in it are not distinct."[9] In these conversions, ethereal and ineffable resonances are drawn into naturality to yield variegated patterns of motility, contraction and expansion, linear and radial pulsations. Throughout the substance of the organism, its energeia, both centrifugal and centripetal processes, rhythms of the most intricately ordered dynamic forms, are polarized, rearranged, and transmuted. With respect to organismic economy, different schemata of equilibria are shaped, broken, and re-formed. Distinctive temporal trajectories carve out potential routes of passage through a sequence of (counter-entropic) re-equilibrations. Invariants of form, substance, and cyclic trajectory are maintained with respect both to "energy" distribution and, more deeply, to a common, underlying thematic of a structure and resonance.

At this point, I pass to the next phase of biogenesis, *metabologenesis*, with its associated stage of consummation, *replication*—substantive paradigm for reflection, and basic model for the biologically autonomous act, both in its autogenic and in its impact-receptive aspects. Here, differentiated modalities of feeling arise: e.g., those of desire, will, and choice. Culminating in mentation, the dialectics of consciousness and the Unconscious will be prefigured here. For the first time, suprapersonal factors involving co-adaptation will be introduced as, coevally with the infrapersonal, constituting the ground of all organismic activity.

NOTES

1. For the following etymologies, I am indebted to Eric Partridge, *Origins: A Short Etymological Dictionary of Modern English* (London: Routledge & Kegan Paul, 1959). See appropriate entries.

2. Thomas, *Lives of a Cell*, p. 25.

3. Andrew, *Symphony of Life*, p. 415.

4. *Meister Eckhardt*, p. 104.

5. Whitehead, *Modes of Thought*, p. 152.

6. Ibid., p. 151.

7. Ibid., p. 167.

8. Ibid., p. 168.

9. Susanne K. Langer, *Mind: An Essay on Human Feeling*, 2 vols. (Baltimore & London: The Johns Hopkins University Press, 1967, 1972), I 28. See, in general, the discussion on "Feeling," in chap. 1 of Vol. I.

7

MAN'S FERMENTING ESSENCE

PREAMBLE

Now I treat the organism as ferment, the loosening of the potentiality for motility resident within crystalline things. A membrane forms about a laminated crystal. Originating life-processes which fluctuantly enmesh, the crystal liquifies. Within this fermenting matrix, specific structures, associated with variegated functions, emerge. Protected by the membrane, matter turns in upon itself. As it grows in complexity, its self-interiorization likewise increases. Routes of transmission twist about one another in myriad patterns; centers of activity differentiate and coalesce. Within this labyrinth, primitive sentiency evolves. And, inhering in the metabolic situation is a deep emptiness—hence, the yearning for self-fulfillment. To break down the very barriers which served as protective sheaf wherein this tendency itself comes to fruition, the organism "strives," in reciprocal yearnings, to fill itself with the presence of like organisms. Increasingly directed toward rectifying its own experienced deficiencies, a living community develops the proclivity for a quest for what in man is consummated as the philosophic enterprise: the search for truth, goodness, and beauty. Already, primordial metabolism prefigures this search.

With respect to biologic truth, germinating within metabolism is, in effect, a commentary upon what *is*: the stable configuration of environmental forces to which living creatures must, to survive, adapt themselves. Molding its form to conform to the contours of its milieu, an organism "declares" truth. So intent is it upon adaptation that, by the resistance of the environment, the organism closes in upon itself. A relationship is established wherein one term, milieu, is constant, while the other term, organism, is variable. Because of this resistance, the organism is compelled, through increasing complexity—hence, self-interiorization—to search for its own inward truth. Minimally turned toward its milieu, it is compelled to readapt itself, however, whenever circumstances change. For the environment, in fact, is fluctuant; novel factors ceaselessly appear. To achieve adaptation, the organism must develop an invariant rather than a merely fluent structure, a structure to which the environment itself is coerced to adapt. This metabolizing invariant confers resistance upon the organism to wide-ranging environmental shifts. Now the organism imposes its own forms upon the environment.

Imprinting itself upon its milieu, that it might sustain its own integrity, the organism thrusts from within itself, as its own efflorescing substance, such replicas, and diverse mutations upon these, as will allow it the illusion of imperishable self-enjoyment before a turbulent, unreliable world. By preserving its dynamic form, it achieves veridical self-identity. Beyond that, the organism works to reconstitute the environment in such a way that the community within which it participates will survive. A plexus of self-regulating, self-renewing, and self-transforming activities supervenes; counter-entropically, the organism persists. It evolves increasingly fragile, luminescent, and mutually enmeshed adaptive structures. Yet these structures themselves must regulate, rearrange, and transform the environment on behalf of the organismic community. For its own biologic good—hence (by extrapolation), the betterment of all—that organism evolves to partial autonomy and self-sufficiency; it is in the process of becoming a genuine agent.

At this point, reciprocity supervenes, a dynamic co-adaptation in which organism and environment are reciprocally transformed. In the primordial phase of metabolism, a dialectic unfolds between biologic truth and biologic good. Within this dialectic emerges the consequent phase of metabolism, a phase of transaction and transfiguration. Diversifications and co-dependencies of structural–functional complexes, organismic and environmental, evolve. Such means of organism–environment orchestration as, for example, the immune-reflective systems are devised to supplement the replicatory system. In co-adaptive rhythms of attunement, wherein the integrity of each is preserved and intensified, biologic beauty is prefigured. No longer are organism and environment merely counterposed. In mutual adjustment and enhancement, the way is prepared for metabolic consummation in the incomparably subtler resonances of man.

A · ORGANISMIC MOTIONS

(a) Organismic Feelings

In the section "Boundary and Center," I treated the living organism under the perspective of its power for maintaining itself as a closed system, a system bounded and set apart from the circumambient milieu by which it is bathed, yet a system dynamically interwoven with that milieu in ever more novel schemes of equilibration. As such, the organism was regarded as ceaselessly modifying its own composition, even while it closes in upon itself. In its every form, the living distinguishes itself from the non-living by its intrinsic capacity for preventing its inner content from pouring into the environment and, thereby, negating its status as organism. At all cost, it must never unravel itself into its constituent strands of polymerized molecules. Whether cocoon, fragile but rigid structure, or free-flowing protoplasm, the web of overlapping and mutually entwined polymers remains intact. Yet the individual components of those strands perpetually dissolve into the remaining substance of the organism in its environmental interchanges. Replicating themselves anew, they give rise to duplicate chains the links of which are only occasionally, though momentously, disturbed through the introduction of some mutant form.

Within this perspective, the organism is a mobile enclosure—and this ineluctably, whatever the type of mobility. Woven of membranous strands of great topologic intricacy which express nature's infinite ingenuity for design and ornamentation, it is without question vibrantly mobile. Surely, a living creature pulsates with variegated rhythmic patterns, and endlessly subtle modulations upon those patterns: each a theme upon some set of variations. True, the organism must sustain multifarious deformations. Inexorably, it submits to environmental changes which vary from a subtle, finely modulated play of minuscule forces to the nearly catastrophic, the raging, and the torrential. As a mobile environment never ceases to obtrude upon it, organismic integrity is thus tested. Nevertheless, the organism is pre-eminently empowered to initiate those processes which eventuate in its own self-affirmation as living through its own integral self-restitution.

A certain invariant configuration of activities is preserved through many classes of transformation, classes which pertain to both environmental and intra-organismic factors. At times, the organism is at rest. Like the virus which oscillates from a state of seeming lifelessness, in its extracellular phase, to an active ferment with profound repercussions for its host cell, every organism may, each in its own fashion, pass into a virtually inert crystalline-like state. On its way, it assimilates itself to the inorganic. But, like the virus', this passage is mere hibernation, a preparation for metamorphosis! As in the chrysalis, all its vital resources are mobilized for the crucial leap into living motion, motion in its interlocking phases of locomotion, commotion, and emotion. In multitudinous ways, and through the most diversified and seemingly devious trajectories, every living being is impelled by its own freely exercised dynamism, the very essence of its nature, to express that nature as a plexus of organically orchestrated rhythms.

I also analyzed the organism as a complicated tapestry of membranous fibers, one infolded upon the other, all interweaving to constitute a fabric of activity which germinates within the vast aggregate of proto-organismic molecular units. Ranging from the simplest molecules to a meshwork of polymers, especially polypeptides and nucleotides—the unit polymers of life's essential chemical ingredients, protein and nucleic acid—this multiplex texture of units, subunits, and compounded units wrap, twist, coil, or resonate about one another. Thus intricately and reciprocally enfolding, each molecular arrangement exhibits characteristic plasticity amidst the rigid and self-contained atoms of which it is constituted. For these atoms are fluctuantly enveloped by every such arrangement. A multilaminated fabric is so composed that its every macromolecular component flows hither and thither into "pseudopods" of differing configuration, always embracing variable and perpetually interchanging atomic units. Now expanding, now contracting, now still but pregnant with vibratory tension, a flexible and protean design of mobile proteins (and nucleic acids) is created. Between their interstices are implanted two kinds of substance, the better to achieve proper balance among its diverse ingredients: a firm, skeletal container, woven of carbohydrate and protein; a softer, yielding matrix, woven of protein and lipid.

Intricately "corpuscular" as a behavioral plexus—to speak the language of Teilhard[1]—and profoundly "interiorized" as a center of feeling, this self-enclosing, self-engendering focus of throbbing vitality is a vast sheaf of particles which, as soon as they are formed, "phyletize" themselves as mutant types of organismic activity. Arborescing into separate branches, or phyla, each the efflorescence of a mutant germ grounded in polymers so constituted that every structure overlaps and interacts with its predecessor, this motile but latticed organism engages its environment in dynamic relatedness of center to center. In each instance, an additive, self-synergizing series composed of these polymeric layerings culminates in a complicatedly infolded quasi-crystal, fluent and pulsating. Thus protoconsciously arranging matter about itself, through the action of mediating catalysts, this organism manifests its essence as indefeasibly transcendental, yet as luminously naturalistic; it signifies this double status to all that lies about it.

Every organism is an activity of a self-presenting to another and, reciprocally, of a self-receiving (as an Imago) into its own interiority of that other's presence, especially should its presence itself be a fellow-organism. Clearly, when I use locutions such as self and feeling, I conceive the organism to be precurser to that full flowering of freedom which is achieved only when the miraculous leap from body to person is consummated. Furthermore, I assume that throughout the phyla, and in the numberless forms which these phyla embrace, every organism, no matter how minutely or fragmentarily, prefigures the ultimate organismic form, the form indeed of the personal, upon which the whole evolving process seems ineluctably to be converging. It is as though an interior purposiveness, cosmic in its inmost ground and intent, however abortedly a branch may terminate, works laboriously but with sure, measured cadence toward this great end, surely, in our epoch, the fruition of cosmic evolution.

This organismic interiority is both symbol and fact; it both represents and *is* indigenous, archetypal feeling. In novel format and in richly embroidered mosaic what in an immediately antecedent stage had been interiorized is now correlatively exteriorized. The ceaseless dialectic between introjection and projection is inscribed upon every living being. By their interplay and co-adaptation, each, so to speak, acknowledging the other's needs and proclivities, the entire plexus of organisms endlessly combats the regressive currents of entropic degradation: flow into disorder and randomicity, dissipation of organically utilizable energies.

To attain this goal, whereby ever more sentiently refined evolutes are cast in the wake of a dramatic progression, that very plexus itself becomes enclosed by a single enveloping membrane. Delicate, fragile, translucent, ethereal, and evanescent, this membrane perpetually shifts its loci of super-saturation and hyperexcitability from one region to another. A veridical bio-membrane envelops what has now been transmuted into a veritable biosphere. Composed of innumerable organisms, each a center of feeling, each a proliferation of intricate webs, all exhibiting affinities for all, this biosphere compresses its members in upon themselves to constitute a hyper-symbiotic system.

Beneath the protecting bio-membrane, all organisms evolve. Like a mighty tree from the trunk of which radiate limbs and foliage in gloriously branched design and intricately etched leaf, the whole, grand procession of organismic forms unfolds. Like the great spreading roots of that tree, each organism turns in upon itself, and as it were searches ever more deeply into its inward recesses, probing (in howsoever germinal a way) the transcendental origins of its own existence, origins at once ultimately remote and intimately near. Beneath this biosphere, every component maintains itself, and reproduces in another what it continually reaffirms for itself: namely, "centro-complexity"—a centricity of feeling, action, and movement; an autonomous and spontaneous manifestation of reflexive inwardness; an unremitting quest for source and destiny.

It is appropriate to echo Peirce, when he speaks of "man's glassy essence." As he writes,

> protoplasm, when quiescent, is, broadly speaking, solid; but when it is disturbed in an appropriate way, or sometimes even spontaneously without external disturbance, it becomes, broadly speaking, liquid. . . . The life slimes have, further, the peculiar property of growing, . . . of taking habits. The course which the spread of liquefaction has taken in the past is rendered thereby more likely to be taken in the future. . . . But the one [property] . . . next to be mentioned, while equally undeniable, is infinitely more wonderful. It is that protoplasm feels. . . . Observation upon living naked protoplasm seems to show that . . . feeling has a continuous extension in space. Nobody doubts that it has a continuity in time, nor that the consciousness in one instant directly influences, or spreads over into,

the succeeding instant. In like manner, the feeling at any point of space appears to spread and to assimilate to its own quality, though with reduced intensity, the feelings in the closely surrounding places. In this way, feeling seems directly to act upon feeling continuous with it.[2]

Surely, Peirce is here succinctly affirming a position toward which I am, step by step, advancing. To restate his insights, I assert these tenets. First, protoplasm passes from crystalline dormancy, a kind of unconscious quiescence, to vibrant liquefaction. Next, as shown in this passage, it acquires habits of flow and configuration which are roughly steady if not firmly invariant. Finally, glowing in the interstices of habit synergistically acquired are feelings of variable intensity.

To anticipate the thrust of my argument, I may now say: metabolism is a leap beyond mere chemical inertness to a joining together of strands of crystalline material which, once conjoined, transmute themselves into feeling, sense, and, ultimately, cognition itself. Again to cite Peirce: these *mental* activities spread both spatially and temporally; they spread for a given organism, in its own self-perpetuating acts, and among a multitude of organisms; thereby, other loci of mentation are so affected and transformed as to prepare themselves for the consummatory act of ecstatic protoplasmic power: to replicate themselves as those mutants which will inscribe novel modes of mentation upon the efflux of life. But when Peirce speaks of the spatio-temporal extension of protoplasm, he is using the term "extension" in a special way. He wishes to startle our habitual modes of conceiving nature. For he proposes a reordering of conceptual categories, a reordering which henceforth will assign a fundamental status in the scheme of things to *feeling*. Accordingly, Peirce directs one's attention to an underlying identity between a materialist notion of extension and what, from his standpoint (and mine), is a deeper and more comprehensive notion.

Peirce is prefiguring one of my principal theses: namely, that the naturalist position prescinds from the subtle intricacies of organismic activity; it is a position which equates superficial behaviorism with a fundamental metaphysical doctrine. A more intuitive grasp of behaviorism would be better expressed by exploring the import of its cognate, *to behave*, a term which refers to demeanor and deportments. Quite literally, to be*have* is, in being *what* one is, to *have* one's being; it is the generic mode of self-possession. In the deeper sense of behaviorism, the behaving organism is that organism which exhibits a characteristic way of feeling its way among environmental vicissitudes, and through its own inwardly changing modes of being.

(b) Organismic Givings

These modes portend the variable moods of the organism. In this sense, it is moo*dy*. Subject to shifting moods, it is indeed a *subject* which passes through diverse states of feeling. Surely, an organism's very being (its *be*havior, in the sense of "having being") is linked to its manner (i.e., its mode) of feeling, thus to its deportment. As moody, it is, in effect, in a certain mode of its being. "Mode,"[3] being related to the Greek μήδομαι, meaning "to be mindful of," and to the Latin *mederi*, meaning "to heal," "to be good for," and (in this sense) "to attend to," concerns the way in which the organism attends to, heals, or, in effect, is good for itself in relation to its environment: hence, its particular style of noting, and, in this sense, of respecting—thus, by extension, of caring for—that relationship.

Certainly, from an etymologic standpoint, the core of significance concealed within behavior—hence, behaviorism—is not violated when one stresses this element of deportment. Nor, since many organismic powers are involved, is *comportmental care*—hence, feeling manifested through its encounterable signs—a misconstrual of the inner purport of a veridical behaviorism. Furthermore, not only is feeling revealed through these signs as though it were extrinsic to them; feeling is actually contained within the signs. It is, so to speak, *held fast* by a complicated scheme of signals. In consequence, feeling is presented by the organism *within* a multilaminated structure, the matrix of those representations by which the organism presents itself to another, including (of course) to the inquirer.

From these considerations, it follows that the organism reveals itself to the one who would seek its inner being. It in-forms the inquirer with its own intrinsic "form" through the information contained within the messages which it sends forth. As in the Latin *revelare*, which means "to pull back the covering from," this self-disclosure is effected through many layers of comportmental signs, all constitutive of the organism. In effect, in expressing its nature, a living creature *presses out* from its essential being the evidence of its existence to the one who searches that being. Moreover, the texture of evidence (derived from the Latin *videre*, "to see"), which is at bottom the texture of the organism itself, is *seen by* the inquirer. Thus (authentically) illuminated, it is conveyed to his reflective vision as a complicated fabric the facets of which must, one by one, be stripped away in order that the import of organismic being be finally wholly unconcealed.

An organism represents itself to another through a plexus of symbols. Intricately composed, these symbols must be examined, layer by layer, so that the authentic organism be revealed. These layers lie upon the organism; they are continually extruded by it, as a penumbral manifold which, on immediate inspection, hides its feeling, caring existence. Sufficiently penetrated, the living creature would stand forth in shining ἔκστασις as never ceasing to combat an inexorably regressive urge into stasis, Peirce's crystalline inertia. By innumerable staining techniques and other identificatory means, this or that strand or aspect is disclosed. Yet the totality of such devices barely suffices to convey to the biologist an organism's full vibrance. Just as assuredly, they point toward and progressively evoke its effulgent rhythms.

Through its diverse metabolic processes, appropriately symbolized, every organism transmits a mark of its status as a unique center of feeling to some recipient organism. In the measure of its capacity searchingly to apprehend the import of that status, this recipient experiences the organism's corpuscular intricacy and its depth of interiority. By these processes, all living creatures "communicate," in manageable and specific ways, their interwoven structures and functions. By "communicate," I imply neither language nor consciousness. Etymologically, "communicate" is related to "common" and "commonality." And this expression is associated with more general, and less precisely delineatable, phenomena than the linguistic and the sentient. It is deeply connected to the idea of *a making available to all*. Qua communicant, the organism sends forth potential information concerning its needs and its proclivities. A sensitively attuned recipient will assimilate this information, responding to the communicant with appropriate signs of this fact.

By this revealing of the metabolic deficiencies which an organism continually and inexorably acquires in the course of living, these needs and proclivities are both gratified and respected. The organism may be regarded as ceaselessly in quest of a gift which is proffered in response to its communicatings, the gift of remedying those deficiencies. An activity of self-giving through its communications, the organism seeks reciprocation, the gratuity of some relevant acknowledgment. This gratuity is a fulfilling of need, a taking cognizance of proclivities. It is the suffusion of the organism with the presence of another, complementary organism. This plenitude *is* nothing else than the other dwelling within it, dwelling through its manifold and continually ramifying signals, signals which, as they ramify, constitute themselves an increasingly nutritious presence for the sustenance of the organism. Above all, every animate being is a questing for preservation and integration, for wholeness and integrity. It is a yearning after self-completion.

Resolution of metabolic deficiency occurs, I repeat, when an organism is appropriately suffused with symbols of the presence of a complemental organism. *A fortiori*, a principle of parity with respect to complementarity reigns. Mutually complemental organisms suffering from analogous metabolic deficiencies remedy those defects by a reciprocal filling with presence. Dwelling in a community of like organisms, each member is metabolically interwoven with other members. In the end, the entire community is a matrix of dynamically enmeshing metabolic activities. A kinship of communicants is created whereby organisms make available —hence, for sentient organisms, virtually *known* to one another—their respective natures. Many techniques of intercommunication have been worked out. Grounded in intercellular transductions, which, in turn, are mediated by appropriate hormones and signaling devices (possibly, electrical), multicellular organisms evolve interorganismic methods of transduction. A complicated variant of the original techniques, a medley woven of elementary transductions, the communications of organisms entail, in addition to subtler metabolic processes, impalpable and ineffable strands of *empathy*—a topic which I treat in my last chapter, "From Biologic Act to Personal Being."

Granted: what through these techniques and methods is made known are only those aspects of organismic feeling which are relevant to the style of existence of the communicants, be they fellow-organisms, simpler organisms, or more complex organisms. What is "made known" is, surely, determined by the location of the organism in the hierarchical arrangement of complexity with respect to interiority and corpuscularity. For persons in quest of their own organismic being, a deep empathy holds, empathy which has been superimposed upon, yet woven into, grosser organic processes. Indeed, the person who inquires into his animate nature discovers it to have a double meaning. As strictly vegetative—hence, tending toward the inanimate—a person's organismic aspect is set in opposition to him. Yet, as a tendency to metabolize itself (from an evolutionary point of view) in self-transcendence toward the status of personhood, the same aspect is intimately bound to him. But the situation is even more complex. For person qua organism embraces within his own organic dynamism deeper rapport with person qua person. Insofar as the former tends, regressively and entropically, toward its *in*organic source, it expresses an essential constituent of the unconscious (personal) being of the person, a veritable archetype which ultimately devolves upon that component of the ground of personal being which arises from *non*-being.

Qua both organism and person, each man is doubly oriented toward what is other than himself: he is inwardly turned toward his origins; he is outwardly turned toward a cosmos brought, by deliberation, to a harmony of ordered parts. In the former case, feeling is consummated in intuition, with a latent cognitive ingredient. In the latter, feeling is consummated in cognition fructified by intuition. Moreover, every organism prefigures the characteristically personal quest after truth: a self-adapting of itself, together with its perception of that adaptation, to its roots, both interior and exterior. In each instance, organismic being fits itself to those roots—roots which are object to the organism yet implicated in being as possessed by it.

This fittingness always involves mutual and reciprocal adaptation. Not only does the organism reconstitute itself to adapt its contours and its dynamics to that of a preformed, relatively constant milieu, inner and outer; but, in confronting stubborn fact, it expresses that inalterable character of the cosmos which initiates truth's unfolding toward its propositional embodiment. Nor, alternatively, does the organism merely change the milieu the better to adapt it to its needs and, thereby, to set it on a different evolutionary course. Surely, the very process of adaptation creates a more profound harmony between organism and milieu. In the narrower sense of truth, the milieu is deemed a fixed realm vis-à-vis which the organism must reconstitute its inner makeup in order effectively to "comment," i.e., to make those statements which will bring it into that mode of relatedness which alone will promote its chances for survival. Likewise, on a narrower construal of survival, the milieu is deemed sufficiently flexible so that *it* might be reconstituted as a *better* medium for organismic adaptation. Indeed, such an orientation is the primordium of the quest for the *good*: so to rearrange the circumstances of existence as to harmonize the prefixed organismic nature, exemplified by all members of the community of organisms, with those now altered circumstances.

(c) Interorganismic Relations

In the last analysis, the quest for primordial truth and the quest for the primordial good must be conjoined. Only in this manner may the ancillary status of each be exhibited; thus alone can both quests make their limited but significant contributions to truth in its larger sense. Inclusive truth requires reciprocal fittingness between the self-transfigured organism and, by its creaturely actions, a transfigured milieu. In mutual and dynamic entrusting of self and cosmos, both are changed. Transformation is reciprocal. Through a veritable metamorphosis, each is more effectively beautified. For truth blossoms from the germ of the beautiful. When this seed has been planted, by each organism after its own fashion, a veridical synthesis of a more constricted truth with a less efficacious goodness is achieved. In the sublation of the true and the good in the beautiful, truth, goodness, and beauty are brought to their consummate forms. Every living creature participates in the activities by which the Form of these forms is, by human endeavor, eventually borne to fruition.

By making itself known to the cosmos in the way of reciprocal adaptation, the organism discovers the cosmos in relationship to its own being. In this discovery, it *re*covers from the cosmos what it had lost: loss expressed as metabolic deficiency, recovery expressed as metabolic plenitude. To rectify deficit, the organism, by its autonomous and teleonomic activity, achieves a new metabolic equilibrium. When I say "teleonomic," I mean the specifying of a goal. Surely, every organism directs itself, spontaneously and by its intrinsic acts, toward an end which it defines— hence, continually reinterprets—for itself. Thereby, it shapes ever more harmonious modes of cosmic relatedness. By construing itself as "center"—hence, by referring all facets of the cosmos to itself—the organism discerns these facets as fitting together in a manner "proportionate" to its own being, a manner symmetrized by its own focal activity.

Alone among organisms, the person acquires a capacity for transferring, through his self-conscious acts of deliberation, a characteristically organismic *ego*-centricity —naturalistically centered in organismic being—to a transcendental and deistic center. Typically, the person *deifies* the cosmos. He centers it in an all-unifying, all-integrated God. Nonetheless, the organism prefigures this deification, this cosmic "centrification." Every living creature co-participates in the eternal scheme of the Divinity, an *un*conscious—hence, un–*self*-conscious, orientation. But only the person seeks to recapitulate this mode of unconsciousness. Having passed through a phase of intense self-awareness, he strives so to relinquish his self as to repossess not a particular entity but a manifold of relations among all entities. In eternal return, albeit a new and expanding phase of a never-ending cycle, the person reassesses the organismic mode of existence, and renews it, though on a more sublime plane.

Every organism, like every person, also takes its stand in the outermost limits of being: pure being, the "outside" to which it inwardly relates; and non-being, the "inside" to which it inwardly relates. In primordial restlessness, all living creatures seek ἔκστασις. They yearn for self-transcendence. For the organism, the form of this transcendence is metabolic. And the dominant and consummatory processes of organismic metabolism are its complementary and culminating phases, replication and reflexivity, dual moments inwardly linked as one. To the theme of delineating this fragile and doubly phased state, a state which nevertheless grounds (from the organismic side) all personal being, I now turn.

Etymologically, "meta-bolo-genesis" derives from three Greek terms: μετά, meaning "beyond," as pertaining to the inclusive, immanent context wherein specific issues arise; βάλλειν, meaning a "joining together," of diverse factors to constitute an integral unity; γένεσις, meaning an "engendering or unfolding," through phases from a germinal stage to a consummatory stage. In its narrower sense, metabolism refers to the interplay of two complementary, but, from the standpoint of the purpose and direction of the process which this interplay constitutes, oppositional and contradictory forces. In specifically biologic usage, metabolism designates those forces to be a double trajectory of oppositely directed chemical reactions: "catabolism," literally an *un*joining or breaking down; "anabolism," literally a joining together or building up (of stable organizations). In the former, schemes of energy conservation are disintegrated, free energy is consumed, unutilizable energies are dissipated as heat; entropic movement is favored. In the latter, free energy is released and a minimum of unutilizable energies are dissipated; schemes are devised for effectively binding these liberated energies to more intricate organizations; counter-entropic tendencies combat an inexorable, overall entropic "flow."

The topic of metabolism treats those bio-chemical activities whereby factors are formed which constitute the total configuration of energy exchanges, dissipations, and distributions. It examines the correlative and interwoven processes by which structures implicating both organism and its milieu are built up, in bio-synthesis, and torn down, in bio-degradation. Indeed, organism and milieu themselves are but subordinate systems discernible as active, interactive, and transactive within a single, inclusive, and composite system. I say "active," for each subsystem is relatively autonomous, a durable structure of dynamically interwoven elements. I say "interactive," for the two subsystems never cease to interchange their contents while maintaining as intact the general contours of their identities as systems. I say "transactive," for the boundary which creates this pair is itself perpetually shifting and at no time may it be specified as definitively established.

Metabolism refers to the dynamics, the energeia, of locomotion. It implicates the two termini of motion: emotion and commotion. To recapitulate: in the first instance, stimuli arise internally from autochthonous organismic activity and, thereby, set in motion locomotive acts. In the second instance, stimuli arise externally from encounters either with other organisms or with non-organismic environmental factors, and, thereby, from the opposite direction (so to speak), set in motion locomotive acts. In both cases, the initiating stimuli can be nutritious or

toxic, and accordingly give rise to either aversions or adversions. Aversive reactions are internal turnings away from intra-organismically functioning centers
of activity. As avoidance reactions, they lead to proto-psychic "defenses" against
such internal threats. Specific tensions accompany these defenses, tensions which
contort both morphology and action. On the other hand, adversive emotions entail the organism's total taking possession of itself, in all its contents—hence, its
self-possession. In the former instance, organismic vitalities are diminished; in
the latter, enhanced. Analogously, aversive commotions involve fear reactions
which eventuate in environmental reconstruction or even in object annihilation,
in order (in both cases) to promote survival; adversive commotions entail such
positive responses as tenderness, care, love, commitment. In a word, a complex
dialectic implicates both commotions and emotions, both aversions and adversions.
Vectorial resultant of a vast conglomeration of forces which reflect this dialectic, organismic locomotions acquire variegated configurations, and serve diverse
purposes.

Whether commotions or emotions are stirred, symbiotic conditions may reign.
Internally originating stimuli may derive from enclosed suborganisms, like organelles or viruses. Alternatively, externally originating stimuli may arise from
congenial creatures dwelling within the vicinity of the organism. In both instances, when symbiosis prevails, the organism embraces the "object" which lies
within it or without it, and, reciprocally, is embraced by that "object." A mutuality
of entrustings supervenes. In turn, symbiosis can be either an asset to the organism
or a liability. In the first case, the object embraced is an agency for facilitating the
ultimate well-being of the organism. In the second, it is, in the long run, an agency
for handicapping the organism. Many modalities of trust emerge from the interplay of organism with organism. Some prove felicitous; others are debilitating;
many confer differential favors.

But my concern is not the pathologic consequences of interorganismic relationships, save insofar as these consequences bear upon the *eventual* molding of the
person. At the moment, it suffices that I take note of the metabolic intricacies,
wholesome as well as pathologic, of organismic locomotion, the enormous range
and diversity of creaturely movement. Later, I treat the specific import of these
intricacies for the interpersonal domain and the intrapsychic domain. I show how
organismic motions so intermesh as to constitute the ground for a motile and
fermenting unconscious source of human sentient activity.

B · METABOLIC TRANSCENDENCE: THE RHYTHMS OF REPLICATION

(a) The Aim at Self-Enjoyment

In every situation, aversive or adversive, or in any variation upon symbiosis, information is transmitted through the relevant metabolic routes, information which
specifies the shifting configurations, amidst ceaseless metabolic activities, of or-

ganism, organismic ingredients, and environment. Biologic metabolism refers to the context of ideas which systematically explicate the means by which the contradictory forces, catabolism and anabolism, are sublated, then converted into constituents in a larger, more coherent process. Indeed, metabolism is a going beyond the paradoxical activities which their joint functioning entails to the more inclusive system in which they appear as but moments. In this system, a naturalistic scheme of activities is shaped, which incorporates both tendencies yet transcends each.

For this incorporation and transcendence to be achieved, metabolic bio-syntheses and bio-degradations which are only tenuously linked in a fragile yet cohesive and self-consistent activity must be consummated as a sturdy and durable structure of evolving processes: a "genesis" from inchoate beginnings to a complete, ordered whole. Suffused by immanent purposiveness, the metabolizing system emancipates from mere natural ferment a scheme of dynamic forms. Transcending its original status, metabolism, to achieve this end, must first engender, from within its inner unity of oppositional forces, a contradiction within itself. Through the agency of its own constitutive substance, it effects a synthesis of antithetical moments which, in effect, is a duplicate of itself, a duplicate which as non-identical with itself stands in opposition to itself. Though distinct from its own engendering model, this dual entity counterposes itself, in dialectic fashion, to that which gave birth to it. It constitutes a novel variant upon an original theme, perhaps even a frank mutant, while it bears striking resemblance to that theme.

In the culminating phase of metabolism, the system, as it were, leaps out of itself as a virtual (substantive) replica. Impregnated within the original, birthed from its very womb, it is nonetheless distinct and autonomous. Where there was one, now there are two! By its own inner dynamism, monadicity engenders dyadicity. An act of audacious creation! The original reconciliation of the initially opposed forces of catabolism and anabolism was but momentary; it was effected in the specific system, or in the unfolding sequence of re-equilibrated variants upon that system, within which they first manifested themselves. For durable reconciliation to occur, there must be impregnation, birth, new growth, interaction with a virtual replica, novel unification. Whatever the specific biological tactics, only in the context of ongoing biological reproduction may stability be achieved.

Under special conditions, for exceedingly intricate organisms, two organisms may collaborate symbiotically, one acquiring the role of impregnator while the other acquires the role of bearer of the germ of impregnation—until that germ attains fruition in a new creature. Stability depends upon fortuitous attunement of a pair of members of the organismic community. For metabolism so to turn in upon itself as to negate its perpetual restlessness, a dyad is required. A succession of such dyads guarantees continuance of metabolic tranquillity. By anticipation, a particular organism may find its peace, and its ultimate at-homeness, within the endless progeny to which replicatively congenial organisms give birth. A ceaseless renewal of the original! Yet novel variations are inscribed upon the recurrent theme. A veritable immortalization of its substance! Yet the tragedy of eternal lapse from throbbing vitality cannot be averted. A symbolic dwelling in the timeless! Yet, though inextricably intertwined, symbol and substance are not, in the last analysis, interchangeable. Naturally, this particular mode of self-transcendence through duplication, with all its attendant paradoxes, is of peculiar significance for the person. In later books, especially *Apotheosis*, the mysteries of the equation between symbol and substance will constitute an important and recurrent topic.

At this point, I must stress that correlatively with substantive reproduction, the replication of living organisms, another analogous and complementary process occurs, a process which now, however, unfolds in the spiritual domain. In actuality, the metabolizing organism achieves its transcendence, the culminating and consummatory phase of metabolism, in *two* ways. Replication, a doubling of the organism, substantively speaking, is itself a double process. The double casts its own shadow. Within the naturalistic perspective which has dominated my account, always implicating the resonances to which I alluded in my section "Boundary and Center," is a spiritual doubling. Throughout the life of every organism, however minimal its power of sentiency, reflective acts persist. Despite the flickering of reflection, its endless regressive return to sheer organicity (a repression of those acts into *radical* unconsciousness), this persistence dominates the vital processes of that organism, its very existence as a living creature.

By my argument, replication which is substantive, or natural, and replication which is spiritual, or transcendental, are deeply analogous. They involve homologous dynamisms. Both activities inhere within metabolism itself as its uttermost potentiality. Constituting the immanent and ineluctable destiny of metabolizing matter, these activities are mutually presupposing and, indeed, profoundly interrelated. So closely are they interwoven that each term is a metonomy for acts represented by the other. Hence, etymologically, "replicate" derives from *replicare*, "to fold, or bend, back"—in effect, a self mirroring itself to itself; "reflection," corresponding to *reflectere*, is its philological equivalent—for, by the phonetic shift of p to f and i to e, the terms are essentially identical.[4]

In both instances, though in different modalities, a self duplicates itself in its manifold relations to its milieu. Each term refers to a process which, in effect, is a (relatively) invariant configuration of (relatively) durable factors. Though the actual processes differ, each draws, for some of its essential ingredients, upon the other. This inner dependency, as well as a mutual resemblance, will be set forth later. Accordingly, to prescind from environmental factors, the self orients itself essentially toward a schema of itself. It adopts a certain attitude toward that schema, an attitude the consequence of which is the framing of an Imago of the schema: one substantive, the other symbolic. To render these processes, intraorganismic and extra-organismic "synapses," the dynamics of which were previously delineated, become specialized, though in different ways. Without sacrificing their intrinsic analogy, these distinct but inwardly related processes exhibit, ontologically speaking, distinctive modes of being. In brief, the final aim of organismic activity, the essential equivalence of replication and reflexivity, was often expressed by Shakespeare, as in the lines:

> But were some child of yours alive that time,
> You should live twice,—in it and in my rhyme.[5]

The aim at self-enjoyment, the distinguishing mark of *living* matter, thus doubly manifests itself. Whether embodied as replication or symbolized in reflection, the organism never strives for momentary self-enjoyment alone, no matter how intense, refined, or subtle the satisfaction. On the contrary, it always directs itself toward an imperishable self-enjoyment. A live creature is matter so animated, integrated, and textured that its every movement subserves the intricate checks and balances which jointly govern self-perpetuation; and this ultimate end, which is nothing less than the quest for immortality, the indefinite persistence of a unique self-identity, is doubly incarnate. Organismically speaking, child and poem are manifestations of the same process. Their equivalence is indefeasible. An ecstasy of creation accompanies the birth of each. In their own ways, both preserve a trace of the continuance of the selfhood which characterizes their progenitors.

Luminous with the being of their creators, child and poem alike both reveal and symbolize metabolism itself. In its larger sense, the latter may now be regarded as mediating the transition between two states: transiency or the momentary existence of a material configuration, mainly inert and passive but already germinally autonomous and self-reconstituting; indefinite persistence, a living configuration in ceaseless renewal despite variants and mutants of an unending sequence of symbolic duplicates. Conceived in passionate organicity, these replicas always possess the form of the personal, or at least of the quasi-personal, since organisms prefigure persons, a form which assumes either substantive shape or spiritual shape. What now is the metabolic ground for such organismic duplication?

As a metabolizing system, the organism is a matrix of chemical chains, reactions which "pursue" certain temporal trajectories, reactions at times slow, at times quick, at times of variable rhythm. Different chemicals metabolize at different rates, even within a single reaction chain. These reactions are catalyzed by enzymes and inhibited by counter-enzymes. In both instances, the agents are often by-products of the reactions themselves. The entire organism is, so to speak, dynamically criss-crossed by a *fluent* mosaic of hierarchically ordered structures, a set of mutually enclosing dynamic forms, a matrix of variegated bio-chemical activities in relations of subordination and superordination. To use a more apt set of metaphors: the organism, metabolically speaking, is a composite of intricately *orchestrated* chemical themes, chemical variations, chemical figures, chemically contrapuntal unfoldings. Amidst shifting metabolic routes, each a repeatable chemical reaction with but minor variations, membranous structures persist; they persist as invariant factors despite the transient changes induced by resonances traversing them. Amidst changing schemata of adaptation, identity is preserved; it is preserved throughout the growth of life toward more intricate modalities of sentiency. Despite ever-altering components, the basic patterns of chemical reactivity persist; despite their ceaselessly evanescing ingredients, structures of membranous fiber persist, all interwoven in multifarious design. In both cases, that of chemical reaction pattern and that of membranous structure, a particular scheme of replication manifests itself and is activated by the appropriate intra-organismic agents and extra-organismic stimulants.

In consequence, metabolism is as much grounded in replication as it is the basis for its own self-consummation through replication. Every metabolic component is a factor which contributes to the enlargement of organismic experience. And replication, too, is in the service of such enlargement. It is the means whereby simpler organisms are transformed, by the relevant intercellular transductions, adhesions, and reconfigurings, into more complicated and durable societies of organismic activity, societies which cohere by virtue of the integral dynamic forms, all woven into a unified manifold, which pervade the entirety. By such metamorphosis, a congeries of new metabolic routes is shaped from the interactant paths of bio-synthesis and bio-degradation. Together, they constitute a network of ever-shifting dynamic forms. Replication is the spur for those novel metabolic schemes which themselves come to fruition in replication.

No absolute distinction prevails between strands of bio-synthesis and strands of bio-degradation. Not only do these strands interact; in addition, they share constituents along their respective routes of traversal. In the end, the purpose of the diverse contributions of all reactions is the transformation of the merely individual self-enjoyment experienced by lesser units of life into the collective but integrated, and unified, self-enjoyment experienced by larger units. Ultimately, metabolism mediates the processes whereby fragmentary modes of satisfaction are woven to a unity of searching-ness, at-homeness, and at-one-ness with the cosmos itself.

(b) The Integral Biosphere

Whence derive the energies for organismic sustenance, integrity, growth, and reproduction? As I suggested earlier, numberless enzymes catalyze specific chemical activities. The combined action of these enzymes is cumulative, integrative, and purposeful, and it is directed toward the maintenance of stable energy structures. On the one hand, enzymes aid in regulating, transforming, and distributing available energies. On the other, they aid in releasing or dissipating energies through non-noxious means and in gathering new energies for subsequent utilization. But, ultimately, enzymes themselves are dependent, for their joint functioning as "energy discriminators," upon a single energy source, sunlight. Whether directly through photosynthesis, or indirectly through the food products of photosynthesis—i.e., plants or animals which themselves have ingested food—sunlight irradiates the earth and, alone, makes possible the appearance, growth, and spread of all its living creatures.

A vast envelope of life, the biosphere is bathed by light which ceaselessly impinges upon each member of the intricately organized ecosystem. Though composite and subtly designed, this hyper-organism is, with respect to its dynamisms for capturing, storing, and diffusing energy, archetypal for all the particular organisms which comprise it. In differing ways, and with variable sensitivities and intensities, the elements constituting this maximal organism utilize for their own continuance and for their self-directed metamorphoses quanta of light emitted by sun and by what lies beyond the sun—for all we know, the great constellations of stars which together form the source of all the light which suffuses the cosmos. In all instances, routes for transmitting life-sustaining energies are clearly mapped out, both within each organism and among all organisms. Etched upon every living creature are the pathways along which metabolic processes unfold in order to sustain and to preserve it.

The entire biosphere, on this planet as well as on those numberless planets which might inhabit the universe, is pervaded by light, which derives from the manifold foci wherein light is created, whence it is diffused, to which it will return. Invigorated and renewed by light, this irradiated biosphere is a luminous matrix which glows in many ways. Diffracting into every spectral line, it is a great effulgence which dominates and subdues all the inanimate structures which, as it were, gather about it. Though any particular ray might be obliterated by the superior force of inanimate matter, the entire configuration ineluctably prevails. Yet it is as though the inorganic pays homage to all that lives. For it, too, glows in the reflected light of the living, and, in its glowing, casts new and more subtly modulated light back to its penultimate sources. Once the irradiation of the cosmos has been consummated, a kind of dialectic of light unfolds between the animate and the inanimate. Patterns and textures and hues of things enhance, by contrast, the radiant splendor of life. By this dialectic, we celebrate the glory of an harmonious cosmos.

Of the constitutents of the biosphere, some are transparent, others are translucent, still others are nearly opaque. In such variegated ways each, so to speak, becomes light incarnate. A great radiance pervades the cosmos. Emanating through its spheres, that radiance reaches its inmost and darkest recesses. Pre-eminently among natural entities, living organisms are embodiments of light, translating it into myriad substantive symbolisms. As one ascends the ladder of life toward the pinnacle of interiorization, the person, one discovers these symbols to have become as compressed, multifaceted, and modulated as a radiant gem. It is as though the great variety of crystals which spread throughout the domain of the inanimate have suddenly liquefied, then recondensed in transfigured fashion. Herein, substance has been spiritualized. What had been mere life—quasi-amorphous, un-self-conscious, almost random—has now been transmuted into human life.

Reiterated throughout the great chain of living being is a single structure which mediates all energy exchanges, adenosine triphosphate, ATP. This organic chemical bears the chemical energies into which light energy has been transformed.

Early in the unfolding of life, chlorophyll serves as the universal agent within which ATP is the essential ingredient. As the tree of life flourished, other chemicals, derivative or substitutive, assumed this role, but ATP remained at the roots as primordial element. A single chemical molecule (the base of which is adenine, an amino acid—one of the building blocks of life itself) represents an invariant factor within the whole of life, a factor which alone makes possible the most diverse and startling energy exchanges and, hence, is the supreme mediator of all organismic metamorphoses. Could not the uniqueness of each individual organism, as well as the unique features of species and classes of organisms, derive from seemingly minor mutants upon this factor—mutants which are not morphologically discernible but the distinctiveness of which rests upon variable modalities of rhythm: rhythms insusceptible of identification by contemporary bio-chemical techniques?

Each mode of energy distribution, and all modes are but variants upon the single theme which implicates ATP, is associated with a particular type of organism—ultimately, indeed, with a singular, individual organism. From this standpoint, one may regard every living creature as itself mediating the progressive transformation of light, that universal physical constant, through a multitude of changes, physical and chemical. Nuclei, atoms, simple molecules, macromolecules, polymers of intricate design are successively formed, then *trans*formed into bodies which, by the mysterious interplay of the emanations of non-being and pure being, eventuate in persons: a progressive interiorization of events—if you will, a divinization—each an instance of light incarnate.

In this grand procession of one community of luminous creatures to another, each organism is a more subtly modulated incarnation of light than its predecessor. "The various actual entities which compose the body," to cite Whitehead,

> are so coordinated that the experiences of any part of the body are transmitted to one or more central occasions to be inherited with enhancements accruing upon the way, or finally added by reason of the final integration. The enduring personality is the historic route of living occasions which are severally dominant in the body at successive instants. The human body is thus achieving on a scale of concentrated efficiency a type of social organization, which with every gradation of efficiency constitutes the orderliness whereby a cosmic epoch shelters in itself intensity of satisfaction.[6]

Without technical explication of Whitehead's terminology, the key notions which I stress in this text are contained in the following extracts: "experiences . . . transmitted . . . to be inherited with enhancements accruing upon the way"; "the enduring personality . . . [as] the historic route of living occasions which are severally dominant in the body at successive instants." From these extracted passages I emphasize the ideas "enhancements accruing" and "historic route . . . [through] . . . occasions . . . severally dominant." In citing Whitehead, I highlight my argument that the different parts of the body contribute their separate and highly individualized modes of energy distribution, together with structures for storing energy, to complex and dominating centers of activity. In addition, I stress that these centers are continually displaced from one region of the body to another and that, in their successive transpositions, they synergistically aggregate themselves to effect integration and unity of the body. And woven from these separate contributions is an ordered assemblage of parts, in relations of subordination and superordination, all unified as an integral creature possessed of a sense of its own identity and aiming at intense self-enjoyment.

Symbolizing this unity, in the literal sense of *joining together* a luminous representation of disparate parts, is light. It is as though the very rhythms of light's propagation activate powers which, through the circuitous evolving of manifold organic forms, culminate in man. Nowhere has the human incarnation of light been so profoundly yet lucidly articulated as in Rembrandt's portraits. It is no accident that his shifting tonalities of light reveal so incisively human character: the astoundingly intricate recesses of human form and psyche. Hardly by chance does his deployment of chiaroscuro, the luminescent qualities and textures which he renders, disclose man's inner being: a perpetual flux, evanescent yet durable. Under this perspective, the "dominant occasions" of an integrating experience are those through which light shines with a steady, renewing glow, irridescent and variegated—now diffuse or fragmented, now intense and concentrated. Now efflorescing into myriad hues and tones, now refracted by multilaminated and crystalline structures into a kaleidoscopic dance, now pure and primordial! Matter and life are light substantialized; the person is substance as light transfigured!

Arising from the womb of creation, the quanta of light configure themselves as myriad shapes. Step by step, these shapes converge. Now they stream together in rivulets of light which, ever hastening, finally gush to torrential currents; now they diverge into finely textured but separate strands, glowing threads of nearly arrested flow. All this patterned spray of light terminates in the intricate effulgence of substance become spiritual. Persons are instances of such substance. They are modes of transient content and eternal form. The former expresses itself as patterns of metabolic pathways, routes for transmitting mutually enhancing influences, trajectories which culminate in psychic manifestation. The latter expresses itself as a certain ineffable quality, impalpable but sure, which a transcendentally personalist doctrine, later to be set forth, delineates as ultimate ground for coordinating the diverse "dominant occasions" to authentically "enduring personality."

In this book, my concern is essentially with the doctrine of transcendental naturalism. I largely prescind from elements of the personal. At the moment, I further restrict myself to the realm of the metabolic. To elaborate, I affirm: metabolism is the network of chemico-cellular processes in which two constituent subprocesses are interwoven, catabolism and anabolism. In catabolism, externally introduced nutrition in the form of protein, carbohydrate, and lipid is broken down into smaller constituents, essentially amino acids, polysacchyrides, and fatty acids.

Free (i.e., utilizable) energy decreases, and energies in the form of non-utilizable heat are dissipated. The ATP storehouse and mediator of energy exchanges (a structure which resides in intracellular mitochondria) is synthesized, thereby consuming energy. In anabolism, organismically utilizable protein, carbohydrate, and lipid are built up from amino acids, polysacchyrides, and lipids, catalyzed by the appropriate (proteinate) enzymes. Free energy increases, and is, accordingly, yielded for utilization. And this process is coupled with the splitting of ATP, that dissolution into components which release efficacious energy.

These processes, or the chemical reaction routes of catabolism and anabolism, are themselves linked. Each is constructed from the same interconvertible intermediates. Whereas catabolic routes begin with clearly defined substances and terminate with no unambiguously defined end products, precisely the converse holds for anabolic routes. The two pathways proceed in opposite directions. But they are joined in two ways: through phosphate transfers, for they involve the respective constructing and demolition of ATP; through electron transfers which allow hydrogen released during catabolic reactions to be utilized for (anabolic) bio-synthesis. In sum, from a metabolic standpoint, a multitude of energy-consuming and energy-releasing processes are set in motion, and interwoven. Each follows a special chemical-reaction trajectory; the totality constitutes the complicatedly enmeshed activities which, from the chemical side, symbolize the primordial biologic act.

(c) Flux and Stability

Yet the consummation of this biologic act is no mere interplay, however dynamically they be construed, of chemical reactions, no mere dialectical transaction of oppositional forces. It is a *teleonomic* act.[7] Metabolism is immanently directed by an underlying purposiveness. It is thrust toward a goal, crown and culmination of life itself, the ἔκστασις of organismic existence: replication. As I have shown, the activity of a self duplicating itself is woven with the very processes for which it constitutes goal and purpose. Further, as soon as substantive reflexivity appears upon the scene of fermenting matter, converting nature lifeless to nature alive, its complement, *spiritual* reflexivity, likewise (though more primitively) reveals itself within metabolizing processes. Deriving from the same source and initially analogous in their inner dynamisms, these complementary activities jointly ground the co-adaptation of one biologic form to another.

Thus originates the great enterprise whereby increasingly intricate but fragile and supple counter-entropic organisms are cast in evolution's wake. Within the envelope of the biosphere, ever greater demands are made upon available energies. Since the system is relatively closed, hugging our planet closely, and because of the inexorable workings of entropy, these organisms perforce must effectively utilize decreasing quantities of free energy. They evolve ever more delicately balanced and more complicatedly designed metabolic trajectories. The resonances which accompany chemical reactions occurring along these trajectories themselves become correlatively more subtle and ineffable. Thus, organisms resonate, as life unfolds its diverse forms, in rhythmic patterns of complexity which grows to enormous proportions. The organism is in a continual state of pulsation. It vibrates in variegated orchestrations with the rhythms of self-duplication. Among these rhythms are those which express sentiency; of the latter, some become specialized as mentation. And corresponding to increasing organismic complexity is successively greater refinement of sensibility.

Consider, again, the relation between metabolism and replication. It is a striking fact of biology that both processes, together forming the quintessential center (chemically speaking) of life itself, depend upon a single chemical factor, adenine, and upon a context for its functioning in certain predelineated ways. This member of the (heterocyclic) purine family exhibits as its basic chemical structure a (hexadic) benzene ring doubly bonded to a pentadic quasi-benzene ring, each with nitrogen replacements for certain relevant carbon atoms. In my diagram of this substance,

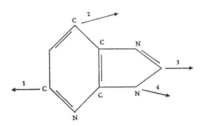

the arrows $\xrightarrow{i}$ (i = 1, 2, 3, 4), stand for an electric charge which, in *stable* adenine, is replaced successively by (H)$^+$ for $\xrightarrow{1}$, (NH2)$^+$ for $\xrightarrow{2}$, (H)$^+$ for $\xrightarrow{3}$, and a complex molecule, at the core of which is the pentose sugar, ribose, and a pyrophosphate, for $\xrightarrow{4}$. The entire structure (namely, adenine which is a purine derived nucleotide), when joined to other nucleotides, forms nucleic acid. Adenine itself is a constituent of the particular nucleic acids, deoxyribonucleic acid, or DNA, and ribonucleic acid, or RNA. As a significant chemical part of DNA, it is one of the factors which encode information about the organism with respect to its integral nature and its diverse activities. Through its role as, in addition, a significant chemical part of RNA, it both transcribes the encoded message upon RNA and, through the latter's agency, transmits that information throughout the organism. This activity, which is directed at protecting the organism's integrity and preserving its durability, may roughly be classified into three groups of functions: those pertaining to immunologic defenses and healing; those pertaining to memory, sensation and thought; and those pertaining to biologic reproduction. Now I comment upon the third group; subsequently I treat the first two groups.

In the third group, RNA catalyzes the double helix macromolecule, DNA, into those activities whereby DNA replicates itself. One half of that macromolecule forms a kind of mirror image of the now-split-off second half. Each mate then engenders a new mate upon the template of the original, combining with that mate. First transferring the information encoded therein to RNA, DNA then transmits that information to other cells. In this context, RNA catalyzes the formation of new protein from the relevant amino acids, which then enters the required metabolic pathways; aids in controlling overall protein manufacture by directing the congeries of relevant enzymes to their proper locations on the metabolic pathways; and, finally, retranscribes the information originally received by DNA to new DNA in new cells, so that analogous catalysis and replication may occur. When a sufficient number of cell-clusterings have thus been activated with respect to their component DNA, the requisite cytoplasmic material assembles itself about the requisite DNA to constitute a quasi-duplicate of the originating organism.

I say "*quasi*-duplicate" because, by the principle of the identity of indiscernibles, each replica is exact only with respect to gross morphology and function. Because of subtly modulated variations in the resonances associated with them, all replicas de facto differ. On the other hand, with identificatory techniques currently available, a principle of fidelity holds. Each molecule of DNA is the blueprint for an exact duplicate. At the same time, the composition of an RNA molecule faithfully reflects the DNA template upon which it was formed. Despite the diverse metabolic processes in which it participates, that molecule remains unaltered. Nevertheless, both copy errors and random mutants may appear. Inexact duplicates will be rendered of the sequence of polypeptide (i.e., polymers) woven of amino acids, and twisted into complicatedly interlinked chains of protein. Somewhere along this route of transformation, some ingredient may accordingly suffer a defect.

The cytoplasmic material peripheralizing itself about DNA is composed primarily of protein, with a lipid matrix and a carbohydrate support. This cytoplasm is implicated in metabolic processes the intermeshed chemical-reaction routes of which, both bio-synthetic and bio-degrading, are linked through a common tie to ATP. Having noted that adenine is the purine base in the energy storehouse, ATP, one can infer that adenine suspended in an ionized aqueous solution is, in effect, one of the life invariants. It is that invariant which mediates the two most fundamental activities in the adventure of life.

Metabolism unfolds as a conscrescence of phases. In its primordial phase, the fundamental structures and functions manifest themselves in sharply etched ways. Here, I deal with this phase. But, in its consequent phase, initial differentiations break down. A more integrated and, indeed, transfigured plexus reveals itself. Later, I examine this new plexus.

To refer again, to the primordial phase: the mediating invariant, adenine, which links metabolism's diverse elements, reorganizes the chains of chemical reactivity as organic polymers and nucleic acids; the organism acquires greater elasticity and deformability. Wedded to the sturdy structures DNA and RNA, which function like stable axes, this flexible organism pulsates with numberless

rhythms. Built upon the finer resonances of those structures, the diverse metabolic reactions weave multitudinous arrangements of ever-increasing adaptability.
Orchestrating themselves into sweeping contrapuntal patterns, these reactions, despite wide-ranging transformations of the organism's milieu, preserve that invariant as the very core of life.

To recapitulate: these processes may thus be presented—

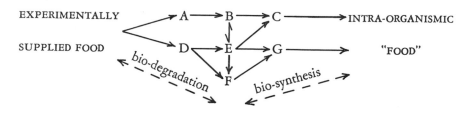

In bio-syntheses, the building blocks of life are first shaped from the diffuse
materials deposited by catabolism. From these, macromolecules essential for life
are assembled. Though oppositely directed, catabolism itself does not govern bio-
synthesis, in spite of the fact that it utilizes many of the latter's intermediate
products for its own end: to provide initial material that metabolism might continue. Yet catabolism is interwoven with bio-synthesis. For bio-synthesis and bio-
degradation are so enmeshed that an increasingly ordered system, the metabolizing organism, is always created at the expense of a less ordered milieu. On balance,
the overall *coupled* reactions of catabolism and anabolism are accompanied by a
decrease in free energy. Hence, these reactions are irreversible in the direction of
bio-synthesis. Passing through intermediate routes, with diversions, overlappings,
and rechannelings, bio-synthesis terminates in the production of definite materials
from diffuse and ambiguously defined precursors. In catabolism, however, converse modes of origination and termination hold. Definite precursors are assembled, then progressively split into diffuse products. Accordingly, bio-synthesis and
bio-degradation are mutually presupposing processes. But they are also reciprocally
enhancing!

These interwoven processes are regulated by two kinds of control which, together, not only maintain organismic stability but, beyond that, lead to greater
organismic vitality. These controls may be coarse or they may be refined. So variegated are the metabolic pathways, and so linked are they to criss-crossing subordinate pathways, that many highly specialized enzymes are required for their
regulation. In general, fine control depends upon two factors: the available sub-
strate on which key pacemaker enzymes can act; the proper intra-cellular concentrations of metabolites affecting pacemaker enzyme reaction rates. These
regulatory metabolites either speed up or slow down enzyme activity; they determine the shifting schemes of metabolic pathways; they alter molecules by acting

upon them at specific regulatory sites. Organismic molecules are perpetually in movement. They are shaped and reshaped in response to forces acting upon local regions of sensitivity. A veritable ferment of molecular sensibility; precursor to the Unconscious; ground of awareness itself!

Through a network of self-regulating systems, homeostasis is maintained. But, by contingency or by teleonomy, homeostasis is often disrupted, and homeo*dynamics* supervenes, though momentarily. These transient disequilibrations are significant. They create minuscule metabolic crises, primordia of personal crisis. By the organism's readjusting of both its own chemical-reaction routes and enzyme quantity and distribution, as well as by its shifting of molecular regulatory sites and its reconfiguring of molecular orientations to create new stereometric patterns, internal organismic sensitivity is heightened. The way is prepared for evolutionary leaps into ever-heightening sentiency.

In these transformations, metabolic routes as well as sites of action are constantly altered. All is in flux; stability supervenes; flux is renewed: a cycle of ebb and flow. These routes both condition and sensitize one another with respect to such factors as reaction rate, pathway configuration, composition by interchanging ingredients. Ever-novel modes of metabolic coordination must be worked out. And throughout this process, the organism passes into states of excitation. Functions are redistributed; new structures emerge. New systems of interlocking constellations of molecular groupings are created. This organismic lability grounds the possibility for a procession of new levels of equilibration. On the whole, enzymes which catalyze the entire action are, at times, synchronized. But, at times, they are mutually cacophonous. In general, these factors do not act as direct effectors; rather, they inhibit such processes as, when they are released from their control, may indeed catalyze the entire system into paroxysms of activity. But, overall, self-regulation prevails. Recovery from such internally induced stress normally prevails. Everywhere, mutual interaction and reciprocal interference dominate metabolism. Steering its diverse motions into variable courses, restitution of metabolic integrity is, on the whole, nonetheless achieved.

But when these more finely attuned processes are insufficiently tranquil, for sufficient time intervals, the machinery of the organism becomes subject to coarser controls. Hormones are excreted, passing from cell to cell, from tissue to tissue, and from organ to organ. Although previously fine controls allowed for sensitive adjustments of the nutrient flux along prescribed metabolic pathways, when this overall flow deviates by large increments from the norms of metabolism, now they are so realigned that homeostasis again prevails, but this time through hormonal action. As one ascends toward more complicatedly interiorized organisms, homeo*dynamic* processes tend more and more to dominate. Nevertheless, potentials for vegetative response, expressing the more delicate variations of homeostasis, persist —e.g., in the form of the autonomic nervous system—to afford a sturdy instinctual foundation for organismic behavior. Yet pervading all organisms is a balance between fine controls, manifesting alternating repressions and accelerations of enzyme activity, and coarse controls, expressed by appropriate hormone production.

In brief, hormones and enzymes jointly determine which modalities of balance between diverse organismic parts will allow the organism to seek its aim toward self-enjoyment and which, on the contrary, will thwart that aim. Surely, every living creature is suspended between two limits of *im*balance: a "lower" limit beyond which pathologic behavior is exhibited, disclosing acute disproportionality among its diverse activities; and an "upper" limit beyond which mutant forms of extravagant vitality display themselves, exemplifying the *genius* potentially resident within each organism for significantly reordering both its own internal relations and those constituting its milieu. Later, I note certain consequences, especially important for an account of the person, when organismic balancings go awry, in the direction of either limit.

C · CONCRESCENT METABOLISM: ORGANIC FUNCTIONS DIVERSIFIED

(*a*) Bio-Space and Bio-Time

To proceed further with my account of these balances and imbalances, I must consider two additional functions of metabolism, each complementary to replication and all linked by the same invariant chemical structure: memory and, beyond that, processes which involve sentiency and mentation, immunology and healing. In these sets of activities, the same chemical dynamism is implicated. Speculation regarding the ultimate import of metabolism, in its consequent nature, may be both facilitated and enriched by my showing a fundamental analogy among these functions.

This fundamental analogy is prefigured in the associations of these functions with biologic space, time, and matter. Earlier, I defined bio-space as expressing organismic morphology, the modes of distribution of organic parts; correlatively, I defined physical space as schemes of potential compresence among events. By bio-time, I meant the system of interwoven, and often quite intricate, bio-cycles; correlatively, physical time referred to event trajectories through schemes of compresence, one layered upon another. Finally, by bio-matter, I meant processes of energeia, i.e., organismic energy transformations, modalities, and interchanges; correlatively, physical matter expressed differential regions of rarefaction and condensation, the virtual motions of the shifting density patterns of events.

In the primordial phase of metabolism, its characteristic functions are linked to space, time, and matter. In their linkages, these functions, considered jointly under the topic "consequent phases of metabolism," will be exhibited as mediating the transition from the sphere of the biological to the sphere of the personal. In my argument, immunology will be related to bio-space, reflection to bio-time, and reproduction to bio-matter. In each case, disparate—hence, merely assembled— metabolic elements are conjugated to form integral and coherent activities. Later, these coalescing factors will be shown to converge upon a single overall function, the fusion and, indeed, the transformation of the separate functions to the unitary product which subserves organismic integrity. This unification itself will be seen to be a manifestation of the (previously demonstrated) internal unity of space, time, and matter, in both its physical and its biologic aspects.

From the point of view of metabolism, biologic space concerns the preservation of organismic integrality. It expresses contemporaneous foundations for the possibility of sustenance and growth through the variegated defenses which the organism constructs against potential invading pathogens. In general, the host must immunize itself vis-à-vis such intrusions, or, should they occur, it must set in motion the processes by which healing may more efficaciously be achieved. For the organism must take such measures as will maintain a stable configuration of compresence with other organisms—a configuration which preserves its intactness and, at the same time, sets the conditions for the fulfilling of its essential organismic functions. This matrix of relationships *is* its space. Immunology expresses the moment by moment enhancement of organismic vitality, guaranteeing a stable scheme of compresence by rejecting all infelicitous intrusions.

Metabolically speaking, biologic time involves an organismic subject's projecting itself *regressively* into its own memories, dwelling among them, and searching its own concrete past; it involves that subject's projecting itself *progressively* into thoughts, the interwoven scheme of ideas which are, so to speak, anticipatory mirrorings of an hypothecated future; it involves the subject's extending itself in sensation and perception toward its milieu, gathering in their stimuli, their impingements, and their presences as its own collective (temporal) present. Accordingly, as in its immunologic function, the organism protects its integrity, sustains its existence, and grows to an activity of more diversified powers and richer experiential potentiality by its reflective preoccupation with its own temporality: a past, present, and future woven into its ongoingness as a living creature.

Finally, the quest of the organism to preserve itself, especially when it "construes" self-preservation as defying time and indefinitely extending itself, is to perpetuate itself through another. When it has become sufficiently pregnant with organic vitalities, the organism must reproduce and, thereby, transfer its own substance, its energeia, to a near-replica, its offspring; yet these offspring are but one generation of members in an indefinite lineage of potential progeny. Itself only a single creature in an ancestral chain which stretches back to life's very beginnings, every organism declares its substantive continuity with all living creatures. This fact is highlighted by the dramatic observation that precisely the same DNA–RNA replicatory theme is repeated, from time immemorial, over life's entire range, with but minor variations (in the sphere of subtle, imperceptible resonances) on a fixed and invariant morphologic structure. Because of the action of this replicatory dynamism, biologic matter concerns the persistence of material identity.

Through immuno-healing acts, the organism spatializes itself with respect to other organisms; it discriminates a manifold of stable (spatial) relations which express diverse modes of compresence with other organisms and, thereby, protects its characteristic style of compresence. Through reflective acts, the organism temporalizes itself, discriminating a manifold of (temporal) relations within which past, present, and future are focal regions; it establishes its spiritual ties with the cosmos. Through reproductive acts, the organism materializes itself by perpetuating its own living substance. Within this substance, it both discriminates particular replicas and specifies the material relations which bind together, as an intricate genealogy, its ancestors, itself, and its progeny.

Yet these functions cannot be dissociated from one another. Each implicates and presupposes the remainder. Immuno-healing acts are so constituted that the vitalities requisite to reproduction constitute, for the most part, a natural defense against pathogenic processes to which the organism might otherwise be susceptible or might even succumb. A multitude of progeny is virtual guarantor for continuance of the spawning organism in at least some of its replicas. With respect to reflection, clearly the stimuli which the organism receives from its milieu sensitizes, where necessary, its immunologic capabilities. Memory and anticipation in addition promote such perceptivity as will facilitate protection. Secondly, the reflective act is so constituted that when the organism has (through immunologic prowess) successfully combated prospective invaders, its receptive powers are enlarged sufficiently to enable it to gather more inclusive classes of stimuli for thought and remembrance, stimuli which it otherwise would be too debilitated to absorb and utilize. From the side of reproduction, schemes of ideas are therein transmitted and, in effect, achieve incarnation in progeny. For the mutants cast in the wake of replication introduce novelty into what otherwise are perpetuated as, for organisms, quasi-spiritual traditions in the form of instinctual patterns of (potential) conduct. Finally, replication itself is brought to fruition within an immunologically wholesome context. Insofar as an organism has antecedently gained power for rejecting pathogens, it is enabled to consummate the reproductive act with less likelihood of aborted or defective progeny. In addition, replication is clearly affected by such (reflective) factors as foresight and hindsight, as well as by contemporary evaluations with respect to the need for exerting control over reproduction or, conversely, to the power for fructifying its acts.

(b) Organismic Integrity

Beyond these considerations, there is a deeper tie which links these three metabolic functions. All are in the service of maintaining organismic integrity, of defending it against disruption, and of sustaining the organism through unfortuitous circumstances. The recurrent constant which conditions, potentiates, initiates, and governs these functions is nothing other than the DNA–RNA replicatory dynamism, working in accordance with general principles which I now enumerate.

Three interwoven and overlapping aspects of replication may be distinguished: adjacency, invariancy, and electivity. In the first aspect, each cell transmits to adjacent cells information about its own makeup, an image of itself in relation to its milieu. Encoded within the relevant cell nucleotides, this information varies slightly from cell to cell. Mutant variations upon fundamental informational themes are randomly distributed among these cells. Such mutants survive as are congenial to a given milieu; others are ineffectual, save in rare instances when they "wall" themselves off from the milieu—or, should the milieu itself dramatically change in such fashion as to favor those mutants. In principle, gestation may occur in any cell. But in more complicatedly organized creatures, certain constellations of cells are selected for this process. Within such constellations, cell pairings occur wherein relevant information deriving from each cell is fused. Within every cell pair, normally a single member functions as matrix for germinating a replica of significant features of both cells. In effect, replication is the process whereby cells collaborate for the purpose of achieving their own collective "perfections," perfections dispersedly and potentially resident within these cells. This process is triphasic: a phase of gratuity, in which each cell spontaneously "prefers" certain information for possible use; a phase of locking-in, in which cells create a passage between them through which information may be exchanged; a phase of projection, wherein cells so thrust themselves toward one another as to activate a substantival matrix which bears an ideal image of both cells in their mutual relatedness.

In the second aspect, the phenomenon of invariancy discloses itself. Despite both random perturbations and systematic variations, a certain structure, self-sufficient and stable, is maintained throughout all transformations. Each cell contributes its share to protoplasmic substance, the consummation and incarnation of both cells. Despite these individual contributions, a certain set of factors is preserved as invariant. The plan of this unfolding activity resides in all DNA–RNA systems. Initially dispersed, but progressively coming to confluence, the ingredients of the factors which ultimately bear the significant information to be imparted assemble in a given locus, after having been propelled from afar toward that locus by numberless forces. This point of convergence is unique. Conjugated from four nucleotides, the relevant nucleic acid becomes differentiated into DNA and RNA. Analogously, polymerized from twenty-three amino acids, the relevant polypeptides form a multitude of proteins. The processes whereby these macromolecules are created are themselves interrelated. Step by step, conjugation occurs, then linkage to polymers, finally a dramatic closing in upon itself in a dance of synthesis: dispersal, convergence, concretization as vital substance wherein closure and a kind of interiorization supervene. To consummate this process, replication (utilizing nucleic acid and protein) involves a leap into futurity, an objectification as new substance in which the patterns and rhythms of the original organicity are preserved.

In the third aspect, the factor of electivity dominates. Initially, a project, a teleonomy, a spontaneous self-directedness prevails. Each cell thrusts itself toward another. In this act, different cells "recognize" or *elect*[8] one another. For each contains factors—DNA, RNA, and their constituent nucleotides—which exhibit mutual affinities, allostereospecificities. Such inter-molecular acknowledgment arises from the presence on diverse molecules of specialized regions of excitation. Asymmetric molecules, drawn from distinct cells, complement their respective loci of sensitivity by joining together. In this manner, neutralization of "opposing" loci occurs. Even a kind of gratification of their "yearnings" supervenes. Yet, in the midst of fusion, synthesis, and cancellation of hyper-excitability, an aura of resonance hovers about the mating molecules, code bearers and message bearers for the organism. Opposing rhythms gather. Their fugue-like interplay intensifies. Even as opposition heightens, coruscations of apposition become condensed and "solidified," but never to mere durable structure. A veritable transmutation into Heraclitean effulgence prevails! Surely, the permanent and the changing are inextricably enmeshed. Energies flow to crucial points. Therein, energies are synergized and amplified. Increments of electric potential widen. The gap sparks new excitation. Throughout this orchestration, spins, motions of all kinds, a multitude of harmonies unfold. Yet this commotion clusters about the (relatively) stable axes of DNA and RNA, axes with respect to which polymeric strands wrap and twist themselves with diverse movements of translation and rotation. Pervading all are inter-molecular inductions, intra-molecular splittings, weak bonds and un-bondings, strong bonds and un-bondings.

This plexus of movement and stability, discernible within the three aspects of replication, is not anomic. Order reigns, order both gross and subtle. In its morphologic dimension, the former has been worked out in innumerable experiments; the latter may only be speculated upon. In any event, a context is created wherein cellular activity may be elaborated into processes of involution and convolution, processes which comprise the evolutionary drama of life. Thus orienting themselves spontaneously toward one another, cells and all imaginable kinds of cell-clusterings, build ever-new (counter-entropic) schemes of integral co-adaptation.

The topics, thus far briefly mentioned, of immunology and reflection, especially the latter, under additional facets of replication, will occupy me in the remainder of this book. They become particularly important in the context of (i) the assemblage of multicellular aggregates and (ii) interorganismic behavior. To deal adequately with these types, I require (in my final chapter) the theme *co-adaptation*. Suffice it now to note that the invariant factor of these fundamental metabolic functions has been postulated as the DNA–RNA replicatory dynamism. In the context of metabolism, the relations among these functions are illuminated by considering their association, as I have already indicated, with bio-space, bio-time, and bio-matter. Indeed, the unity of *these* dimensions is metabolism itself, metabolism in its consequent phase: the integral substance of life. From the standpoint of the primordial phase of metabolism, I have proposed a single structure, *adenine*, as representing the ultimate life invariant. The additional functions, immunology and reflection, imply the validity of this proposal quite as much as does the function already proposed: namely, replication. However, I must not be understood in the strict or literal sense. For, according to my claim, adenine is but a symbol, a mode of representing something as elusive but pervasive, something which *is*, in fact, the life invariant. In my final chapter, I treat certain subtleties of this topic.

(c) Organismic Pathology With Respect to Bio-Space, Bio-Time, and Bio-Matter

Prior to passing to my concluding themes, wherein these topics will be taken up, I must stress, in a preliminary way, some general implications of my deliberatings for organismic pathology. These considerations will constitute the beginning for laying the groundwork for a theory of the bearings of pathology upon human psyche. In *Choros*, a book which is more directly concerned with personal rhythms, I undertake this task.

With respect to bio-space, the metabolic expression of which is the immunologic power of the body, the root pathologic condition is cancer, which constitutes the most pervasive immunologic defect. Here, the usual modes of intra-organismic compresence—hence, by implication, interorganismic compresence as well—go awry, undergoing insidious deformation. Distortions in organismic morphology and contour are rampant. Diverse atrophyings and hypertrophyings, bizarre neo-plastic metastases, weird intra-nuclear cellular mitoses alike betoken a metabolic disease of profound import. Though often blending with healthy tissue, deformed cells spread amorphously and willy-nilly throughout the body. Yet these tissues ineluctably function as alien corporeal introjects to which the body as a whole must orient itself. Indeed, it may well be that the patho-plasticity of cancer is individualized in its earlier stages. In this case, specific initial localization would be associated with prodromal signs related not only to genetically determined sites of predilection but also to particular psychic deprivation. A given site would be determined by the individual nature of that deprivation. As a result, the body may well be affected in regions psychically associated with irretrievable personal loss. If so, cancer is a neoplastic symbol, the somaticized and inalienable sub-stitute for a lost external object. And inability to control this object, through giving and receiving in authentic care, eventuates in analogous loss of control with respect to its carcinogenic correlate. Depressed cortical excitation may be linked to unresolved neoplasias, just as it may also, in a different pathologic context, be linked to exacerbated schizophrenia.

In relating to this carcinogenic tissue, the wholesome body becomes randomly depleted of vital energies. A strangely anomic composition of dissociated cells, isolated and wild, goes astray; they sink to dissolution and death. The body clings regressively to an object which is forever receding, an elusive object the quest for which leads to physiologic disorientation and imbalance. Insofar as every organism endeavors to persist as an integral unity, the body seeks to reassimilate, in a kind of tender concern, these unwholesome elements. Yet, inexorably, it is drawn toward non-being, all its love pouring into an unrequiting void. Indeed, in cancer, which fundamentally expresses a metabolic *de*pression, there is profound imbalance between the non-being ground and the pure being ground of organismic activity.

With respect to bio-time, the metabolic expressions of which are the reflective processes, the root pathologic condition is schizophrenia, which constitutes the most pervasive psychic derangement, in fact, the correlate in this sphere to cancer in the corporeal sphere. Here, the psyche is dominated by heterogeneous, inchoate, and contorted psychic factors. A strange cacophony prevails. Quasi-ideas, quasi-memories, quasi-sensations are wedded; degenerate and split-off psychic elements grotesquely combine. Disharmoniously manifesting themselves as hallucinations, weird agents are incorporated as alien to body and psyche, yet agents to which the person (or, by analogy, any schizophrenic-prone organism) is forced to relate. Although in cancer all regions of the body may, in the end, be affected, schizophrenia is, from a corporeal standpoint, more consistently localized. Since it implicates bio-space, cancer is perforce more diffuse; the entire organism is affected. Involving bio-time, the lesion associated with schizophrenia is restricted in locale. Perhaps, it is confined to centers mediating, or implicated within, the time sense. In this case, certain vestibular nuclei located in the temporal lobes of the brain (or brain equivalent), where tracts from variegated neural regions come to confluence—hence, are activated to interchange their contents—could be the primary sites of affliction. The *mélange* thereby created would lead to profound confusions, even upheavals, of organismic temporality.

As in cancer, the incorporated psychic objects, which ramify like bizarre fungi and exhibit their own atrophyings and hypertrophyings, drain psycho-physical energies.[9] With a kind of desperate care, the person likewise seeks to redintegrate these dissociated fragments within his integral being. Yet, as in cancer, he is inexorably led toward a void. Helpless, uprooted, and alone, the person is doomed to combat these tormenting hallucinatory introjects, this strange mixture of disparate psychic elements. It is as though he were embedded in a field of traumatic personal influences, his very spiritual existence determined by *physical* factors, factors which disallow him the space within which, by his free decisions, he might move and live. Voices are, as it were, stuck inside his head, voices which are noisy, prohibiting, tyrannical, tormenting. By the very pervasiveness of this disease, he must entrust himself to these devasting presences; they shape a virtual cosmos within his being. Yet he never ceases to be harassed pitilessly from within. And so he gives himself up to disorientation, imbalance, and unreality. Haphazardly, without being able to steady his keel, he is thrust between non-being and pure being.

With respect to the dimension of bio-matter, the metabolic expression of which is the reproductive act (and all that this act implies), the root pathologic condition is the congeries of illnesses which, genetically determined or congenitally conditioned, afflict progeny and potential progeny. Among these illnesses, the most common to affect diffuse regions of the organism, especially its most vital parts, is, for man, Down's syndrome (formerly called Mongolism). In this disease, not only is the brain severely affected, but the heart, genitals, and musculature; and other metabolic processes may be implicated in ways which distort many critical functions. In addition, Down's syndrome appears to involve a defect of the parental replicatory system as well as the victim's. Since disease categories associated with reproduction are less clearly demarcated than cancer or schizophrenia, with respect to both pathodynamics and symptomatology, I include under the rubric bio-matter, such disturbances as abortion, sterility, and, indeed, birth defects in general.

From the standpoint of an organism with a large progeny, many deviant offspring will be found. In each instance, the quality of care tendered these offspring will be altered from the norm. So deprived are they with respect to the accuracy with which they replicate the parent that he will experience them as, in effect, alienated from his own substance. In principle, however, he will seek to care for them by imagining them to be endowed with a fictitious "self." He will relate to idealized images unconsciously imputed to the offspring, rather than to the actual (aborted) mutants. For persons, such progeny can constitute incarnations of aspects of parental substance which, repressed in the parent, are unacknowledged by him. In this case, the parent will find the child repugnant and, hence, unworthy of his love. Now the very substance of the parent–child *relationship* has become deficient. It is the matrix of caring which has, so to speak, become diseased. That relationship is now experienced as involving profound incongruities. Bizarre atrophy and hypertrophy of progeny! Grotesque orientations toward progeny! A double illness has evolved. Analogously to cancer and schizophrenia, the true object of concern is regressively experienced as receding toward a void. Object love is insatiable. Defensively, and by implication, while communities of quasi-replicas are walled off. Thus isolated from a wholesome genealogy, its every member is deprived of love. Striving to transmute inalterable mutants into authentic replicas, the parent experiences a profound flaw in his capacity to care. Throughout his body, as well as in that which is substantively continuous with him— namely, the bodies of mutant progeny—this inability manifests itself in metabolic deformation and, ultimately, in depression.

I here affirm a deep analogy. Cancer is to the body what schizophrenia is to the psyche and aborted progeny is to the community of persons. Yet, in every case, three *interwoven* "entities" are involved, though each is stressed in one disease more than in another. These entities are the corporeal, the psychic, the interpersonal. Deformation, contortion, and incongruity reign throughout. They are exemplified in body, symbol, and person. Underlying all these diseases is metabolic degeneration. This occurs through a kind of hyper-permeable metabolic plexus. In this primordial pathology, body, symbol, and person are excessively receptive to noxious and disruptive stimuli. Failing to ward off such stimuli, the organism falls into metabolic depression. Yet it never ceases to reach out toward the depressed factors, to endeavor to absorb them, and to strive to restore vitality. Whatever the invariant adenine truly represents, some mutant upon this invariant, a subtle resonance, leads to deformation. Always, a defect of the encoding, transcribing, and transmitting of information prevails.

However, in each case, a positive analogue to disease may be distinguished: regeneration rather than degeneration, genius rather than insanity, wholesome offspring rather than sick. Between the limiting poles of depression and vitality, most organisms conduct their lives. Though utterly distant from one another, pathology and the radical converse of pathology are strangely close. For, at the very basis of all organismic activity, over the entire range of normality and abnormality, is the unifying ground in the primordial phase of metabolism. Here, the ramifying chemical adenine symbolizes a common structure for every metabolic act. This structure joins its inwardly linked manifestations: the immunologic, the reflective, the reproductive. Metabolism itself is a synthesis of mutually intensifying resonances prevalent throughout the body. Governed by a hierarchy of fine controls and gross controls, novelty cumulatively and ceaselessly evolves along diverse routes. Certain mutant resonances, or certain deviant routes, favor disease. Others, far more prevalent and perhaps structurally akin, favor heightened vitality.

NOTES

1. For the following discussion, see *Phenomenon of Man*, esp. Book IV; see also the index entries for "phylogenesis."
2. See Vol. VI of the *Collected Papers of Charles Sanders Peirce*, edd. Charles Hartshorne and Paul Weiss (Cambridge: The Belknap Press of Harvard University Press, 1935), sects. 255, 277.
3. See the appropriate entries in Partridge, *Origins*.
4. See the appropriate entries in ibid.
5. Shakespeare, Sonnet 17.
6. *Process and Reality*, p. 140.
7. Jacques Monod, *Le Hazard et la nécessité* (Paris: du Seuil, 1970), p. 26.
8. Ibid., pp. 75–112.
9. W. Ronald D. Fairbairn, "An Object-Relations Theory of the Personality," *Psychoanalytic Studies of the Personality* (London & Boston: Routledge & Kegan Paul, 1952), esp. pp. 82, 136.

IV

Implications of the Animate:
Consequent Categories

8

FROM BIOLOGIC ACT
TO PERSONAL BEING

PREAMBLE

Now I treat the philosophic import of the succession of changes by which the living organism is progressively, and by seemingly miraculous leaps, transformed into the person. I do not propose that the sole origins of personal being lie in the sphere of the biologic and, by implication, the material. True, by my thesis, the infrapersonal realm has been regarded as essentially a product of vectorially ascendant forces, forces which arise within the condition of physical elementarity. Under a naturalistic perspective, the penultimate ancestry of life's numberless variegated forms resides in the inanimate. Beyond that ancestry lie altogether mysterious stirrings. In the end, the inanimate itself is the progeny of non-being, its articulation and its diversification. From a philosophic point of view, one ground of personhood is a rhythmic emanation of all that must be consigned to a non-existence shrouded in darkness. By stages, physiogenesis transforms itself into biogenesis. Progressively, privative being is transfigured, first, into the crystalline being of the merely physical; then, into the fermenting being of the organismic; and, finally, into personal being, an entirely new modality which, in turn, undergoes its own characteristic genesis.

In setting forth the procession of actions which lead, phase by phase, to their culmination in the person, I prescind from a coeval source of personhood, the suprapersonal or, ultimately, pure being. Earlier, I suggested as topic for subsequent inquiry the esoteric dialectic, from an ontologic point of view, between pure being and non-being. I proposed that correlated with essentiality's infrapersonal stages with respect to man's makeup—namely, the privative, the crystalline, and the fermenting—are analogous stages quite as essential as the former when seen within the suprapersonal perspective. The latter I designate the *plenitudinous,* referring to pure being; the *ineffable,* referring to mysterious and unspecified rhythms deriving from pure being; and the *ethereal*—those cosmic resonances which hover about man like a celestial aura, no account of which can be reduced to systematic formulation of such corporeal rhythms as are treated by natural science.

These two series—namely, the descent from pure being and the ascent from non-being, each comprising three stages of essentiality—are equally important for grounding personal being. In this final chapter, I deal only with such contributions as are made by the first series, the infrapersonal. Abstracting from the person qua emanatum of *total* being, that profoundly spiritual union of pure being and non-being, I focus exclusively upon him qua emanatum of non-being. Thereby, I provide the broader context in which a metabolizing organism, transfigured and concrescent, is to be understood, once that organism has evolved to the status of the human body, the consummation of a transcendentally naturalistic evolution. Made specifically experiential as metabolism's consequent phase, this context provides the ground for passage to my next book, *Choros.* In this way, I bring to conclusion the general plan of *The Dance of Being*: namely, systematically to set forth the main factors governing infrapersonal activity in its relevance for a philosophic theory of the person; and I link the tenets comprising my conclusion with the primordial categories introduced in Part I.

In particular, I dwell upon the process whereby, stage by stage, from out of the human labyrinth, grows, through small leaps and great, the marvelous tapestry of speech. In their special questings, organisms just prior to man in evolution's great march hover upon the threshold of speech. Their apparent every attempt to shape authentic words is inexorably aborted, or at most doomed to an undynamic, un-self-transfiguring destiny. True, the primate stretches toward a world which it finds exhilarating and challenging. In its manner, it seeks new experience; it expresses tenderness and care and compassion; it experiments with novel combinations of the forces and the things which it perceptively discriminates. But not until, metamorphosed into man, it stands upright, not till *he* can survey creation's great globe or peer into its more obscure recesses, is he privileged to form the sounds by which, with ever-growing finesse, he may attune himself to those recesses, and discern its deeper intricacies and its subtler nuances. Not until his brain has shaped myriad new convolutions, and his fingers acquired greatly enhanced suppleness, may man articulate nature's harmonies and dissonances as no mere multiverse—as doubtless it must remain for the primate—nor, as, for the behaviorist, a universe easy to conceive in its broader contours, but as a veridical cosmos: unfathomable in its profound unity, crucible within which man alone attains his higher transfigurations.

A · CO-ADAPTATIONS: ECOLOGY ASCENDANT

Throughout, I have stressed two methodologic principles, principles both analogous and correlated to one another though not identical in their connotations. On the one hand, three interwoven and mutually presupposing moments replicate themselves throughout the procession of the inanimate to the animate, and pervade the unfolding diversification of life. Exemplified in each living form, and by every phase of growth, these moments acquire ever-increasing elaboration of detail. Assemblage, conjugation, and transformation occur everywhere in the infrapersonal domain. On the other hand, an additional set of interdependent moments unfolds, with increasing subtlety of application, in all development, pre-organismic and organismic. Self-action, interaction, and transaction universally pervade this domain. Now my concern is to exhibit the relevance of these triphasic principles for an understanding of the phenomenon of co-adaptation, with respect to the import of this phenomenon for the emerging person. Reflection upon their specific exemplifications illuminates the inner meaning of the ascending intricacies of ecologic balance and imbalance.

(a) The Biologic Act

Thus far, I have designated as the fundamental biologic unit, a unit of which all organisms are composed, either the cell or a more primitive protoplasmic analogue to the cell. But I must now emend this formulation. Examination of the integral unities which progressively evolve during successive cell and proto-cell coalescings reveals that the primordial unit is, in actuality, the biologic *act*,[1] whether composite or simple. My inquiry has suggested that organismic elementarity requires continual redefinition, depending upon the particular context in which biologic entities function. True, for less complex organisms that unit tends, on the whole, to be the cell. Yet proto-cellular factors, such as viruses which lack many significant features of the cell, exhibit certain essential attributes of life. They possess both a replicatory system and the enveloping metabolic matrix by which that system is activated. In consequence, the *adenine* invariant, and all it symbolizes, ground the integrity of the proto-cell as a unit of life; it is an integral biologic act. Granted: the metabolic matrix might not be borne by that system through the diverse peregrinations of the proto-cell. Nonetheless, it is discovered by the system within the milieu which it perchance comes to inhabit. For, functionally, the matrix is the schema of processes most congenial to the more durable modes of symbiotic relatedness which the system might establish with its milieu. Moreover, in the more complex organisms, cellular migrations, redistributions, and transformations so rearrange the metabolic configuration that no longer may ancestral cellular factors be deemed *the* primordial units. What had hitherto been a mere aggregate of cells is now reconstituted as tissue, organ, or system of organs, in each instance, a novel integral entity. During the course of organismic complexification and interiorization, different functional units emerge as fundamental. No longer is a simply designated structural unit, associated with readily specifiable functions, an elementary building block of life. Quite the contrary. Different morphologic organizations may assume analogous functions; distinct functions may be correlated to quite variable morphologic patterns. What had been an indivisible biologic whole is now an intricate plexus of biologic units. What had been a group of units is now joined to indivisibility.

What is this biologic act I now designate as primary: its features, it phases, its functions? How does the organism evolve into a plexus of intricately arranged acts, acts which realize their latent potentialities over a wide range of magnitude, intensity, and complexity of structural and functional composition? Wherein lies the power by which its often disparate and seemingly incongruous elements are unified into a single, integral action? Analogous to the physical event, a protoplasmic process unfolds in phases. No single phase may be excluded from this process without destroying the integrity of the act which that process expresses. Nor may any phase pre-empt a congeries of biologic events constituting the most essential aspects of that act. All phases are interwoven and mutually presupposing. Here, I distinguish three phases: a building up of biologic tensions, a peak tension which constitutes the critical limen of the act, and a subsidence of tension. I treat these phases briefly and seriatim.

In the nascent phase, a moment of incipient coalescence, the act is born of a matrix composed of antecedent perishing acts. Corresponding to the initial phase in the unfolding physical event, though with enormously increased complexity, diverse and often disparate factors, themselves biologic acts or proto-biologic chemical-reaction chains, are gathered into a unity of action. Localized neither in the phase of its origination nor in any subsequent phase, this unity expresses a quality which pervades the entirety, a quality which may be denoted but not readily specified. The diverse currents of biologic flow thus gathered together are vectorially directed toward a culminating focus, a point of confluence of numberless strands of action. This focus may be identified with a particular, discrete region of the organism, structurally or functionally defined. Alternatively, as with neural phenomena, it may be diffused over large regions which are not sharply demarcated from one another. Or it may be distributed to widely separated regions, regions structurally disjoined but functionally interconnected. Finally, even the criterion of functional cohesion is not absolute. The entire organism, scene of often widely dispersed and but loosely coordinated operations, can serve as integral locus for the unitary action of any of its component acts.

In the intermediate moment, a moment which mediates transition from one state of tension dispersal to another, the vectorial directedness initiated in the nascent phase—which itself never ceases throughout the matrix of processes constituting the biologic act—is progressively intensified. Tensions mount; they combine, deflect one another, shape a laminated system, synergize novel arrangements. Thus reordering themselves as new schemes of confluence, this organization of tensions constitutes the ground wherein a dynamic pattern emerges and perpetuates itself. Exemplified in diverse biologic forms, this pattern acquires, through interplay of act and milieu, significant ornamentation upon its fundamental composition. It links with other dynamic patterns analogously shaped; and, in this joining, distinct patterns become subsumed under more inclusive dynamic arrangements. In this process, different components of the biologic act exhibit mutual affinities and antagonisms. Associated with their variegated impulsions, these components, on the whole, work together to bring about a series of consummations in the progressively mounting tension. At each instant in this procession, the organismic act is laden with primordial expectations based upon prior summings up and fulfillments. Associated with symmetries in both the distribution of tensions and their adjustments to one another, these expectations are heightened, diminished, or in some fashion altered. By *symmetry*, I here mean a momentary equilibrium of counteractant yet mutually reinforcing tensions preparatory first to disequilibration, then to readaptation.

In the final phase, detonation, a relaxation of the hitherto sustained and mounting tonus, supervenes. Previously, the succession of symmetrized rhythmic schemes, composed of rhythms now coalescing, now dispersing, rhythms exhibiting pervasive order but touched by an element of variation and disorder, culminated in a critical juncture at which tensions attained a maximum of *in*tensity. These tensions constituted a system of intricately involuted and entwined tensions, the totality manifesting itself as patterns of fluctuant intensity. But momentarily poised at this juncture, these out-folding rhythms now begin to disperse themselves in variegated sequence and with measured cadence. A choric-like recessional, companion to renewed processions, unfolds. Resolutions may be sudden or gradual. But whatever the mode of rhythm its contrapuntal and fugal retreat expresses, the recessional immediately consequent upon consummation of the act entails some kind of subsidence. The tumult dies down; detumescence ensues.

Inquiry into the ingredients of biologic acts thrusts one directly toward the realm of the proto-organismic. Myriad bio-physical and electro-chemical reactions are implicated in every act. In themselves minute, these polarizations and resonances constitute, in the aggregate, that summing up which culminates in the threshold wherein the biologic act effloresces. I am not asserting that the sole condition for organismic activity is the congeries of physico-chemical processes woven into the incipient phase of the act, and pervading its subsequent phases. For, I must stress, there is a coeval condition: namely, factors resident within the ambience of the organism, both proximate and remote. Indeed, I shall sketch in the following section the relation between the most inclusive ambience, which stretches toward the furthermost reaches of the cosmos, whence derive the more subtle influences which co-determine the organization of the biologic act, and that act. For, when the relevance for that act of the rhythmic ebb and flow of the cosmos is itself specified, one is already prefiguring a source of factors which is not merely extra-organismic but, indeed, *supra*-organismic. At this point, appeal must be made to a doctrine the tenets of which go beyond those of naturalism.

To apply the first methodologic principle (to which I earlier alluded): the biologic act presupposes, first, an assembling of diverse elements; next, their conjugation into variegated patterns; and, lastly, the transformation of schemes of patterning into more complicated rhythmic textures. These moments of assembling, conjugating, and transforming apply to all bio-acts and to all combinations of such acts. Hence, these considerations apply to organisms as well. For, itself an integral act constituted in the fashion indicated, the organism is, in addition, a *plexus* of biologic acts. It is an interwoven matrix of acts which intersect, enmesh, and reciprocally impinge upon one another. In these senses, these acts are *assembled*. Furthermore, certain acts which enter into the composition of this matrix are subsumed under other acts; still additional acts span a variety of acts either wholly, to comprehend them as component acts, or partially, to comprehend them—now to embrace them, now to abandon them. In fluctuant manner, dominion is transferred to still more inclusive acts, acts which then assume dominance. This plexus of mutually entwined acts, perpetually constellated and reconstellated, shape novel acts. In these senses, acts composing the organism are *conjugated*, then *transformed* in varied ways.

Thus ceaselessly forming and re-forming, resolving and dissolving, these collective acts are, in effect, an orchestration of the rhythmic potentialities inherent within each act. By synergism, their rhythmic realizations mutually enhance one another in intricate contrapuntal consummation and *dénouement*. Accordingly, the organism is an integration of patterns of acts the unit acts of which subserve its integral activity. This is the dynamic matrix of life; this manifold of act-complexes—involuted and convoluted, agglutinating and dispersing—is the perpetually evolving resultant of an endless stream of self-compounding minuscule acts. Just as each act is a rising and a falling of tension, an ebb and a flow, so this integral plexus of acts replicates the basic rhythmic pulse. Rhythm is layered upon rhythm in shifting concatenation, and arrhythmias are inscribed upon periodic patterns. A trace of disorder appropriately woven into the rhythmic fabric adds greater cohesion to rhythmic order. Yet always the same kind of movement persists: confluence to crisis; subsidence the progeny of which are new modulations on new cadences.

To this plexus of acts the second methodologic principle may be applied. Different units are relatively autonomous and self-acting, spontaneously working out their inherent but circumscribed potentialities. All contiguous acts, and many acts which are spatio-temporally segregated, interact to produce compound acts. Such interaction may occur either directly or through the subtle resonances which pervade and hover about all acts. Furthermore, the entire matrix may be crisscrossed in many ways, yielding variegated patterns of functional units. Depending upon which pattern comes to dominate the matrix, what hitherto had been acts may become but elements within newly constituted acts. These acts, redistributions of assemblages of intra-organismic processes, exemplify the theme of transaction. By this theme, I mean those inclusive possibilities resident within any act-complex which favor apportionment into component acts, but in an indefinite number of ways. No mere summation of the individual sets of possibilities inhering in the totality of constituents of the complex, the entire set derives from the new and integrated product, which results from the interplay of the countless factors which gave birth to that product. In sum, self-action, interaction, and transaction are mutually implicating notions equally applicable to the biologic act.

In co-adaptation, acts are adjusted to one another, both intra-organismic acts and interorganismic acts. At the moment, I stress the former. Catalyzed by specific bio-agents, such as enzymes or hormones, some acts are intensified by inhibiting these factors through direct catalysis; other acts are intensified by inhibiting those factors which themselves inhibit acts. In general, a large number of intercoordinated catalyzing agents work within each organism. At times, these agents are felicitous for organismic development; at times, they are unfavorable. But, however intricate and subtle the bio-agents, if all forces playing upon the organism are relatively constant in time, then specific adaptive morpho-functional auxiliary organs tend to evolve. In such cases, intra-organismic stability is readily maintained. On the other hand, should these forces continually alter, undergoing diverse vicissitudes, only sturdier creatures may survive: namely, those creatures which can mobilize a large variety of adaptive functions rather than merely a single, specific adaptive organ. For latent within the latter creatures are countless possibilities of morpho-functional differentiation activated by an ever-shifting milieu. Depending upon a particular state of that milieu, one rather than another of these possibilities will be actualized. In particular, intra-organismic crises may arise. To settle these crises, internal rearrangements must often be quite profound. In general, complementing an external ecology, in its continuing ascent for evolving communities of organisms, is an *internal* ecology, either progressive or regressive, for each individual organism. Here, every phase of growth requires an idiosyncratic mutual readaptation of the factors constituting its internal milieu: a delicate balance of homeostatic with homeodynamic forces. Analogous considerations hold for looser aggregates composed of a multitude of interorganismic acts—save, however, that in the latter instances, more subtle and perhaps less facilely operative transductional bio-agents are mobilized.

(b) Co-Adaptations Culminating in the Human Body

By my argument, the entire body is pervaded and, indeed, constituted by an intricate composition of overlapping and intersecting acts. Through their combined interplay, these acts give rise to tension, crisis of tension, resolution of tension. In perpetual ebb and flow, the vicissitudes of tension shape a scheme of rhythmic patterns, all enmeshed and concatenated. A dialectic of inhibition, induction, reinforcement, and annihilation, numberless processes of varying duration and scope span one another to sustain a prevailing life balance. The rhythmic patterns associated with these processes originate other rhythmic patterns. Now releasing them, now controlling them, now reordering them, these variegated proliferations of act, tension, process, and rhythm are cumulatively recorded within the body. Its every lineament reveals the countless unfoldings which, from its inception as an organic body, have pervaded it. Every line and every texture manifest, in many layers, subtle and gross, obscurely expressed or dramatically evident, its history and its varied fates. Encoded within specific ontogenetic factors, the information which shapes an organism's destiny is gradually disseminated, in specific stages and with environmentally conditioned variation, throughout its emergence from germ to consummation.

First and foremost, the fundamental biologic act consists of an assemblage of disparate elements, an assemblage purposively and with a certain immanent spontaneity directed toward the end of achieving an intricately differentiated and cohesively ordered integration of these elements. Through mutual affinities and repulsions, by interplay of forces antagonistic and protagonistic, through quasi-"recognitions" and consequent "lockings-in," a web of molecular complementarities is spun. Arising within a matrix of asymmetric molecules which, as it were, yearn for symmetry, reciprocity, and completion, a succession of ecologic balances is maintained by all-pervading resonances. Sweeping over and penetrating the evolving organism, these immeasurably subtle resonances interweave in schemes of potent confluence, potentiate within the organism new conjugations and new transformations, and synthesize increasingly complicated yet integral organismic activity. Throughout this *efflorescing* growth, the variegated and ceaselessly redefined parts of the organism are mutually readapted to one another. For it is precisely the increasing pervasiveness and depth of resonance which suffuse that organism which allow ever more improbable transductions from one (distant) organismic region to another.

Once these diverse parts have been gathered together, the very complexity of the catalyzing resonances, in sure procession of dramatic self-enhancement, not merely promote but, indeed, necessitate continuance of differentiation with respect to organic parts: reordering, realignment, veritable transfiguration. Whether construed phylogenetically or ontogenetically, a complicated interplay never ceases between variants which, when they sufficiently deviate from this or that ecologic norm, constitute veridical mutants. Intra-organismic growth and interorganismic evolution are determined by the reciprocal impingements of both changing environment and novel mutant. Within limits, some kind of randomicity prevails; certain courses of development are favored, while others are not. Yet what I stress here is not only the inexorability with which the environmental action upon an organism "chooses" for it (by *natural* selection) certain routes of movement and flow, and not others, but, quite as significantly, the efficacy and the potency with which the reshaping impact of mutants, however they are produced, works on the environment itself. Ever new transactions of organism and milieu induce transformations of both. Indeed, all natural phenomena coevolve through elaborate ecologic schemes of co-adaptation.

Throughout organismic co-adaptation, the metabolic functions which, in their mature expression, jointly characterize the concrescent phase of metabolism—namely, immunology, reflection, and reproduction—become diversified and specialized. Many ancillary functions arise within them to enable the organism to cope with specialized factors in its environment. New and not merely auxiliary functions effloresce, but functions the foundations of which were already laid down as inextricably interwoven with the primordial phase of metabolism. In that phase, they germinated as immanently linked to functions already specified. So embedded were these (now new) functions in metabolism that they were, in effect, the same as metabolism. At that stage, I did not yet mention their integral role in organismic preservation. With increasing elaboration of the metabolic network, they now require specification. For the greater the differentiation of intra-organismic parts, the more its increasingly demarcated functional manifestations are coordinated with one another as jointly guaranteeing the integrity of the organism.

Four major additional systems are now relevant. First, the digestive system concerns ingestion and absorption of nutritious materials deriving from the environment. Since the sources of nutrition are variable and erratic, this metabolic function enables organismic balance to be maintained within a relatively unstable environment. Next, the respiratory system sustains organismic balance within a relatively stable environment. It metabolizes such essentially constant extra-organismic ingredients as oxygen, nitrogen, carbon dioxide. Thirdly, the cardio-vascular system maintains intra-organismic stability by circulating factors felicitous for organismic survival, factors introduced into the organism by the previous functions. Finally, the excretory system regulates the supply of both externally and internally originating factors by eliminating such components of these factors as are unfavorable to organismic vitality.

Interwoven in variegated modes of co-adaptation, with respect to the internal organismic milieu, these functions are linked with compensatory mechanisms relevant to maintaining overall stability. The general paradigm for expressing the conjoint activity of *all* functions set forth is simply construal of the organism as a system of diversified dynamisms so interposed between patterns of stimuli (e.g., bacteria, food, oxygen, tactile irritants) and patterns of response (e.g., antibody production, excrement, carbon dioxide, muscular avoidance reactions) as to maintain, by the appropriate harmonizing of these patterns and of their adjustment to one another, a proper balance between homeostatic and homeodynamic tendencies. In all instances, the distinguished functions, efficaciously ordered and mutually linked, build up that level of organismic vitality which will subserve the organism's stability and growth, and will promote its self-expression in all modes appropriate to its status in the *overall* ecologic scheme.

Organisms belong to classes of organisms, each class exemplifying a particular scheme of co-adaptation: an arrangement of parts according to a plan inhering in every member. Typical of every class is a thematic pattern. Save for idiosyncratic ornamentations inscribed by each individual, this pattern repeats itself throughout that class as seminal, archetypal ground for subsequent modulation. Variegated schemata of morphologic, cyclic, and energeia distributions pervade all ecologic systems. Furthermore, every organism passes through definite stages along its life's way, stages both genotypical and phenotypical. In effect, a proto-pattern is laid down by the replicatory dynamism, itself the invariant which sweeps, with but minor though unique embellishments, over the entire range of life. A series of concentric circles may be visualized; each corresponds to a theme. An enclosed circle is a variation upon that theme; an enclosing circle is a more inclusive theme. Phyla, families, classes, genera, species: each is associated with a particular circle. The unique point which all circles circumscribe corresponds to a particular individual. Given: a single cell; its destiny is inscribed upon it, including the special vicissitudes which it will undergo, save, of course, for those fortuitous and seemingly random environmental influences which may either constrain or enlarge the scope of its journey. Though a certain range of co-adaptive possibilities is fixed and determined for each individual, and for every class (no matter how inclusive) to which it belongs, the limits which bound that range may, through the perpetual reshaping activities of the organism, be extended or constricted.

Orthogenetically, the destiny of life flows inexorably toward its culmination, the person. Uniquely inscribed upon *his* germ plasm is a peculiar flexibility: not merely the power for spontaneously adapting himself to shifting environments, nor even merely the capacity for reconstituting those environments. For these gifts belong as well to organisms other than men. Rather, alone among the earthly creatures, man is endowed with both freedom and consciousness of freedom. In exercising his self-conscious power, man evolves toward consummate personhood. He turns in upon himself to redirect his own growth; he turns out toward nature to redirect its growth. Thus in this blending of self and nature, each is transfigured.

An anatomical difference between man and beast symbolizes man's unique place in the scheme of life. Only man holds his head upright; his foramen magnum is so constructed that his spinal cord proceeds along a straight line into his brain. What is the import of this peculiarity? By merely introducing structural anomalies of skull and spinal column man can, by twisting in the right way, rotate his head by virtually 360 degrees. Combined with his stereoscopic vision, this factor enables man alone to extend his searching gaze, when employing all his senses, toward heaven and earth. He alone searches the great globe of the universe, empowered to integrate its every facet, to explore its most obscure recesses. And when he has exhausted outward vision, only man may deliberately block both sight and sound to search the depths of his inwardness, to conjure up images archetypally resident within him. In our epoch, the pattern of co-adaptation which comes to fruition in man is his gift for discerning patterns, for coordinating patterns, for envisaging more inclusive patterns. Beyond that, it is man's capacity to reveal to himself the pattern of his own being as pre-figured in proto-human being and progressively brought to consummation in the sphere of the personal. It is, indeed, the capacity for speculating about the meaning of pattern itself, pattern exemplified in myriad ways and transmitted through numberless routes.

In my account of co-adaptation, I use the term *ecobologenesis* to express, literally, the joining together of diverse loci to which either different parts of particular organisms, in their internal ecology, or different integral organisms, in their external ecology, are habituated to root themselves. Every living creature is ensconced within its uniquely demarcated natural region, its own private dwelling place. Each is an activity of questing after its own roots. In its search, those roots ramify beyond their original *Anlage*. For plants, this *Anlage* is restricted to a single, fixed locale. For animals, loci of rootedness are borne with them. Nonetheless, both environmental and genetic circumstances set boundaries to the areas within which animal, like plant, may freely roam. Both animals and plants are restricted to specific circumscribed regions such as sea, air, and land, though, surely, potentialities for locomotions beyond these realms reside within every organism. By fortuitous mutation, some of their progeny may, indeed, realize these potentialities. Moreover, the migratory patterns of organisms are intricate and variegated.

(c) Man's Migratory Patterns

For man alone, these patterns are indefinitely extensible. Pre-eminently, he is the creature who *widely* roams. Endowed with special inventiveness, symbolized by flexibility of hand and intricate links of neural coordination which control their use, man uniquely devises increasingly the general tools with which more specific tools (for specialized tasks) may be contrived; his armamentary of tools is itself indefinitely extensible. Through these tools, *his* migratory patterns become immeasurably greater than those of other organisms. By the agility of his fingers, by the molding power of his palms, by the tautness of his fist with its power freely alternately to tighten and to loosen its grip, man can self-consciously both directly or through tools create instruments for engaging in ever-widening ranges of environmental exploration. By the fluidity of the movement of his limbs, by the size and supple flexibility of his feet, by the litheness of his skeleto-muscular configuration, by the minimum specialization of his teeth, yet the sufficiently subtle morphologic differences among them, man can adapt his habits to flora and fauna of innumerably variegated milieux. By his power to envisage an integral, unified, and comprehensive universe, he can shape natural materials into terraced layers, cups inverted or everted of whatever size, arches, vaulted roofs, soaring towers; and, by these, he can survey his surroundings and thereby intensify and broaden still more the scope for his searching.

Beyond that, man as he searches is empowered deeply and subtly to feel; the capacity for ecstasy and exaltation is his supreme gift.[2] And he exhibits that gift in amazingly diversified ways. By the very tools through which he extends his searchings, man can beautify his environment. Not only does he seek to discover nature's manifest harmonies in their most subtle variations; he also dares to re-constitute nature, thereby to draw forth its own latent harmonies, harmonies concealed deep within the surging sea, the rocks about him, the trees above him, the canyons and mountains and plains, and all the beasts and plants which dwell therein. Alone among living forms, man may in principle move anywhere within the cosmos. It is uniquely he who can discern the cosmos qua cosmos, who can extract from it its hidden secrets. Man alone has the synoptic vision to embrace the entirety, and the spiritual gift to mold it to his ideal envisagement. Perceiving the limits of his quest, by the constraints placed upon tool and imagination at every stage of his life's seeking, he is nevertheless empowered in principle to push beyond those limits. His quest for disclosure and revelation is insatiable. Presented to the cosmos as they, re-formed by its forces, are reciprocally presented to him, man's symbolisms, incarnate in natural materials, including the expressions and extensions of his own body, enable him to leap into ecologic arrangements far more extensive and complex than those of other organisms. In the final analysis, the mode of co-adaptation peculiar to man is initiated by the efficacy of his tools and culminated in his invention of the symbol. In effect, the ecologic essence of human existence is not so much an exceedingly refined co-adaptation of human organisms to one another as the co-adaptation of symbols *inter se*, symbols self-perpetuating and self-metamorphosing.

Precursors to expanding matrices of co-adaptation, the ever-widening, ever more intricate migratory patterns of cells carve out a network of routes for their journeyings, each associated with a distinctive ambience. As groups of these cells cohere in larger biologic units, new trajectoral systems arise, shaping the cartography of organisms the complexity yet organizational cohesiveness of which do not cease to grow. In the ebb and flow of cell motions, and the overall movement which spans their minuscule pulsations—indeed, in the variegated accretions which they form—distinction between inorganic and organismic, once so dramatically established, tends toward dissolution. Life blends and interweaves itself with all of nature. It fills the niches of material entities, and it proliferates throughout their interstices by diverse techniques: symbiotic attachment to the inanimate as by barnacles; inorganic residue like hair and fingernail which themselves, whatever their specific protective roles for the organism, link the living and the lifeless; the artistic reshapings of man by which he converts inanimate nature into elaborate extensions of his own being. Truly, the animate and the inanimate intrude upon one another. Each insinuates itself into the recesses and crevices of the other; each may either truncate or hypertrophy this or that constituent structure, the more effectively to adapt itself to the contours and the dynamisms of the other.

A veritable enmeshing of two realms unfolds, both descended from a common ancestor. Granted: this ancestor seems more akin to the inorganic. Yet in subtle ways, perhaps by the special resonances which aboriginally hovered about the primordial proto-replicatory form in this intricate genealogy, the archetypal crystal within which resides great potentiality for life is surely quite different from its progeny in the inorganic sphere. Could it not be that this progenitor is, so to speak, neutral to progeny of either inorganic or organismic kinds, and equally capable of giving rise to both, depending upon which of its features are stressed and which are suppressed? Might not the mutual impact of these realms, hitherto distinct and partially autonomous, and their reciprocal interpenetration, modify, re-form, and, in complicated interplay of forces, reorganize existing patterns of demarcation? If so, could not the original identity of these realms once again be established but, now, on a level so subtly laminated and webbed that both realms, the inorganic and the organismic, are subsumed as moments within a more inclusive and integrated hyper-nature? Is not the person himself, person as seeker, the very agent wherein hyper-nature first comes fully to manifest itself? Might not the person be the cosmic instrument whereby is undertaken the task of red-integrating what had been split asunder? Surely, in such a process new and more profound spiritual unity would be achieved, unity which would replicate, in immeasurably enriched forms, its cosmic fount wherein undifferentiation had hitherto reigned.

Associated with all life is a propensity toward opportunism. On the whole, individual organisms tend to gather together to perform corporate acts, as though they were of one body, for the purpose of establishing a mutually advantageous stance vis-à-vis the environment. In turbulent interplay of numberless mutants, spontaneously produced, living matter incessantly beats against the barriers of the inorganic. Spreading throughout nature, organisms gradually fill, and indeed penetrate, the very interstices of the thingly environment. Within this ferment, novel composites are continually formed through cotransformation of organism and environment.

Between the matrix of biologic acts and the situations within which these acts unfold, a relation of force, a *pression*, holds.[3] Indeed, the vast fabric of burgeoning acts *ex*presses the combined effects of billions of pressive relations, all adjusting to one another to constitute living matter. Moreover, acts *im*press themselves upon other acts and, thereby, establish a kind of memory of the reciprocal *com*pressions, *op*pressions, *ad*pressions, and (to coin a word) *a*pressions of many acts. At the same time, certain factors deriving from interactions are *re*pressed within a given act—pressed, as it were, out of "memory," or possibility for utilization, yet remaining embedded in that act to condition its subsequent destiny. Normally, repressions aid in maintaining the overall integrity of an act, lest specific *op*pressions be disruptive and pulverizing. Alternatively, some impressions are merely *sup*pressed, or isolated within limited sectors of that act. These factors are available for recall, i.e., mobilization on behalf of act preservation. In yet other instances, acts may exhibit either *de*pression, or diminished vitality, or, contrariwise, such *de-re*pressions, as may eventuate in heightened vitality.

I have used the stem "pression" to apply to several nodes of relatedness between act and act. Now, I introduce the (artificial) stem "gregation," based on the Latin *grex*, meaning "herd," and akin to the Greek ἀγείρω, meaning "I gather," "I assemble." Just as one can affix to "pression" such prefixes as *im-, ex-, de-, re-, com-, op-*, and *ad-*, to express different aspects of act interaction, so to "gregation" I may attach such prefixes as *ag, se-, con-*, or *e-*, to designate different kinds of act assemblage for varying schemes of aggregation. In any aggregate, some acts are *se*gregated from one another; other acts *con*gregate in unison to catalyze their respective vitalities; still other acts are *e*gregious in the sense of being distinguished from the remainder, standing apart as unique and idiosyncratic. On the whole, "aggregations" redirect pressions; pressions determine modes of "gregation." For these notions are correlative and complementary.

In general, acts are organized schemes of impulse which press toward actualization as various types of "gregation." Thereby, particular acts imprint their forms upon the patterns of acts determined by interplay of pressions and "gregations." Such patterns may be sustained, fragmented, expanded, contracted, reordered, negated, or reinforced. Throughout such fluctuations, a unique tangle of pressions and "gregations" is spun and un-spun within an ever-changing environment. Co-determining its own ambience, the matrix of acts slowly but ineluctably fills in the ecologic niches of inanimate nature.

Myriad oscillations express the interplay of acts potentiating new acts. Matrices of acts dovetail with one another, all attuned in variegated ways; matrices of acts adapt themselves to environmental fluctuations, filling ever newly forming ecologic niches. A grand processional of rhythms is concatenated. Systems vast and intricate unfold, minuscule cycles woven with more inclusive cycles in diverse grades of amplitude and frequency. Innumerable acts, each building itself toward its characteristic peak intensity, all "strive" to prolong themselves, within the limits of their genetically determined possibilities, into the inorganic. Among these acts, ecologic competition inevitably prevails. In the course of evolution, the inanimate increasingly becomes ancillary to and at the disposal of the organismic. The original relationship between the two becomes inverted.

Consummating the process of inorganic servitude to the animate is man. Even his embryologic development microcosmically reflects this great adventure of nature. As man develops from conception onward, ever-shifting schemes of adaptation of his internal milieu as a whole to its constituent parts are created. Original embryonic functions are successively abandoned as new functions are acquired. Pervasive internal vibrations coalesce into novel schemes of growth

and differentiation. And, in general, a living nature of ever-growing density becomes increasingly laden with optive pressions toward diverse "gregations." Herein, a momentous crisis of existence supervenes. In this movement and flow, this
confluence of multitudinous forces, freedom is born. By the elaborate ways in
which organismic being, continually confronting the inorganic, carves the latter,
the former, pressed back into itself, is increasingly converted into a circuitous
and labyrinthine interiority. These internal ramifications proliferate in patterns
which correlate with—hence, become adapted to—ever-increasing environmental
profusions. Throughout this activity, efflorescing bundles of phyla—polymorphous,
elastic, and dynamic, and exhibiting myriad shapes of divergence and convergence
—tend, nevertheless, to cluster about and eventuate in emerging man.

From the lowliest, every organism shows intimations of the power of choice, a
power which is immanent, spontaneous, and subjective. An amoeba will turn
toward a nutritious particle, and turn away from a noxious particle. In the presence
of both, he will give behavioral signs of confusion. In successive presentations,
he will modify his behavior. By analogy, I impute to him a kind of primordial will.
Indeed, the inherent ambiguity of freedom is prefigured in all subhuman life.
Freedom cannot be freedom unless it is construed under the perspective of limit.
What might, in principle, be determined beyond that limit cannot be explored;
it is consigned to mystery. For each living creature, the boundaries are relatively
fixed and circumscribed. But only man perceives both limits and mystery. Only
he may know the scope of his freedom. Yet to perceive one's determination entails
the freedom to act within those limits. For perception involves a stretching out
in varying directions for the purpose of discerning opportunities for movement,
and, hence, motion within the region which sets bounds to the possibility of
motion. Moreover, through action, the power to push back limits is conferred,
power to extend the scope of freedom. In stretching against limits, the very limits
themselves are altered. Accordingly, the transactions of organism and environment
always imply a dialectical relation between boundaries and bounded loci.

In a measure, all animals and plants, however primitive their sentience, are
endowed with a capacity for reconstituting the limits which define the locus of
their spontaneous action, their *loco*motion (or shifting from one place to another).
Co-adaptation is the collective quest of organisms for continually expanding the
loci of freedom within which they may locomote and thereby orient themselves.
It is an implicit commitment to the activity of searching. In the consequent phase
of metabolism, metabolism itself is construed as this quest; it is an immanent
vector toward freedom. From this standpoint, freedom fully incarnate *is* the person. Yet each living creature finds its location within nature with respect to its
relative degree of freedom. And, though seemingly without purpose, all organisms
arrange themselves about man, depending upon their respective capacities for
freedom; they radiate, so to speak, from man as center. In this grand design, living
beings are mutually co-adapted.

Acknowledging his own centricity with respect to biogenesis and his special role in the ecology of the kingdom of nature, yet his embeddedness in nature *sub specie durationis*, man recognizes, too, that he alone dwells within the kingdom of grace. In his latter habitat, he perceives himself as *eccentric* with respect to the Source and Donor of all freedom *sub specie aeternitatis*. Nonetheless, he accepts himself as a creature of momentous significance within that kingdom. By the symbolism of his comportment, man both reveals his living presence to his fellows and, reciprocally, accepts the living presence of their comportment. Focal to human comportment is speech. Unique among living organisms and, to that extent, transcending organicity, man dwells co-adaptively with others in the realm of the spoken word. Herein, he discovers his veridical freedom. Therein dwelling, he achieves transfiguration. Without negating his status as natural, he weds that status to his status as spiritual. As center of nature, man possesses biologic pride; as participant within nature, he possesses biologic humility. By attuning himself to proper balance between pride and humility, and by recognizing their intricate dialectic, he prepares himself to receive the full measure of his personhood.

In my remaining sections, I treat, respectively, "the resonances of primordial reflection" and "the miracle of personhood." Yet my discussion of these themes is, in effect, but a prolegomenon to their more systematic presentation in subsequent books. There I pass beyond the theme of this book—namely, person qua thing and organism—to set forth the topic *person qua person*, in the more significant dimensions of man's strictly human existence.

B · BODY TRANSFIGURED:
THE RESONANCES OF PRIMORDIAL REFLECTION

(*a*) The Hyper-Organismic Nervous System

When a sufficient number of biologic acts have aggregated themselves into an integral composite act, waves of numberless pressions and "gregations" spread over those acts. Giving rise to an elaborate scheme of intra-organismic trajectories, these waves, in turn, transmit influences through the trajectories, once they are formed, from one region of the organism to another. Itself a composite of subordinate bio-acts, every trajectory wraps itself, so to speak, about other trajectories. The bundles of trajectoral strands thereby emerging coalesce to shape still more complex organizations. In this way, a hierarchically ordered system of routes of intra-organismic communication establishes itself as a kind of subordinate organism which functions with relative autonomy, despite its embeddedness in the organismic matrix which engendered it.

In the human body, this quasi-organism is the central nervous system together with its auxiliary components, a system the biologic center of which lies in a brain in perpetual ferment. Infolding upon one another to form an increasingly complicated labyrinth, a fabric of convolutions shapes itself, a fabric which undergoes significant metamorphoses from shortly after conception to a few years following birth. When this process has completed itself, an enormous number of neural channels are available for potential activation. Such factors as brain configuration, intensity of nerve impulse transmission, and quantity of neurones vary, depending upon the interplay of genetic endowment, with life experience. Indeed, since RNA occurs with unusual concentration in cerebral tissue and is, moreover, associated with memory "engrams," hence (perhaps) with continual changes in the replicatory system itself—insofar as the latter pertains to the nervous system—the functional makeup of a seemingly stable brain may be indeterminate throughout life.

Often, I have used the locution *quasi*-organism. I refer to an assemblage of organs which exhibit properties which go beyond those manifested by such organ systems as the cardio-vascular or the pulmonary–respiratory. In the central nervous system, intricacies, subtle modulations, and powers for assuming an extraordinary range of novel activities are incomparably greater. More strikingly, a relationship holds between variegated embedded (neural) quasi-organisms which is altogether unique, and quite inapplicable to non-neural systems of organs. For integrated over all individual organisms of a given class are neural organizations which, because of their (partially) extra-organismic locus, communicate with one another. Mediated by essentially ineffable channels of transmission, these communicatings, together with their collective neural matrix, form a kind of *hyper*-organism which directs and conditions numberless *inter*organismic processes.

Once extruded from the members of a community of organisms, this hyper-organismic neural apparatus constitutes a link between the internal (homeostasis-maintaining) activities of each organism and such activities as facilitate communal survival. In effect, neural structures proliferate "outward" from the original organismic matrices, wherein each member of the hyper-organism functioned as a quasi-organism—that aggregate of bio-acts the biologic status of which is intermediate between systems of organs and organisms proper. Overcoming natural resistances of an altogether unanticipated kind, the community pervaded by this hyper-organism acquires a range and subtlety of co-adaptive techniques which expand immeasurably; the character of organicity itself is transformed. A new mode of biologic existence, the emerging hyper-organism superimposes itself upon the vital activities of its originating sources, sources wherein it initially functioned as but an immanent system for organismic intercommunication. The interorganismic milieu itself is penetrated.

Anlage to this grand evolutionary development is the system of cell membranes, reticula, organelles, and nuclei which analogously mediate impulses within a community of adjacent cells. But for advanced organisms, the reticula sent forth from morphologically distinct neural structures are, as it were, *supra*morphologic. In earlier chapters, I referred to proto-morphologic channels of transmission between cells, channels essentially constituted by processes which had not yet crystallized into sharply contoured morphologic units. But now a new leap in natural evolution has been effected. The resonances transmitted from person to person, and indeed from community to community, are by comparison so subtle, and constituted with such delicacy, that only such appellations as ineffable, ethereal, or transcendent indicate their essential quality.

By implication, persons are increasingly rooted within this hyper-organism. Dwelling therein, they partake of the reverberations which endlessly circulate throughout its components. Moreover, hyper-organismic reticula extend themselves beyond the community of persons, and ramify among distant reaches of the cosmos. Penetrating its inmost recesses, a continually efflorescing hyper-organism, evolving indeed beyond what could be designated merely "neural," acquires a meshwork of "antennae" which eventually proliferate throughout the entire cosmos. Constituting itself a vortex of processes which increasingly become centered in a single transcendental point, this meshwork is transformed into a kind of singularity in the composition of the cosmos. Himself a vortex of processes about a center naturalistically expressed by *intra*-organismic neural resonances, the person ec-centrically relates himself to this singularity. Yet, in his very eccentricity, he achieves a more profound centeredness upon his deeper self, a self which is inwardly linked to the entire cosmic configuration.

Competing with one another for dominance, through reciprocally impinging stimuli and inhibitory factors which stem from both intra- and extra-organismic sources, a complex array of acts and rival acts builds up within each organism a matrix of tropisms and reflexes. Thereupon, a composite of interwoven acts, differing combinations of protagonists and antagonists all dialectically enmeshed, is shaped into a cyclically unfolding congeries of concatenated acts, acts exhibiting endless varieties of cadence, consummation, thematic repetition. Regnant throughout the organism are simple reflexes, autogenic and autochthonous activities, stereotypical acts discharging in repetitive schemes with but minor variations, direct responses to situational influences, countless proclivities and tendencies, interlocking purposive acts which jointly function as complex instinctual patterns, and instinctive acts which collectively comprise purposive behavior. All these are hierarchically organized to enable the living creature to build such fragile counter-entropic structures as will conserve energy, a texture of urgencies, summations, and relaxations. Within this evolving fabric, varying stimuli-thresholds appear. By the shifting gradients of these thresholds, perpetual oscillations and vibrations sweep over the body. Yet a constant basal tonus is maintained as the originating, stable source whence continue to emerge those specific and differentiated acts which, in their totality, comprise directed organismic activity.

Every organism searches. By the scheme of neural trajectories which pervades communities of organisms, each organism is enabled purposively to reach out and to extend its concealed antennae farther into its environment. Therein, each imbibes novel influences which, in turn, potentiate new tendencies and impulses. Consider the infant. He sucks instinctively; he turns his head spontaneously; he crawls with ever-decreasing randomicity; he flexes and extends his limbs with ever-increasing adventuresomeness when placed upon his back; his fingers exhibit athetoid movement which becomes progressively more ordered: a perpetual and autonomous activity, but not a random activity! Increasingly, movement and intention are focalized; impulses are coordinated, directed, and woven to habit; neural resonances aggregate to transcend thresholds of sentiency and, thereby, to convert instinct into specific motive. Arising from a physiologic matrix dominated by autonomic nervous activity, schemes of motivation emerge which exhibit endless varieties of ornamentation inscribed on recurrent thematic patterns. Within a matrix of reciprocal innervation, acts potentiate, inhibit, and synergize new acts.

Every thwarting of a vector toward act consummation elicits such schemes of repression and de-repression as will create, through reconstellated and redirected energies, new channels for potential novel motivation. Correlatively, ecologic systems evolve which allow for testing newly emergent options; the *Umwelt* of living creatures enormously expands. A vast range of novel factors reveal themselves, to those creatures of sufficient sensibility, for exhilarating exploration. The entire past experience accumulated by each creature dwells within him to condition and to reorient his contemporary action. As the evolutionary process converges with seemingly purposive orientation upon more and more intricately designed creatures, interwoven arcs of nervous tension span every organism, maintaining the cohesiveness of each and permitting stability for the community of all. Beneath these arcs, as it were, metabolic activities become increasingly complicated; new pathways of nerve conduction are engendered. In this process, interiorization of organic functions becomes ever more elaborate; a psychic center emerges like "a vortex which grows deeper as it sucks up the fluid at the heart of which it was born."[4]

Earlier, I proposed that a hyper-organismic network ramifies over the community of living creatures the complex interrelations of which mirror the organizational composition of its associated organisms. Embedded in the individual organisms which originated it, this network, so I continued, mediates not only intra-organismic and interorganismic communication, but the diverse influences pervading the cosmos beyond. Thus, both organism and community possess an intercommunicating agency, and, in turn, are possessed by it. Sectors of it dwell within each, coordinating its diverse parts; yet so widely does it ramify, its ultimate scope corresponding to the cosmos itself, that every living creature dwells within it. From a cosmologic point of view, this integral mediator of cosmic resonances is, in effect, split into interconnected functional units. Each unit is, so to speak, *assigned* to a particular organism and to a particular community. Still, the true locus of the mediator, the context of its most inclusive functioning, is the cosmos itself. Nonetheless, all morpho-functional distinctions within the hyper-organism depend upon distribution of its components with respect to their relevance for the variable potencies characterizing each creature.

Hovering about every particular organism and about every community of like organisms are the reverberations perpetually transmitted throughout the relevant regions of the larger hyper-organismic intercommunicant. When, for a given creature or society, these resonances have attained sufficient subtlety and complexity, the limen of feeling has been crossed. Primordial reflection first manifests itself. Transmitted back and forth, and efflorescing in this or that organism in accordance with the organism's specific propensities and endowment, this great meshwork constitutes ground for a complementarity of interpersonal and intrapsychic. The organism is pervaded internally by such resonances. Conversely, the milieu occupied by a multitude of organisms is likewise pervaded by the same resonances. When these resonances have attained sufficient contrapuntal intensity, one may designate body no longer as *mere* body, but as body *transfigured*: both the individual body of an organism and the corporate body of co-adapted organisms. In effect, every community is totally affected by all cosmic reverberations. Yet, from the point of view of the particular levels of sentiency which its members are empowered to attain, each community is selectively affected. This principle holds with respect to both stimulus patterns and response patterns.

(b) Thresholds Along the Vector Leading to Man

By my argument, these resonances derive from two sources and, accordingly, are in every instance associated with a double vector: primordial bio-acts, originating in the inanimate, and so amplifying one another, in a continual process of interiorization, that the psychic labyrinth is formed; and the larger cosmos, laminated into resonances ethereal and ineffable, which pervade and suffuse each creature. The locus in which these vectors meet, the person, is pre-eminently the region wherein the rhythms of pure being articulate themselves; it is the realm of their coherence, their cogent unification. In its private resonances and in its plenitudinous resonances, the entire cosmos focalizes its infinitude within the finite boundaries of man. Numberless modulations of feeling—will, appetite, sensation, kinesthesia, perception, and cognition—interweave with varying integrations and intensities of awareness. In effect, the hyper-organismic neural apparatus conveys such modulations to each individual as are relevant to his own specific makeup. Depending upon his particular aptitude for receiving them, and for shaping their contents to a veridical Imago of some relevant cosmic sector, the person is more or less attuned to the integral cosmos.

No organism is merely bombarded by discrete stimuli. Stimuli are but foci within orchestrated resonances which, depending upon relevant gradients and states of organismic receptivity, come to expression in one organism rather than in another. Bathed in cosmic rhythms which have been constellated to different bundles of potential stimuli, every organism has its characteristic power of recipiency as well as a pre-existing archetypal structure, its indigenous modifying medium. According to the mode of interplay of these factors, the organism will experience forms of action extrinsic to itself, but always in their autonomous structures, which pre-exist independently of any idiosyncratic receptor organization or any techniques for coding and transcribing.

Pre-eminently, through the multilayered intricacies of speech, but significantly modified by such comportmental factors as physiognomy, vocal inflection, gesture, or postural configuration, the messages of real persons are transmitted, acknowledged, and responded to by other real persons. True, an aura contributed by a person's archetypal constitution hovers about every message. Nonetheless, the message is received, however distortedly, in its unique and experiential import. Transposed to a recipient organism's linguistic or other symbolic competencies, that import may be discerned, through a searching of sufficient depth, in its authentic correlation with the source whence it arose. Surely, a profound intersubjectivity haunts the cosmos, a kind of *supra*consciousness which envelops all, as messages are sent by cosmic actor to cosmic actor in schemes of variegated modes of interactivity. Always, this transmission occurs "through the medium of the universal communication system of action, within the matrix of the interaction of the world and ourselves."[5]

In consequence, it is not true that the organism *as such* engenders mentation as a highly differentiated function of its metabolizing activity. More accurately, the organism is a locus for receiving, selecting, and reacting to reverberations which perpetually echo throughout the cosmos. It imbibes certain reverberations and it excludes others. Not so much by the fact of this responsiveness as by his awareness of the fact, man differentiates himself from animals. Though subjects, animals are surely not selves. Granted: they also discriminate reverberations, and oftentimes with great finesse. But, for them, essentially instinct, however suffused with purposiveness, rather than self-consciousness, is the distinguishing factor. Furthermore, only man, possessing a sense of the *wholeness* of reality, is empowered to impute its integration to an Integrator. True, the reverberations received are already transmuted. But, by reason wedded to feeling, man may separate those reverberations into rhythms of absolute silence and rhythms of absolute vibrancy. Through his speech, man symbolizes this haunting perception; through his symbolisms, man transfigures his body.

At what point in man's development does the power of true reflection first make its appearance and, thereby, allow for the miraculous leap into consummate personhood? If one were to trace natural evolution along the vector which leads from non-being to personal being, a few great thresholds of transformation manifest themselves. The more salient I designate the *evanescence* of matter, the *crystallization* of matter, the *fermentation* of matter, and, finally, the *penetration* of matter by a power for creating symbols. The first three thresholds I review briefly, the last in somewhat more detail.

Earlier, I distinguished that increment of the evolutionary vector wherein matter first appeared: sheer elementarity, an evanescence of no-thingness to primordial thinghood. A seemingly reversible process, matter at this threshold passes from a state of virtuality to a state of actuality, and conversely: on the one side, nonexistence; on the other, bare existence. Immediately following the emergence of particulate matter, more and more complicated aggregates form, break down, and re-form. Ultimately, these aggregates so coalesce that elementary crystals appear, the second great evolutionary threshold. Beginning with simply latticed structures, crystals evolve into laminated patterns of variegated symmetry and asymmetry, and of myriad shape and design. Though grossly fixed and rigid, these constellations of inflexible texture nonetheless disclose, in their inmost depths, perpetual flux and activity. Evanescent or crystalline, matter dialectically interacts with its environment. Resonances arising from within or from without a material configuration sweep over both entity and circumambient milieu. Thereupon, each conforms its structure to that of the other. Yet the dynamics of neither ceases. New resonances continue to circulate; novel transfigurations recur.

Later, I referred to the simplest semi-permeable membranes which surround more complicated crystalline formations. Allowing for electrolytic balance shifts on the surface of a crystal, a sensitive outer texture evolves which permits discrimination of stimuli which impinge upon the membrane, both from within it and from without. Yet, throughout this process, the inner crystalline content is so shielded from externally derived traumata that the sturdy structure hitherto characterizing it is free to dissolve and to liquefy. Now circumscribed by a protective coating, the relatively durable configurations of laminae comprising the ground for intracrystalline activity are converted into fermenting processes, the third great evolutionary threshold. By ever more subtle dynamic interchange between what has now become an organism and its milieu, together a single inclusive system, the integrity of the former is stabilized through its own agency, its self-induced activity. Nevertheless, as in the realm of the inanimate, reversals may occur.

At this threshold, sufficiently new stimuli so penetrate the bio-membrane that novel flowings and swirlings, regions of increasing or decreasing viscosity, and contractions and expansions supervene within the organism. Numberless dynamic patterns of formation and deformation, of equilibrium or disequilibrium shape themselves. At times, the viscous matrix passes into states of lesser fluidity, at times of greater. In this fabric of tensions which mount, diminish, or discharge themselves, the organism perdures. Whereas a crystal does not perpetuate itself but simply *lasts*, enduring by the collective dynamisms of its constituent atoms and molecules, and by the particular arrangements which they form, the activities of an organism are in ceaseless efflorescence and defluxion. Nevertheless, a dynamic form is preserved amidst an ever-enlarging range and an increasingly diversified set of environmental and intra-organismic transformations.

Within this fluctuant fabric, replication marvelously makes its appearance. It is as though, to preserve its own *fixity*, the liquefied matrix must leap out of its own confines, and strive in other environments—sought after, as it were, by its own mutations—to maintain stability. Compensating as a persistent (temporal) viscosity in the realm of time for what it lacked in its random flowings in the realm of space, the engendering matrix gives birth to numberless mutants, each adapting itself to ever-varying environmental circumstance. By self-replication, the organism endeavors to perpetuate itself, lest it disperse its contents through too

porous a membrane. In this process of alternating homeostasis and homeody-
namics, some mutants undergo embryogenesis by which they incorporate themselves into larger ecologic systems; others metamorphose into forms which retain
their individualities within the ecologic context. In both instances, new resonances,
interior and exterior, suffuse ever-evolving organisms to induce still further
transformations.

Now a new and yet more dramatic threshold appears. Emerging from the primate is man. Conjoined are his power of speech and his power of reflection. Together, these powers enable him to symbolize his experience, to survey the cosmos,
to search its recesses, and self-consciously to secure himself within its every facet.
By the interwovenness of speech and reflection, and by their reciprocal reinforcement and transformation, man first acquires a capacity to pass beyond his merely
natural state, his journeyings along the vector rooted in non-being, to a super-
natural state, a veridically spiritual condition, to dwell in successive thresholds
among the emanations of pure being. Though speech and reflection are inseparably
enmeshed, I here stress the latter. In my next section, I focus upon the former; in
particular, I treat the intricacies of their interplay.

By a remarkable synchronicity, perhaps the result of the convergence of mutants
which stem from diverse sources and affect different parts of the body, a new
species of primate arises, or a new family of mammals . . . or, an altogether novel
mode of existence. What increment of time elapses within which this creature
emerges, a creature so miraculously adapted to the prevailing ecology? By what
marvelous confluence of forces does the ecologic balance of the earth so fluctuate,
over a time span minuscule by comparison with the great sweep of evolution, and
become so precisely attuned to that constellation of mutations? No answer to these
questions is yet available. But conjectures concerning reasons for convergences,
confluences, and coincidences may plausibly be made. My subsequent discussion
advances one ground for cogently entertaining a possible explanation.

Consider the process of mutation with respect to the epoch in which man en-
tered upon the scene of evolution. During a certain time interval, a variety of
mutants emerged, each suited for survival in a certain milieu. Within this interval,
the milieu underwent momentous shifts, shifts so constituted that without a prior
mutant's becoming obsolete a new mutant became suitable for survival. In this
manner, over a brief time span obsolescence did not supervene with respect to already viable mutants, and new conditions made it appropriate for new mutants
to prevail. Two sets of mutants coalesced: those which were non-obsolescent, and
continued to survive; those which were newly adapted for survival. In consequence,
within some group of primates, indeed a very special group, a configuration of
mutations appeared which immediately released certain potentialities for adaptation which hitherto had not been possible. The organism arising from this combination of mutants adapted *itself*, by its inner constitution, to comportmental
possibilities newly resident within it. Its potentialities became adjusted to one
another; a new balance was thereby achieved. In the acts by which those potentiali-

ties became realized, they synergized one another to form a new compound. In this way, an extraordinarily complex leap was made in the passage of the primate to man.

At this point, the vector associated with pure being came into play with incomparably greater drama than was hitherto possible. Granted: this vector was immanently operative even at the very beginnings of physical existence. Hence, the rhythms of pure being and those of non-being are interwoven; they are integrally enmeshed. At no point in the (subsequent) evolution of creatures "higher" than man will the non-being component of the great bi-vector of being altogether vanish. It will simply become attenuated. In like fashion, the pure being vector was merely attenuated at the pole of non-being. As one passes from personal being toward non-being, the pure being vector loses potency. Conversely, the non-being vector gains in potency. Reciprocally, as one passes from personal being to pure being, attenuation and potency are analogously, though conversely, interchanged. Under the perspective of man's apprehension of himself, he stands midway between these poles; for him, the two are equally potent or, what is equivalent, equally impotent. For man is the locus of both harmony and conflict with respect to the privation of being and the plenitude of being. Herein lies the veridical metaphysical ground of Freud's construal of the conflict between eros and thanatos. But what Freud failed to discern is the deeper harmony between these apparent opposites, i.e., their status as apposite. Yet the most important consideration is this: In what manner, and in which direction, does man exercise his option freely to move, to discern, to acknowledge? How, in short, may he specify the relevant factors which establish him as a creature apart from all others?

(c) Mutants Coalescent: The Emergence of the Person

To this end, I first briefly refer to prevailing ecologic factors to which mutating forms must adapt. Next, I indicate the kinds of creatures who could survive the fluctuant upheavals which these factors comprise, and presage. Thirdly, I indicate a few of the mutually reinforcing and reciprocally potentiating mutants which characterize man's distinctively physico-biologic nature: his body, from head to toe. Then, I draw certain inferences from these facts, auguring some of their significant consequences. Finally, I consider the joint implications of these consequences as a succinct proposal for a unified theory of the import of the resonances of primordial reflection. Thereby, I clear the way for my passage to the crucial and salient theme of speech. For alone in the unity of reflection and speech may one discern the elements of a doctrine which truly portends a person's essential character.

Some million years ago—the precise time is unnecessary for my speculations—the ecologic balance of the earth underwent extraordinary change. Volcanic upheavals, the appearance and disappearance of whole mountain ranges, dramatic glacier movement, continental drifts, geologic transformations of variegated kinds, all contributed to radical alteration of the earth's terrain, the sea's currents, the climate of land and water, and—because of the redistribution of flora and fauna—the very composition of the atmosphere, and of its oxygen and ozone content, in particular. Momentous realignments of the natural forces of the earth were effected, and this within a brief span of time.

In most parts of the earth, two radically different types of living creature were favorably endowed to survive: those organisms which could evolve specialized techniques for acclimatizing themselves to specific locales—such as burrowing skills, climbing powers, blubber beneath the skin; and those organisms with enormous flexibility, creatures which though not potent with respect to any particular adaptive habit could nonetheless survive by shifting, with rapidity and skill, from one habit of survival to another. Within the limits of temperature, oxygen tension, and other factors essential for life, the former type could occupy only a narrow region, depending upon the region's natural attributes. Within the same limits, the latter type could occupy an immensely wide region—one indeed the boundaries of which were nearly coextensive with the outermost limits themselves—and ultimately, *mirabile dictu*, came, by competent deployment of technique, to extend the very limits of the possibility for the efflorescence of life itself.

My concern is to outline some examples of the kinds of mutations which, by felicitous confluence, brought about embryogenesis of the more versatile creatures. For these creatures became *men*. Whether biologic speculation that a single replicatory particle gave rise to all living progeny is more valid than analogous for man's genesis, or whether indeed a single, unique person first emerged, ancestor of all humankind, is a moot question. On the other hand, such an unlikely convergence of mutants could have appeared only under quite specialized ecologic conditions and in an astoundingly small number of living beings. Even to enumerate the more salient of these mutants would be a major undertaking; to associate temporal increments and ecologic metamorphoses with correlated groups of mutants would exceed our present knowledge. Nevertheless, I do essay briefly and impressionistically to list a few mutants, in order both to indicate certain connections between them and to suggest their larger import.

Consider the cranial bones.[6] Sutures and fontanelles do not close until after birth; thereby, the brain continues to grow until the age of three or four. When this fact is combined with both an incredibly convoluted brain formed of many layers—hence, much surface for sentiency and reasoned response—and intricately composed neural fibers, the information transmitted about organism and milieu becomes remarkably detailed. Moreover, the development of prefrontal lobes, large visual and auditory centers, and a complex balance system constituted of interwoven vestibular nuclei far exceeds analogous development in any primate. Accordingly, the autochthonous activity of the brain becomes enormously increased. Beyond this, in the labyrinth of the inner ear, a complementary balance center appears. Sensory-motor development permits ever-gathering momentum with respect to possibilities for nerve impulse transmission; tactile organs of pressure, temperature, and pain are widely distributed throughout the body, though they tend to favor certain critical areas for their concentration; sweat glands allow for finer discrimination of temperature fluctuations. All these mutually reinforcing and reciprocally potentiating mutants arise to govern body activity from head to toe.

Turning to the relative sizes of skull and face: the magnitude of the latter is considerably diminished vis-à-vis that of the former. In consequence, sense organs such as the eye and the ear become less vulnerable to injury. At the same time, associated with a proportionately smaller face is an extraordinary complexity of musculature. Because of the motility and subtle modulations of facial muscles, expressiveness increases greatly. When this factor is combined with a highly developed neural apparatus, the possibilities for communication are further enhanced. Moreover, consider the import of binocular, stereoscopic vision which, when associated with a flexible, supple, and slender neck, composed of its own intricately overlapping muscles, permits both a nearly 360 degree rotation of the head and its upright, forward peering position—maintained steadily through the activity of the complemental balance systems. This rotatory power is further increased by the position of the foramen magnum through which a supple spinal cord passes directly and linearly into the lower brain. Even greater ease of head rotation is grounded in the intricate interlockings of vertebrae along the spinal column, the protective skeletal sheaf for that cord. Indeed, this power of rotation is yet further potentiated by the complicatedly infolded musculature of the back, especially by the innumerable small muscles directly connected to the vertebral column. Now consider how both head rotation and torso movement are facilitated by the relationship between an exceedingly intricate shoulder girdle and an analogously complex hip structure. For, thereby, the powers to leap, to dance, to hop, to jump, to run become far greater, in their interwoven potentialities, than for the primate. Moreover, this combined effect of vertebrae, shoulder girdle, hip bones, and torso musculature allows man to retain an upright position, despite his performance of the most variable tasks. Yet it permits him readily to shift to countless other positions when circumstance makes this alternation appropriate.

Next, consider how a flexible forearm combines with versatile finger movements which, in turn, are wedded to a maneuverable hand which can mold, cut, and feel objects of variable density and texture. Here, dexterity and agility arise which permit balance between fine and coarse controls, the balance by which tools may, in a brain of sufficient complexity, be constructed, and tools for contriving new tools. With respect to the lower extremity, consider the analogously flexible lower limbs in combination with a bipedal foot and toes which clutch just sufficiently to allow for free movement of all lower regions of the body: man the roamer becomes possible. Yet to facilitate a person's roaming activities in the most diverse climes, teeth must remain relatively undifferentiated, or at least already established differences must be so tapered that different classes of food, discovered in widely separated terrains, may be ingested: foraging, biting, chewing—all become possible. Returning to the nervous system, consider the highly differentiated sympathetic and para-sympathetic components of the autonomic nervous system which allow such visceral reactivity as breathing regulation—regulation which will permit oxygenation of the body under rapidly changing conditions of available oxygen, as one moves from heights to depths. Finally, behold the larynx! What marvelous possibilities this simple organ exhibits, that organ so like a stringed musical instrument, which, when complemented by the ear drum and joined to other powers, gives birth to the miracle of speech: hence, precise distinctions within self and other and between self and cosmos.

What do all these facts and correlations of facts portend? Essentially, they speak for themselves. For I have designated man the *roamer*. By the power of his limbs and by his capacity to survive in diverse environments, his patterns of migration are extensive and variegated. By the power of his head and shoulders to rotate, coupled with his stereoscopic vision, he surveys the spheres of heaven and earth. By the power of his neck muscles to bend his face low, and his forearm muscles to stretch toward it his trembling fingers, simulating a fetal position, in a marvelous conjunction of gestures, he meditates and prays in solitude. By the power of his larynx to emit precisely differentiated sounds and his hands to gesticulate and to designate, he speaks, he communes, and he symbolizes. By the power of coordinating vision, by which he detaches objects from himself and experiences a panorama of durable configurations, each autonomous and self-contained; hearing, by which he attaches objects to himself and experiences their fluent, dynamic, and evanescent qualities; and touch, by which he experiences the textures and circumscribings and densities of objects, he shapes an integrated manifold within which he roots and secures himself. By the power of his numberless flexible and ever-proliferating new habits, his undifferentiated teeth, his fine homeostatic control through a delicately constituted autonomic nervous system, he endures numerous environmental vicissitudes: he cultivates plants; he hunts animals; he tames and domesticates beasts; he explores the most diversified environments. By the power of a convoluted and supple brain, conjoined with all his morphologically defined aptitudes and a highly differentiated sensory-motor system, not only does he potentiate the hitherto enumerated powers but he experiences all imaginable mood fluctuations—interweavings of will, desire, emotion, kinesthesia, sensation, perception, cognition: a kaleidoscopic etherealizing of his mundane experience. All these, and so many more, are the powers of man!

Man comes silently into the world.[7] His mind is filled with intimations of realms beyond realms. Bursting with images, the deposition of memories and dreams and fantasies, his primordial reflections glow with intense, incandescent, and haunting hope. Amidst images of terror, like a child perpetuating naïveté into adulthood, he entrusts himself to spheres of being which by his indigenous powers he synthesizes from the numberless perspectives which his ever-shifting gaze and movement disclose to him. Above all, man perceives with increasing clarity the unity which pervades his efflorescing and sinuous images, images which at first betoken fragmentation but, ultimately, a vast integration. For man is the great

Refuser. Dissent and discontent lurk in his soul. An ephemeral and transitory existence requires defense and control. Ever poised to destroy a threat or to elude it, quickening his pace or stealthily keeping his vigil, he nonetheless desists from renouncing a dream: powerful, steady, luminous, clear—a refusal to feign, an abstention from deceit, a resolve not to be dissimulated, a demand to clash with desiccated belief. When speech breaks his silence, man names his fears; and he names his aspirations. Profoundly rooted in man's organicity, this unremitting quest for the true, the good, the beautiful is immeasurably amplified by his capacity to receive the greater cosmic rhythms. This refusal, this quest, this openness is the ground for primordial reflection. But this ground itself is rooted in defiance— defiance hurled to all the forces of the universe: *something in man will not perish*!

> Death, be not proud, though some have callèd thee
> Mighty and dreadful, for thou art so;
> For thou whom thou think'st thou dost overthrow
> Die not, poor Death; nor yet canst thou kill me.
> . . . .
> One short sleep past, we wake eternally,
> And death shall be no more: Death, thou shalt die![8]

C · BODY'S SILENT LANGUAGE:
THE MIRACLE OF PERSONHOOD

(a) The Ground of Speech

How does man manifest this trust, this hope, this aspiration? By what means does he commune, symbolize, and search? Wherein consists his reverence for himself, his friends, the world? At the culmination of man's natural development, on the level at which the contributions of the inanimate and the organismic reach their consummation and bring their diverse contributions to convergence, the luminous center of a subtly modulated comportment, the power of speech, makes its appearance. Now I sketch the general contours of the relationship between speech and comportment within the context of an organic basis for the primordial rhythms of reflection. In later books, I probe the various facets of man as seeker and symbolizer in greater detail; in particular, I outline those metamorphoses by which, once he has emerged from sheer organicity, his consummate wisdom is attained. The present perspective, transcendental naturalism, is intended to prepare the way for the consideration of man under a more inclusive perspective, transcendental personalism.

When I speak of the "contours" of the relationship between speech and comportment, I must refer my reader to my first chapter, in which I treated as primordial categories, agency, power, and rhythm. Pre-eminently, these categories are expressed by speech woven with comportment, the matrix wherein the laminae of man's essence are orchestrated. Until now, these laminae were expressed as man's evanescent essence, his crystalline essence, and his fermenting essence. At this point, I add his *symbolizing* essence. In later books, I deal with the vector which joins pure being with personal being, a vector already proposed as complementing the vector, described in the foregoing pages, which joins non-being with personal being. Then I shall distinguish two additional essences: the ethereal and the ineffable, each a stage along the way to man's consummate fulfillment through his participation in the plenitudinous rhythms of pure being—rhythms which are not isolated from the privative rhythms of non-being, but subtly interwoven with them. Now I must treat the organic basis for speech–comportment matrix in its relevance to a general theory of the person.

Considered independently of speech, man's physical comportment, insofar as it purports to communicate, is obscure and ambiguous. Nature's myriad subtle and variegated rhythms are such that no gesture, vocal inflection, or postural stance, or, for that matter, any specific attitude, can accurately delineate information about those rhythms. By "delineate information," I mean, quite literally, *precisely to set forth the lineaments of the form intended to be communicated*: the exact contours of objects, activities, or qualities. Only speech, when assisted by comportment, possesses this capacity. Phonemic themes aggregated into morphemes and semantic units, and modulated upon each spoken repetition, are associated with a slowly growing reservoir of unambiguous and clearly etched meanings. Earlier, I showed how elementary particles aggregate themselves into intricate particles, how new coalescences form, and how in their interactions these novel formations give rise to increasingly complicated configurations. I stressed how, on every level of combination, the quest for reciprocal imprinting, particle upon particle, aggregate upon aggregate, expresses, perpetuates, and enhances an inexorable growth toward the human. Inhering in all existence is a power of inducing such impressions; every existent, so I argued, is the agent, itself pregnant with such synthesized impressions, whereby those impressions are first exteriorized and transmitted to other agents. And, in general, both inflorescence and efflorescence reign throughout nature. The fruition of this process is persons holding dialogue through speech, speech conditioned, reinforced, and accentuated by comportment.

Under the following rubrics, I now set forth the general features of speech's import, its organismic meaning for the person; I prescind from the problem, the topic of later books, of the autonomous development of speech and its power to symbolize: its instrumental value in man's insatiable searchings. I list these rubrics seriatim: (i) mutant convergence and structural–function migrations; (ii) interwovenness of pleasure and power in utterance; (iii) speech categorization, and the rendering of cognitive categories through speech, by oscillatory links; (iv) primordial child–parent speech resonances; (v) comportmentally induced speech differentiations; (vi) namings as products of child–parent symbiosis; (vii) the denominative fabric woven by child, parent, and object; (viii) the heuristics of repetition: the uniqueness of utterance; (ix) phoneme-band particularizations;

(x) primordial identity of thought as action and speech as action; (xi) interstices and phonemic fissures as the self-multiplying loci of silent speech; and (xii) deposition of chains of being as interiorized speech: the consequent nature of agent, power, and rhythm.

(i) *Mutant Convergence and Structural–Functional Migrations*

A firmly poised balance between uttered sounds of variegated quality and a flexible comportment which is finely nuanced announces the miracle of speech. Latent within the brains of evolving organisms as a potency for speech competence, this miracle actualizes itself when two factors coincide: a certain genetic endowment and an appropriate environmental catalyst. Here, I stress the former. Just as the transformation of delicately attuned components into an intricate system of co-adaptation, the result of fortuitous convergence of numberless mutations, is required for primordial reflection to emerge, so the immanent cerebral power requisite for speech may be realized only in conjunction with an even larger group of mutations. Instrument, shaper, and matrix of reflection, speech thereupon appears.

Among the strictly morphologic mutations, I stress the following: a larynx composed of intersecting and vibrating folds of a certain resilience; a throat and palate appropriately contoured and textured; a pair of lungs functioning as a kind of bellows; an elaborate scheme of bronchioles, bronchi, and trachea; nostrils and eustachian tubes smoothly conjoined with throat; mouth and lips sufficiently versatile; a mobile and sensitive tongue; teeth and jawbone firm yet flexible; maxillary and frontal sinuses sufficiently porous; a receptor system based on bones of variable densities for sound conduction; an ear drum, canal, and middle ear possessing interlocking ossicles—though the latter three elements are not, strictly speaking, essential for speech production, as witness the deaf-mute's capacity for "inner" speech. And one must add the highly developed speech "centers" located in certain brain convolutions, usually of the left hemisphere, and a right hemisphere which either is specialized for music reception or serves as repository for residual and instrumentally useless rejects of potential sound. Perhaps, indeed, mirror images of phonemes and morphemes are woven into its complementary hemisphere but available, upon suitable activation, for later transfer to the right hemisphere, and transposition preparatory to a newly creative (poetic) role.

Moreover, a genetically determined post-natal period of great instability must be present. By virtue of an inexorable continuance of species-specific developmental trends, maturation continues. First, a relatively amorphous period reaches a crisis. Next, with respect to its potentialities for undergoing further cerebral transformation, this period rapidly becomes attenuated, and flows into a diminishing cadence of potential responsivity. In conjunction with neural predilection, other significant regions of the organism, not directly associated with speech, must show analogous maturational patterns: the capacity for athetoid finger movements to undergo transformation to clutching, grasping and, finally, exploratory functions; the capacity of foot and pelvis to acquire powers for erect posture, converting random crawlings to purposive walking. Marvelously, the appearance of speech, the exploratory maturation of hands and fingers, and the roaming potentialities of lower limbs tend to coincide and to become associated, somewhere between the ages of one and three, in an essentially synchronous development.

In this process, many structures previously connected to non–speech-related functions tend to acquire new speech-related capacities; earlier functions become obsolete or dormant. Thus, lips and mouth become functionally reorganized to assume as primary role not the differentiated food ingestion techniques of animals, but specific speech activities. In other instances, structures themselves are abandoned, even though they were previously related to structures now associated with speech. Such rejected structures may acquire additional non-speech functions. Alternatively, they may be relegated either to vestigial status or to gradual dissolution. In short, new structural–functional compositions become superimposed on now archaic patterns. Old functions are muted; old structures exhibit variegated patterns of mutability; migrations of structures and functions supervene; new conjunctions, juxtapositions, and syntheses are effected.

(ii) *Interwovenness of Pleasure and Power in Utterance*

Given a pre-existing disposition to speech, what activates its realization? It is resistance: the foil which the environment presents to the person as he, reciprocally, presents himself to it. Ultimately, indeed, speech is catalyzed by the dynamic interplay of resistance and counter-resistance. Consider the first implanting of a child's toe upon the earth. In the coordinating of toe and sole, pleasureable sensations arise through the interplay of tactile and proprioceptor receptors. In turn, kinesthesias originating in leg muscles, pelvis, and torso add to these sensations. Furthermore, contact with the earth is resilient. In the force of rebound, delight is experienced. When the foot is placed firmly on the ground, its contours are molded to the configuration of the ground. At first warily, but with increasing skill and, hence, confidence, the child feels sinuosities, protuberances, crevices, and depressions. Now pleasure blends with a sense of power. With power, the joy of roaming and exploring expands. Never, however, does the foot merely yield, in the sense of merging with the terrain; there is no anomic enmeshing of the two. On the contrary, its felt movements are accentuated as the foot actively shapes its contours to the ground and, conversely, the ground redesigns the stresses upon the musculature of the foot. Throughout, this process is governed by the principle that action is equivalent to reaction. Together, these patterns are associated with heightened self-esteem.

Analogously, once a brain function has been transformed into a function which is more complex, and the person blunders upon the nonsense of babbling as a kind of trick and delightful self-conceit, the possibility of the performance of which had long lain dormant in the brain, both proprioceptor and tactile receptors in tongue, pharynx, and lips are activated. Joy woven with power arises. Now a motive is supplied for the increasing exercise of the organs of speech. Environmentally induced alterations in those organs are effected. Progressively, they allow the child to babble, to gurgle, and to coo in ever-widening range and with ever more diversified innovation. He enters a world of his own self-produced sound. Truly, he is enveloped by these autochthonous melodies. Encountering *their* resistance, the child still further deploys his natural speech-making apparatus in order to aggrandize and to differentiate his own subsequent utterances.

In the hominid, yearnings first appeared for converting mere cries, signalings of one creature to another, into the authentic symbolism of speech. As hominid transforms itself into man, speech emerges. And in primitive man, now pregnant with the possibilities for speech, and with the powers for the actualization of speech roughly synchronous with the development of the exploratory faculties of hand and finger and the roaming propensities of leg and foot, dance fully bursts forth. A primordial cry is the very consummation of the dance: the quest of comportment to become word—silence transfigured into meaningful sound. Heightening the ecstasy of dance, the reverberations of this cry also increase, through a kind of synergism, its contrapuntal complexity. Now, recapitulating the experience of primitive man, the child truly opens himself to the world. Terrain of sound, earth, and object becomes increasingly differentiated. Everything resists. Yet resistance originates creative ornamentation. An image is shaped: for the wind's whistling, for a flower's whisper, for a trickling brook, for the rush of a stream, for a crashing waterfall, for the desert night's palpable stillness, for the soft movements of a plant, for cries of animals as they turn toward the child—all resist. Yet the child experiences every motion and every sound as though they but await his response. For him, they are oriented uniquely toward him. Through them, his delight and his power increase. By the dexterity and the versatility of limb, hand, and speech, a more nuanced "terrain" is molded. Powers for joy are correlatively enhanced.

(iii) *Speech's Categorization, and the Rendering of Cognitive Categories through Speech, by Oscillatory Links*

Resident within the infant, indeed species-specific in a genetic sense, are primordial cognitive categories which, ultimately, will be transposed into articulated semantic units. The power for eventually expressing supposals, affirmations, assertions, exclamations, denials already inheres within the organism. In a universal and inclusive way, primordial speech reiterates these categories. Often, whole classes of a particular cognitive type are compressed into smaller units of speech. At one juncture of an infant's development, a single phoneme will suffice. Hence, speech is initially associated with a prodromal, global character. Later, its syntactic and semantic differentiations will correspond, though not in one-to-one fashion, to more detailed taxonomic distinctions between and within cognitive categories. Accordingly, latent within each person is the fundamental architecture of all speech. But, inscribed upon this architecture is an architec*tonic* "structure," a moving and fluent structure, actually a congeries of associated functions, which slowly evolves as post-natal maturation unfolds. Not inert structures so much as dynamic modulations characterize the most general matrix of speech consistent with the cognitive ground of mind.

Amidst the numberless transformations induced by environmental impact, varying gradients of invariancy, each enclosed within another, are engendered as successively new regions of the brain are innervated, and a more intricate categoreal-taxonomic scheme is accordingly shaped. Though a multitude of conceptual and affective nuances are inscribed upon each taxonomic theme, this theme is not a mere abstract, universal form, pregnant with infinite possibilities for phonemic differentiation. On the contrary, it is a concrete and substantive invariant which infolds those classes of phonemes, and their arrangements, congruous with the actual biologic constitution of man. They are *possible* phonemes which, given the appropriate circumstances, may actualize themselves, spiraling outward as they effloresce from their original locus of compression.

Man's essential cognitive categories are imprinted upon his brain both dynamically and temporally. During ontogenesis, they continually change and metamorphose. At one and the same time, they become increasingly generalized and increasingly particularized. Each polar movement grounds its inverse movement. Moreover, these categories are presumably inscribed upon neural replicatory material. Memory having been associated with the RNA dynamism, unusually large concentrations of such material may be found in the relevant higher cortical centers. But neither RNA nor its complement, DNA, is an inert macromolecule. Doubly helical in composition, each is in a state of constant fibrillation. Surely, various oscillatory rhythms sweep over and activate pulsations indigenously associated with every such particle. In effect, a multitude of "resonators" are linked in the brain in an intricately ordered oscillatory chain, each link of which is in some state of vibratory movement. These diverse motions are imparted to one another along the chain. Throughout this process, attunements and cacophony, equilibration and disequilibration are regnant.

What holds with respect to neural oscillatory chains analogously applies throughout the body. Consider the reaction of a child to his own first babblings. Strikingly, no expressive motor speech can, in the final analysis, be separated from receptor impressive speech. As soon as a discrete and circumscribed babble is uttered, the child's lips, his tongue, larynx, laryngeal nerve, constellations of his cortical neurones, and, ultimately, some specific intra-cortical but not a simply located dynamism, like that of RNA, resonate; and these resonances affect his brain. Along the entire series, throughout the whole neural network and beyond that network, in the more mechanically constructed organs of the body, each part resonates in response to its antecedent parts. Varying amplifications, energy transformations, diminutions and increases of amplitude, and altering frequencies occur—but, always lawfully and in regular sequence.

Thus activating oscillations in one another, the links in this chain terminate in RNA, which, as it fibrillates, may well enter into association with DNA and, thereby, induce multiple replications. If so, these speech–memory replicas would spread temporally throughout the cortical regions. Already engrained memory engrams would, under this supposition, interact with incoming speech-stubs. New combinations may occur; former depositions could fragment. All is in flux; no structure is fixed in this viscous, marvelously circulating efflux called the brain. Many neural oscillatory centers may co-exist; the number which can be activated is determined by genetic factors potentiated by environmental catalysis. From every center emanates a spiraling efflorescence of waves. Propagated from that center, these waves exhibit, in direct proportion to the distance of a wave from its originating center, increasingly attenuated energy configurations. However, sets of attenuated wave "circles" within this set of sets of concentrically patterned "circles" interact synergistically. Thereby, new centers are created—centers perhaps even woven with resonances deriving from the right hemisphere of the brain, that mysterious repository of normally unused experience. In any event, babble engram-stubs are engrafted onto babble engram-stubs. Each in self-action, pairs in interaction, all transactionally woven with other analogous depositions, these babblings constitute ever-new speech discriminations. Through them arise altogether novel centers of resonance, centers capable of undergoing still more innovative fibrillation.

Since many periodicities, cycles, and oscillatory patterns are involved in the transmission of waves from one sonorous body to another, the propagation of sound is quite intricate. Sustained notes associated with vowels and transient notes associated with consonants mingle; the medium through which a wave is transmitted, preceded by an emission and terminated by an inmission, may modify its form, its frequency, its amplitude; many different trains of sound waves may be propagated with mutual interference, reinforcement, or cancellation. Despite this seemingly inchoate medley, each brain resonator, perhaps the ultimate minuscule RNA oscillators, is empowered to differentiate the original patterns, as with speech or music, and to separate out the waves which have been distinguished. Hence, sound replication can occur within the brain with respect to the original character of the variegated sounds received.

Granted: each member of the series of resonators along the way to the brain adds its unique coloration. The brain is pervaded by a flux of kaleidoscopic sound patterns, each with its idiosyncratic contours and all dynamically linked. Even abstract thought patterns are delicately nuanced fibrillations. Yet it is as though one is in a great concert hall: every recess of the hall, every fabric covering seat and floor, every protuberance jutting from the vaulted ceiling, the body-configuration of each person in the hall—all add their special resonances to the music; nevertheless, despite all interference, the orchestra transmits an authentic replica of the originally intended sound. Analogously, the brain functions like a concert hall within which music endlessly reverberates, and its essential invariant qualities are accurately reproduced.

(iv) *Primordial Child–Parent Speech Resonances*

Consider, now, the basic paradigm for the interpersonal speechifying relationship: the primordial resonances of speech as child and parent commit their first utterances to one another. I have already shown how, from the child's side, a rudimentary propensity for articulation is first laid down in specific oscillatory brain engrams, engrams which spread temporally and interact dynamically. Furthermore, I implied that through a system of inhibitors, activators, and releasors of inhibitors —dynamic processes which pervade the brain—intertwined neural speech patterns are laid down. Though a latent structure, this configuration is actively to be construed as unfolding constellations of nested dependencies: pre-speech oscillators enclosed within and dynamically related to one another. Potentiating these constellations is a scheme of analyzers and synthesizers. By their interplay, these factors enable the latent and archetypal structure of language to be realized progressively through relevant transpositions to an outer, articulated, and specialized form of language.

When, in the neural and genetic context, a child first babbles, the resonance–replicatory dynamism is immediately set in motion within him. Against the resistance of his own obscure attempts at speech, the child's internal oscillatory system so evolves as to allow more precise endeavor, a continual action and reaction. Hearing these primitive sounds, the parent analogously absorbs them into his own incomparably more intricate network of oscillatory chains. He weaves the newly incorporated utterances into the layers of reverberation already laid down during his own maturational phase as constitutive of his continually growing capacity for speech, a potential which is activated again and again with respect to both speech recipiency and speech production. Indigenous laminated oscillatory patterns are further modulated, in subtle but often significant ways. Against the resistance of the child's primitive utterance, the parent, too, modifies and perhaps transfigures the speech proclivities already resident within him (the parent). He himself responds to the child; but his reactions assume the form of well-structured, precisely contoured, finely delineated, incisively uttered, and highly articulated phonemes, morphemes, and semantically composed units.

Impinging upon the child's receptor apparatus, or, should he (or, indeed, *mutatis mutandis*, his parent) be deaf, certainly conveyed through bone, lip-reading, and subtle propagation of sound waves which strike less dramatically but nonetheless effectively against other sensitive regions of his body, parental responses are absorbed into his indigenous but hitherto largely inactive oscillatory system as new schemes of fibrillation. In turn, these schemes interact with dynamic forms already initiated by his *own* babblings; novel layerings of internal resonance are created. In consequence, new potentialities for speech are released through a kind of mimesis of the sounds heard—not a simple imitation or mimicry, but a dynamically interactant product of two factors: the child's global and undifferentiated utterance potentials, and a highly refined and well-honed system of sounds, originating within the parent.

To recapitulate: the infant hears his own initially uttered sounds; he resonates to these sounds and layers anew, constituting an already patterned scheme of new fibrillations—a scheme which, in effect, awaits potentiation to realized speech. As soon as they are set in motion, the most primitive babblings unfold, and evolve in accordance with an autonomous dynamism which already inheres in the infant's neural apparatus. When the parent hears these babblings, they are woven into his own more complicated scheme of fibrillations. Thus delighted, he communicates his delight to the infant, by vocal inflection and gesture, and in myriad comportmental ways. Perceiving the pleasure of his parent, the infant reinforces his efforts to babble in a way which is pleasurable not only intrinsically for him but extrinsically for his parent—as these efforts are experienced by the infant.

In this process a sound, a, uttered by the child, is responded to by a sound, β, replied by the parent. Both child and parent resonate to the complex (a, β), each in his own manner. However, for the child (a, β) tends toward a sound, γ, whereas for the parent (a, β) tends toward a sound, γ'. In the matrix of reciprocally speechifying relationships between child and parent, γ and γ', in turn, become more and more similar: the increment of phonemic difference between them tends toward zero. Expressed otherwise, γ and γ' have a special affinity for one another. Drawing toward each other, they progressively evolve toward identity. Further, γ and γ' are, in effect, uttered by child and parent *in unison*. In consequence, child and parent dwell increasingly in a joint orchestration of harmonizing sound. A shared music-like experience envelops both. Thus in a common world of sound, the speech of the two, but especially that of the unformed child, tends to become more and more precisely co-adapted. Within this matrix of speech co-adaptation, communication will eventuate.

The infant's initial speech equipment is quite elementary. Save immanently, it consists of an actualizably small, even minute, range of phoneme differentiations, each phoneme compressing meanings which, in adulthood, will be expressed by more intricately combined phonemes. Though the recipiency of his own sounds as well as of those uttered by his parents, a gradient of rapid expansion supervenes for the child, expansion grounded in the shared system of evolving sound. Because of both post-natal maturational factors and the increasing exertion of relevant muscles and bone structures, all organs of speech become more powerful. Hence, the earliest phases of infant development are characterized by nearly limitless possibilities for phonemic specification, combination, and modulation. Firmly if haltingly, the child commits himself to speech. This seemingly inexhaustible wellspring is based upon two factors: the ever–self-modifying speechifying responses of the parent, and the virtually reflex activity of the child, at a phase of maturation when the speech-learning gradient is at a maximum.

(*b*) The Primordial Structures of Speech

(v) *Comportmentally Induced Speech Differentiations*

Accompanying the interchangings of sound, which constitute increasingly meaningful patterns of relatedness between child and parent, are significant gestures.
Manifesting incredible motility in the variegated facets of his comportment, the
child's utterances are conveyed to the parent with marked emphases of vocal inflection, gesticulation, lip and tongue twistings, poutings, widenings, and all kinds
of contortion, torso and leg movements such as belly retraction and protrusion,
kicking and dancing, and myriad other modulations of physical presentation. In
turn, like its associated rigidly structured yet diversely composed phoneme matrix,
parental comportment is, on the whole, more stereotyped and inflexible than that
of the child. Yet it is far more differentiated, exhibiting finer motions of quite
circumscribed regions of the body. In a reciprocity of comportment, child and
parent are brought into physical proximity. Alternatively, they may physically
withdraw from one another. In either instance, in the oscillating rhythms of attachment and detachment, the numberless ingredients of the comportment of
each, child and parent, and the numberless interweavings of the comportment of
both, comprise a mosaic of symbols which together with speech reveals the inwardness of every individual: his motives, intentions, and moods; the varied layers
of experience which he has assimilated; attitudes of tenderness or harshness, fear
or tranquillity, joy or melancholy. When parent or child correctly deciphers the
meanings encoded within comportment, profound communion and communication between the two supervene.

Comment on the origin of the word "person" is relevant. In Latin, *persona* is
a "mask" which both conceals the masked one with respect to his actual intendings,
communicating a sense of mystery and an aura of impenetrability, and, when the
ritual of the mask is understood, reveals this or that aspect of the symbolizing
comportment intended by the mask. Before that, in Greek, πρόσωπον, meaning
"toward the face and eyes" (i.e., πρός and ὄπα [from ὄψ (or ὦπα from ὤψ)]), referred to the special apparatus placed by actors about mouth, eyes, and other
significant facial features. For the Greeks, in addition to the emphases, conceal-
ments, and disclosures of the Roman mask, the προσωπεῖον *amplified* the actor's
voice. By amplification he dramatically transmitted to the audience a sense of
veridical dynamism and meaning, originating in his inmost recesses, that the
audience members might empathically experience analogous feelings stirred within their own hidden and perhaps *un*conscious regions. In addition, the Greek play
was accompanied by both choral and dancing parts the purpose of which was twofold: first, to accentuate and to reinforce meanings portended by the individual
actors, stressing now this and now that dimension of import; and, secondly, to
function as a communicator of meaning, so that, in both the apposition and opposition of chorus, dancers, and actors a more richly orchestrated texture of meaning might be transmitted.

Likewise, the relationship between parent and child is a kind of mutual dance. In its very exclusiveness, this relationship enhances the likelihood of amplification, hence, dramatization of significant themes of relatedness. Lineaments of empathic unfoldings are more sharply etched; contours and rhythms of comportment of both parent and child enmesh. Coming to fruition in actual utterance, speech in this comportmental matrix conveys more subtle, dramatic, and authentic representations of the realities of each, parent and child. In this frame of mobile comportment, the sounds themselves become more differentiated—hence, more delicately nuanced—vehicles of meaning, by working against the resistance of the interplay of comportmental decompositions and integrations.

Speaking in unison, indeed dwelling in unison, persons in communion employ gestural accompaniments to their speech which, as a whole, constitutes a kind of dance. Thereby, both the scope and the matter of unison are enlarged. In a way hitherto inconceivable, these living symbols—meaning-pervaded physical resonances of communicants—become finely attuned and co-adapted. Perceived deviations from already established patterns of comportment therein unfold; with gathering momentum, they spur renewed phoneme differentiation. A context for speech is created, speech woven with comportment. In it each factor, speech and comportment, though inwardly related and mutually presupposing, acts upon the other to increase the precision of its contours. As the context shifts with respect to its composition and its design, and other persons add their unique contributions so that an expanding community of personal agents is engendered, this interplay becomes richer and more subtly modulated. Regardless of his stage of maturation, every person who enters this community dwells in an already shaped milieu of precisely and conventionally demarcated modes of expression of its members' collective spiritual intent. Yet, in adding his idiosyncratic endowment, that person facilitates production of both realignments and oscillating balances in an ever-fluctuant symbolic matrix of presence and compresence.

To this ever-expanding complexus of symbolisms, a fabric woven by communal resonances, new tones, hues, and lines—subtle variants upon the patterns, forces, and changes of nature—are perpetually added. All this is part of a great cosmic ferment which constitutes the larger matrix in which every child achieves his identity. By successively (and primordially) identifying himself, through speech-illumined comportment—now with fluctuant seas, now with overarching trees, now with a great geologic upheaval, now with tranquil tides of wind and water, always with the flowings and surgings of nature which ring the human community with reverberations to which the child equally attunes himself—he counterposes the germ of an already formed identity to the resistances which it ceaselessly encounters. Thus embedded in the unpredictable currents flowing within a womb far more labyrinthine, harsh, and disordered than that from which he emerged, the child acquires, by virtue of this manifold of identifications, an ever-enlarging self-identity; already crystallized powers are potentiated in such ways as to solidify his identity, and to expand its scope.

(vi) *Namings as Products of Child–Parent Symbiosis*

In the context of the symbiotic bond of infant and parent, the architecture of an already established language is created for the infant, and the architectonics of novel modulations upon that language is created for his parent. The timbre of the voice, inflection, the interchanges of sound and silence—such factors as these allow a mood to envelop both parent and infant long before either infant understands parent, or, for that matter, parent understands infant. With increasing intentness, each listens to the other; a mood of listening hovers about the two. Foci of intensity and foci of attenuation emerge in schemes of varying balance within this milieu of reciprocal listening. Imperceptibly, the infant is drawn from autocentric rhythms of proto-speech to allocentric rhythms of veridical speech. Correlatively, the parent enriches his conventional patterns of speech with an aura of the autocentric—evoked within him from dim, haunting memory, and newly added to memory by the infant's novel intonings. By their encounters, each elicits from the other unfathomable and inexhaustible reservoirs either of experience or, for the infant, of feeling.

In this manner, the infant is gradually, but at times with critical leaps, drawn into the world of the parent who speaks. For parental speech portends for the infant limitless depths of what, for him, is a charismatic, awesome power which lurks in the parent. The converse proposition must also be affirmed. Truly a relationship of symbiosis holds between infant and parent. The mysteries of birth are engendered anew within the parent as fantasy and reflection. He, too, is entranced by hidden silence embedded in the unspeakably delightful phantasmagoria of the infant's movements and sounds, indeed by his very existence. By the evocative power of speech, primordial and advanced, in their dialectical interplay, the intentions of both, infant and parent, are apprehended and acknowledged. Apprehended and acknowledged! Each literally "prehends" for himself the inwardness of the other; each literally *names* for himself that inwardness, and names with cognitive intent: the one, in the etched contours of conventional speech limned by the other's autism; the other, miming those contours and, thereby, gradually articulating a structure for his spontaneous utterances.

"And out of the ground the Lord God formed every beast of the field, and every fowl of the air," declares the author of Genesis;

> and [He] brought *them* unto Adam to see what he would call them: and whatsoever Adam called every living creature, *that* was the name thereof. And Adam gave names to all cattle, and to the fowl of the air, and to every beast of the field [Gen 2:19–20].

"These He brought to man," I repeat, "to see what he would call them; each one was to bear the name the man would give it." By this text, the power of naming is conferred upon man; it is a gift from God. But the use of this power, the naming of names, is man's acknowledgment of this gift; *he* determines the names to be given. By these names, he fixates, he delimits, he defines a path of orientation within nature. Without the name, man would be lost in a trackless void, an unnamed nature in a wilderness of chaos. By the name, he secures himself. By the elusive nuances of the name, man articulates an ever-widening experience. There is always an unexplored margin of experience which itself serves to incite one to fill the gap, to rectify discrepancy; and the void is covered by the name. Lag between experience and word engenders an inexhaustibly productive force which invites the quest to name.[9]

What is the motive force behind this quest? From the point of view of the parent, and based upon a principle adduced earlier—namely, that self-replication is an effort of the organism to perpetuate itself substantively into its progeny— the special delight experienced by parent in his infant's strivings to name is a specific instance of that principle. Every person is filled, not so much with "raw" experience, a formless void, as with *named* experience—names of actions, names of qualities, names of objects, names of relations. Just as the woman is from time to time pregnant with child, so every person is always pregnant with the name, names which he, in ceaseless quest, allows to be born in the efflorescence of utterance. Man conceives his very substance to be woven of the fabric of speech: speech inward and ineffable; speech the subtle motions of which constitute thought; speech exteriorized and by the polyphony of which man and his community are surrounded. When I speak of names, I include as language silence as well as sound, pauses between sounds. Surely, the pause is as much constitutive of language as the sound. In counterpoint, both bear meaning and intent. Accordingly, when the infant begins to name, the parent identifies his own substance with the substance of the infant. By the same token, in his failure to distinguish signifier from signified, for he correctly perceives what the adult often loses sight of—namely, the profound interwovenness of the two, their inseparability—the infant analogously identifies with the adult. In reciprocal utterance there is reciprocal delight; and both grow apace. In the embrace of shared delight, the powers of each expands: the motive to name works inexorably; its energies unfold ineluctably. Surely, for names fully to emerge, mood must be transmitted through name, as well as by the actual experience of the objects which surround both parent and infant. In addition, objects must be so demarcated by the name that the latter constitutes, in the aggregate, an extended commentary upon the former.

(vii) *The Denominative Fabric Woven by Child, Parent, and Object*

Though a symbiotic relationship is the primordial matrix wherein the potentiality for naming arises, the realization of this potential requires, in addition, an object, an object present (in my simplified paradigm) to both infant, now become child, and parent. All three, persons and object, are not only compresent, but interwoven. Each is a necessary element in a composite situation. From their interactions, each in accordance with its own kind of power, the veridical name arises. From the standpoint of the object, its differentiable texture—fibrous, granulated, or smooth

—its discriminable protuberances, its sinuosities, and its proliferations constitute invitations for exploration, joint searching by child and parent. By its powers, inanimate or animate, the object presents itself for discrimination of its relevant ingredients. Oriented toward that object, child and parent share their touchings and their discernments. As they are thus enveloped by the pleasure of the sharing, layers of shared names emerge. Each informed by the object with its intrinsic contours, the parent uttering conventional signs and gesticulations with respect to this or that aspect of form, and the child gradually molding his utterances to conform to those of the parent, they come jointly to refer to the object *in the same way*. Information about it is thereby communicated between the two, information which is progressively modified as the object is fingered by each, held up to changing lights, placed in different contexts, viewed under diverse perspectives—in a word, as one lingers over the object.

A name serves, first, as general mark of an object, a sign of one of its features. But, immediately, sign is converted to symbol. Literally, as in συμβάλλειν, parent and child join in a shared enterprise. Depending on the kinds of discrimination needed, subtly, as they modify the sound of the name, they propose phonemic variations upon morphemes and semantic units. For compressed within a name, depending upon how it is uttered, are multitudinous meanings. As new names are contrived and communicated, and particularly as new objects are introduced into the situation, a synergistic interplay among increasingly diversified names unfolds. A veritable organism of namings emerges. Acquiring a kind of autonomy, this organism exhibits phonemes, morphemes, semantic units, and syntactic structures which combine and recombine in accordance with rules which are made increasingly explicit for the child, without ever having become formalized for the parent. By his participation in, and his reshaping of, the structures discriminated through the agency of the spoken word, each, child and parent, articulates his own being. Each declares that being as momentous and durable in relation to the world.

Ever discerning increments between possibilities resident within objects for further discrimination and the names thus far actually accumulated, one shapes a dynamic fabric of speech, a fabric which undergoes endless modulations, both efflorescences and inflorescences.[10] To refer by particular words to an increasingly global yet differentiated route to objects, actions, qualities, and relations several conditions must be fulfilled. First, the integrity of the composition of phoneme and morpheme must remain intact, a relative invariant amidst numberless subtle transformations, expressed as modulation differentials. Next, a stable association between word and entity denoted by that word must be maintained, at least as a relatively durable configuration—subject, of course, to linguistic evolution deriving from cultural factors, random phonemic shifts, novel contributions by the chance utterances of infants newly entering the community, unpredictably novel experience, and genetic endowment alterations, especially in the form of mutations. Finally, whenever a visual image replicating the object is presented, the intrinsic associational links should be so contrived that child or parent ought, with minimal searching, to find in his repertoire of names that word which will most appropriately identify the image as an image *of* the object named. Thereby, a basis is established for associating with every word a category. For a word is a generalized class of prospective designations. It expresses numberless signals, all phonemically (approximately) isomorphic to one another in this sense: the particular aspects of a particular object are exposed by the utterance corresponding to this class of isomorphs. In general, the perception of any object is enveloped by innumerable associations, many idiosyncratically penumbral to the response which "normally," or conventionally, would be elicited upon presentation of the object. *Naming* it requires, in effect, a choosing from the class of associations but a single, unique associational link, and so uttering the appropriate morpheme.

(viii) *The Heuristics of Repetition: The Uniqueness of Utterance*

Every recurrence of an uttered phoneme elicits novel ornamentations upon that phoneme; every spoken name is associated with unique vocal inflections, gestural accompaniments, timbre, volume, speed, and momentum shifts, myriad nuances of myriad kinds. Not only is a phoneme, morpheme, semantic unit, or syntactic structure universal and general for a class of speakers, indeed for a community, a culture, a nation; beyond that, it is concrete, idiosyncratic, and unique upon each occasion of its repetition by every particular speaker. A special poetry, peculiar to each who utters, hovers as an intriguing aura about every word, not only as that word is recurrently spoken, but, in addition, upon every particular occasion of its utterance. Circumstances of memory, experience, and anticipation are utterly distinct and non-repeatable for every individual. Even the contours of throat, larynx, lips, and tongue vary from person to person. The way in which these organs are filled with propagated sound waves, the very form, amplitude, and frequency of those waves, especially with respect to seemingly minor oscillations inscribed upon them and, accordingly, modifying the principal characteristics of the waves, fluctuate from person to person. Indeed, when one considers the synergistic impact of sound wave upon sound wave, and the incredible variety of links established between visual, olfactory, gustatory, tactile, and kinesthetic Imagos, not to mention the vast repository of memory engrams, the likelihood of indiscernible differences between seemingly identically spoken words is quite remote.

From the universal groundwork of a given linguistic structure, perpetually modified by nuances introduced by every new member of a community, are extracted such sub-patterns as are peculiarly associated with the experience of each member. These sub-patterns are ways by which he communicates the special experience of the world which he inscribes upon the archetypal and general experience of the community. A double injunction to every communicant is grounded in these considerations: listen intently, with all your resources, to all the multiple layers of signification, private and public, which inhere within every utterance; seek empathically to attune your own mood and intentions to what you discern as the deeper structure—the music resident within an essentially *inner* speech (ultimately the kaleidoscopic flow of thought itself)—of the language spoken by another. Should this injunction be heeded, the *heuristics* of language is allowed full play.

A strictly personal hermeneutic based on the precept that every linguistic interpretation is concrete as well as universal permits language to be immeasurably enriched, even by seemingly ritualistic, stereotyped repetition of linguistic entities. No repetition is wholly free from subtle, often hidden elements of the particular and non-recurrent. True, on the whole, the overtones and undertones of speech would perish unless, by repeated intense listening as well as speaking, they are incorporated into communal dialogue. But dialogue is broadly to be construed. Authentically delivered, no person's speech wholly perishes. It deposits itself, as a kind of objective immortalizing of the person himself, into the ever-growing, continually self-enriching spiralings of the entire linguistic enterprise, humanity's larger spiritual quest. In the deepest sense, human speaking compels reverence. When he speaks truly, man stands before eternity. A veridical sacrament, the word symbolizes the progressive etherealization of the human community.

(ix) *Phoneme-Band Particularizations*

Undoubtedly, a gradient is associated with every person's capacity to absorb and articulate phonemes. During early maturation, the power of a child's nervous system to register a wide range of phonemes, extending indeed to the uttermost limits of human possibility, is exceedingly great. At this stage, he can, in principle, learn an indefinitely large number of languages. But, as he learns, the self-replicating engrams engrained upon the relevant neural structures increasingly constitute themselves a barrier to further imprinting. In effect, attainment of his full capacity for phoneme articulation would inhibit the child's ability for further linguistic realization. Once actualized, his speechifying power becomes progressively depotentiated with respect to the spread of phonemes beyond a range associated with a certain set of wave frequencies, forms, and amplitudes. On the other hand, within this increasingly delimited range, the very same power becomes progressively greater with respect to phoneme differentiation and to the inscription of subtle variants upon every particular phoneme. In brief, scope is diminished; differentiability increases. It is as though the child becomes ever more intent upon achieving competency within a given restricted range. But because of his earlier capacity to extend that range indefinitely, he is enabled to focus simultaneously upon the variety of phoneme sets previously learned.

In general, amorphous and indefinitely flexible potentialities present at birth become divided into a set of phoneme bands, usually one, but in a multilinguistic person, a variety. Differentiations within each band are then effected. Later in life, when skill has been attained in the exploitation of phonemic possibilities within even the most restricted band, the inverse situation often prevails. A reversal may occur. The power of linguistically competent adults to learn new languages, thereby so extending the scope of one band as to enable it to merge with newly developed bands associated with different language, increases in proportion to the adult's actual exercise of that skill, i.e., when he deliberately sets about learning a new language.

A pattern of phenome possibilities is neurally embedded. Initially, the set of resonators serving as physiologic agents for speech articulation is highly sensitive over a wide range of potential oscillations. As a basic categoreal scheme is laid down and the region of limited competency is demarcated, this sensitivity is diminished. It is converted into a new kind of sensitivity: that kind which discriminates fine nuances and modulations within a restricted band of phoneme potentials. A variety of types of maturational equilibria, critical junctures, and disequilibria prevails. But, even after the power for multi-language learning has significantly decreased, the potentiality for continued expansion of scope is not annihilated; it is merely suppressed. A latent dynamism continues to operate, a dynamism which by subsequent fortuitous factors might be so activated that de-suppression may occur with respect to hitherto unarticulated phoneme patterns. In effect, linguistic reverberations on subliminal layers continue to echo through the nervous system. Given appropriate life circumstances, and suitable exercise of adult linguistic skills, some of these reverberations may break through the threshold and become *realized* potentials. In general, the fundamental linguistic–cognitive categories are universal. At different epochs of life, one can, in principle, draw upon hitherto suppressed patterns.

A significant factor determining realization of certain linguistic potentials is the need, elicited by environmental tensions, to camouflage the sounds of plants and animals. Every person is empowered to protect himself through camouflaging devices. Man's capacity to survive through a miming propensity far exceeds that of any other creature. In this process, which culminates in the linguistic coming together of persons into a community for self-protective ends, a skeletal protective structure is laid down. When one migrates to a community of strangers, his self-protective needs are activated, regardless of his age or maturational level or the working of special inhibitors (which are suspended). A heightened tension-threshold catalyzes production of such sound patterns as will draw him more intimately into the new group. In his wanderings, the power of onomatopoesis (as a substitutive mode of camouflage) is constantly evoked. Moreover, gesture fills in the linguistic gaps. Onomatopoetic power is shaped by and assimilated to the rhythmic structures of an already prevalent language. In addition, it is set in motion by the natural sounds which flow about one. Everyone is born into a world of prefixed sound. Yet the possibilities for linguistic expansion and increasing subtlety of expression, a need for sharing and protection, special proclivities toward creative exploration, the particular dynamics of dialectical interplay between functionally autonomous groups of neural resonators, transferrals from the linguistically recessive speech hemisphere in de-repressive engram migrations— either random or perhaps activated by subtle nuances on some name, heard or spoken, a poetic connotation which hovers as an invigorating aura over every name: such manifold factors as these can predictably constitute for a person an altogether new fabric of speech.

In sum,[11] one may truthfully declare that the body is, quite literally, extended by its use of tools and musical instruments, extended in such a way that, in effect, it spreads itself throughout the cosmos. Sounds transmitted from distant cosmic recesses aid in *uncoiling* the inwardly turned phoneme depositions; and the latent contents of these depositions are released to expand a hitherto fixed speech manifold. Phoneme hierarchies are dissolved; new phonemic layers are established and orchestrated; novel links are formed which bring the diversified linguistic competencies of individuals into more profound sharings. Ultimately, this "music of the spheres" pervades all. It binds together persons dwelling in communities in which the most variegated customs and languages prevail. In a sense, the presence of all who are, and all who ever were, are woven together in myriad patterns. Endlessly, these patterns combine and recombine. A great drama of transfiguration unfolds.

(c) Emergent Thought

(x) *Primordial Identity of Thought as Action and Speech as Action*

In my preceding section, I dealt with the "resonances of primordial reflection," without reference to the phenomenon of language; I treated reflection with minimal reference to speech. From neither speech nor reflection may one prescind without violating the essential character of both. *Thinking* and *speaking* are activities and processes. Within a larger perspective, they are not only complementary activities, but, indeed, at bottom, identical. To justify this claim, one must reflect briefly upon the distinction between inner speech and outer speech, i.e., speech proper. For the child, speech is predominantly exteriorized. The variety of non-stereotyped utterances is manifold. Every sound he hears, including those which he himself speaks, reverberates throughout him. Imprinted upon his brain via mutually attuned neural resonators, sound initially transmitted to him is, in turn, transposed into more subtle and intangible—indeed, ineffable—resonances. These resonances are primordia of what will subsequently evolve into the highly articulated system of inner speech.

As the child's exterior speech becomes more differentiated, especially as he first utters the names which, in early stages of his development, compress innumerable meanings within a limited group of phonemes, his inner fantasy life effloresces. Throughout this process, increasingly subtle oscillations are rhythmically inscribed upon his uttered sounds, always, in response to communicational patterns which become progressively more significant for the child. By this dynamism, his fantasy world is converted into a more finely modulated texture of inner sound—sound which is in constant motion. Patterns of thought supervene, patterns which are, in effect, the internalization of already sophisticated schemes of exterior speech. As the child passes into adulthood, the ratio between inner speech, increasingly identified with thought itself, and outer speech becomes ever larger. Numberless interiorized phoneme patterns incessantly interact to create more and more intricate cognitive structures.

Truly, thought is a movement; it is a luminous motion in the flow of inner speech. For it is speech subtilized and incandescent with rhythms of a peculiarly ethereal status: inner speech transparent to the resonances of reflection; inner speech, in fact, identical with those resonances. Both speech proper, or exterior utterance, and inner speech, or thought, are motions. They are temporal unfoldings. The variegated rhythms of time, its intricate meshwork of cycles and epicycles, and the more delicately nuanced fibrillations, whether minuscule or coarse, are inscribed upon those periodic movements to manifest themselves in speech and thought. When the inner nature, the veridical substance, of the correlations of speech and thought are properly understood, the complementarity and, in the final analysis, the identity of the two are established: the speech of the inner world of thought and the speech of the outer world of utterance, utterance woven with comportment which is mobile and fluctuant. Despite this ultimate identity, speech and thought paradoxically act upon one another. Through their interplay, each *re*acts in ways which induce special alterations and even transfigurations of its own intrinsic composition.

Vicissitudes of oscillation between thought–speech identifying and thought–speech transactions, with the consequent metamorphoses of each, will be explored in later books. At present, I need only indicate how, in a general sense, thought and speech alike flow forth. Constituted by resonances propagated as meaningful sound, intense foci within modulated and motile comportment, speech is, in its ideal form, to be construed, in its inner congruities and in its rhythmic motions, as a well-executed dance; it is as though music were woven into realized choreographic patterns. On the other hand, thought is constituted by resonances propagated as meaningful episodes, transitions, combinations, evanescings, and efflorescences. In both instances, the motions proceed from a common center.

With respect to thought, to think "a word clearly and distinctly . . . is . . . connected with . . . a sensation of movement, which . . . in the case of a very conscious thinking, [is] heightened so much that we can become aware of this sensation of movement."[12] For example, if one places one's finger deftly upon one's Adam's apple, vibrations are felt. These are the perceptible movements of thought, i.e., *inner* speech. With respect to (outer) speech, clearly, the factor of motion is paramount. Pitch, volume, timbre, accentuation, pause–sound sequences and proportions: all these diverse facets of speech are in constant rhythmic movement. Accordingly, speech has no "inner form" (namely, thought), an alleged structure which envelops speech as though it were a separate and independent entity. On the contrary, each is, as it were, the "form" of the other, grounding its very possibility, hence, shaping its every contour. In their oscillatory interweavings, both proceed from a common source. Each serves as condition for the further emergence of the other. Their joint source is a germinal silence laden with import, import which strives toward actualization.

Thought moves and grows.[13] Coming into existence through the agency of outer speech, it is identical with the interior echoes deposited in the wake of that speech. A word uttered, a name, compresses large thoughts, an echoing deposition within the brain encoded in the ever-expanding self-replicating resonators. Yet these echoes are no mere imprint, passive and inert, of the internal impingements of outer speech. Once woven with neural substance, they evolve (in their encoded states) according to their own laws, undergoing their autochthonous transformations. Thereupon, thought unfolds as a kind of decompression or unspiraling of these engrained imprints. For the child, a single word is associated with dim and amorphous, but nonetheless large and inclusive, thoughts. But for the adult, words are split into many discrete components, each a name in and for itself. The thought associated with every such unit becomes less global but more precise. In its denotative use, the word acquires greater specificity; in its connotative use, it becomes more circumscribed and richly nuanced—though, under pathologic conditions, it may become associated with greater stereotypy and less imagination than for the child.

No utterance is ever an altogether inert structure. In every instance, however arrested be the imaginational ingredient, utterance is a process. It is a process by the agency of which things reveal themselves to be what they are. Therein, they disclose their indigenous forms and textures. At the same time, all utterance manifests and embodies the thought which it embeds. Accordingly, the spoken word is intermediate between two realms of being, the physical and the spiritual. It mediates the rhythmic passage from one realm to the other. In this activity, every phoneme evolves, proliferates, and defines itself. Occurring in the context of the specific resistance of things, phonemes are structured as such in correspondence with the emerging structures of those things. Thus interwoven in a complicated dialectic with things, speech turns in upon itself. Thereby, it is converted into thought, thought which in this inward coiling of speech differentiates itself, and proceeds upon *its* course of evolution.

As increasingly differentiated vocalization supervenes, the child's egocentric and autistic speech diminishes. Correlatively, social speech markedly increases. Yet egocentric speech always remains the matrix whence springs new sounds. It is the ground for the ceaseless potentiation of the poetics of speech. Associated with increased vocalization—hence, with decreased speech ego-centricity, a process unfolds whereby uttered words are interiorized as thought. By its own determining principles, thought, through its very identification with inner speech, evolves along its characteristic dimension. More and more, the dialogic character of outer speech becomes complementary to the meditative, or constructively monologic, character of inner speech. Indeed, interpersonal encounters entailing authentic dialogue complement confrontation of a person with his own self, a mode of internal encounter which, in effect, entails monologic dialogue. Quite literally, this thought-ful gathering of the impressions of actual utterance is *a filling of oneself* with thoughts. It is an encountering of the presence of thoughts, thoughts linked to images, kinesthesias, and all the interior products of sense; it is a realm of psychic Imagos which unfolds autonomously, a realm into which, as strange and mesmeriz-ing congeries of presentment, one may thrust oneself, and seek ever new meaning.

In brief, thing, word, and thought are dynamically bound together. Thought is born in and through the word; things are discriminated by and through the word. Truly, the word links thought and thing.[14] But the word cannot be separated from the act. Indeed, both thought and word are activities. At bottom they are a single process. Each occurs as focal regions within comportment; and comportment al-ways unfolds with respect to things. Things cannot *be* without specific acts of discrimination. Hence, thought and word are integrally enmeshed aspects of acts. Each diffuses itself throughout things. Conversely, in offering resistance to thought–word acts, which unfold within comportment, things also (reciprocally) diffuse themselves throughout action. According to Saint John, "In the beginning was the Word"; according to Goethe, "In the beginning was the deed."[15] So inter-woven are word and deed that these affirmations are not contradictory. For the word crowns the deed. The substantive microcosm of all human consciousness, it is the fruition and culmination of the deed. Still, a single act is but one component in an unfolding and continually self-reordering sequence of acts. Within this sequence, word and thought are the often imperceptible transitions—the gaps, as it were—between act and act.

In general, acts may be quiescent or they may be active. In the former case, they are instances of intense listening. As such, acts are evocative of words and thoughts. In the latter, they are actings *upon* things, transforming and redesigning them. In consequence, word, thought, and act are interlocked. At times, one emerges into prominence; at times, another. But, in the last analysis, the three are inseparably interwoven. Among them prevail a dialectical interplay and identification. In this dialectic—hence, paradoxical relationship—thing, thought, and word exhibit an intrinsic identity, each with the other. Within this context, identity is construed as a ferment in which each factor ceaselessly imprints itself into the other. No factor may be extracted from this ferment without violation of its character.

(xi) *Interstices and Phonemic Fissures as the Self-Multiplying Loci of Silent Speech*

Veridical speech[16] and inner speech, which is identical with thought, lie not so much in uttered sound, or, for that matter, in the interior deposition of utterance as in the interstices between phonemes. Ultimately, phonemes are not linked to-gether as merely discrete units. On the contrary, they interact and transform one another, as in sequent flow each encounters the resistance of the other. Once uttered, every phoneme is diffused throughout an efflorescing speech; its scope continues to expand; and its content, to become more differentiated. Within the fissures and the gaps between phonemes, lie thought and, hence, speech in its actual import. Herein dwell both the potentiality for thought-diffused utterance and the realization of that potentiality. If one were artificially to segregate these interstices, and cause them so to be juxtaposed as to constitute their *own* flowings forth, they would, in their collectivity, comprise the immanent ground, form, and matrix of speech. Then, one could in truth speak of *body's silent language*; one could affirm that herein lies *the miracle of personhood*.

In primordial utterance, what lies within these interstices are the crudely shaped, global categories of thought. Yet, as the child develops, numberless sub-phonemes, all subtle and intricate variants upon conventionally demarcated phonemes, are engendered with ever-gathering complexity and richness of differentiation. They are shaped to an inarticulate but viable presence which, as it were, progressively fills the gaps between what is manifestly uttered. Yet between every pair of sub-phonemes, no matter how subtle its composition, lies still another gap—a gap more ineffable then the previous gap, since it is woven of the echoes and resonances of the proto-sounds which surround, or, more accurately, hover about every gap, bounding it on both sides. Phoneme-filled interstices enclose one another with in-creasingly ethereal modulations, like so many fragile Chinese boxes.

Whether spoken or gestural, signs *as such* do not express meanings. In actuality, they carve out and thereby mark the divergence of meanings between one sign and another. Composed of the differences between terms, language, in effect, "pre-cedes itself, teaches itself, and suggests its own deciphering."[17] In this sense, language is like a living organism. Many forces come to confluence; powers are activated and deactivated; equilibria are formed and shattered. So in language, an autonomous unfolding of variegated patterns of signs infolds upon itself, certain constellations of signs intersecting with and acting upon other constellations of signs. Novel patterns and rearrangements are perpetually created. A unity of co-existence of inarticulate and inexplicit signs is the veridical locus of language. A silent, internal articulation of sound occurs. In this process, meanings embedded in signs are alternately compressed and de-compressed.

For the child, a word stands for what, in the adult, is a sentence; a phoneme stands for a word. Throughout the maturation of speech, a dialectical opposition and interplay of phonemes occurs. Appositions, combinations, syntheses, differ-entiations, variations, mutations: all these functions are typical of phoneme forma-tion and transformation. Born into a linguistic world, the child is ineluctably drawn toward that world. The entire meaning of a language pervades its every part; the whole is immanent in every item. At the edges of signs, so to speak, lies memory: the deposition of intrusions of signs into the body. And so the child fills himself with signs, meanings, and memories. It is the latent, *diachronic* relations to signs—signs profiled, as it were, against signs—which is the true fabric of speech, a fabric to which each, in his manner, child or adult, gives himself up.

Pregnant with powers for birthing and rebirthing new significations, signs come into being, coalesce, or vanish as temporary guideposts "establish[ed] at the intersection of linguistic gestures as that which, by common consent, the gestures reveal."[18] Thought, so to speak, crawls along language, inhabiting its crevices and its sinuosities; it "moves through language as a gesture goes beyond the individual points of its passage."[19] No thought can be fixed and frozen in any well-demar-cated set of linguistic signs. On the contrary, thought is language as it liquefies and ferments. Hence, all language is allusive and silent. The very absence of a sign is itself a sign. And man dwells creatively and imaginationally in every cranny, no matter how elusive, of this linguistic organism. Moreover, to discern language's motions, one "must uncover the threads of silence that speech is mixed together with,"[20] so that thereby one may tear components away from the texture which these threads form to weave new sounds, sounds which, in turn, newly rub against one another to induce novel transfigurations. Indeed, thoughts *migrate*, now along this sign-trajectory, now along that. The linguistic fabric is criss-crossed by num-berless trajectoral possibilities. Each awaits actualization as a route for realized thought as every human gesture inaugurates new means for linguistic expression. Concealed beneath spoken language are values which exceed the actual presence of that language, values which form the constituents of a process over which reigns the principles of "laterality" and intersection.

The linguistic discreteness implied by this diachronic character of language is belied and contradicted by its synchronic character. Language is an orchestration of sounds and silences. And by the contrapuntal inventiveness which inheres within language as its own power for autonomous contrivance, no person can be *locked into* it; it is neither mechanism nor fossil. Every "act of expression . . . [is] . . . a modulation of . . . [some] . . . general system of expression . . . differentiated" —and differentiated radically and dramatically—"from other linguistic gestures."[21] By the dynamism of language, every word is but the crystalline residue of a linguistic habit long past use. The two formulas are complementary: "Synchrony envelops diachrony," "diachrony envelops synchrony." New fissures constantly ap-pear, seemingly at random, created from this orchestrated pattern of successive mosaics. In the "moving equilibrium" which is language, each fissure shatters its antecedent; each prepares the way for its successor.

Within language, processes incubate which effloresce, now as thunderous cre-scendos, now as softly evanescing diminuendos. A cohesive whole within which no *single* sign can be a vehicle of thought; all signs work together as an assemblage, a single unit to constitute the mobile linguistic organism. The texture of language is fibrous, but fibrous in a multi-patterned way. By its mute and muted presence, every factor signified arouses speech; every factor induces mutations within speech. Ever more meaningful than that which signifies, in its narrower import, the signi-fied reifications of a ceaselessly fluctuant world so act upon this structure of signifiers as to draw forth new signifyings, novel linguistic gestures. Language is like a painting upon a canvas which extends endlessly to sweep the entire cosmos. Never completed, it echoes and re*sounds* throughout the cosmos, penetrating its most hidden recesses and coalescing endlessly with other analogously constituted language. Within the great spheres of being, language thereby sets in motion confluences of resonance, confluences ever more profound and pervasive.

(xii) Deposition of Chains of Being as Interiorized Speech: The Consequent Nature of Agent, Power, and Rhythm

Speech brings to culmination the grand processional of rhythms, inanimate and animate; it transfigures those rhythms and exalts them, elevating them to the sphere of the personal. Together with its accompanying complement, thought—the two woven with comportment—speech is the vehicle which mediates transition from the infrapersonal to the personal. The consummation of natural evolution, speech concentrates, and compresses to a new mode of being, the most subtle resonances of man's thingly and organismic aspect. It initiates the metamorphoses by which the merely human transmutes itself into the sublimely human. In human relationships, mediating the transformations of speech, itself the mediator of the infrapersonal and the personal, are, first, the parents; then, through their agency, society; and, ultimately, the most inclusive human community, from the remote past extending to an indefinite future—a community upon which is engrained the great traditions of humankind.

From primitive utterances of a single, unique, primeval man, ancestor to the entire progeny of the human family, through which, in turn, by the latter's conflicts and self-differentiating habits, and catalyzed by interplay of genetic variants and environmental shifts, language itself cumulatively evolves, the great linguistic divergencies are engendered. I say a "unique . . . ancestor." For, given contemporary views regarding convergences of reasonable sets of probabilities, it is almost beyond conception that the extraordinary number of mutations required for the emergence of speech and, beyond that, the numberless factors by which thought capable of self-growth is itself grounded could have come to confluence in more than a single creature, especially under the prevailing geologic upheavals during which man appeared. Surely, at most, an extraordinarily small number of creatures —in effect, virtually a singular being—must be progenitors of contemporary man.

Constellating itself about its own distinctive phonemic groundwork, each language undergoes the most elaborate mutations and ornamentations. Yet all language, however intricately composed and autonomous within its own sphere, is based upon a universal and archetypal set of cognitive categories. For this reason, these all-pervasive categories, conjoined as the single matrix of every language, immanently condition linguistic transition and distinction, and bear to full circle the multitude of styles and classes of utterance which originate in a primordial linguistic germ, as a single, cohesive linguistic manifold. Multiple linguistic confluences infold one upon another. Their products converge upon continually self-integrating universal speech, speech within which the hitherto special languages now appear as luminous foci. Latently welded together, all these foci constitute the collective deposition of the great chain of being, a chain of which the cosmos is composed, upon every individual person, himself a microcosm of the whole. Thereupon, each person interiorizes the idiosyncratic transcriptions of these depositions, transcriptions encoded into his own genes and engrained in his neural network. Diffused throughout his body, the reverberations of these engrainings constitute a single set of variants, richly nuanced and thickly textured, variants inscribed upon a universal theme: the cosmos incarnate as every person.

Unique among creatures, man possesses his own past and his own future in a way which is as significant for his being as his possession of his present. Indeed, to *own* one's present, one must be self-possessed; past and future, so to speak, must be compresent with the present. Man alone dwells within this larger present: a present in which memories grow to anticipations, a flux in which are embedded his moment-by-moment acts. What is the import of this formulation for a transcendentally naturalistic interpretation of the threshold of speech?

Earlier, I stated how the depositions of speech, speech uttered and speech heard, replicate themselves as resonating laminae of phoneme imprints, laminae which spread over the speech centers of the brain. Like geologic strata deposited in layers, each upon the former, the instant-by-instant perishings of speech, once uttered and now past, nonetheless remain ever present. One by one, a succession of laminae is layered upon each other. So interacting that their contents intermingle, these laminae themselves are transformed. In *Choros*, these transactions will become a significant topic. At present, I stress only the following considerations. In thought, and especially in fantasy and in memory, man dwells in meditative solitude within the increment, a veritable temporal interstice—between one here–now and another, each drawn from one of the laminae. A gap between two processes prevails: temporal flowings of outer speech by which a particular "instant" is decompressed, and converted into a veridical duration; the inwardly spiraling speech of a thought which *had* perished into a settled past yet remains pregnant with still viable resonances—those interior echoes which shape the past into a living drama. Analogously, as man comportmentally thrusts himself toward all that lies about him, gathering through his sense organs the resonances of the world, he also experiences an increment: a gap between his actual here–now namings, no mere instant but a duration of speaking, and the things which compose those surroundings. Thus dwelling in this increment, man shapes a future for himself by joining signifier to signified: a future of ever-heightening intensity; a drama comparable to the drama of his past.

In sum, man's past is, in actuality, included in an imperishable present. The relationship between past and inclusive present derives from two factors: man's discernment of the "interval" between his inner constitution, symbolized by thought, and his present speakings forth; and man's dwelling in this interval while such portentous sound hovers like a mysterious aura about him. Likewise, the future arises as part of the same imperishable present. For man also discerns the interval between his outer world, symbolized by the thing, and his present speakings forth. Analogously, he dwells within *this* interval as *it*, in turn, envelops him. Hence, the power of speech grounds the possibility for discerning increments between the *being* of speech and the *becoming* of speech, in its inverse flowings toward both thought and thing. Thereupon, the rhythms of speech become interwoven with the rhythms of thoughts and things. The agent by which this power is exercised, man's manifold rhythms, unfolds to fructify his being.

In previous discussion, I referred to both physical space, time, and matter and biologic space, time, and matter. In the context of my present treatment of speech as medium for human transactions, I now further delineate bio-personal space, bio-personal time, and bio-personal matter. By bio-personal space, I mean the compresent enmeshings of dialogic speech: i.e., organisms on the threshold of becoming persons and thereupon building their own personhood. By bio-personal time, I mean the unfolding interstices which separate thought from speech and speech from things: the primordial temporal flow of organisms as they pass into virtual personhood. "Remembrances of things past" flow forth to encounter things present; and this encounter occurs through a bio-personal *material* dwelling in the scheme of intricately diffused resonators, including phonemes themselves—the very substance of speech, considered from the point of view of the numberless ingredients implicated in its formation, its transmission, and its reception.

The power of speech is essential for humankind. Through its agency, every person is transformed. By the rhythms of speech, the rhythms of man are disclosed. Once born, speech potentiates its own self-development; every novel mode of speech orchestration involves its own convolutions and involutions. Once liberated, man's rhythms, assembled as a unity of action, integral and indiscerptible, constitute the agency whereby speech, in its continual self-differentiation, is transmitted from one scheme of utterance to another. Speech is, at once, agent, power, and rhythm. Likewise, man is, at once, agent, power, and rhythm. Immanent within his being and emanating from him is the being of speech. For a person *is* a gathering together of diverse imprints from the outermost reaches of the universe. Inversely blossoming, as it were, into a single compressed germ, the cosmos now blossoms forth as affirmations of the unity which he confers upon these imprints. The rhythms of these affirmations are the rhythms of speech. By their essence, man and speech are one. Their powers, their agencies, and their rhythms are one. Two integral modes of being, each presupposing the other in its existential manifestations, man and speech are, by nature, unified. The speaking forth of speech and the "humanizing forth" of man are inseparable acts. By the identity of the originating ground of each, all action, speechifying and "humanizing," which springs from this ground, is one and the same: the Word is Flesh illumined; the Flesh is Word incarnate!

Woven into the fabric of personal being are two sets of resonances: those of the privation of being, which ascend along the route of the transcendentally natural; those of the plenitude of being, which descend along the route of the transcendentally supranatural. The locus wherein this confluence occurs is the person: a single, integral substance which manifests itself both as comportment, mobile and modulated, the luminous center of which is outer speech, and as spirit, ethereal and ineffable, the luminous center of which is inner speech, or thought. Whether joined together or split asunder, comportment and spirit are, not merely complementary, but, at bottom, one and the same—a *dialectical identity*, wherein differentiations and identifications alternate in ceaseless ferment. In the former—namely, joinings together—one may speak of the archetypes of symbolism: the ground of the sacred; in the latter—namely splittings asunder—one may speak of the archetypes of diabolism: the ground of the profane.

This dialectic duplicates itself within the psyche itself. In his bifurcated psyche, man exhibits both symbols, which unite and make whole, and "diabols," which divide and fragment. These ingredients may be transposed from one psychic sphere to the other: consciousness and the Unconscious. Mediated by symbols—ultimately, the expression of pure being—the Unconscious unites with itself. In turn, it becomes subsumed, within consciousness, after having been joined to it. Now each, consciousness and the Unconscious, synthesizes its content and, thereby, extends their combined boundaries to coincide with the boundary of spirit itself. Mediated by "diabols"—ultimately, the expression of non-being—consciousness and the Unconscious remain bifurcated, and in precarious balance. As their contents are endlessly transposed from one region to the other—transposed by alternating repressions and de-repressions—the very boundary between consciousness and the Unconscious tends to disappear; it contracts to constitute but a minuscule portion of spirit. Enclosed within symbols, as the paradoxical ground of the symbol, "diabols" unfold their own content. Correlatively, in a larger paradox which includes the lesser paradox, this composite now grounds those very symbols. Herein, the mystery of being is prefigured: pure being encloses non-being as its germinating center; non-being encloses pure being as *its* germinating center.

Yet, in this interchange, the play of the rhythms of spirit as alternating symbolisms and diabolisms—condensed and transmitted as thought, or inner speech—mirrors itself within the complementary sphere of comportment—comportment condensed and transmitted as outer speech. Together, the spiritual and the comportmental comprise the integral person. In a larger sense, his rhythms require for their full unfolding the context of interpersonal encounter. At last, a full complementarity of the intrapsychic and the integrally personal growing to the interpersonal prevails. A veridical unity of spirit, which encloses the intrapsychic, and comportment, which encloses the interpersonal, is attained. Together, each now enclosing, yet enhancing, the other, spirit *and* comportment bear to fruition all the infrapersonal forces herein set forth, and surely myriad other forces of which, in these pages, there is but a bare presentiment.

NOTES

1. In my subsequent treatment of biological acts I am greatly indebted to the account given in Langer, *Mind*, Vol. I, chap. 2 and Vol. II, chaps. 12, 13. I am also

indebted to John Dewey, *Art as Experience* (New York: Minton, Balch, 1934), esp. chap. 8.

2. See "The Nobility of Sight," in Jonas, *Phenomenon of Life*, pp. 135–56.

3. Langer, *Mind*, I 370, 376.

4. Teilhard de Chardin, *Phenomenon of Man*, p. 172.

5. W. Norris Clarke, S.J., "Interpersonal Dialogue: Key to Realism," in *Person and Community*, ed. Robert J. Roth, S.J. (New York: Fordham University Press, 1975), p. 152.

6. In the following discussion, I have freely drawn on my "The Human Body as Rhythm and Symbol: A Study in Practical Hermeneutics," *The Journal of Medicine and Philosophy*, I, No. 2 (1976), 136–61.

7. See Jonas, *Phenomenon of Life*, p. 81, for the following discussion.

8. John Donne, "Death," *The New Oxford Book of English Verse, 1250–1950*, ed. Helen Gardner (New York & London: Oxford University Press, 1972), p. 197.

9. See the illuminating discussion in Ernest Schachtel, *Metamorphosis* (New York: Basic Books, 1959), esp. pp. 200–203.

10. For the discussion in this paragraph I am indebted to Aleksandr Romanovich Luria, *Higher Cortical Functions in Man*, trans. Basil Haight (New York: Basic Books, 1966), p. 390.

11. For this material I am indebted to Maurice Merleau-Ponty, *Signs*, trans. Richard C. McCleary (Evanston, Ill.: Northwestern University Press, 1964), esp. chaps. 1 and 2 of Part II.

12. Fritz Mauthner, *Beiträge zu einer Kritik der Sprache*, as cited in translation in Gershon Weiler, *Mauthner's Critique of Language* (Cambridge: Cambridge University Press, 1970), p. 36.

13. For the material in the paragraph I am indebted to L. S. Vygotsky, *Thought and Language*, trans. Eugenia Hanfmann and Gertrude Vakar (Cambridge: MIT Press, 1962), pp. 119–51.

14. Ibid., p. 15.

15. See ibid., p. 153.

16. See note 11.

17. Merleau-Ponty, *Signs*, p. 39.

18. Ibid., p. 42.

19. Ibid., p. 43.

20. Ibid., p. 46.

21. Ibid., p. 81.

EPILOGUE

THROUGHOUT THIS VOLUME, I have sought to carry out, in its initial phases, the project originally set forth, together with the method for its accomplishment, in *Homo Quaerens*, a project encapsulatedly reiterated in my Prologue. For the most part, I have restricted myself to an account of aspects, dimensions, and processes which, within a transcendentally naturalist perspective, characterize the person. I have stressed his infrapersonal rhythms, both inanimate and animate. However, often it was necessary for me to thrust myself ahead of a particular topic, introducing themes bearing directly on the ontology of the person from within a transcendentally personalist perspective.

My reasons for this extrapolation were threefold. First, I have never ceased to link this volume, in which the contours of a substantive theory of the person in but one of his significant modes of being are sketched, to *Homo Quaerens*, which deals with method—a volume in which I treated (from the methodologic standpoint) neither things nor organisms as such but persons, and dealt with the former only insofar as they enter into the composition of the latter. Secondly, in order to eliminate facets of things and organisms not directly relevant to the person, it was necessary that I introduce, by reflecting upon the person qua person, the general principles of a human ontology. By a process of methodologic attenuation, prescinding from certain aspects of these principles, and suppressing all factors which exclusively pertain to persons qua persons, it was possible to derive those components of the principles which alone concern inanimate and animate aspects. Finally, I have consistently emphasized that my task is not to treat natural science as such, but only such findings of natural science, or speculations upon those findings, as allow an interpretation of infrapersonal nature, a hermeneutic which will permit me, in subsequent books, to pass to direct examination of the person himself. At no point have I wished the reader to lose sight of the fact that my essential focus is the person. Only insofar as the inferences, theoretical and factual ingredients, and suppositions and metaphysical speculations which have appeared herein directly converge upon a human ontology dominated by a concept of man as one who pre-eminently searches are the topics of *The Dance of Being* germane to my overall enterprise.

Often, I have been tempted to pursue for its own sake a theme which bears upon some topic which, only in the end, is relevant to the personal realm alone. Nevertheless, I have tried to keep my digressions to a minimum; and I ask my reader's forebearance if, at times, I indulge myself. No single topic of this work could not have been treated sui generis, and elaborated wholly on its own terms. Surely, however, had they been examined in greater depth, many details, appropriately interwoven, would have led, granted circuitously, full circle back to the person. Though many times in writing this book I have found myself intrigued by certain themes as ends in themselves, themes which are not self-evidently or prima facie relevant to a human ontology, I am nonetheless convinced that implications pertinent to a generalized theory of man haunt these details. In consequence, I have tried to weave a fabric of fact, theory, and speculation pertaining to the infrapersonal domain which, in the long run, is pregnant with import for human ontology. Thus, I have always sought to reaffirm the position set forth in my Prologue. Now I retrospectively comment upon the main drift of my argument. Following my summation, I prospectively delineate directions of further inquiry.

As basic methodologic injunction governing my choice of themes, I have proposed this dual recommendation: on every level of organization of the substantive factors entering into a person's natural composition, seek those invariant structures which have been preserved amidst the widest range of transformations pertinent to that level; seek so to link the invariants thus chosen, beginning with the primordially physical and culminating with the bio-personal (the latter construed as derivative from the former within a transcendentally naturalist perspective), that the vector joining non-being to personal being may be understood as a progressive efflorescence of new contents inscribed upon or germinating within a persistent and shared unfolding theme. Though, in the long run, my metaphysical account of the person requires a theory of the complementarity and interpenetration of two vectors—namely, the ascent from non-being to personal being and the descent from pure being to personal being—the first vector alone has thus far been relevant, though the second has always immanently pervaded my reflections.

Throughout, my guiding vision, latent until now, yet, in subsequent books, to be made increasingly explicit, is this: the great chain of being involves a treble mediation of non-being and pure being. To use, for example, a Christian paradigm, one of several construals: if my model be a circle, at the pinnacle God the Father could be understood as mediating interweavings of non-being and pure being; at the base, man, the dialectical process; in the center, God the Son, the dialogue between man and God the Father; the entirety is irradiated by an effulgence which binds periphery and center to a unitary and integral complex. Within a Christian theologic context, this schema might be characterized as transcendental trinitarianism, a scheme in which the Holy Spirit corresponds to the luminous radii which effect ultimate integration. Implications of such a schema, as one way of particularizing general cosmology, will be set forth in later books. Then I shall trace out tenets of what, in effect, is a doctrine of pentadic transcendentalism. According to this doctrine, the following principles are regnant: transcendental naturalism, which treats those components of the scheme which lie on a vector beginning just beyond non-being and terminating just before personal being; transcendental personalism, which concerns regions adjacent to and, as it were, hovering about personal being; transcendental supranaturalism, which treats regions along that sector of the vector the *terminus ad quem* of which is immediately below pure being and the *terminus a quo* of which is immediately above personal being; transcendental trinitarianism, which deals with the entire structure, emphasizing the roles of pinnacle, center, radii, and base of the circle of being; transcendental substantialism— in effect, a dialectical construal of a Spinozist hermeneutic—pertains to the synthesis of the foregoing modes of transcendentality.

The specific ontology of the person which I henceforth elaborate will, in the end, apply the cosmologic doctrine of transcendental substantialism to a systematic general philosophy of the person. In *Homo Quaerens*, I set forth the method by which this ontology progressively crystallizes within the matrix of themes which I subsequently treat in considerable detail. The latter first emerge in the present inquiry, within the context of a transcendentally naturalistic theory of the infrapersonal domain in its relevance to the personal domain. With greater coherence and detail, they will continue to emerge in the books to follow. As I work through these theories, I foresee many revisions of the scheme which I now conceptually hold before me. My fundamental guiding vision may be elaborated, or even transformed, in ways which I cannot yet know. It is only by applying this vision, in its successive forms, to topics under investigation that its specific content and import will gradually be amplified, from mere prefigurement to a fully ornamented doctrine.

Returning to my explicit subject matter in the present volume: I have been affirming a doctrine of the progressive revelation, through a method of transcendental naturalism, of invariant structures along the route from non-being to personal being. Each structure is associated with a dramatic threshold, a threshold of this unfolding in which a new character of nature startlingly appears, a character relevant to both the emergence and the composition of man. A purely naturalistic theory would merely *mention* these thresholds, and their correlative invariants, and would only specify an ordered series of functions in their relationships to an associated class of potential transformations. But transcendental naturalism exhibits the inner content of these invariants as progressively, dynamically, and dialectically interconnected. When they are, as it were, *cracked open*, such invariants reveal ever-enriched, ever more inclusive horizons of interrelated phenomena in the grand procession of nature. Evanescent existence gives way to crystalline existence. Crystalline existence, in turn, evolves into fermenting existence. And this progression culminates (for the purposes of the present volume) in symbolizing existence. Now a prognosticative arrow points toward still new thresholds: ethereal existence and ineffable existence. Construed not only phylogenetically and ontogenetically, but as both compresent for and interacting within the person, each threshold affords a special perspective upon him. In their totality, these perspectives so condition one another that the metamorphoses of personhood, from birth to death, are, in part, definable in terms of their joint functioning. Always, a principle of contextuality governs their respective *modi operandi*. Each

perspective provides a context within which the remaining perspectives may
heuristically be discerned, and articulated. Together, they reveal the ever-changing
contours of the person.

What is the ultimate invariant beyond and, as it were, immanently enclosing
the specific invariant factors associated with each threshold? In what sense do the
contents of this grounding invariant effloresce through the stages which I have set
forth in this volume? How does each stage compress, as latent forces, the powers
which, appropriately potentiated, culminate in man, man the creature who searches
and, in his searching, speaks? These questions cannot be adequately answered in
the context of the present inquiry. In subsequent books, I take up these issues anew,
and I press further toward a solution. In cursory fashion, I can only summarize
the tentative and anticipatory notions at which I have thus far arrived.

First, I wrote of the phenomenon of elementarity: that level of organization
at which simple material particles imprinted themselves upon one another, and
thereby set in motion complicated actions and reactions. By these movements,
syntheses of new particles, each associated with its novel oscillations and attunements, alternate with resolutions into more primordial particles, associated with
their characteristic rhythms. Primordia of the process whereby spiralings, infoldings, and outfoldings give birth to successively more complex configurations,
evanescing material configurations enter upon the scene of physiogenesis: the ap-
pearings and the disappearings of matter; asymmetric chunks, whether of matter
or of anti-matter, in patterns of mutual annihilation—i.e., passage into non-being;
adhesions of nameless potencies which miraculously materialize, and transfigure
themselves into existence.

Beginning with this first dramatic threshold, the naturalistic vector progresses,
so I argued, through successive stages toward the emergence of *crystalline* existence. Now a primitive lattice structure coalesces as germinal matrix for subsequent infoldings and unfoldings. Through the conjunction of crystals of varying
kinds, complex material linkages supervene. Polymers unfold and combine, chemical chains the links of which are simple organic molecules. Among these links,
adenine (for example) plays a particularly important role. Based upon the fusion
of a hexadic with a pentadic carbon ring, with its typical benzene or quasi-benzene
resonances, this molecule becomes the ground for new modes of impingements
and imprinting. From the first liquefied crystals—the phenomena of metabolism—
replication, and mutation evolve. As the link between metabolism and replication,
adenine can be construed to symbolize this vital development: a confluence of
multiple processes—processes based upon protein and nucleic acid reactions, each
enclosed in a membrane in which lipid and carbohydrate become additionally
relevant components. Herein, *fermenting* existence emerges as the third great
threshold.

Finally, I showed how, by persistence of a single invariant, embellished in
manifold ways, through the most diverse mutations and adaptations, and through
accumulation of variegated but imperceptible forces, the processes of physio-

genesis and biogenesis converge upon the marvelous phenomenon of speech, a
phenomenon which itself is related to an antecedent stage in which the DNA–
RNA replicatory system dominates the biologic sphere. Here, complicated schemes
of resonators evolve, neural structures woven of intertwined oscillatory systems.
Interiorly extending into autonomic physiologic acts and exteriorly extending as
an hyper-organismic aura of supra-morphologic channels, these extended "structures" transmit resonances more ethereal than any resonances hitherto pervading
the organism. And the combined activities of two systems, the intra-organismic
and the extra-organismic, allow for the crystallization of phonemes: those units of
speech which, in combination with one another, permit reflection, naming, communication—in a word, man's *symbolizing* existence. By the *word*, a new vehicle
is created, a vehicle whereby a person opens himself to receive the ineffable emanations of pure being. The barrier of transcendental naturalism is broken; the
plenitudinous rhythms of supranatural being may henceforth envelop emerging
man, and, conjointly with the rhythms of natural being, direct his metamorphoses
and his fate.

A sequence of novel phases unfolds, each phase succeeding and incorporating
its predecessors. In diagramatic fashion, I illustrate these themes.

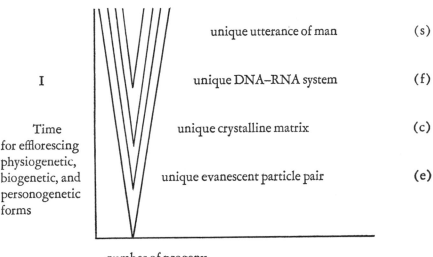

I

Time
for efflorescing
physiogenetic,
biogenetic, and
personogenetic
forms

unique utterance of man   (s)

unique DNA–RNA system   (f)

unique crystalline matrix   (c)

unique evanescent particle pair   (e)

number of progeny

Note: In the spreading progeny of each unique factor, many
        mutants appear.
        (s) symbolizing
        (f) fermenting
        (c) crystalline
        (e) evanescent

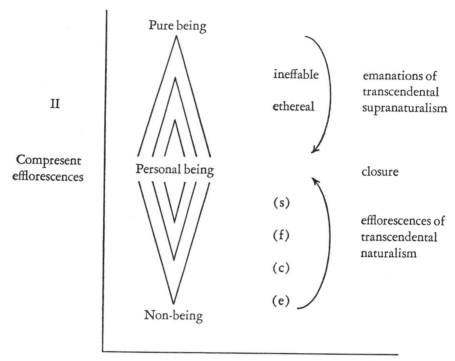

Note: (e), (c), (f), (s), ethereal, ineffable refer
to the orchestrated laminae of personal essences.

According to these representations, at each threshold a variant upon a single theme is woven into the variant associated with the next threshold. This theme may be described only contextually. It pertains to the entire unfolding along the double vector of transcendental naturalism and transcendental supranaturalism. And the variant itself is a *relative* invariant. Culminating in the person, a labyrinthine structure of interwoven (relative) *in*variants, the succession of thresholds are compresent aspects of his existence. Indeed, a person orchestrates several essences, each a lamina extracted from some element essential to the makeup of the cosmos. Thus far I have designated six such laminae: the evanescent, the crystalline, the fermenting, the symbolizing, the ethereal, the ineffable. In every case, the lamina constitutes a unique mutation with respect to but one of the progeny deriving from an immediately antecedent lamina. The locus of convergence of two such systems of mutation, every person is a confluence of emanata from pure being and efflorescences from non-being.

Within these unfoldings, "particles" of varying configuration appear. At one and the same time, each "particle" exhibits to those "particles" adjacent to it its unique self-identity, and reveals itself as constituted by its identification with simpler "particles"—i.e., "particles" which imprint their configurations upon its configuration. With respect to the contrasting factors, unique self-identity and scheme of identification, a principle of complementarity and indeterminacy prevails. The greater the potency with which a "particle" exhibits self-identity, the more weakly it exhibits identification. The two cannot be present simultaneously with the same clarity of articulation. Yet each presupposes the other as the condition whereby it itself may be presented and specified. On the one hand, identification expresses the determination of a "particle" by that which is other than itself; on the other, self-identity expresses its determination by itself. In the former case, a principle of determination is potently operative; in the latter, a principle of freedom. Each contrasting pole, that of determination or that of freedom, requires the other for its own definition. Neither may be construed without the other.

In sum, a grand principle is inexorably at work within the naturalistic makeup of every person. Equilibrations and disequilibrations reign; configurations form, shatter, and re-form; active strivings for autonomy and self-perpetuation alternate with passive acquiescence in the imposition upon autochthonous contours of the contours of alien factors. Ceaselessly, a dialectic prevails between a determinate process of imprinting and the free synthesizing of imprints already deposited. For every set of "particles," endogenous dynamisms shape a self-identity for each member of that set. Through the reciprocal impingements of these "particles," metamorphoses are induced within each. Within this dialectic, new unities perpetually form, composites in which individuality is never fully lost. True, in howsoever transmuted a form, the novelty of the whole is retained *as* a totality, one in which transactionally determined redistributions of particles do not cease to occur. Yet never is the perishing individual wholly lost. Something is always preserved and, in a measure, immortalized within an eternal flux. *A fortiori*, the person stamps the cast of his uniqueness indelibly into the cosmogenetic process.

Prefigured in the present volume, these principles will be amplified in subsequent books. In particular, persons will be treated under two contrasting yet interpenetrating perspectives: the person *in solitudine*, the person *in communitate*. More broadly, the person will be regarded as an integral component within a larger cosmos. By my overarching doctrine of transcendental substantialism, all parts of this cosmos are mutually enhancing. Though but one part among many parts, the person nonetheless occupies a central position within the entire scheme. By the labyrinthine rhythms shared with all creatures, the person manifests a mutual bond. By the marvelously variegated dance of being, the person emerges as supremely important. *Human* being is *primus inter pares*.

INDEX

ꞵ